Lala Sreeram

Vicharsagar

The Metaphysics of the Upanishads

Lala Sreeram

Vicharsagar
The Metaphysics of the Upanishads

ISBN/EAN: 9783743423343

Manufactured in Europe, USA, Canada, Australia, Japa

Cover: Foto ©Lupo / pixelio.de

Manufactured and distributed by brebook publishing software (www.brebook.com)

Lala Sreeram

Vicharsagar

THE METAPHYSICS

OF

THE UPANISHADS.

VICHARSAGAR.

TRANSLATED WITH COPIOUS NOTES

BY

LALA SREERAM,

PLEADER OF THE COURTS,
AND
LATE TEHSEELDAR OF DELHI.

CALCUTTA :
HEERALAL DHOLE
127, MUSJIDBAREE STREET.

1885.

[All rights reserved.]

VEDANTA PRESS,
NILAMBAR VIDYARATNA,—PRINTER.
MUSJIDBAREE STREET, CALCUTTA.

TO

SIR CHARLES U. AITCHISON, K.C.S.I., C.I.E., L.L.D.,

LIEUTENANT-GOVERNOR OF THE PUNJAB AND ITS DEPENDENCIES,

FOR HIGH CHRISTIAN MORALITY, THOROUGH CONSCIENTIOUSNESS, NEVER-CEASING ANXIETY FOR THE WELFARE OF THE PEOPLE HE RULES OVER, AND HIS APPRECIATION OF OUR ANCIENT LEARNING AND PHILOSOPHY,

AND

IN GRATEFUL REMEMBRANCE OF A LIFE-LONG SERVICE UNDER GOVERNMENT,

THIS WORK IS BY PERMISSION DEDICATED,

BY

HIS MOST OBEDIENT AND DUTIFUL SERVANT

SREERAM,

Tehsildar of Delhi (retired) now Pleader of the Delhi Court.

PREFACE:

A WORK that is already well-known needs no word of commendation. It has made it's way in the outlying districts of the Punjab, and every *Sadhu* who knows to read and write receives instruction from his Guru, on this very work, so that by perusing it, he learns all that is worth knowing of the Upanishads. It embodies a mass of instruction which cannot be otherwise had, unless a large number of original works difficult to understand, and requiring the life-time of an individual, are gone through. It is the only work of its kind in the vernacular. To increase its utility, and to make it easily understood without any extraordinary pains, or the assistance of Pundits, its present garb will be unusually facilitating to those who understand the language in which it is written. Where the text is obscure or requires elucidation by reference to other subjects beyond the pale of the work in hand, ample notes and references have been given to avoid the necessity of consulting the original works. No pains have been spared to increase its utility, and give a true and correct rendering of the text, so that it can be confidently recommended. The original work abounds in the technicalities of the original Sanscrit from which our author has drawn largely, and their rendering into English has always been given in the plainest terms, so that there may be no mistake. But no philosophy can be taken up like a romance, or a book of travel ; it requires deep thinking, and constant reading, with patience and tranquility of mind. The times we live in are extremely auspicious for works like the present. Thanks to the late Swamy Dyanand Saraswati and other allumini, there is an increasing activity noticeable everywhere for a study of our *Shastras* and what they teach ; and the English education which had hitherto turned our young men into rank materialists, or scientfic atheists, is now giving way for a more healthy spirit of inquiry for our ancient philosophies. The impulse to this novel movement received no mean help from the Theosophical Society. The noble and self-sacrificing career of Madame Blavatsky and Colonel Olcott for regenerating our ancient literature and faith, deserves the highest encomium everywhere. Had it not been for their example and co-operation it would have taken several lengthened periods before the revival of things as they are, could have been accomplished.

Thus then, if the present work would tend to increase the national spirituality, if it would be the means of inviting the active sympathies of our young men and old, and stimulate them to study our ancient writings and the faith they inculcate, if it would stem the tide of materialism and supplant it with the noble and high aspirations which Non-duality teaches, if it will suppress bad *karma* and incite the good of our fellow-creatures, we would think ourselves highly gratified and amply repaid. It cannot be insisted too often, that a nation without spirituality is but on the road to ruin and self-destruction. It is indeed a sorrowful sight to find the struggle for existence gaining a strong ascendancy over us everywhere ; hungering for material comforts and thirst for accumulation of wealth is omnipotent here as in Europe, we are now no longer satisfied as our forefathers used to be, increased civilisation means increased luxury, that has become a necessity and for its gratification we must have increased resources and that again signifies our best attention and energies in pursuit of wealth. It cannot be expected, the present state of things will suddenly collapse, no, there are cycles in the life of a nation, and all these are to be passed as surely as night follows day, and day, night. But if our inner consciousness may be roused to perceive and feel the utter worthlessness and unreality of this world, and if we draw our lessons from the sad experience of nations that have preceeded us, we may receive a check in our headlong path to ruin. That this may so be is the earnest prayer of the

TRANSLATOR.

INTRODUCTION.

With a view of facilitating an enquirer of self-knowledge to comprehend the main doctrine of the Upanishads, which forms the subject of the accompanying treatise, a few explanations, are needed; and it is hoped that they will be of much help to him. Non-duality or the oneness of the Individual and Universal Spirit is the subject to be demonstrated, and an elaborate and critical analysis of the rival systems which look upon them as different and otherwise, have been fully discussed. That does not concern us for the present. What we propose is to lay down a few salient points, to give a skeleton sketch, leaving the rest to our author. In the discussion of his subject he has brought in, a mass of arguments from all available sources; the work itself is a result of a vast amount of reading, and whatever is worth knowing of the Vedas, Mimansa, Nyaya, Sankhya, Puranas &c., has been included in it. It contains likewise a discussion of the merits of personal and impersonal forms of worship, and seeks to satisfactorily account for the apparent and seemingly anomalous dictum of the several Purans, wherein each sets up a different form of worship and particularly insisting upon it, in lieu of others. In this way, the different sects of worshippers—Vishnuvite, Sivite, Ganpat, Sakta,—who have hitherto been taught to regard his especial Deity to be superior to the rest will find much to unlearn. Reason, and analogy, with the proofs derived from the *Shastras* have been amply introduced to help the comprehension, and to erect at much labor, a neutral ground where the most inveterate bigot will cast away his rancor, and shake hands in fraternal love and harmony with one whom he had hitherto looked upon as a fool and knave. Thus then there is much to engage the attention of the reader; caste and creed, stands not in the way of acquiring the knowledge inculcated here; for we find no mention about it by our author. The only caste he seems to recognise is that of qualification, and any person having the necessary qualities may profitably engage himself in its study. He will find much to interest him, much to engage his attention, much to evoke his sympathy; the scale from his eyes will be dropped of and it is hoped, he will rouse to realise a new existence; the clue to solve the mighty problem of existence, the end and aim of human life is here spoken out with as much fervour, as its dignity demands, and though to realise it and form the basis of turning a new life can only happen to the fewest of the few,—to those who have sown the seeds of knowledge in their previous births—yet it can be profitably made use of by all alike.

With this preamble, we enter into the few necessary explanations which we have promised at the outset. *Brahma* is described as "*Sat-chit-ananda,*" '*Sat*' signifies Existence, '*chit*' Intelligence and '*ananda*' Bliss. It is therefore essentially Existent, Intelligence and Bliss. In the *Mundaka Upanishad* the story is related of the illustrious son of Sanaka, who desirous of knowledge, repaired to Angiras the sage, and enquired of him "what that was, which being known, every thing else would be known." He was told in reply, that the wise regard "the invisible, intangible, unrelated, colourless one, who has neither eyes nor ears, nor hands and feet, eternal, all-pervading, subtle, and indestructible as the cause of all that exists". This is the Impersonal God of the Vedâs, called severally by the names of *Parabrahma, Brahma* and *Paramatma*. It is said, pior to the evolution of the objective world there was present only '*Sat*' the ONE EXISTENCE *Parabrahma* without name or form, for name and form are indications of creation, and what is created is open to destruction hence non-eternal, therefore *Parabrahma* being eternal is devoid of both. The three expletives 'one' 'secondless' and 'Existence' (*ekam, ebam, adwaitam*) with which *Parabrahma* is always connected are only for differentiating it

INTRODUCTION.

from bodies similar and dissimilar. That is to say, as It is one and secondless, and there exists not another body of Its kind, inasmuch as It is eternal,—while the world and its contents are non-eternal—It has only one indication. But a sect of Buddhists *(Madhyamiks)* contend that in the beginning there was present *'Asat'* or nothing instead of *'Sat.'* Virtually they teach that nothing produced everything, which is clearly impossible. Now if it be said, as *Parabrahma* also existed in the beginning, whence did the materials come from which the world was ushered into existence ! The reply is as steam exists potentially in water, so was *Prakriti, Maya* or *Ajnana,* so many names of matter residing potentially in the supreme *Brahma.* To be more explicit, *Parabrhma* is the supreme force residing within Matter in its primordial condition, or cosmic state. Thus then, we have both Matter and Force, or Matter and Motion, as the Western Scientists would have it, to satisfactorily account for whatever that exists. So much in common with the Materialist only, the difference is yet more marked. For, while Materialism discards any hereafter, the Vedântin looks upon metampsychosis as the inevitable lot of humanity, and as life means suffering and an incessant struggle, he wants to crush the seed which produces the tree of life, and lays his axe at its root, so that there be nothing left to produce it again.

We purposely refrain from entering into the arguments both for and against, as they have been amply dealt with by the author, ours is only a pencil sketch and this the reader is requested to keep in mind. Now then with regard to intelligence ;—there are three states of consciousness called respectively the waking, dreaming and dreamless slumber. It is said, that consciousness of all the three conditions is one, the difference consists in the multiformness of the objects which consciousness covers : in other words, the several acts of cognition brought about by the sensory organs (sight, hearing, touch, smell, and taste) relate to one consciousness, though the objects which that consciousness takes possession of, to render them perceivable, may be many and varied ; and what is one is always eternal ; hence the Supreme *Brahma* being eternal is also Intelligence. In the *Mundakya Upanishad*, *Brahma* is described as "neither conscious nor unconscious" neither is it cognizor, nor the object cognized ; the purpose of all that is to shew that it is knowledge in the abstract, indicating cognition and not the subject of cognition ; for that would be incompatible with truth and infinity. Now infinite cannot be marked or limited by any thing in any direction, and a knowing subject must have objects and cognitions to limit it, hence *Parabrahma* is not a cogniser. Moreover in that case, a dualism would be involved, for whenever there is consciousness there is relation and rleation, implies dualism. In this way, the knowledge of the Supreme *Brahma* like the heat in fire is "the abstract essence itself." Man derives his powers of discovering or discerning from reflection of intelligence in the internal organ, (*antakaran*) or mind. Now this reflex intelligence is a reflected shadow of the Intelligence of *Brahma*, which for its close proximity sheds its lustre, in the same way as a red flower kept close to a crystal sheds its color on the glass and it appears red ; or to quote a familiar illustration as a needle is moved by a magnet when held close to it. Thus then, *Brahma* is self-luminous ; and all objects derive their luminosity from it. The word Intelligence is here intended to convey a very wide meaning. It may be taken for vitality, or life essence too. Because, it is universally present—from the insentient molecule of atomic dust to the huge Andes or Himalayas, from the rank weed infesting a stagnant pool of rain-water collected in the road-side ditch to the gigantic Banian, and from the tiny fly "dancing and frisking before our eyes" to man, each and all has its particle of vitality—its individual unit of intelligence, which keeps it in its present condition of activity ; all are equally dependent on *Brahma* hence its another name or designation is "the source of all."

Brahma is likewise described as bliss. 'Bliss' signifies cessation of misery. As in deep sleep, when there are no dreams to trouble him, a man cuts off his connection with the objective world, and is perfectly insensible to pain, he may therefore be said to be in the highest enjoyment of felicity, and his personal experience also goes to establish it ; since on rising from sleep he exclaims "I was sleeping happily I knew nothing then ;" or in the condition of being absorbed into *Brahma.* Here every thing is joy, and there is no pain. We all have it in common. Ignorance is an obstacle to our perceiving it, and if that can be destroyed by knowledge, all illusions are at an end, the relation we establish with our connections and worldly goods lose their hold, and we are on the road to *Nirvana.*

The importance of knowledge is thus clearly established. But of all knowledges, that which tends to know the nature of self is paramount, and this is called a crown. But we may be asked, how can Matter have any resemblance to Ignorance and why is it called so ? We proceed to answer.

Ignorance is called in the *Veda,* as neither existent nor non-existent, and something indescribable. 'Existent' in so far as it is everywhere present, for no one can say that he knows every thing, consequently he is ignorant; and 'non-existent' because knowledge drives it away, and with that object it has been described as antagonistic to knowledge. It is quite distinct from real, and unreal as neuter is neither male nor female. In this way, though Ignorance is universally present, it cannot be mistaken for *Brahma* which also is universally present; likewise there is another similitude, for both of them are declared to be unborn. Because Brahma is eternal, and Ignorance is not—for with the advent of knowledge it disappears, or is reduced to non-being, therefore it is unreal ; while Brahma is Real,—therefore, as Ignorance cannot be particularized one way or the other, as it is neither real nor unreal, neither existent nor non-existent, and as it cannot be said to be with or without shape, it is hence indescribable. It cannot be contended, want of knowledge is Ignorance. For, want is negation, non-existent and unreal, while knowledge is positive, existent and real, therefore they cannot be connected with each other. Ignorance abounds in darkness and knowledge abounds in luminosity, that again constitutes another difference between them ; and for this darkness which is identical with insentiency, Ignorance and Matter are one. What has just been said in regard to Ignorance applies equally to *Maya*. But *Maya* is called illusion, and it may be asked why? Because it is the very nature of illusion to make an unreal substance appear real, like objects seen in a dream.

Illusion can be removed only by knowledge, hence the imperative necessity of acquiring Self-knowledge cannot be too often repeated. We regard the world as something real, and hanker after the acquisition of property, and accumulation of riches with the false hope that they will procure bliss and felicity. It is an illusion to think so. Likewise the attribution to Self, of bondage, and to regard him as an agent or instrument, or one who is a doer of works is also due to illusion. "All our sense, perceptions, the cold in the hand, the smell in the nose, sight and hearing are illusions yet essential to existence." For as in the instance of a snake created in a rope,—an illusion of sight—the mistake is removed when the rope is fully known, so the mistaken attribution of bondage ceases only with thorough knowledge of Self.

Having thus done with Ignorance and Illusion it remains only to consider Matter or *Prakriti*. The best definition of Matter is that which occupies space, but a *Vedantin* says it to be indescribable. Because we are so little acquainted with its nature and properties, and the ways in which it works that the above epithet is very appropriate. Matter is said to possess three attributes. These are the *Satwa* or good, *Raja* or active and *Tama* or dark; and as every object in nature is derived from the elements ether, water, fire, air and earth, therefore all of them have these properties more or less. In one sense, the so-called properties are nothing else but distinct forces, and we have thus a parallel of the forces of attraction, and gravitation etc. Now this can be established in the following wise :—

It is said, the first (*Satwa*) is light, the second (*Tama*) is heavy and the active force. Now *Satwa* and *Tama* can do nothing till overpowered by *Raja*. Thus then what is light has an upward motion, as gases, blazing fire &c. ; the sensory and active organs for their acute perception and ready prehension are likewise said to be derived from the *Satwavic* quality. It is likewise possessed of luminosity. Motion is due to the active quality or *Raja*. It induces action everywhere. It sets the air in motion. The mind for its unsteadinesss is also said to be a product of this quality. *Tama* is said to be heavy, because it obstructs the luminosity of *Satwa*, hence Ignorance is said to be a product of *Tama*. The first and the last have no velocity or motion, till acted upon by the second, which also receives a check from the heavy *Tama*, so that *Raja* or the active quality cannot lead *Tama* anywhere and everywhere; for by its force *Tama* counterbalances its action, hence there is no breach in the order and synchonism of natural laws. We have here a satisfactory explanation of intelligence in Nature. It is a sterotyped argument of anthropomorphism, that law signifies a law-giver, and as there is a display of intelligence in natural laws, that proves the presence of mind, and for that mind to remain there must be a requisite body, hence God almighty has a body etc. But a pantheist says, such a creator can neither be infinite, nor all-pervading, his pervasion must be limited by his body, for he cannot be present everywhere at the same time.) The especial pleadings of both these views need not concern us, as they are beyond the scope of the present notice. We thererfore pass on to consider the elements.

At first sight, it may appear strange that our forefathers were taught to believe the so-called elements as simple bodies. That would imply their ignorance of physical science and chemisty notably. For, we in our time have been taught by Western Science to regard water, air, and earth as compound. There is Hydrogen and Oxygen in water; air contains oxygen and nitrogen besides an admixture of carbonic acid &c., and earth is a mixture of several substances. But there is no necessity for such an apprehension, for their elements find no place in Western Science. The so-called elements of the West are liable at a future period, when chemical analysis and synthesis will have attained more perfection, to be decomposed or resolved into other simpler substances. But with regard to our classification, that shall never happen. It is said, the elements of which we have knowledge and which we are accustomed to use for our daily wants are different from what they were in the beginning, hence we have the subtle and gross elements. The latter are a result of peculiar form of mixture called quintuplication (*panchikarana*) as follows :—Divide each element into two equal parts ; of the remaining ten parts, take the first five of each element and divide into five equal parts, then leaving the undivided second half of each element, add to the above mentioned four parts, the second halves of the other four elements, each to each. Thus then we have one element each, an eighth part of itself, while the rest is made up by the other four elements. And their presence is demonstrated in the possession of qualities which naturally belong to them. That is to say, ether is said to possess the quality of transmitting sound, while air has sound derived from its cause ether, besides its individual property of touch ; in the same way fire has sound, touch and form ; water—sound, touch, form, and taste, while earth has sound, touch, form, taste, and smell. From the same elementary combination have originated the seven abodes placed one above the other, Bhur, Bhuvar, Swar, Mahar, Janas, Tapas, Satya, and the seven nether spheres, one below the other severally called Atala, Vitala, Sutala, Rasatala, Talatala, Mahatala and Patala, together with Brahmánda, the four varieties of physical bodies with their adequate food and drink.

In respect to air and water we find them mentioned in the *Sruti Mimansa*, *Naya*, and other systems, that they are compound and not simple bodies. Their composite nature is easily demonstrable. For instance, water if left to stand will deposit a sediment of mud which is nothing else but earthy particles. Even in the clearest sample of water it is easy to detect the presence of earthy salts. But this cannot be practically proved in the case of the other four elements. Moreover, it is said that some of the five (*vutas*) elements in their subtle form have been mixed with similar subtle atoms of a second element, and have thus helped the production of the gross, while other atoms have produced similar results without any mixture. In short, the gross is a changed condition of the subtle with and without a blending of their atoms. In the gross elements we have a prolific cause for the material universe.

What is ether? The atmosphere which surrounds the globe does not extend beyond thirty or forty leagues, and diminishes in substance, in proportion to its elevation above the earth's surface. It is therefore not very high; beyond it, is the planetary ether of physicists and astronomers. It fills all space, and is drawn into the interstices of the solar systems, the stars, nebulae etc. It is all-pervading. It may be called a fluid, but it resembles the air we have, though much rarefied than it. In calculating the speed of heavenly bodies, resistance of ether is taken into account by astronomers, hence it is impossible to deny its existence.

Thus far we have been mainly concerned in introducing our readers to the signification of the technical terms abounding in the philosophy which forms the subject of the present treatise. Without a proper comprehension of the terms that will frequently occur, it is impossible to master the subject in all its details, hence it was necessary that they should be explained. We purpose now to touch upon the cardinal doctrines of Vedantism. These are, besides non-difference of the Jiva and Brahma, the doctrines of *karma* and metampsychosis.

'*Karma*' is the collective totality of works good and bad which an individual performs in life. They determine his future existence both subjectively and objectively. That is to say, in proportion to a person's merits, he inherits a better sphere of existence after death. That may bring forth an abode in heaven, but after the consummation of happiness he is sure to be hurled back to an objective life. Actions are transient, and their fruits are likewise so, for the properties of a cause are transmitted to its products. Hence to abstain from works is of paramount importance. But it may be said, it is impossible for a man to live without doing any thing either by the active organs—hands, feet, etc.,—or by the mind; even if he turns into an ascetic and retires from the world, to live in a mountain cave, certainly the necessity for appeasing calls of hunger and thirst, of defæcation, and urination, and sleep must yet continue so that if works cease to produce re-birth, literally no one can be freed. To avoid this difficulty, knowledge is credited with powers of destruction. But all works cannot be destroyed. Apart from the daily and occasional rites, and forbidden works, or those sanctioned in the sacred writings, there are other works *viz.*, accumulated, fructescent and current :—that is to say, the first refer to works which have accumulated in several previous births, the second refer to those which have resulted in the present life and have already commenced to bear fruit, while the third comprise the works performed in the present life. They will bear fruit in a future life. The fruits of accumulated and current works are destroyed by knowledge of Self and his identity with *Brahma*. But the fructescent, can only be exhausted by enjoying their results during the present life. It is beyond the scope of the present notice to enter into details. Suffice it to say, that in this '*Karmaic* law,' we have a satisfactory solution for the puzzling questions which so often harass us. We mean, in the instance when "virtue starves" as said by Pope in his *Essay on Man*, or a learned and able person with difficulty scraping together the means of a sorry meal for himself and family, and struggling on from day to day, not knowing when and where his troubles are to cease ; or a young and handsome wife suddenly deprived of her husband in the heyday of his youthful career ; of a poor widow, poor and friendless, aged and infirm, suddenly deprived of her son, who was her prop and support and the main-stay of life. Now instances like these can be multiplied indefinitely, they are too common to escape the attention of any one, but what we have said will suffice. Here the *prarabdhakarma* is the key. 'Fructescent works' have already commenced to bear fruit, and as that fruit is to bring forth pain and suffering or the reverse, according to the nature of previous works, consequently an individual is seen unaccountably to suffer while another who is worthless, has for his portion all material comforts. In the case of children dying, there is the same operation of the *karmaic* law. But it is said that a person may, apart from physical circumstances, for his bad *karma*, be born blind, deaf or dumb and thus be a cause of anxiety to the parents.

In this way, it will appear that heaven and hell are relative conditions of happiness and misery brought forth by the deeds of an individual. But opinions differ, for which a *Vedantin* is bound to accept the teachings of his Sacred Scriptures ; he necessarily pins his faith with the truth, there taught. He may look upon the blissful abode of the seven upper spheres already mentioned, as a result of merit or good works, but after their consummation he must revisit earth in human shape and rehabilitate a body that must be a net result of his unexhausted *karma*. Kapila on the other hand, lays down the doctrine of a man's being reincarnated into a beast or Deva, in proportion to his demerit or merit. Buddhism teaches, after humanity, there is no more retrogression ; that is to say, when a human being dies he must always be human in his furture reincarnations and not take his chance with beasts and birds, or vegetables and stone.

Though equally believing in *Karma*, yet Kapila maintains with much show of reason and strength of argument, his doctrine of *Bhavanamayasarira*. A person in his deathbed is overtaken with a fixed thought ; if he is a lover of horse-flesh, his mind will be centered in a horse, so that when he dies, his astral body assumes the desired body of a horse. In this way, a person may be a rogue all his life, and yet escape the torments of subjective or objective suffering. In his last moments, his thoughts may overtake *Brahma*, *Vishnu*, *Shiva* or any other *Deva*, and sure enough he goes there to reap happiness. A practice still prevails in Bengal and other countries to bawl out the name of Ganga, Narain and Brahma into the ears of a dying person ; to one who is unacquainted with its signification it may sound unnecessary and cruel. But there is a fixed object in view, it means the momentous question of sending that person's soul to be received in heaven. If perchance, the reiteration of name does come to occupy his mind so as to be moulded after it, if it would direct his mind mentally to worship or remember his *mantram* given by his spiritual preceptor, he is saved from hell-torments.

The question of heaven and hell, is a relative existence. Our ancient writers are not very unanimous. Each author has made ample mention of them, but there are others who maintain quits an opposite doctrine. For instance, heaven and hell are for the enjoyment of happiness or suffering of misery. But who is to suffer ? Let this question be first answerd. A *Vedantin* says the *Atma* or seventh principle is neither an agent or instrument, he is passive, and does no works, he is neither subject to re-birth, consequently death cannot affect him, and he is free, therefore he is not subject to pleasure and pain. Under such circumstances the *Atma* is clearly neither responsible for the works performed by the *Jiva* in his career on earth, nor is it necessary for him to appear on the day of judgment to receive his sentence—of eternal happiness or eternal damnation in hellfire, as taught by the Christian Church. Ours is much simpler and more reasonable. It is said, for enjoyment or suffering, a body is required, not the subtle astral body, but the physical body which we have all got, hence it consequently follows, reincarnation is the scene of fruition as it is for fresh action. In this sense, there is neither heaven nor hell beyond the world. Heaven and hell are in our own keeping. By turning the mind away from objects of sensuous gratification, if we live for others, abolishing all selfish ends, and reverently perfom all virtuous actions, we do what is best for weak and frail man to do. The reverse of what we have just been saying leads to a life of ineffable misery in next. Existence itself is admitted as a twain condition in which both happiness and misery are the unavoidable lot of all and every one of us ; a man rolling in riches attended by servants in rich livery, living in a style befitting his rank and means, courted and flattered by his friends and relations may appear happy to all of us, but you will find, that he is in fact as miserable as an average human being without his advantages. Perhaps he is childless, or the slave of an insatiable thirst for accumulating more wealth, or he is a miserable wretch so far as health is concerned, or he may be very unfortunate in his wife ; no one loves him, none cares a straw for his person, all his relatives are so many parasites anxiously waiting for the hour of death, so that they may be remembered in his last will. Such is the rule. Here we can expect no unalloyed happiness ; the poet's dream of love and bliss are too holy to have a place here : our journey through life embraces a long period of time, of which a part goes in acquiring the usual training and experience to befit us in this up-hill struggle; another part is spent in fulfilling Darwin's law of survival of the fittest. In this way, is spent the best part, landing us now into the ladd of reflection, and decripitude, with hairs hoary sitting reverently as a crown for all the struggles we had in the past. Now if in all this, we maintain an unflinching honesty,—honesty of word, deed and thought, we are then more than human. Show us the man who will say that he has been honest all his days, from the time when he arrived at years of discretion and we say that he is an exception. No doubt there are men, who are fit to be worshipped in every sense of the word—men who have retired from the sad turmoil of an empty and deceitful world to study self, to meditate on the mystic 'OM,' or to dwell in *Samadhi*. These sages or wisemen or call them more properly theosophists, guard our destinies, a wide range of philanthropy actuates them, nationality they know not, man is the object of their solicitous care, and to teach and instruct is a favorite occupation with them. We cannot say that the world has become denuded of them, but their number is extremely few. The present writer has the good fortune to know one, who is his preceptor, and he can hardly express his gratitude adequately to Baba Purdumun Sing, Sadhu Nirmala.

To return from this digression to our subject, we find it laid down, that with death we part with our physical body just as a snake casts of its coil. Our conceptions and *Karma* remain impressed in the body called subtle or astral (*linga sharira*) which is again subjected to re-incarnation. It is everywhere the unanimous opinion that the astral body continues to come and go till emancipation. This is a very shadowy duplicate of the gross body, and has seventeen characteristic features. The five vital airs—*Pran* and the rest; five sensory organs,—sight, hearing etc.; five organs of action—hands, feet, mouth, anus and genitals, together with mind and intellect [the human soul and animal soul] constitute the *linga sharira*. By the practice of *Yoga* it can be projected out at a distance from the physical body, wherever a *Yogee* wishes it to be; in this way even the natural barriers offer no impediment to its passage.

The reader will find it mentioned in its proper place the need of a continued residence with a Guru, supporting him by begging and satisfying him in all manner by doing menial services, never troubling him even for food but waiting to receive whatever he offers, neither asking for instruction but bidding his time and pleasure—even these require no ordinary amount of patience—by a pupil duly qualified for receiving the necessary instruction on *Brahma Vidya*. Under these circumstances, it is easy to conceive, why the number of such qualified pupils have been getting less and less day by day. One must leave the world to all intents and purposes, and lead a life of absolute purity before he can acquire that knowledge. If it be asked what is the necessity for knowledge? For if the Jiva be one with *Brahma*, and if the natural felicity and intelligence of the latter be alike a part of the former, there is no reason why a person is to make such a sacrifice ; or it may be argued, as in common practice, we do not trouble ourselves any more concerning a thing already got; similarly the felicity of *Brahma* and destruction of misery being already present in the individual, there does not exist any paramount necessity for the acquisition of knowledge. But the reply is, as a person with a piece of gold in his hand forgets about it and is seen to busy himself in its search, and when pointed out by another, he recovers it to all intents and purposes, though it never left his possession and he had it already ; similarly the enveloping or concealing power of Ignorance hides the perception of felicity which naturally belongs to him and knowledge alone enables him to recover it. Then again, that knowledge, as it is antagonistic to Ignorance, which again is nothing more or less than matter, destroys the materials out of which the seed for the future body of the individual is to grow, hence being removed from the fetters of consecutive re-births, he will abide for ever in the *Brahma* whose sole essence is joy. Destruction of grief is eagerly sought after by man, no matter whatever may be his position, and as it can only be effected by knowledge, we have here another incentive. But it may be replied, that for every kind of misery there are particular remedies, therefore the application of remedies is equally capable of destroying it. Clearly, to say so, is a mistake. For instance, medicine removes or cures a great many diseases, that is true indeed; but there is no certainty that the disease would not return again in the life time of the individual; in the same manner pangs of hunger and thirst are removed by a good dinner, and drink, but there are yet a good many miseries which refuse to be destroyed and there is no remedy for them, beyond knowledge. When a person loses his only son, his grief knows no bounds, and no remedy is more potent to destroy his grief save the knowledge, that his so-called son was nobody; that it was a mere illusion which tied him in bonds of affection; that it is the ordinary lot of humanity from which there can be no escape; that the world itself is unreal and transient, and full of grief.

We are extremely selfish: without an expectation of deriving sure benefit we never undertake a work. The authors of the *Shastras* understood human character too well to allow it to escape their notice, hence we find it mentioned there are 'four incentives.' Of them 'necessity' is the last. That is to say the necessity of studying the *Shastras* is pointed out in all its bearings.

The philosophy of the *Vedanta* embraces two subjects, metaphysics and physics. The first has been considered in all its aspects, including a critical review of the arguments of the other contending systems, pointing out their mistake and establishing truth. In the elucidation of truth, a *Vedantin's* analysis and mode of arguing is simple as it is convincing. Our author has ransacked the whole ground covered by the partisans of especial theories, and though he had added nothing, yet he had, by bringing the arguments together in one place, rendered ample service to the cause he represents, to deserve the gratitude of his readers. In regard to the latter he is rather reticent, he dismisses the subject with the remark that the world and its contents are unreal, therefore deserve no especial or particular mention. Evidently he could not have done justice to it, without putting in another volume before the public, and the labor of the undertaking might have stood in his way. To every religious minded person, the physics are unattracting. Even in the present day, we find a conflict between religion and science. The Church in the West, had received severe wounds from the artillery brought in by science (physical); these wounds are now being dressed up with care and skill by her custodians—Bibliologists; and the recent authorised translation of the Holy Writ has been purged of several very objectionable points. In this way, to fit in with the facts of scientific evolution, the six days of the world which occupied God to create it, are said to cover an immense space of time. We happily, are not similarly placed. For we have our Brahmâ's day and night, that means time enough, and we have nothing to be ashamed of.

Turning from Physics to Metaphysics, we find a vast array of subjects, the sum total of which is to shew the illusory nature of all phenomena; they are therefore unreal. The world and its contents are relatively and not absolutely false. As in the instance of an illusion of sight, when a person conceives the presence of a snake in a dark night, in a bit of straw, rope, &c., the so-called snake is discovered to be false when a light is brought to shew what the thing lying in front is. By the help of light, person derives the necessary knowledge of the rope, of all its parts, when the illusion is dispelled. Similarly the illusion of the world is only removed by a thorough knowledge of Self, who is no other but *Brahma*. In the foregoing instance, the reality of the site of the snake, the rope itself, is not at all denied; on the other hand, everywhere it is maintained as something substantial. Because without a site there can be no illusion. In the absence of the rope there can be no mistake of a snake. In other words, we must have something resting on the background, so to speak, on which to superimpose or project through a force of ignorance the necessary mistake or illusion. In the case of the world and its contents, what we objectively recognize through the medium of the several sensory organs are so far real, having an objective existence with the usual form, taste, touch, &c., but they are non-eternal, and it is an illusion to consider them otherwise, for there is only one entity of that nature and that is *Brahma*. Now in regard to our body, we are apt to confound it and the several organs of sense, &c., with self. It is the business of metaphysics to establish a correct knowledge of Self, and to shew that the body is not Self. Neither are the organs of sense, the vital airs, nor the mind come under that category. They have been fully dealt upon and with the help of the foot-notes, the reader will have enough to clear his mind of preconceived and incorrect ideas. Therefore we need not stop for considering them in this place. " All our sense perceptions are illusions." This requires a proof and we have in Astronomy a trite illustration. Stars are classified according to their magnitude. The higher are placed in the ascending scale, while the lower ones are nethermost. A star of the fifth magnitude will make its ray of light appear in the earth at an immense distance of time ; all the time the light has been travelling with its accustomed velocity to reach our globe, and the telescope can find its site nowhere ; the *rationale* is, by the time it reaches us, the star itself is lost. Now here we have a ray of light coming from a body that was existing in the time when that light started on its onward journey, but since then, the law of change has so worked upon matter, that the star is lost in the infinity of space.

To connect happiness and misery with Self is a common mistake, universally present. We find it commonly said by all classes of persons, and there is hardly any exception " I am very miserable" " He is very happy." These are a few of the instances in common use daily with all individuals according to their experience of grief or happiness. Opinions are divided according to the several Schools of Eastern Metaphysicians. From the Vedantin's standpoint happiness and misery are created by Jiva,—upon the relations created by him. They are not *Iswar's* productions. For instance, a father has his son residing abroad on foreign service, his neighbour has also one of his sons in a similar service, distant from home. Now when the father of the first son, receives intelligence of the demise of his son, by a person returning from that country, he is extremely depressed and his grief knows no bounds ; similarly that other father is elated with the information that his son was doing well and intended shortly to return home laden with wealth, accompanied by a large retinue ; but the fact is otherwise, his son was actually dead, while that other son was very prosperous. But the man who gave the wrong information owed a grudge to the family and that is why he put the father into unnecessary grief, but when the mail brings the good tidings, in the hand-writing of the absent son hitherto taken for dead, his father is extremely delighted. Thus we find, that the relationship of the first father with his son artificially created by him, is the source of his grief and happiness. If the son were the seat of such grief and happiness, then for every son, each father would feel pleasure or pain, but that is not the case. But how is this relationship artificially created? By the internal organ. It may be argued the ties of affection are natural and it is improper to call them artificial. For throughout nature we find even in the lower animals the same feelings for their young ones. That indeed is correct. But what is here sought to be conveyed amounts to this:—*Iswara's* creations are natural. While those of a *Jiva* are artificial or imaginary. If *Iswara* would have created happiness in those who are called sons, another father would have felt equally for all sons of other persons equally with his own. Thus then, an imaginary connection or relationship created by *Jiva* in his internal organ through the medium of *Maya*, leads him to be a source of his own misery. The conclusion is therefore evident, that all objects have neither pleasure nor pain in them; but what pleasure or pain we vainly attribute to them is due to our ignorance. This can only be rendered plain by example. Wealth is generally believed to be a source of happiness. If it were so, all persons having wealth ought to have been happy. But is this really the case? By no means.

We all know how fireflies are attracted in autumn to the light of a lamp, they dance and frisk, hover and fall into the fire, you cannot keep them off; to them it is a pleasure thus to be present near the fire. If fire were endowed with such pleasing sentiments or say happiness, everyone would have likewise felt it. In the cold winter with a bitter frost, and sharp winds blowing, it is indeed extremely pleasant to sit by the fireside, but when the dogdays come and the hot blasts try our nerves, we never think of fire, we avoid it and court water; this should not be if any subject had in it the particles of happiness or misery. The *rationale* according to the *Sidhanti* is, when a firefly is actuated with a desire of touching fire, its *Boodhi* loses its changibility, and by a relationship with it and desire, it is made steady, when perception of happiness is realized. When a person desires for an object, a relation is established between his desire and the internal organ, it loses its unsteadiness, and therefore he cognises felicity. Thus we find happiness is not situated in a subject, the same thing may be a source of happiness in some and pain in others. We all know the function of the internal organ is never fixed, or steady, it is ever changing according to the subject which demands its attention : it is therefore said to be subject to birth and death. But knowledge is not so.

What is knowledge ? This is the subject of *Vedanta*. Knowledge is Self. That is the shortest and best answer. But it may be argued, knowledge is only an attribute or quality of Self, through which he discovers all objects. In that case the question is whether that knowledge is eternal or transient ? If the answer be in the affirmative that will establish Self and knowledge identically the same. For Self is eternal and not-self non-eternal. Therefore to say knowledge is eternal brings it in the same category with Self. You cannot regard knowledge as a distinct substance from Self, in that case it will be non-eternal ; so that to speak of knowledge as eternal and yet distinct from Self, will be clearly impossible as indicating existence of properties directly opposed to one another. If on the other hand it be contended, knowledge is not-self. 'Not-self' is insentient, and devoid of intelligence, as for instance 'a jar.' It is non-eternal too. Because when a thing is non-eternal it is insentient. Therefore knowledge cannot be maintained with any show of reason to be non-eternal; on the other hand it is eternal. But there is only one substance that is eternal and secondless and that is Self or *Brahma* therefore knowledge is identical with Self. Apart from what we have been saying there are other considerations leading to the same conclusion. For instance, a quality of a substance may or may not be present all along. It may appear in a subsequent state of development, remain for a short time, then disappear.

We find this notably in flowers and fruits. The rich juice and sweetness of several edible varieties of fruits are only produced in a subsequent stage of development when they are ripening. In the prior stages these qualities were absent, as they will disappear when over ripe. Therefore starting with these premises, if knowledge were a quality of Self, he would be sometimes conscious and at others unconscious, at least his quality will be short-lived *i. e.*, transient. But since knowledge is eternal in duration, his resemblance with Self is complete.

What continues in all conditions of time is called eternal. We have only three divisions of time—waking, dreaming, and profound slumber. In all these states knowledge continues. Even in the condition of profound slumber the continuance of knowledge is proved by individual experience of felicity. A person on rising from sleep exclaims " I was sleeping happily, I knew nothing then." This should never follow, if there is no actual perception of felicity, and the subsequent remembrance is a fact of positive knowledge; for an unknown thing never crosses the memory. The sensory organs have no relation with knowledge. For in that sleep, the senses are at perfect obeyance; they cease to carry on their functions yet there is no absence of knowledge. Thus then knowledge is eternal and as Self never exists without it, they are therefore one.

The 'necessity' for knowledge is emancipation. Works and devotion are quite powerless in that way, they may lead to a better abode but they cannot make a person free from future re-births. There are various opinions on the subject : but from a *Vedantin's* view there can be no freedom from metempsychosis without knowledge, so a theosophist has nothing proper for him to do. He is beyond the pale of works and devotion. They are only the nethermost rungs by which the top of the ladder is to be reached. Good works make the mind pure, and remove its blemishes, devotion helps to make it steady, they are therefore only means to the acquisition of knowledge. All works are undertaken with a distinct desire of reaping their benefits hereafter. That means re-birth, but a theosophist has no desire of continuing his existence; he abstains from *Karma*. He waits only to see his cup of fructescent works—which have already commenced to bear fruit, and have produced his present existence—drained; he is no hurry about it, he does not wish for his death to come at once and make him free, but patiently abides his time. Prior to knowledge, whatever acts he had undertaken, and what have already been done cannot produce any more fruits, for they are destroyed by it. It is for inculcating this grand truth that we find an emphatic mention in all treatises dealing on the *Vedanta*, that a wise person has no more need of works and devotion, when he has obtained a thorough knowledge of Self; as a result of that, he exclaims " I am *Brahma*." Just as a torch is extinguished by a traveller when he arrives at the door of his own house, or as the husk is thrown away after the grains have been gathered.

It will thus be found, that knowledge and works with devotion are naturally opposed to each other. For which the former brings on emancipation, the latter an objective existence in a better sphere, or its reverse, according to the merit of the works and the dignity of the object worshipped. It remains also to be observed that with thorough knowledge, actions are incompatible. Why? Because Self is regarded by a person engaged in works, as an agent and instrument. He is apt to exclaim " I am doing virtuous actions and their fruits must be my portion." A wise person has no such desire, he is devoid of virtue and vice, happiness and misery, and he knows Self is unconditioned, the Absolute, *Brahma*. As regards devotion, a theosophist knows not any distinction of worshipper and the object worshipped. He knows everywhere there is the same play of that one Intelligence which is nothing more or less than *Brahma*. Hence he has no inclination for devotion. To look upon Self as subject to the bondage of future re-births is the greatest of all mistakes, which knowledge only dispels. And in this, there is nothing unique; for as we have had occasion to mention, just as a snake is removed from a rope, when it is fully known, so knowledge of Self establishes his oneness with *Brahma*, and he is eternal and free. As for the destruction of the snake, knowledge of the rope alone is enough for the purpose, so in regard to emancipation, knowledge of Self alone is capable of bringing it about, and there is no need of works and devotion. In the *Shastras*, knowledge is called emancipation. It means, knowledge alone is a source of release. And works and devotion are not included in it.

At first sight, one is bewildered to find works, (good, of course) and devotion are helpless. They are helpless in cutting off the chain of consecutive re-births. That is in strict accordance to the *Karmaic* Law which knows no exception. Because every action must produce a fruit; the meritorious works in this way bear good fruits, which a person to enjoy must reincarnate in a better sphere ; after their consummation he is hurled back into an earthly existence, to reap what he had sown in the past. Similarly the bad works lead to a nether sphere. Works and devotion are simply means to knowledge. If it be said, no theosophist in that case, can ever succeed in attaining emancipation. Prior to his knowledge he had been engaged in devotion and good works, and they must necessarily subject him to re-births. The reply is, there is no need for that ; save and beyond the ' fructescent works' which have commenced to bear fruit, and which terminate with the present life of the individual, knowledge is capable of extinguishing the seeds of past *karma* which are to fructify hereafter. The natural acts of eating and sleeping, and satisfying the natural calls are a matter of habit, they cause him no injury. Because there is an absence of desire in him. In other words, he is never desirous of eating this or that, or discarding another, makes no choice of his bed. It would thus appear that desire plays no insignificant part either in our present or in determining the future life. But opinions are divided, and the reader will find the arguments for and against, in the usual place. In connection with this subject, it is worth mentioning, there are two extreme views advocated by their respective partisans, *viz.* :—Restraint and Immunity from restraint. The learned author of the *Panchadasi* upholds the first, as there are others of equal authority maintaining the latter view.

In the *Brihadaranyakopanishad* we find it mentioned, a theosophist liberated in life is absolved from works good and bad, unsoiled by sinful works, uninjured by what he has done and left undone. Anandagiri says:—" The theosophist so long as he lives may do good and evil as he chooses and incur no stain, such is the efficiency of knowledge. The commentator of the *Vedantasara* Nrisinha Sarasvati reviews it in the following words:—Some one may say, it will follow from this that the theosophist is at liberty to act as he chooses, that he can act as he likes, cannot be denied in the presence of texts of Revelation, traditionary texts and arguments like these 'not by matricide, not by paricide.' 'He that does not identify not-self with self, whose inner faculty is unsullied,—he, though he slay these people, neither slays them, nor is slain.' He that knows the truth is sullied neither by good actions nor by evil actions.'...... In answer to all this we reply: True, but as these texts are only eulogistic of the theosophist; it is not intended that he should thus act." Thus then, we find the supporters of Immunity from restraint basing their authority on the *Vedas* and *Upanishads* advocate *Yathestacharana*, forgetting the impossibility of such freedom of action in a person who has acquired the supreme wisdom.

Frequent mention has been made of Illusion, and it requires a passing notice before we close. The source of an illusion is ignorance. A trite example is to mistake a rope for a snake. But it may be asked, how is it produced. There are several ways to account for it. For instance, a *Naiyayika* would say a person must have the impression of a snake seen in a previous period of time, and a defect in his sight. Given these two conditions and the snake illusion is sure to follow. In other words, when a person has seen a real snake in the past, its impression remains ever afterwards, it may be roused by the stimulus of an object resembling it, or by the force of words adequately representing it, so that in the dark when he comes across a bit of string, that stimulates the dormant impression of a snake seen in the distant past and he fancies he has a snake in front of him, which he avoids either by running away, or avoiding it anyhow; or he may have defective vision and that also brings it about. But on the other hand, it cannot be urged that a person whose sight is good, is not liable to be the subject of a similar illusion; therefore this view is not a correct one. The *Vedantin* accounts for it in quite a different way. His method is called. "The indescribable." In the visible perception of an object, the internal organ plays an important part. When a substance is seen, its cognition takes place by the internal organ establishing a connection with the object through the sense of vision; then it assumes the shape of the object to be cognized, drives away the ignorance resting on it, and at the same time illuminates or cognizes it. "The stock illustration of this is that of water flowing from a well or tank by means of a narrow open channel, emptying itself into the square beds with raised edges into which a field is sometimes divided, for the purpose of irrigation, and assuming the shape of those beds. The illuminated internal organ is the water, and the operation is called an evolution or modification of that organ." In the case of an illusion when a rope is mistaken for a snake, the function of the internal organ projected by the eyes, establishes a connection, with it, but the obstacles or defects as they are called (darkness etc.,) do not determine the modification of that organ, as to make it assume the shape of the rope, consequently its envelopment of ignorance continues to be present. No snake is actually created in it, for if it were so, a light brought to discover what the thing lying in front is, discovers no more snake, but only a bit of string; this should not be; therefore we find, knowledge of a rope is an obstacle to the existence of a snake: so long as we do not know it to be so, the snake created or superimposed on it, by the force of ignorance, exists to all intents and purposes (relatively though) to the individual subject to that illusion. Then again, it cannot be said, no snake exists in the rope, for on appealing to individual experience, it will be found, that in all such instances men have been known to behave exactly as they would, if they had a real snake before them. Since therefore you cannot particularize one way or the other, "Snake is or is not existent" it is called 'indescribable.' It is a modification of ignorance, or better still, its changed condition. There are two causes at work for its production and discovery. Its formal cause is the particle of external ignorance situated on the rope, which transforms it into a snake, while the particle of ignorance situated on Intelligence discovers it in that changed condition.

The other doctrines of illusion need not detain us, as the reader will find them amply mentioned and argued with all the resources of our author's vast erudition. Illusion and knowledge are opposed to each other. Illusion is a modification of the dark quality of Ignorance, while knowledge is a modification of its good quality, which is light itself. There can be no illusion after knowledge has once arisen.

The student of Self-knowledge is to mould his internal organ into the modification of *Brahma*. Now, modification signifies assuming the shape of an object. In the case of formless *Brahma*, how can thought be moulded after it. This is a question that is easily met. What is meant, implies no contradiction; you are constantly to dwell upon non-duality of Self and *Brahma*, and when that has been firmly fixed in your mind, by repeated practice, you are indissolutely one with the subject of your thought. In this way, "I am *Brahma*" is the acme of knowledge and height of felicity. When that has been fully realized, there is no more any hankering left after material comforts; pleasure and pain, hunger and thirst, heat and cold,—nay the most adverse circumstances will fail to unruffle the calm equanimity of a face radiant with beatific light. Various are the means of arriving at this knowledge. The usual means 'Discrimination,' 'Indifference' etc., only pave the way to it; constant study, hearing the precepts of a Guru versed in *Brahma Jnana*, consideration and profound contemplation are the chief factors. *Yoga* is a sort of Self-training that helps to make the mind unwavering and steady, and leads to the same goal finally. All our *Shastras*, how muchsoever they may differ in theory, are entirely of one accord so far as *Mukti* is concerned; their processes may differ, but the finality is everywhere the same. In this way, that staunch advocate of Materialism, Kapila, sees no necessity of discarding final disenthrallment from consecutive re-births. With him, *Prakriti Sakhyatkar* is supreme knowledge. The ordinary description of knowledge answers not the sense in which we have used it. An ignorant person is called one who has a conceit for his body ; one may be a man of vast reading, yet so long as he mistakes Self with this or that, his physical body or the sensory organs, he must come under the category of the ignorant. Because he can no more be freed till his mistake or illusion is cleared away. Thus we find the ignorant and the wise are the respective seats of bondage and emancipation ; for the first is marked with desire, while the last is perfectly indifferent. The potency of desire even shakes a man of firm intellect, and whatever indifference he may have, is put to an extreme stretch, so that he has always to keep a thorough watch, to mount guard on the door-way of his *antakaran*. His desire may unruffle him momentarily, but the firm knowledge which he has acquired can never bring back the perception of reality in what he has once discovered to be unreal. He knows phenomena are unreal, material comforts equally so : unlike a dull person, when he shews an indifference for worldly goods, at best, it is but an invisible knowledge of their unreality and not a visible perception ; or it may have been brought about by the presence of defects, so that, no sooner the defect is removed he is after them again, bent more for the accumulation of riches. But the indifference of the wise is caused by the visible perception of unreality, and if ever he shows any true regard for them, that unreality is removed for the time being, but it cannot continue ever afterwards. Just as a snake is removed, when the rope is discovered, and there is not a possibility of its being mistaken again. Thus then, as a wise man never becomes a subject of illusion after he has once discovered it, his indifference is therefore called firm. Whereas in the ignorant, his indifference is apt to come and go, hence it is said to be produced by the presence of defects. That is to say, just as a person after coitus feels an aversion for a female and is extremely indifferent to her, so in wealth and riches there are defects too, which produce indifference for the time being, till a person is re-agitated with a desire of acquisition. The ignorant look upon their self as a mine of affliction, while a theosophist looks upon him as one with *Brahma* whose sole essence is joy. But for such knowledge to arise, there are several grades. Hence it is said to be ordinary and particular. Now the particular variety comes after ordinary knowledge, by means of what are called Indications. In comprehending the transcendental phrases "That art Thou," and their like, the meaning can only be cleared by Indication of abandoning a part of the meaning ; for instance 'That' refers to *Brahma* and 'Thou' *Jiva*. The proposition is to prove their identity. But there is a conflicting element in their composition, for both are Intelligence, yet one is marked with visibility, and the other with invisibility, therefore by deleting them from both sides of the equation, we have Intelligence equal to Intelligence.

The reader will constantly meet with the words Intelligence and Consciousness, Self and not-self, Being and non-being. They require a passing notice. From a *Vedantin's* standpoint, there is one Intelligence pervading everywhere ; no matter a thing may be insentient,—a bit of stone for instance, yet it is prevaded by it, and that is *Brahma* ; our next word is only another name for it. Modern science traces in all substances the presence of a subtle force called *Odyle*. It was first discovered by Riechenbach, who wrote a treatise on the subject but only to be laughed at. In his experiments, very carefully conducted and including a large body of metals metalloids and other substances, he had found the presence of magnetism sufficient to influence a sensitive. It is everywhere present. We have therefore sufficient grounds based on science to connect intelligence with bodies appearing to all intents and purposes a mass of insenticiency. Self and *Atma* are synonymous, they refer to the principle of individuality the perception of "I am I." He is 'existence,' 'intelligence' and 'bliss.' What is uncreated and eternal is called 'being' or 'existence.' Not-self includes all other objects—in short phenomena ; while self is noumena. 'Non-being' is the opposite of 'being.' It signifies unreality. What is not eternal is called unreal. Therefore as the world we live in, with its contents, are liable to destruction, they are unreal, while self alone is real.

Destruction of the world is called '*pralay*' as *Mahapralay* means total destruction. But in reference to it, opinions are divided. The general belief is that no such total destruction ever happens, and we have *Sankhyakar's* protest against it.

It was not intended that the whole ground covered by the accompanying work should figure in this preliminary notice. We had touched on the main features of the Vedantic Doctrine to impart an idea of its philosophy and help the reader to form correct notions of the technical terms, with which every philosophy worth the name must necessarily abound; and in this, we believe, we have done our best to succeed. It cannot be too often repeated that the subject is as vast as it is important, and requires a patient study. There is much to profit by, and a great deal more. To succeed in mastering it, will depend a great deal on the personal endeavour and the amount of labour and time spent.

And in thus bringing to a close, we cannot but acknowledge with thanks the valuable assistance received from Babu Heeralal Dhole of Calcutta, for the labour devoted in correcting the proofs as they were passing through the press and expediting its publication. Labour of an anxious professional work leaves little inclination for continued literary effort and that will account for any shortcomings, so far as its English version is concerned. We had aimed at correctness more than beauty of diction, and have followed the text closely and faithfully.

S. R.

VICHAR SAGAR.

ON THE ASCERTAINMENT OF REALITY AND THE HAPPINESS IT YIELDS.

INTRODUCTORY STANZA.

I AM* that pure and infinite Self, who is bliss, eternal, manifested, all-pervading, and the substratum of all that has name and form. Whom the intellect cannot discern but who discerns it,—imperishable, without a beginning—Hari, Vishnu, Mahesh, Sun, Moon, Varun, Yam, Force, Dhanesh, Ganesh—an object of meditation for devout sages everywhere, who is all kindness and consciousness. "His associate am I," thus to consider Him (as an associate) is illusion or false knowledge. Who knows not him, confounds the objective world

---

* To one acquainted with the mode of worship which a non-dualist adopts, the introductory stanza needs no explanation. But it is otherwise with the generality of readers, who may conclude it an height of impertinence thus to raise one's own Self to the dignity of the Supreme BRAHMA, the Absolute and Unknowable of Western Pantheists, as the author evidently does in the opening line. On this subject the *Panchadasi* (Book IX. Verse 73.) says, "Self indicated by the signs of bliss, sentiency &c., is the Impartite Supreme-Self. 'I am that Self,' in this way is he to be worshipped." But then BRAHMA is an impersonality, actionless, without any attributes, yet to differentiate It by the indications of felicity, intelligence &c., may appear puzzling and inconsistent, inasmuch as it virtually amounts to an admission of personality in impersonality. We find it distinctly laid down in all *Vedántic* works that this is neither inconsistent nor unauthoritative. In the *Sháriraka*

for something real, in the same way as a snake is created in a chord; but who looks the world as poisonous as a snake is a real knower of Self—and such Self is to be recognized as actionless, pure and beautiful. To Him I offer my salutation.

(Obs.)—What is eternal, bliss, Self-manifested, all-pervading and substrate of name and form.
Whom intellect cannot discern, but who discerns it.
I am that pure Self and infinite.

[This is its paraphrase.]

The purport is to establish non-duality, that is to say the Individual Spirit or *Atmá* is non-different from the Universal Spirit, PARABRAHMA—the Absolute, after the manner of the transcendental Vedic phrase "That art Thou" or "I am BRAHMA" &c. But that Supreme Self or *Brahmá* has peculiar charterising traits—his predicate—which are being set forth as follows:—He is joy, self-manifested, all-pervading and substrate of all that has name and form. Moreover intellect cannot discern him, but he discerns it. That is to say, the function of a word's strength cannot influence the individual's intellect in such a manner as to help the cognition or perception of *Brahma*, but he can only be perceived by the indications of a word acting upon the function of the internal organ. A person whose intellect is faulty and impure, cannot perceive him, but one whose intellect is pure and faultless discovers him. It is to be understood from this interpretation, that a person pure in intellect knows the *Brahma* not by the pervasion of the result, but by the pervasion of the

---

Sutras (Chap. III. Book II. Verse 11 and 33) Vyas expounds BRAHMA in the concluding portion of his chapter in that way. As a Pantheist, the author is at perfect liberty, with right and consistency in his side, to put his BRAHMA in Hari, Vishnu, Mahesh, in short anywhere and everywhere. For Brahma is here a first Principle and not a Personal God; as such it is everywhere present, and at all times; even the meanest tadpole that thrives in the smallest accumulation of water collected in a roadside ditch has its PARABRAHMA equally with the mightiest emperor that rules the mightiest nation on the surface of the earth.

modification of the internal organ, and as the light of a lamp discovers another object, the modification of the internal organ has not a similar power of discovering the *Brahma*; but like a covered object discovered by breaking the cover which conceals it, so by removing the ignorance which rests on *Brahma*, It is discovered for its self-luminosity and therefore *Brahma* stands in no need of the intellect. He is the discoverer of all objects, consequently He is said to be not a subject of discovery for the intellect, though He discerns it.

In this manner is established his self-luminosity.* Moreover *Brahma* is pure and infinite. These are the indications of differentiation. That is to say, if *Brahma* were only bliss, then it would be mistaken for material happiness, or with the property of felicity which a *Naiydyika* attributes to Self. To prevent such misconception,

---

* It is needless to say the Commentator leaves the matter quite unexplained. By introducing a learned metaphysical interpretation to a plain piece of poetry he misses his way and is bewildered himself. But it needs clearing up hence we subjoin our interpretation as explained in the *Vedantasara* :—" For whilst the need of the pervasion by the modification of the internal organ is admitted, [for the cognition of the veiled *Brahma*, as of other unknown object] the need of its pervading the result *viz.*, the unveiled *Brahmá* is denied. As it has been said " For the removal of the Ignorance [resting] on BRAHMA, its pervasion by the modification of the internal organ is requisite ; but the authors of the *Shastras* deny that [in His case] there is need of its pervading the result." For, " As *Brahma* is self-luminous, the light [necessary for illuminating the jar &c.,] is not employed [in His case]." As He is self-luminous, no sooner has his enveloping darkness of Ignorance been removed by the internal organ, He is revealed, and the reflection of intelligence on the internal organ required for discovering all inanimate objects &c., is not needed in His case. It may be asked what is the necessity of creating such a subtle distinction ? The reply is. *Brahma* is regarded neither as an object of cognition, nor a subject. According to the VEDANTA, cognition follows only when the intellect or its reflected intelligence assumes the shape of the object, (jar &c.) it seeks to cognise through the sight and other sensory organs. If *Brahma* were a subject or object of cognition, a relation will be created and relation always implies dualism. Hence *Brahma* is knowledge in the abstract.

the blissfulness of *Brahma* is said to be eternal. Material happiness is non-eternal and the attribution of felicity to self is also non-eternal according to the *Naiyâyikas*. If BRAHMA were only eternal then as ether, time &c., are also regarded in *Nyâya* to be eternal, consequently there will be a pervasion of mistake, that is to say, *Brahma* would in that case be mistaken with ether, time and the rest. Hence with the eternal *Brahma* the indication of self-luminosity is added, because though ether is said to be eternal, yet its luminosity is not admitted in *Nyaya*, on the other hand, it is said to be insentient. Thus then, coupling luminosity and blissfulness as indications of *Brahma* with Its eternal nature, all sources of fallacy and misconception are removed. For the luminosity of the Sun, and the luminosity of intelligence—a property of self—can lay no claim of identity with *Brahma* as they are transient and non-eternal—[because the supporters of the transient theory of intelligence, say all acts of consciousness follow like a continuous current of water, in which a second conception succeeds a prior one, and so on ;] while *Brahma* is pervasion. The sun is luminous but that luminosity is finite and not all-pervading. A *Naiyâyika* does not admit the pervasion of Self, but looks upon him as finite. In the same way, the transient intelligence or consicousness is also regarded as finite and not all-pervading. Therefore *Brahma* has been described as self-luminous and all-pervading.

If you say *Brahma* is only all-pervading, then as ether (*akas*) or space, time, quarters &c., are similarly regarded in *Nyâya*, and as the different other schools (*Prabhakar, Sankhya* &c.,) put a similar construction on the properties of Self, *Prakriti* &c., there is a likelihood of *Brahma* being mistaken with all and every one of them, hence to do away with such a misconception, *Brahma's* pervasion is coupled with 'substrate.' That is to say, It is not only pervasion but substrate of every thing that exists. [For name and form are indications of creation.]

Now, ether and the rest are pervasive, but they are not the substrate of name and form, similarly a *Naiyayika* and *Prabhakar* regard Self (*Atmâ*) to be pervasive, but they do not admit him to be the substrate of name and form ; Kapila looks upon his *Prakriti* in a similar light of pervasion, but not as the substrate of all things that have name and form. Thus then Its difference is clearly established by the indications set forth in the above manner, and there is no chance for a mistake or misconception.

Simply to regard *Brahma* as the substrate of name and form is open to misconception, inasmuch as the illusion of a snake in a chord produces both name and form, which are perfectly unreal, hence to prevent such a fallacy, it is said to be undiscernible by the intellect but is the discoverer of that intellect *i.e.*, self-luminous. Now coupling it with this one predicate (self-luminous), precludes all sources of mistake with other substances (set up by the other sects) from the indications of *Brahma*. Moreover according to the *Vedánta*, in the illusory creation or superimposition of a snake in a chord, the substrate of the snake's name and form is said to be the intelligence associated with the rope and not the rope itself; and that only ordinary (or gross) perception of the snake is produced for the time being, to be removed after the discovery of mistake. Yet even here, the instance does not clearly apply, because for the presence of that one predicate already indicated, with the other indications of *Brahma* 'undiscernible by the intellect' &c.

If *Brahma* were only admitted to be self-luminous, then as there are worshippers who regard their object of worship as Self (*Atmá*) in the same light, there is consequently a mistake of *Brahma* with self.* To prevent it, *Brahma* is said to be pure. Now those worshippers regard Self to be self-luminous, but then he has the impurities of Ignorance (*Avidya*) present in him. Thus then

---

* To a non-dualist who regards BRAHMA and Self to be non-different, what is more proper than that mistake (as it is called here) to be confirmed. It is the dictum of the *Vedanta*, *Upanishads* and forms the subject of the present treatise. But the doctrine of non-duality is in the opposite direction, Self is mistaken with BRAHMA and taken for such, so that no separate cognition of Self remains. This is meant. Nothing was further from the author's mind than to introduce a contradiction in the opening passage of his work. He has taken pains to establish non-duality and yet to introduce duality is absurd.

by connecting the self-luminosity of *Brahma* with purity, the apparent contradiction is cleared. If it be affirmed that *Brahma* is pure only, then a source of fallacy crops up. For according to Kapila, *Atmá* is regarded as pure, hence *Brahma* will be mistaken with Self. To preclude it, *Brahma* has another indication and that is infinite. Now the author of the *Sankhya Philosophy* does not take Self to be infinite, hence this distinction is enough for the purpose of distinguishing *Brahma* from Self. Time, place, &c., are all considered as indestructible in the *Sankhya* system, but all material substances dependent on them are prone to destruction, hence they are not infinite. But *Brahma* is infinite to the best sense of the term, It depends not on time, place &c., hence indestructible.

Though for the purpose of removing all unnatural inferences it may be remarked that the connection of two such predicates as joy, eternal &c., is enough, the introduction of several predicates has been used to help an enquirer of truth, to know BRAHMA by Its several indications from different standpoints. And, I am that BRAHMA which has all those predicates. This is the purport of the stanza.

But it may be alledged, that in the introduction, the usual valedictory address ought to be made either to Vishnu, Siva, or the other Devas, and to throw them into the shade and introduce Self in this manner is improper. That imputation is cleared in the following verse.

"From Vishnu, Mahesh, it is an infinite succession
To Law [nature] Sun, Moon, Varuna, Yama, Sakti,
                                            Dhanes and Ganes."

Like a never ending sea, with its continuous train of waves, Vishnu, Mahes and the rest are all a continued succession of Devas, indicated by the waves of the sea, and infinite too, and they are each and all of them equally identical with myself. Thus then in praising Self they have all been duly praised, and the impropriety of praising Self is removed.

But it may be said that Vishnu and Siva can properly be looked upon as *Iswara's* waves, and not of yours or your self, hence it is necessary that the work must open with a praise of *Iswara*; as by watering the roots of a tree, its trunk and leaves are all satiated, so by praising *Iswara* alone, all Devas are praised; and by praising your individual Self, no praising of the Devas can follow. But there is no such apprehension, as will appear in the sequel, immediately.

"That kind [God] who is omniscient,
An object of contemplation for the wise,
Whom to connect with an associate is false knowledge."

That kind *Iswara* is contemplated by all devout sages and his associate of *Maya* is as unreal as a snake in a chord, or a city created in a dream, so that by seeking to praise him if Self be duly praised it applies to him, for to contrive his difference is only imaginary.

But that *Iswara* resembles the pure *Brahma*, and as you cannot claim an identity with It, consequently it is proper that the Impersonal BRAHMA (without attributes) be duly mentioned in the introductry stanza, and by speaking well of It, all will be equally praised. That cannot follow from praising yourself. But it is otherwise.

Without Its knowledge the world appears real.
But like the knowledge of a rope removing the snake,
Its knowledge reduces the world to nothing.
And Self is identical with It.

As ignorance of a rope produces a snake on it, which is removed when all the parts of that rope are fully known, so a full knowledge of BRAHMA reduces the objective world into its normal condition of unreality, [and there is no more any hankering left either for the world or its goods, and a man is so to speak, on the road to emancipation] and I am that Pure BRAHMA. And there is no difference whatever between them, when regarded in the light of a part and whole, modified and modifier, or worshipper and worshipped. And in the absence of that difference, there is likewise a want of the other subservient conditions or relations *viz.*, of cause, and luminosity;

container, and contained; consequently my self is proved to be without them, so that by praising Self, BRAHMA is duly praised.

Now there is yet another difficulty :—You belong to the sect of *Dadupuntis* who are worshippers of Ramchandra and as such, it is very proper, that you should invoke a blessing from your guardian Deity, by duly propitiating him with the necessary praise or valediction. For a satisfactory solution of this point the concluding lines of the verse* say :—

> "One must want a good perception and have good deeds to worship Ram without motive.
> I am that Ram and him I offer my reverence."

That Ram, who is only to be worshipped by good deeds performed without a motive of reward either here or hereafter, (when only can a person have his perception cleared in a manner, as to perceive him) is non-different from myself, hence in the absence of an object of worship or of devotion, to whom am I to offer my reverence? that is why I pay my respects to no one. Or it means :—A person who for a clear perception of the Supreme BRAHMA† has served Ram with good actions without any aim of being benefited, and whose self is non-different from PARABRAHMA, has no other object for his reverence, as all are included in his Self, who is the abiding intelligence; and in the absence of such another object different from Self, no proper worship can be tended to it.

---

* Fifth couplet.   † This word is neuter.

REMARKS PREFATORY.

The *Sutras*, their Commentaries, and other works in Sanscrit,
There are many and several ;
Yet I speak in vernacular
For them, who are dull in intellect.

Though the Sanscrit is replete with the *Vedanta, Sidhanta* and similar other works, yet the present one cannot be termed futile, inasmuch as, persons of dull intellect will fail to profit by the instruction imparted in the learned language, while no such apprehension needs be entertained with regard to "VICHAR SAGAR," as it is written in the vernacular, which men of ordinary calibre shall be able to comprehend. Hence for them it is useful.

By poets many works have been written in vernacular,
Well known are they in the world.
But without seeing the *Vichar Sagar*
Doubts cannot be dispelled.

And, so far as language is concerned, there may be many other works like it, but none of them can remove the doubts concerning the Reality—Self—which the "VICHAR SAGAR" alone is capable of doing. For, several of the authors have written their works after hearing, and are therefore full of errors; besides, in some places, they impart instruction in direct antagonism to the sacred writings, owing to their author's inability to comprehend their real signification, as for instance the work known as *Panchbhakha*. Then again, there are others, who have written with a partial knowledge of the sarced writings such as *Atma Bodh*. Hence they are quite incompetent to clear away the doubts in regard to the (*Atmá*) Spirit or seventh principle in man. While there are others, who have not thoroughly adopted the method of the *Vedanta*. Moreover, the present work is complete in itself, it follows the *Vedanta* text closely, and is nowhere opposed to it. It deals particularly on subjects that help knowledge of Self, hence it is unlike the rest in the vernacular (*bhakha*), but superior to them all.

SECTION I.

[THUS having the *Vedanta* doctrine for its subject, the present work is moved by similar considerations. Without them, a seeker of knowledge will have no inclination for the work, hence I proceed to consider them. These are:—

  I. The qualified person or fit vessel (*adhikārī.*)
 II. The relation (*sambandha.*)
III. The subject (*vishaya.*)
 IV. The necessity to dispel ignorance concerning the non-duality to be demonstrated, and to acquire the blissfulness of *Brahma* (*prayojana.*)

There are three defects in all subjects of the 'internal organ' (*Antakarana*) namely *mal*, *vikshepa*, and *āvarna*. Abstaining the mind from works done with a desire of reward, will cleanse it of all impurities (*mal*).

'Devotional exercises' (*upāsana*) will remove misapprehension (*vikshepa*); and knowledge, concealment or want of apprehension (*āvarṇa.*)

> One free from impurity and misapprehension,
> But only ignorant,
> Who is possessed of all the means,
> Is called, a person qualified (in intellect).

I. The 'qualified individual' is a person, who by the performing of actions without a motive of reward, and devotional exercises, have got rid of all impurities, (*mal*) and misapprehension, (*vikshepa*) and who is subject of one ignorance call it (*avarna*) concealment or want of apprehension, and endowed with the four means of knowledge.

The 'four means' (*sadhana*) are:—

(1.) Discrimination between things eternal and non-eternal, *i.e.*, transient (*viveka*).

(2.) Indifference to the enjoyment of reward in this life or the next. (*Vyrag*).

(3.) Possession of quiescence, self-restraint, faith, concentration, abstinence, and endurance; (*Shat sampati*) and;

(4.) Desire for emancipation.

(1.) Discrimination between eternal and non-eternal is to know Self to be eternal, imperishable, and actionless, and is the only substance of his kind, while the objective world is non-eternal and perishable; that is to say, antagonistic in nature to Self. It is the basis of the other 'means;' for 'indifference' and the rest are produced from it, (without it, they are absent,) hence it is the source or cause of the other 'means' from 'indifference' to 'emancipation.'

A sage acquainted with the drift of the Vedas, calls him 'indifferent' who bent on the attainment of a BRAHMA, discards all other things for they prevent his wish being realized.

(2.) Indifference to the enjoyment of reward in this life or the next. This consists in an utter disregard for enjoyments either in this life or the next. For as shown in the Vedas they are the products of actions, and actions are non-eternal, hence such enjoyments, be it nectar or the blissful abode of heaven, must necessarily be of short duration, [and with their cessation or destruction, the individual will be hurled to re-births], all wise men therefore discard them.

(3.) Quiescence, Self-restraint and the four other substances are:—

(*a.*) Quiescence, (*sama.*)

(*b.*) Self-restraint, (*dama.*)

(*c.*) Faith, (*sradhā.*)

(*d.*) Concentration of thought, (*samādhāna.*)

(*e.*) Abstinence, (*uparati*) and;

(*f.*) Endurance, (*titiksha.*)

[They are now being defined]:—

(*a.*) Quiescence or passivity (*sama*) is to keep the mind aloof from subjects which stand in the way of attaining knowledge of Self; one possessed of it is called tranquil.

(*b.*) Self-restraint (*dama*) consists in the restraining of the external organs of sense, and a person who has so subdued his senses is justly called an intellectual hero.

(c.) Faith *(sradha)* is to believe the utterances of the Vedas and one's Spiritual preceptor.

(d.) Concentration of thought *(samadhana)* is the destruction of all mental objects; [they distract the mind and hence prevent an individual from concentrating his mind, already subjugated and turned away from sensuous objects, on Self.]

(e) Abstinence *(uparati)* is to abstain from all works after having been possessed of the four means of Self-knowledge; to look upon all sorts of enjoyments as poison, [or to abandon, the prescribed acts in the manner laid down in the *Shastras* by turning into an ascetic.]

(f.) Endurance *(titiksha)* is to bear the extremes of heat and cold, hunger and thirst, (pleasure and pain &c.,) with equanimity.

These six 'substances' constitute one of the means, and are not reckoned so many, by a person possessed of discrimination.

The acquisition of 'quiescence' and the rest, called the six substances, is looked upon as one of the four means of practice to attain deliverance; and not as so many distinct or new, and a person, possessing them is called one full of 'discrimination,' for they help to produce discrimination, whereby an individual is enabled to distinguish the eternal from the non-eternal.

(4.) 'Emancipation is to attain BRAHMA, and to destroy bondage, (what subjects a man to continued re-births is called bondage); one desirous of release is a prince of sages. The attainment of BRAHMA and destruction of evil are indications of emancipation or deliverance and to wish for them is known by the term 'desire of release, *(moomooksha)*—this word and emancipation are synonymous.

These are the four means of practice for acquiring self-knowledge. With the three, *(a)* hearing, *(sravana)* *(b)* consideration, *(manana)* *(c)* profound contemplation *(nididhyāsana)*; and the ascertaining of the real signification of 'That' *(Tat)* and 'Thou' *(Twam)* [in the transcendental pharse That art Thou] they are altogether eight in number. That is to say, 'discrimination' and the three others together with 'hearing,' 'consideration,' 'profound contemplation,' and the ascertainment of the real indication of 'That' and 'Thou' [non-duality], constitute the eight means for acquiring knowledge of Self.

These eight are the 'internal,' while sacrifice and other offerings are the 'external' means. One engaged in the practice of the 'internal,' parts company with the 'external.'

The eight means already mentioned commencing with 'discrimination' and ending in the ascertainment of the real signification of 'That' and 'Thou' are called internal, while sacrifice and other similar works (*yaga*) are the external 'means' of acquiring knowledge [of Self]; of these the last are to be avoided, and the former alone to be practised by a seeker of truth. They are called 'internal' because from 'hearing,' or 'knowing them,' apparent or 'visible results,' (*prataksha*), are produced. Discrimination and the other three, are subservient to that 'hearing,' inasmuch as a dull person without them cannot ascertain the drift of the sacred writings from 'hearing' them; and in the same way, 'hearing' 'consideration' and 'profound contemplation' are subservient to knowledge [of Self], for one cannot have any knowledge without them. In like manner, without the ascertainment of the real indication of the words 'That' and 'Thou' the knowledge of non-duality [the individual and universal Spirits are one] cannot arise. Thus is determined the subserviency of the four means 'discrimination,' indifference &c., to 'hearing' and the subserviency of 'hearing' 'consideration' and 'contemplation' to knowledge, hence they are called the eight 'internal means.'

The 'external means' do not yield visible* results, but clear the mind of all ill wishes by hearing or practicising them, as for instance, the sacrificial offerings and similar other works.

[As a rule] they are the ordinary practices of our daily concern in life, and hence worldly, and it is quite possible that a person engaged in their performance with a motive of reward, becomes pure in mind, but then they hurl him to consecutive re-births hereafter, to which, they stand as cause. [For consummation of works is life; and therefore, what he has sown in this, he must reap in the next, and so on till final deliverance.] But for one, who is without any desire of reaping any benefits from them, [or who assigns all actions to the Lord (*Iswara*) and acts as guided by Him], the above sacrifices and other works are merely conducive of making his mind pure and faultless, hence their cause. Thus by his purity of mind he derives knowledge of Self and hence they are its source; and therefore they are called the external, or 'distant' while the internal are the 'proximate.'

Practice of the 'external means,' sacrifice and the rest, or abandoning a wife, children and property &c., are for the acquisition of Self-knowledge; they constitute a qualified person. But for such a qualified person it is very unlikely that he shall be engaged in sacrifice and the above works, hence they are distant. 'Discrimination' and the rest behooving of a qualified individual are therefore 'near' or proximate. But then, there is this difference, that discrimination &c., are beneficial to hearing as 'hearing' is beneficial to knowledge. In such a consideration of discrimination &c., hearing and the rest are comparatively speaking internal, while with regard to the latter the former are 'external.'

Though 'discrimination' and the rest have been described as the internal means for the acquisition of Self-knowledge, and not the external means, in all works, yet they yield visible results in connection with 'hearing,' which are therefore as acceptable to a seeker of truth as hearing and the rest. But that does not hold true with reference to sacrifice and similar works, which are therefore unacceptable to him. Hence they are called internal. In relation to sacrifice &c., they are also internal. Here even, they are recognized as the internal means of Self-knowledge; and if it be duly considered, it will be found that, prior to such knowledge ascertainment of the real indication of That and Thou in the transcendental pharse 'That art Thou' is the principal means for such knowledge. Moreover 'hearing' and the rest are not alluded as such means. For,

'Hearing' [*Sravana*] is to ascertain the drift of the Vedas by analysis and argument,

'Consideration' (*manana*) is the unceasing reflection on the non-duality of the individual self and the secondless Reality *Brahma* with arguments for and against;

'Profound contemplation' (*nididhyasana*) is the continuance of ideas conformable to *Brahma*, to the exclusion of the notions of body and such other inconsistent things with It:

'Meditation' (*Samadhi*) is a ripe condition of the above profound contemplation so that it is included in it, and not a separate means.

Now all these are not the direct means for practising Self-knowledge, but they cause the destruction of impossible and inconsistent ideas, and thus clear the intellect of all its blemishes and frailties. Doubts are looked upon as impossible ideas, and antagonistic, are the inconsistent.

'Hearing' (of the Vedanta doctrine) clears away any lurking doubts concerning the proofs adduced to support the subject.

'Consideration' removes such doubts in regard to what is to be proved :—

Whether the utterances of the Vedanta seek to expound the secondless Reality *Brahma*, or something different, any doubts as to the proofs adduced in support of the subject, it seeks to demonstrate, are cleared by 'Hearing.'

Moreover 'consideration' removes all doubts as to whether non-duality or duality is true; and of them, non-duality is the subject that is to be explained.

To know the body [organs] &c., as real, and to consider the individual self and *Brahma* as twain, are called 'inconsistent ideas.'— They are antagonistic to Self-knowledge and are removed by 'profound contemplation.'

In this way 'hearing,' 'consideration,' and 'profound contemplation' destroy impossible and inconsistent ideas which stand in the way as obstacles to such knowledge; and inasmuch as such obstacles are removed by hearing &c., therefore the latter are looked upon as the source of knowledge and called so. But then they are not the direct or evident cause. The direct means for Self-knowledge is to hear the utterances of the Vedanta that is to say, to ascertain their drift as has already been explained while defining 'hearing.'

Vedântic utterances are of two kinds (1) *Avantara* (2) *Mahavakyá* or involved, and transcendental.

The first signifies such words as help the cognition of either the Supreme-Self or the individuated Self.

The second has reference to non-duality, and establishes the oneness of the individual self and *Brahma*. Hence the words employed with this object are termed transcendental.

The first produces knowledge marked by indivisibility as *Brahma* is (existent), while the second establishes knowledge marked by visibility as " I am *Brahma*."

'Thou art *Brahma*,' is pronounced by the teacher to create a relation between the pupil and *Brahma*, which he no sooner perceives than he exclaims, 'I am *Brahma*' and thus acquires visible knowledge, [knowledge in which *Brahma* is established as a visibility, inasmuch as, the first personal pronoun used in conjunction with the subject of his knowledge (*Brahma*) is involved in no mystery, but something tangible, apparent and visible, and when such tangibility is extended to *Brahma* by the non-difference existing between the two, then the last also is rendered alike apparent and visible]. For this conditional relationship between the pupil who hears the words, and the precepts conveyed by them, through the means of hearing, the words relating to that hearing, are determined as the cause of knowledge, with this difference, that the 'included' or 'involved' words relating to that hearing are called the source of invisible knowledge, while the transcendental, under similar conditions, are the source of visible knowledge.

Thus then, the transcendental words bring forth only visible and not invisible knowledge to every one. But it has been alleged by the professor of another province, [dissenter] that, by means of 'hearing' 'consideration' and 'profound contemplation' in connection with the 'words' is only produced the visible knowledge, and by words only, (without hearing and the rest) the invisible, and not the visible knowledge. For it is sure, if words will produce such visible knowledge, then the necessity for 'hearing' 'consideration', and 'profound contemplation' ceases altogether. But this apprehension is unfounded, inasmuch as they are needed for excluding or removing the impossible and 'inconsistent ideas' which one may hold concerning the *Brahma*, or its non-difference with individual self.

Hence we find, though 'words' help the cognition of the *Brahma* as visible, and 'hearing,' and the rest are useful in the manner aforesaid (as expounded in the *Sidhanta*), yet one may contend, that, after the knowledge of the visible kind has been attained by a person, he is no more apt to blend it up with impossible or inconsistent ideas, so that, to an advocate of 'words' as the only means helping the visible knowledge, the ascertainment of the real signification of the transcendental phrase,—"That art Thou" is alone sufficient, not only to produce such knowledge, but also to exclude all impossible and inconsistent ideas; and consequently 'hearing' and the rest are futile and unnecessary.

[Now for the opposite doctrine.] Words only produce the invisible, and the practice of 'hearing' 'consideration,' and 'profound contemplation' produces the visible knowledge. In such a view, 'hearing' &c., are not looked upon as futile; but though this doctrine has been adopted by several authors, it is not true. For, it is in the nature of words to discern dimly an object which is covered,* and they cannot reduce it to a visible condition; as for instance the knowledge derivable from the sacred writings about heaven and its Devas, Indra and the rest; and when an object is uncovered, then it is rendered apparent or visible by words as well as inapparent or invisible. When words are used to indicate the existence of an uncovered object, then only the invisible knowledge is proved as "the tenth person† is." Here the neuter verb implies existence, which refers to the tenth, that is near, hence words establish the invisible knowledge. But when words bring in the conception of a

---

* *Vyâvahit* literally signifies what is contiguously placed, an intervening situation, relatively it is distant and mediate as also covered, I have adopted the latter term as easy of comprehension in the same way *Avyâvahit* has been rendered into uncovered; but elsewhere it has been translated into near, and immediate,—all of which the reader will meet with as he proceeds.

† A party of ten persons were crossing a river, on alighting at the opposite bank, one of them counts the rest and as he forgets to count himself, necessarily he stops at number nine. His companions thinking

near object, and reduce it into the condition of 'this is' then only visible knowledge is said to be established by them, and not the invisible. As for instance " *Dasamata* (Tenth) is". In this way, words establish the existence of the 'tenth' and render it visible. Similarly, BRAHMA for its being the all-pervading spirit present in every individual self, is extremely close or near; hence an included word rendered existent is capable of reducing BRAHMA into a visibility. Moreover, like the example '*Dasamata* is' BRAHMA as the soul of every being, and therefore 'near' is determined by the transcendental words, so that such words cannot imply the invisible knowledge of BRAHMA, but indicates visible knowledge, and as has already been mentioned that, when a thing is rendered visible, there cannot exist any impossible or inconsistent ideas concerning it, consequently 'hearing' and the rest are futile. Such a view is inadmissible. Like a Raja, in spite of a visible knowledge of his minister by name Bhurchhoo, who could not know he was his minister, because his knowledge (though visible) was mixed up with inconsistent ideas, so the transcendental words help the cognition of BRAHMA and render it apparent or visible; but to such persons, whose intellects are clouded with impossible and inconsistent ideas, their blemishes stand in the way of knowledge, and 'hearing' and the rest are necessary for clearing the mind; and—one who has already been freed from them, stands in no more need of 'hearing' 'consideration' and 'profound contemplation' and he may not practise them.

Thus in effect, the transcendental words and pharses are the means of the acquisition of Self-knowledge, not so 'hearing' and the rest, which simply destroy the obstacles to such knowledge; so that, they are called the cause. Then again hearing &c., are

him to be mistaken, repeat the same process over and over, always forgetting to count the one who was counting. Thus finding the tenth person missing, they take him for drowned, and bewail at his loss; meanwhile another person coming up to them enquires of their grief and on being informed that their tenth is missing, he points their mistake and shews that none of them is drowned. They now give vent to feelings of joy, as ere now they had been expressing their sorrow.

caused by 'discrimination' and the rest, consequently these last are called the 'means' for practising self-knowledge, and one endowed with the four means, discrimination, indifference, quiescence, and desire of release, is called the qualified person '*adhikari.*'

II. RELATION.

The relation between the subject and the work which treats it, is characterised as the condition of the 'explainer,' and the thing to be explained. Here what explains is termed the explainer, and that which is fit to be so explained is called 'the thing explained.' Then again, between the 'qualified person' and the 'result' (*Phala*) is a relation characterised as a condition of obtainable (*prápyá*) and obtainer (*prapaka*), inasmuch as the result is obtainable to the qualified person who is therefore the obtainer. Hence the obtainable (*prapyá*) is that which is to be obtained, and the obtainer, (or *prapaka*) is the individual who obtains it. Between the 'qualified person' and consideration of the subject is a relation characterised as the consideration of an agent or doer and 'what ought to be done.' Here the qualified person is the 'doer' or 'agent' and consideration or deliberation of a subject by the exercise of reason is 'what ought to be done' (*kartabya*.) Therefore the agent is he who does, makes, performs or practises what he knows; and what deserves to be so done is called *kartabya* 'or proper to be done.' Between the work and knowledge is the relation characterised as the condition of 'product' and 'producer;' because due deliberation of the work produces knowledge, hence it is the parent of knowledge which is a product derived from its study. So that, what produces is called the parent or producer and what is produced, is called its product or offspring. Thus is relation set forth.

III. The Subject is the identity or oneness of the individual-Self with the Universal Spirit *(Brahma)* which is to be demonstrated in this work, and which is the purport of all Vedic utterances; and one contending against such non-duality, or who thinks them as twain, is unwise and a disputatious antagonist of the Vedás

IV. The necessity is the acquirement of felicity which is the essence of *Brahma* and to be one with it, and the removal of

Ignorance,—the source of the world—as injurious to and destructive of it. For, Ignorance is the progenitor of this vast expanse, and an efficient cause of [birth and death] and its attendant miseries, hence it is called injurious and harmful. The attainment of supreme felicity by the removal of Ignorance is called 'Desire of release' (*moksha*) which is the principal aim of the book, hence it is called the 'supreme necessity,' while the intermediate (*avantar*) necessity is knowledge. Now the subject of desire or in other words, what an individual desires to have is called 'supreme necessity' or the chief purport of human life; and as such desire is for the removal of misery and the acquirement of happiness, it is applicable to all individuals. But it is the same as 'desire for release,' hence such desire for release is the 'supreme necessity' or the principal aim of human life. It cannot be construed as knowledge. For knowledge is the means of procuring cessation of misery and happiness, and not their actual destruction or acquirement, hence it is an intervening necessity. Now an intervening necessity is such as helps the attainment of the supreme necessity or the principal aim; of such a nature is knowledge. For, the knowledge derived from a study of the work will procure emancipation, which is the supreme necessity. Hence knowledge is determined as an intervening necessity.

But doubts may accrue as to the validity of what has just been said in the following wise:—The individuated self is like supreme happiness itself, so say the Vedâs; then for him to procure what he has already got is absurd and inconsistent. For, that can refer to a thing which one has not in his possession, and not to what he has. To introduce the least trace of such a doubt is injurious to belief. Determine it well by repairing to a kind preceptor for instruction and it will be found, that the apparent contradiction in the obtaining of that which has already been obtained, resembles the mistake concerning a bangle, said to be lost, but which is all along present in the wrist.

The oppositionist might say that the destruction of *fruitless**

---

* Unreal is the proper word for *anarth* used by the author.

things, and acquirement of supreme felicity is said to be the necessity for the work. But such is impracticable, because in the Vedas '*Jiva*' has been linked to supreme bliss—which you also admit—moreover acquirement can have reference to a thing which one has not, to apply it otherwise, is to create a contradiction, for to obtain what has been always in possession is wholly impossible. Hence the acquirement of supreme bliss by Self which is always such blissfulness himself, is in every respect contradictory. If any one be so disposed to question, then that need not create any disbelief in the necessity of the work, but on the other hand, he should repair to a kind preceptor for instruction on self-knowledge, so that his doubts may be dispersed by illustrating examples.

These examples are :—As one having a bangle in his wrist may through mistake [caused by forgetfulness or absence of mind] consider it to be lost, he then exclaims "I have lost my bangle" but on discovering his mistake at the instance of another who points to his bangle already there, he is apt to say "I have got it." Here the bangle never left the possession of the owner, yet he took it to be lost from mistake, so that when it was pointed out, he says "I have got it," In other words, practicability of obtaining what is already in possession is thus established. Similarly, by the force of Ignorance, a like mistake as to the supreme felicity of Self is brought about, and he is inclined to the belief, Self is unlike such bliss, but *Brahma* is ; and that a separation has taken place between him and *Brahma*, which by devotional exercises he gains over. A large body of persons are labouring under this mistake. If the greatest of the *Pandits* will admit the individuated self and *Brahma* as twain, and not one, he is no better than a dunce. If such a dull person, fortunately (for good actions) come to hear the precept of a professor on the Vedantic doctrine, and acquire it, that is to say, become master of it, by ascertaining its real signification then he exclaims "I possess the supreme felicity through the kindness of the preceptor and the work itself." Now such an expression amounts to this :—that though Self is supreme blissfulness always, and as such, it did exist prior to my being initiated into the meaning (teaching) of the sacred Scriptures, yet as I could not make it out, that does not necessarily establish there was a want of it; but on the contrary from the precepts of his professor he has learnt it all, and knows (through intelligence) such felicity to be his. Therefore he says, he has now acquired the supreme felicity.

Thus is established the necessity of the work for procuring happiness to one, who was already its possessor, [though from Ignorance he could not appreciate, till stirred up by the kind instruction of a professor] and it need not imply any inconsistency. Similarly, the destruction of unreal (*anarth*) is practicable as in the following illustration.

As a fact, no snake exists in a chord at all, yet illusion creates it, which is removed no sooner the person comes to know that it is a bit of rope. In the same way, Self is quite a separate entity from the world, which is unreal like the snake, yet from Ignorance we confound him with it [sometimes with the gross physical, at other times with the subtle body, son, sensuous organs, vital airs, intellect and nothing]; but by the advent of knowledge we discover our mistake, and as this work seeks to impart the necessary instruction for attaining self-knowledge, consequently its necessity to stop what has already ceased to exist, and to procure that which one is already master of, is fully established and that does not imply any contradiction.

Now cessation of the world with its cause (Ignorance) and the acquirement of supreme blissfulness is the purport* of the work. But from what has already been said this is clearly impossible. For cessation means destruction and the two words are convertible terms, so that they reduce a thing to a condition of non-existence. Hence the existence and non-existence of 'desire for release' are both expounded by them. If we say that it causes the cessation of an 'useless thing' then such cessation reduces it into a condition of non-existence. So the acquirement of felicity refers to a condition of existence. Hence both of them cannot be present at one and the same time in the same object. For want and non-want, or existence

---

* Purport and necessity both stand for *Prayojana*.

and non-existence are antagonistic of each other, hence they cannot be present at one and the same time in the same substance. Thus then one may say the necessity for the work is not clearly established.

To such a contention the reply is:—

Between cessation of the world and its occupation, the difference is nil, just as the cessation of the snake in the chord is its knowledge.

The removal or destruction of Ignorance and its product the world, is possession of *Brahma* (*i. e.*, knowledge of self). Hence, between such knowledge and the removal of Ignorance the difference is nil, just as the removal or destruction of the snake in a bit of chord, is to possess a knowledge of it (*i. e.*, proceeds from knowing a chord thoroughly). Thus then, the destruction of all fancied or imaginary objects, in a manner, resembles an occupation of them, and the two are non-different, according to the opinion of the commentator. Hence the destruction of this apparent and tangible objective world, which is also called fruitless, for it yields no results, is *Brahma* itself; for *Brahma* which occupies it all, is essentially existent, and its destruction indicating the same existence [for they have been shown to be equal, and things which are equal to one another are equal to the same thing, here existence is the same thing and *Brahma* and destruction of the world with its cause 'Ignorance' being equal, they both refer to existence] the necessity of the work is established.

Thou kind Guru! deliver him at once from the chain of consecutive re-births, who reads this first section.

Thus are the moving considerations ordinarily declared.

SECTION II.

THE moving considerations of the work have been ordinarily declared in the former Section, this one will treat them particularly. Of the four means of practice which constitute a 'qualified individual' the 'desire of release' is counted as one which is synonymous with emancipation. Destruction of Ignorance with its product—the world, and the attainment of *Brahma* is called emancipation.

Now, a class of writers, who may be properly designated dissenters (*Poorvapakshi*) contend, that such a 'desire of release' as is tantamount to the destruction of the world and its cause 'ignorance,' we seek not to have.

No one desires the destruction of the world with its cause Ignorance, save the man of 'discrimination' who seeks for the destruction of the three kinds of miseries.

The destruction of Ignorance—the source of the world—or call its removal, and its expectation, signifies a desire for it; such a desire actuates no person. But then say, what do they do instead?

There are three kinds of miseries which a man possessed of discrimination wants to get rid of.

They are:—
    (1.) The spiritual or inherent *(adhyátikam)*.
    (2.) The natural *(adhibhuta)*.
    (3.) The accidental *(adhidyva)*.

(1.) The 'spiritual' or 'inherent' are those caused by disease, hunger and thirst &c.

(2.) The 'natural' are those caused by thieves, tigers, snakes &c.

(3.) The 'accidental' are such as are caused by a Yaksha, Raksha, Preta (evil spirit), the planets, winter and heat.

All persons have an equal desire for the destruction of the miseries just cited, and a man of discrimination has no desire to seek the removal of a thing different from misery, hence it is established, that the destruction of Ignorance with its result the objective world, is not the prevailing desire.

Moreover, if a *Sidhanti* will say, "since all are alike desirous to be free from miseries, and as such freedom can only be produced by the destruction of the world with its cause Ignorance, therefore the destruction of the world with Ignorance, is absolutely needed, before such respite can be had;" such an assertion is clearly inadmissible.

For, the *Ayurveda* contains medicines for every form of disease, whose use will cause the removal of the disease and its accompanying pain; in the same way hunger and thirst are appeased by food and drink. In this manner every individual kind of misery can be removed by particular remedies, so that the destruction of Ignorance with the world is no more necessary for the removal of misery.

The destruction of the material world, with its cause Ignorance, and the attainment of *Brahma*, is called 'desire for release;' now that portion of the 'desire for release' which wants a person to reduce the world with its cause into a state of non-existence, is clearly impracticable, as has already been said; the same holds true in regard to that other portion, 'the attainment of *Brahma*,' according to the view of a *Poorbapakshi*.

Desire can only accrue when a person has experience of a thing. *Brahma* is never experienced, hence no one desires to have it.

Here experience refers to knowledge, hence a desire to obtain it, can only proceed from such knowledge or experience of a thing, and what one knows not, nor has experience of, he never desires to obtain.

Now such an extremely unknown substance is ignorance, consequently no one desires to have it. Then again, a qualified individual has no knowledge of *Brahma*, inasmuch as one with such knowledge is not a qualified individual, but an emancipated being; and for such a one, a desire to obtain *Brahma* is no longer possible, [for he is already a *Brahma*] so that, prior to hearing the precepts of the *Vedanta*, as he was full of ignorance, or ignorant of (Self) *Brahma*, he can have no more desire for it (*Brahma*) again. This is why no one desires for release, by causing the destruction of the world with its cause, and attaining to *Brahma*. Hence there is no such person who is desirous for emancipation.

The absence of a 'qualified person' is established in another way by a *Poorbapakshi*;

Desire of material comforts actuates all, but none seeks the road to release.

Merely reading or hearing the work does not constitute a 'qualified person.'

That is to say, all persons are bent after the acquisition of property, for enjoying happiness; moreover such of them as have left all such pursuits in the present life, and have entirely given themselves up to religious asceticism, undergo severe hardships only that they may enjoy happiness hereafter; so that there is everywhere a prevailing desire for the enjoyment of happiness either in the present or the next life. And such desire for material prosperity cannot be determined as one with desire for release; hence it is said the road to release is not sought after by any one. Thus is shown why a 'desire of release' or emancipation is no where present amongst men.

Further, as the prevailing desire is everywhere manifested in the intense thirst for the acquisition of property &c., therefore no one can be said to be subject to indifference, quiescence, self-restraint and abstinence. Thus in the absence of the 'qualified individual,' the necessity for the work exists not.

Thus is set forth the contending view in regard to the 'qualified person.'

THE SUBJECT.

Say [then] *Brahma* and *Jiva* are one and riches cruel.
Brahma is devoid of pain; its [knowledge] destroys all sorts of pain with the root.

It is not possible to establish non-duality which is the subject of the present treatise, inasmuch as *Brahma* is devoid of Ignorance, conceit, anger, spite and a fixed pursuit, [which are called the five sorts of pain) all-pervading, and secondless, *i.e.*, without another thing similar to, or resembling it, while the *Jiva* is subject to pain, finite and many in number—for there are as many *Jivas* as there are bodies—so that if there would have been one *Jiva* present in all bodies, then pleasure or pain affecting a single individual would have been equally felt by all.

Moreover, what the *Vedánta* says in reference to pleasure and pain as functions of the internal organ, such an organ is present in each body, and therefore, its number is many. Hence is it, that pleasure or pain affecting one is not felt by the rest. Besides, a witness (*sachhi*) is without pleasure or pain, secondless, whole and free from pain; hence is it that *Jiva* cannot be said to be one with *Brahma*. For the *Jiva* is an agent or doer, and beyond him to recognize another as a witness is tantamount to the saying "a sterile woman's son"—a clear impossibility.

Then again, if such witness be admitted, then as it is not one, for there is present one in each body, you will have to recognize several (and this will introduce a contradiction, for *Brahma* is one while witnesses are many in number).

Now for the conclusions of the *Vedánta* against such contention.

Pleasure and pain are the functions of the internal organ. The internal organ and its functions are not the subjects of the organs of senses or the modification of internal organ, but are so to the witness; because the subjects of the organs of senses are derived from quintuplication of the elements; the existing difference between the two amounts to this:—The organ of vision covers or takes possession of a thing that has form, in so doing, it cognizes the visibility as well as the receptacle of such visibility, which thus constitute its subjects; as for instance, the form of the blue or yellow pitcher, and the receptacle of the form—the pitcher,—are at one time covered or taken possession of by the organ of vision; and thus they form its subjects. In the same way, touch is cognized by skin, along with its receptacle, where such touch resides, and which communicating to the individual's skin enables him to feel it.

The tongue, nose and ear cognize taste, smell and sound respectively, by covering each individual subject only and not its receptacle. Hence these three, as also sight and touch are quite helpless to cognize the internal organ. For, form and touch are due to the quintuplication of element or elements, and they are subjects for the organs of vision and touch respectively to cover or take possession of, to render them apparent. But on the contrary, the internal organ is the resulting product of elementary non-quintuplication, which is quite different from elementary quintuplication, and for this existing dissimilarity, the result is the inability of the organs, which are the products of quintuplication, to cognize such other products, to wit, the internal organ, which is derived from non-quintuplication. Moreover, the external objects are the subjects which the organs of sense take possession of, or cover (in other words cognize), but as the mind (here means the internal organ) is internally situated in reference to the organs (of sense) they cannot take cognition of it. Similarly the internal organ is not the subject of its function inasmuch as it is its receptacle hence the internal organ cannot be said to be the subject of its function.

Illustration. As fire supports combustion, and never forms the subject of such combustion, but on the other hand, things dissimilar to fire such as wood &c., are the subjects of combustion, so things dissimilar to the internal organ constitute the subjects of its product, its function, (*briti*) and not its own. In the same way, the attribute of the internal organ is not the subject of its function. Because, if the subject of the internal organ be determined by its function, then its attributes of pleasure and pain will be converted into its subjects. But such a subject-forming-function of the internal organ never appears before it; consequently the mental attributes (pleasure and pain) are not the subjects of its function.

Then again, the rule constituting a subject is the distance of a certain thing from the function; the thing distant is the subject of function; and not what is brought quite close to it. As for example, antimony besmeared in the eyelids cannot be called the subject of vision [the function of the eyes], for its close contiguity; in the same way, the attributes of pleasure and pain from their close contiguity to the mind (internal organ) cannot constitute the subjects of its function, whose receptacle is the internal organ. Hence the internal organ with its attributes are incapable of being cognized by the senses or by its own function; but can be taken possession of by the witness; and if one such witness be admitted, then it is necessary that as it is quite capable of concerning pleasure and pain, affecting one mind, it should feel them alike in all, which it does not. Now this introduces the admission of several witnesses; it is not faulty then. Because the mind (Internal organ) which consists of intelligence, is the associate of witness; hence it is natural that it (witness) should be able to determine the knowledge of the attributes of its own associate only. Therefore it is quite unable to illumine the totality of pleasure and pain as present in all individuals. In this manner is declared why several witnesses cannot be one with *Brahma.*

Now for the *Práyojana* or necessity of the work the *Poorbapakshi* continues:—

Knowledge alone cannot cause the destruction of bondage which is without illusion and there are no substances to prove it as illusory, therefore abstain from the expectations arising out of knowledge.

'Bondage' refers to Egoism and other things not pertaining to Self. If it is present as an illusion, then knowledge removes it; without it, knowledge is powerless. For it is the nature of knowlege to remove Ignorance and illusion concerning a thing which it takes possession of; as the knowledge of a rope removes ignorance concerning its parts as well as the snake illusion, so when an unreality is covered with false knowledge, it is called 'Illusory attribution.'

When the subject is real, knowledge cannot cause its destruction; therefore in relatian to Self (*Atmá*) the bonds are Egoism and the rest. These are likewise called illusions; and because they are unreal, therefore knowledge removes them; then again as Self has nothing unreal in him like those comprised in bondage, which is explained as something real, therefore to expect its destruction by knowledge is futile.

ON THE COMPOSITION OF ILLUSION.

Knowledge of the Reality produces conception.

In the three defects and ignorance are recognized the
substances of illusion.

The text is thus explained:—

Conception is the product of the knowledge of Reality. The three varieties of defects are those of the (1) demonstration (2) demonstrator, and (3) what is to be demonstrated [demonstrable]; and particular ignorance and ordinary knowledge of the demonstrable. These are the five component entities of illusory attribution without which it can never arise. As for example from a nacre, illusion of silver, and from a rope, snake is created.

Here, a man who has seen a snake and nacre and knows them, is apt to mistake a rope for a snake and nacre for silver, but one who has neither seen, nor knows what a snake or nacre is, can never make such a mistake, consequently we find the rule to be, conception of the real substance as cause of illusory attribution. Then again, contrariety cannot determine it, hence a snake cannot create the illusion of nacre, nor can silver do that of a snake. Thus is established the necessity of a similarity or close resemblance, [which is looked upon as a defect inasmuch as it creates illusion] of the demonstrable and 'what is to be demonstrated' being present so as to cause the mistake, and it is therefore looked upon as its cause. Similarly, defects in the 'demonstrator' as temptation, fear &c., as well defects in the 'demonstration' caused by bile and other impurities in the eyes and other sensory organs are looked upon as the source of illusion. Also ordinary knowledge concerning a nacre caused in this manner "nacre is" and not its particular or differentiating knowledge as "This is nacre," can produce it. Similarly in the absence of ordinary knowledge, no illusion can be created. Thus is established the sources of illusion are presence of ordinary knowledge, and particular ignorance of the demonstrable.

These are the substances which create an illusion. All of them must be present to bring it about, otherwise in the absence of even one of them, no illusion results. As for instance, for making an earthen pitcher, it is necessary that there should be present a potter, a wheel, a revolving stick and clay, and in the absence of one of them the pitcher cannot be produced; so the whole of the substances must necessarily be present to create an illusion.

Moreover, in reference to the illusion of 'bondage' there is not even present one of its causes. If 'bondage,' is sometimes looked upon as real, then the 'conception' for its knowledge creates in Self a mistake that he is subject to 'bondage' which is thus explained:—Self alone is Real and excepting him, there is not another thing that is real; consequently bondage is non-real, and no conception can establish it otherwise; hence in the absence of conception concerning the reality of bondage, no illusion can arise. Then again, 'Self' and 'bondage' have no existing similarity in them; but on the contrary like light and darkness they are opposed to each other. Further, Self is internal, bondage external; Self is discoverer, bondage is the subject of discovery. Here discoverer signifies the agent or instrument who discovers; the 'subject' is what is discovered. No illusion is possible between the subjects of the 'internal' and 'external' or *vice versa*. As for example, in regard to son and his son's son &c., the body of his father is the 'internal' while they constitute the external. Now these cannot be mistaken for each other, that is to say the son and the rest for the father, or the latter for the former. Nor can it arise between the instrument or agent, and the subject or *vice versa*. As for example, a pitcher is the subject, and a lamp which discovers it is the instrument, here no illusion can convert a lamp into a pitcher, or a pitcher into a lamp. Similarly, from want of an existing similarity between the 'internal' discoverer or instrument—Self—and the external subject which is to be discovered—Bondage—no illusion can arise concerning Self so as to convert him into a subject of bondage. They are antagonistic of each other, for Self is the discoverer, and bondage is the subject which he discovers. Then again, they are not similar but dissimilar. Hence no illusion can possibly arise. Further, defects of demonstration are alike wanting. Because according to the Vedânta, from the 'demonstrator' to every thing else,—the whole objective world is unreal and illusory,* and they are the veritable bonds.

---

* There is one Reality—Self—every thing else besides is unreal, their apparent reality of objective existence is due to illusion of the special organs of sense, sight, hearing and the rest.

In this way prior to the illusion of bondage, to introduce a demonstrator and demonstration for determining it, is illogical; hence also, their defects are inadmissible. Therefore, the illusory attribution of bondage to Self, cannot apply. Nor can particular Ignorance be mistaken for Self, as they are opposed to each other. *Brahma* is self-illuminated Intelligence and light, hence it is unlike Ignorance which is darkness, therefore the first cannot be mistaken for the latter. As the sun is opposed to darkness, so is intelligence which manifests itself [and requires no adventitious help from another,—much less from Ignorance, which is itself darkness] opposed to Ignorance.

Moreover, even admitting the presence of particular Ignorance in Self, it cannot create its illusion with bondage, for what is entirely unknown cannot be mistaken for that which is perfectly known. But on the other hand, a subject covered by particular Ignorance, can create an illusion with a subject whose knowledge is of the ordinary kind. But then *Brahma* is free from both the above conditions, it is so to say unconditional, hence it cannot either be said to be a particular form of Ignorance, or ordinary Intelligence.

Then again, if you are tempted to create an illusion, you will have to reduce *Brahma* into the conditions of particular and ordinary as cited just now. That will virtually tell against the only logical inference as to the self-manifestibility and Intelligence of *Brahma*.

In this manner as the non-particular manifestation—which is *Brahma*—is unlike the particular Ignorance concerning it, or its ordinary knowledge is wanting, no illusion can arise concerning its subject. Hence bondage cannot be admitted as the illusion concerning the subject of *Brahma*. But, that bondage is real, and as such it cannot be removed by knowledge, consequently to say that, the present work is necessary for procuring knowledge whereby to remove the chain of bondage and obtain deliverance is alike inadmissible. Then again, the conclusions expounding knowledge as the source of the desire for release are not true; but actions alone can create it (emancipation). Such an assertion is determined after the manner of (*Ekbhavikbad*) one whose principle is that every individual is liable to be born only twice in the following manner:—

Real bondage cannot be destroyed by fullness of knowledge, but he who wants to be released must always be engaged in practising the daily rites.

'Fullness of knowledge' in the above sentence implies 'unreasonable conclusions' that is to say, to admit the cessation of bondage from knowledge, is looked upon as an unreasonable inference; inasmuch as the performance of daily rites at all times can alone procure emancipation. Such is its meaning.

Actions are of two kinds
(1). Lawful; and
(2). Forbidden or prohibitory.

(1). 'Lawful' actions are such as are determined in the Vedâs as produce an inclination in the individual to perform them [for they are beneficial]. (2). 'Forbidden' are those interdicted [which one should not do, for they are harmful.]

'Natural acts' (calls of nature) are not considered 'actions'; for actions are those either enforced or prohibited in the concluding portions of the Vedas, to induce or prevent a person to perform. Hence actions are of two (and not three) sorts.

The lawful actions are again subdivisible into four varieties.
  (a.) Daily rites (*nitya*.)
  (b.) Occasional rites (*naimittika*.)
  (c.) Optional things (*kamya*.)
  (d.) Penances (*prayaschitta*.)

(d.) 'Penances' are for the destruction of sin; as for instance fasting for three days and abandoning the thing that has been taken by mistake.

(c.) 'Optional actions' are done with a motive of obtaining results; as the sacrifices done with a view of procuring rain, and the offerings to fire for attaining the blissful abode in heaven etc.

(b.) Occasional rites, if left undone produce sin, but their performance brings forth neither virtue nor sin, they are not for constant practice, but are occasionally have recourse to, for certain purposes; as the rites done during eclipse, or the *Sradha* ceremony. It also includes actions done with an effort; as for instance, to rise from a seat on the approach of a person old in condition, caste, state of life, knowledge (*vidya*), religion, and consciousness (*jnana*). Here '*vidya*' refers to knowledge inculcated in the *Shastras* and to act up to them, and *jnana*, relates to knowledge of the Invisible (*Brahma*) so that the last mentioned is superior to the rest.

(*a*). Daily rites produce sin if not performed, but their performance brings forth neither merit nor demerit. They are always to be done, as bathing, *Sandhya* &c.

These then there are the four sorts of lawful actions, together with the prohibited, their number is five.

One desirous of release abstains from works done with a motive of reward (*kamya*, or optional) as well as the forbidden; for the former procure a better and the latter a nether state of existence, [and as he desires no more re-births] he avoids them. But he is always engaged in the performance of the 'daily,' and 'occasional rites' only, when there is any necessity for them,—for some especial purposes. For if daily and occasional rites are left undone, they will beget sin; and as sin reduces a person to a lower state of being [hereafter] he seeks to destroy it by practising the 'daily' and 'occasional rites,' in the manner just mentioned. They produce no other result, their non-performance is sinful, but their performance is not so. Here then is the necessity why a person 'desirous of release' should always be engaged in their practice. And, if from inadvertency or mistake he does something which the *Shastras* interdict [and which he ought not have done] he must have recourse to 'penances' for atonement.

'Penances' are likewise necessary for the destruction of sin caused by actions done in a previous state of existence [former life] though so far as his present life is concerned he has done nothing which the *Shastras* can take objection to (*i. e.,*) prohibit.

But then there is a difference [as to the method of penance to be observed].

Penances are of two kinds:—

(1). Extraordinary (*asadharna*).
(2). Ordinary (*sadharna*).
(1). 'Extraordinary' penances are those laid down in the sacred

writings for the destruction of particular (specified) sins; of this nature is fasting, already mentioned.

(2). 'Ordinary' are actions enforced in the the *Shastras* for the destruction of all sins, as bathing in the Ganges, pronouncing *Iswara's* name and similar others.

Now sins committed knowingly are destroyed by means of the extraordinary penances explained in the *Shastras*; while the 'unknown,' as for instance, those done in a previous life, require the ordinary penances for their removal.

Because, the 'extraordinary' has reference to specified and particular sins, whose nature is known, and for which the *Shastras* provide particular means of expiation, hence they are enough for causing the destruction of all sins committed either with knowledge, or which have subsequently come to the knowledge of the person. But as the sins of a past life cannot be particularized in the above manner, nor can their nature be possibly known, hence ordinary penances are laid down as a means for their destruction. For, they cover *all* sins and remove them. [Of such nature are bathing in the Ganges, pronouncing the name of *Iswara*, and the others mentioned in the sacred writings]. These are not penances simply, but they are included among optional things as well; for they are done with a motive of obtaining reward. For instance, bathing in the Ganges enables a person to obtain a better sphere of existence, as also pronouncing the name of *Iswara* does. Hence they are (*kamya*) optional and as they cause the destruction of sin therefore they are penances. As the 'horse sacrifice'—(*Aswameda*) &c., destroy sin and secure the blissful abode of heaven, so is the case with bathing in the Ganges. They are penances so far, as they cause the destruction of sin, and 'optional' as they procure a better life hereafter. Hence 'one desirous of release' does not desire for them [for his business is to cut off the chain which produces re-births]. But those who wish for a better sphere of existence in the next life, secure it by bathing in the Ganges at the same time as their sins are destroyed; as regard the others who have no desire for a better existence, its result is simply to destroy sins. Hence when it is practised with a desire of obtaining reward, it forms what is called 'optional penance.' When such a desire is absent, it is 'simple penance.' As the whole range of actions when actuated by a desire of reaping benefits therefrom, hurl a person to consecutive re-births as is said in the Vedanta, and in the absence of such a desire they purify the internal organ, and by the help of knowledge procure his emancipation; so either bathing in the Ganges or pronouncing *Iswara's* name has the double property of penance, and optional thing, to one desirous of reaping benefits; while to that other who has no desire, it is purely a penance. Hence a person desirous of release undertakes the 'ordinary penances' which destroy all sins of a previous life though their specific nature cannot be known. For him, the optional things of a past life produce no result; inasmuch as the desire present at the time of undertaking an action determines the result, according to the Vedantic doctrine, so that when a desire of obtaining heaven co-exists with the performance of an action, then its doer enjoys such a result in his next life after death, and when a person is unactuated by any such motive of obtaining benefits, actions produce no result. In the same way, a desire originating subsequent to the performance of an action determines beneficial results. But as all such desires for obtaining desirable results have ceased in a person desiring to be released, his optional works of a prior birth produce no results for him, in the same way as a person with a desire of becoming rich undertakes to serve a rich man, and though his desire of becoming rich may be removed, yet so far as results are concerned he is just the same as before, without the ostensible means to constitute him rich; therefore it follows that the optional works of a previous life produce no result, in the absence of a desire to be benefited, to a person desirous of emancipation. Thus is determined how actions alone are enough to produce emancipation.

A man of 'discrimination' never has recourse in this life to optional or forbidden works which procure an upper or nether stratum of existence. Actions commenced in a prior birth—optional as well as prohibited—can only be destroyed after reaping their fruits. The harmful effects of daily and occasional rites when left undone, do not accrue to him who is desirous of release, and engaged in their practice; moreover the accumulated prohibitory works of a former life are destroyed by the ordinary penances. Then again, the accumulated optional works produce for him no fruits, as the desire for their enjoyment is wanting. Therefore such a person is engaged in practising the 'daily' and 'occasional rites,' and penances of the ordinary kind. And if in his present life he has done knowingly prohibited action, then he practises the extraordinary penances; or only the daily and occasional rites and no penances, because the accumulated works, both prohibitory and optional, are destroyed by his desire for release. As the destruction of cumulative actions for a knower of Self is admitted in the Vedanta, so by abstaining from the prohibitory works and practising the daily and occasional rites, a person desirous of release causes the destruction of cumulative works in his present life. Or, the cumulative optional and prohibited actions together, subject him to one more existence, and he has therefore to enjoy another objective existence. Or, like a devotee's body—which is a consummation in one time of all the accumulated works commenced in several previous births,—the qualified individual consumes the fruits of his future subjective existences [in his present life]. Or, as the hardships suffered by him in the practise of the daily and occasional rites are the results of his cumulated prohibitory works of the past life, so they do not produce for him the commencement of another future existence after death.

The accumulated optional works commence one body, or several bodies in one time, so that the person desirous of release is never affected with any pain in his future life, but has all bliss for his share of enjoyment. For the cumulated lawful actions have produced his body, and the cumulated prohibitory actions have ceased to be productive of any results (for the pain attending the practice of the daily and occasional rites have consumed them already in that life) hence for him penances are no more necessary, but the daily and occasional rites are enough to procure him deliverence from future re-births. Hence he is to practise the occasional rites when the necessity for them arises, and the daily rites always.

This doctrine is called 'Ekbhavikbad' in the Shastras. Here even, the destruction of bondage by knowledge is not the necessity for the work. For what cannot be done by another substance, constitutes the chief necessity. As without sight, nothing is capable of ascertaining the form of an object, so as to render it visible, here sight is the necessity for seeing the form; so actions alone are sufficient to cause a cessation of bondage, without any assistance from the present treatise. Hence there does not exist any necessity for it. In the same way, there does not exist the necessity of the 'qualified individual' and 'subject' for the present work. Further, in the absence of the qualified individual and the rest, no 'relation' can be created. Because in the absence of the subject, conditional relationship of explainer and what is to be explained, subsisting between the work and its subject (which it seeks to demonstrate) is also wanting. Then again, from the want of qualified person and the absence of a productive result, the relation of obtaining such result and the individual to obtain it (that is to say the conditional relationship of obtained and obtainer) is not created. Moreover, in the absence of a qualified person and the ascertainment of the subject to be explained, no conditional relationship can be said to exist as that of a 'doer' and 'what is to be done.' Also, as knowledge is unproductive of the result aimed at—desire of release or emancipation, that is to say—in the absence of fruitfulness in knowledge, the relation of effect and cause between such knowledge and the treatise, cannot be said to exist. For the effect can only be produced by a thing which is productive and not barren; and as has been just said, knowledge itself is unproductive, besides knowledge of the thing is also wanting. Hence between it and the work no relation can be said to subsist.

For the ascertainment of *Brahma* and *Jiva* as one is called knowledge, (in the *Sidhanta*) and such non-duality is not produced, because they are not one; for this has already been determined in connection with the 'subject,' or that the determination of non-duality [existing non-difference of the two] is not produced. In the same way from an absence of 'moving consideration,' 'qualified person' and the rest, the present work cannot be commenced.

[*Vedantins'* reply]. Now for a reply to the contention about actions:—It is said that a desire of release which is the first item of contention, cannot be created in any one. Because such 'desire' is composed of two parts of which one is the destruction of Ignorance and its effect the objective world; and the other is the attainment of the *Brahma*: of them, the first no one has got; but all persons are equally desirous of destroying three kinds of misery instead, and such can be done by the help of the individual means assigned for each different kind of misery. Hence a person with a desire for the destruction of the world and its cause cannot be termed as one 'desirous of release.' This argument is untenable as follows :—

Without destruction of Ignorance and its effect the material world, proceeds not the destruction of three kinds of misery. For this every one desires the first portion of 'release.'

Here the root of the objective world is called Ignorance, and without destroying it, cessation of three kinds of misery by other means, does not follow. Also with the destruction of the root Ignorance (*avidya*) all sorts of misery and their cause disease &c., and the receptacle of such disease &c.,—the body—cease to exist. Hence for destroying the three kinds of misery, all persons seek for the first portion of 'release' which is the destruction of Ignorance, the root of the world. Its purport is this :—Even persons capable of providing adequate medicines for their disease are not, as a rule, free from misery, which is inevitable. Some may get rid of a disease by suitable treatment, and be free from pain, and some may not be equally fortunate; thus medicines &c., are powerless to remove the pain accompanying a disease in every instance; and even those freed from a disease by the help of medicines may be subjected to a fresh attack from the same or another disease; therefore medicines are powerless to cause entire (extreme) destruction of pain. One who has got rid of his pain and may be exempted in the future from being subjected to a fresh attack, such exemption is termed the extreme destruction. From medicines etc., cessation of pain as a rule does not inevitably follow and it is apt to re-appear after it has once been stopped, hence they are unable to cause its entire or extreme destruction.

Moreover, if all the means conducive of misery be destroyed then only can all misery be at an end, hence for cessation of misery all men are equally desirous of destroying the *means* which conduce to bring it forth.

These means are Ignorance (*ajnana*) and its effect, the objective world ;—as described in the *Chandogy Upanishad* on the subject *Bhoomā Vidya*, where it is mentioned that the sage Narada one day appeared before Sanat Koomār, and said, Oh ~~Vagaban~~ Bhagv ! (Lord) a knower of Self never experiences grief, whereas I am full of it. I am therefore full of ignorance ; give me that instruction which shall remove my ignorance. To this, Sanat Koomar replied, *Bhooma* is without all sorts of grief, and is blissfulness ; save and beyond *Bhooma* things are worthless, and undesirable, and conducive of misery. *Bhooma* is the name for *Brahma.* Therefore the things different from *Brahma* are the means of misery. Ignorance and its active results are different from *Brahma*, hence they are its means, so that with its destruction, entire destruction of all miseries follow, as a rule. Hence, for the destruction of all miseries, the removal of ignorance with its product, the world, by all persons, which again constitutes the first part of the 'desire of release,' is clearly established. And, as mentioned by a (*Poorvapakshi*) dissenter, that as desire can only arise concerning a thing which one has experience of, and as no one has any such experience of the *Brahma*, consequently to attain the Supreme *Brahma*, which is the second component unit for deliverance, is never desired by any one. To this the *Sidhanti* replies as follows :—

Every one has experience of happiness ; *Brahma* is extreme bliss ; and hence the prince of a discriminating individual wants only to attain the supreme felicity of *Brahma*.

All persons have experienced happiness, hence all are desirous of acquiring it. Moreover, *Brahma* is eternal blissfulness, and is so called in the *Shastras*, hence a man possessing discrimination of things real and unreal (called prince of discrimination) is desirous of attaining *Brahma*.

Every one desires for happiness only, [and] wants not the subject to have ; that constitutes the qualified individual and not the discriminating.

Here " happiness refers to material comforts, and such every one intends to be possessed of, but then it cannot bring forth 'deliverance,' or 'desire of release' (which is the subject of the work and which ought to be the chief aim of all) but makes him more worldly (*i. e.*,) attached to the world; consequently in the absence of a 'qualified individual seeking for emancipation, the necessity for writing the present work does not exist. In other words, it is fruitless, and something worthless for him who is undesirous of release, or already emancipated; for them an inclination for the subject of the work is absent."*

But thus to say that there does not exist a person desirous of release is absurd; because all persons want to destroy affliction and to acquire eternal happiness; and desire of release is nothing else but removal of misery in all its various phases, and the acquisition of happiness. Hence is clearly established that all men are 'desirous of release' and not for material comforts, as have been said. They desire happiness, whether it proceeds from the acquisition of property &c., or its reverse. If the happiness created by the acquirement of wealth &c., be only desired, then there will be an absence of a desire for that bliss which attends the condition of profound slumber. This last proceeds not from the acquisition of property and riches; and as happiness only, that is all happiness, is desired and not the particular one that of wealth, hence the possession of property excludes that other. But on the contrary, he desires self-contentment and not material prosperity, for, so far as the latter is concerned, every one has it more or less, and there is a constant yearning for ineffable bliss which is never destroyed, such bliss is the 'desire for release' and resembles (the blissfulness of) Self.

Thus is determined that all men are desirous of release and it is absurd to say that no such person exists. Moreover, if it be said,

* The passage does not imply a contradiction. For, an emancipated individual has no more need for a desire of obtaining release which is the subject of all Vedantic works and such others which have taken them for their standard like the present, for he is already freed.

there is no such person as that, consequently there cannot be any desire for the present work, which is therefore a fruitless attempt; that as the work is not a means for obtaining deliverance, the absence of any inclination (for its study) or those other means, apart from this work, inclination for which does not constitute a bias for the subject of the work itself; or that as the qualifications 'quiescence' 'self-restraint,' &c., whose possession entitle a person to study the work, and help self-knowledge—as there is no such 'qualified individual'—hence there is a want of inclination for the book. To say that the study of this book is not a means for kindling a desire for release, is absurd. For such desire is, as a rule, actuated by knowledge, as the Vedâs have it ; and knowledge is produced from hearing the precepts of the sages and ascertaining their true signification.

Hearing is of two kinds. The first is the relation existing between the utterances of the Vedânta and the ears; the second is the ascertainment of the real signification of the Vedânta sayings. The first only, for its close relation to the ears,—not the second—is the cause of knowing the *Brahma* (self-knowledge).—Hearing of *avantara* words as has already been explained, is the cause of 'apparent knowledge.' And hearing of transcendental words leads to a knowledge of the unapparent or invisible variety. What is thus known, is apt to be mixed up with inconsistent and improbable ideas along with it; hence, for their exclusion the second variety of hearing [*i. e.*, the ascertainment of the real signification of the words 'That art Thou.' 'I am *Brahma*.' 'All this is *Brahma* &c.'] together with 'consideration' and 'profound contemplation' is to be practised. Impossible ideas are removed by the 'hearing' of the Vedânta sayings. The Vedânta either expounds the *Brahma*, or is the explainer of a different signification ? Of this nature are the utterances of the concluding portion of the *Sam Vedâ*—impossible ideas—which are removed by analysis and reasoning whereby their proper signification is determined.

'Consideration' removes the improbable ideas concerning what is to be proved or demonstrated. The oneness of the *Jiva* and *Brahma* is the doctrine 'sought to be proved' in the Vedânta ; and either this non-duality is true or its opposite duality—(the Individual and *Brahma* are twain and different from each other).

Such doubts concerning the subject to be demonstrated are called impossible ideas. They are removed by 'consideration.' Antagonistic or inconsistent ideas are cleared away by 'profound contemplation.' In this way is determined that knowledge derived from hearing* is first the cause of kindling in a person a desire of release; and ascertaining the real signification† with 'consideration' and 'profound contemplation,' as they cause the destruction of inconsistent and antagonistic ideas, is the cause of deliverance. Vedânta, the concluding portion of the Vedâs called *Upanishad*, though different from the present work, yet this one is equal to it in its indication; the difference is in the matter of language (the first in the learned Sanscrit while the latter is in the Hindee dialect); and its hearing also enables a person to acquire Self-knowledge. This will be demonstrated in the sequel. Thus then is determined that the work by procuring knowledge is the source of the 'desire for release,' to say otherwise is to show stubbornness. Moreover if it be said, that 'desire of release' proceeds from the work, and that the other 'means' are equally capable of it, so that the work is futile; it can then be enquired what the other means are? If the reply be, that, in Sanscrit there are several works which establish the non-duality of the *Jiva* and *Brahma* as for instance the *Upanishads* &c., their commentaries, all these tend to knowledge, and knowledge procures emancipation, and that it requires no separate qualified person, hence the present treatise is futile. Even if such be true, then one who cannot determine the true interpretation of the Sanscrit works *Upanishads*, their commentaries &c., but at the same time is desirous of release, can derive no profit from them; for such a dull person the present work is surely not profitless. Also, if there be others who say that 'desire of release' is produced from the work, and the Sanscrit works cannot be read by a dull person for his want of comprehending them; and that there are persons who are really 'desirous of release' but yet

---

* 'Hearing' of the first variety.   † 'Hearing' of the second variety.

have no inclination for the subject of the present treatise ; because to find out a qualified person with discrimination, indifference, profound meditation (already explained) is very scarce, hence from an absence of the individual means of practice for acquiring Self-knowledge there can be no inclination for studying the work, then it can be asked:—Is there no such qualified person ? Yes, there are not many such qualified persons, and if he says so (that there are not many qualified individuals) all this, I admit indeed.

Then again, if another will say that there is not a qualified person fit for knowledge of self ; such a statement implies a contradiction and cannot be therefore entertained. For there are three defects in a subject of the internal organs *viz.*, blemishes, projection* (*vikshepa*) and concealment ; [here] blemishes (*mala*)† stand for evil (sin) 'projection' for fickleness or instability.

Good actions destroy evil or sin ; 'devotional exercises' remove the fault of instability ; and knowledge destroys want of apprehension. A person who is fickle and inclined for evil mentally, cannot be a 'qualified person.' But then one who is freed from mental blemishes and instability either in this life, or in a prior state of objective

---

* Projection, misapprehension, evolution, or power of creating is fully illustrated in the apt illustration of a 'snake in a chord.' Here no snake exists, but misapprehension concerning the chord, projects the form of a snake on it, or creates one. Similarly *avarana* is concealment, or want of apprehension. It can likewise be called envelopment, as, for instance, from the interposition of a small cloud obstructing your field of vision you are apt to say the sun is clouded. And this is a great mistake, for the sun is infinitely larger than the cloud, and therefore it is quite impossible for the latter so to enshroud the former as to cause total darkness, and this proceeds from a want of apprehension. In the same way, Ignorance clouds a man's intellect, and prevents him from realizing self, situated quite close to it, as the infinite, everlasting and uncreate, such want of apprehension, enshrouding or concealment is '*Avarana.*' For further information consult Dhole's *Vedant-Sára* p. p., 18. 19. 20.

† *Mala* literally filth, dirt, excrement, hence converted into blemishes and defects, and faults in other portions of the present work.

existence, by good actions and devotional exercises (literally therefore faultless) is duly qualified for knowledge of self. For him, an inclination of the work is possible.

"And as has already been mentioned, all persons have a particular tendency for material prosperity, and no one wants either to have the eternal blissfulness." This is untenable; for, there are four sorts of persons:—

(1) Stupid, (*pamara*) (2) worldly, (*vishayi*) (3) enquiring (*jijnāsoo*) and (4) liberated (*mukta*.)

Stupid persons are inclined in this life for prohibited actions, but have no tendency for works sanctioned in the *Shastras* or their conception; to enjoy the world as laid down in the sacred writings or be engaged in action for the enjoyment of happiness here or hereafter, such a one is called worldly. And an enquirer is one, who for his good conception, derives benefit from hearing the precepts of the true sacred writings. Such a good man can only discriminate things real and non-real in the following manner. All worldly comforts are non-eternal, even then there is an accompanying pain along with them, and in the end they are the cause of happiness or misery (pleasure or pain). The very knowledge of their being non-eternal and that those comforts will soon die out is a cause of pain even in their enjoyment. In this way he is engrossed in all material comforts and their reverse; so that misery is substantial,* and its cessation cannot proceed from the ordinary means in vogue with men; for he who is to find the remedy for its cessation is himself subject to it, or if he is free from it, is liable to get it anew; and so long as the body lasts, it is impossible to be entirely free from misery; because the body is the resulting product of accumulated good and bad works, and a human body is the result of such mixed works as well as the body of Devas. If the latter were only a product of good and virtuous actions, then after seeing such body of a Deva different from one's own, the other Devas may envy it,

---

* *Rupa* is form, and as a thing with a form is a substantial entity therefore it has been so rendered.

this need not occur. Even Indra, the principal among the Devas is actuated by fear concerning many other Devas and *Danavas* this is said in the *Shastras*. If, therefore, the Deva's body is only a pure product of good and virtuous actions, then there will be an absence of pain arising from the fear of others as just stated. Thus is determined that such bodies are the result of the good and bad actions mixed. The purport of the *Sruti* saying "A Deva is sinless" is this:—Human body alone is entitled to works, (and no other body) so that good and bad actions done in the course of a Deva's life do not produce their effect in the Deva's body, but the good and bad actions done in a prior life do produce their effect in the Deva's body, thus such body is produced from mixed actions. Moreover, reptiles, quadrupeds, and birds are also the result of mixed actions done in a previous state of existence, for the known miseries to which they are subject are the result of sins, and the pleasures of sexual intercourse &c., are the result of good actions.

> Those that crawl on the body are called reptiles (*tirjaka*.)
> Those which move by wings are called birds,
> Those that walk on four legs are quadrupeds;
> Hence birds and animals are also sometimes called
> (*Tirjaka*) as crawling by the abdomen.

Thus it shews that all bodies are the product of mixed actions; some are the result of a small share of sin and a greater one of good actions, as for instance, the body of the Devas: for the presence of a large share of meritorious actions and a small portion of bad, the Deva *sharira* is made up of a small amount of bad and larger one of good works; with this view the *Shastras* lay it down that such bodies are produced only from good actions. That is to say, as for many Brahmins residing in a village, it is called Brahmin's village, though other castes may be also residents in a small proportion, so for a preponderance of good and meritorious actions a Deva *sharira* is said to be the product of good actions only. The body of reptiles, birds and animals are not the product of good actions only; but that of a small fraction of it and a preponderance of bad.

Good men have a disposition similar to a Deva, while bad persons resemble snakes and other animals. Thus are all bodies produced from good and bad works, and the result of bad is misery; hence misery cannot cease to exist so long as the body lasts and such body is the result of good and bad actions, [virtue and sin]. Without their destruction, the body cannot be discontinued (future births cannot be stopped) inasmuch as after the destruction of the present body, a person must inherit a fresh one for the fruition of his good and bad actions done in his present life; so that until the good and bad are alike destroyed he must continue to inherit fresh bodies after death, and virtue and sin cannot be destroyed till passions are destroyed. Because even after the fruition of the present good and bad works is exhausted, passions and envy will produce another train of good and bad, so that without the destruction of passions and anger, good and bad works cannot cease to produce their usual results, and these proceed from the 'supporting and antagonistic knowledge.'

'Supporting' or 'conformable' produces love and the 'antagonistic or unconformable, produces anger; hence without their destruction, love and anger must continue, and such conformable and unconformable knowledge can only arise from a knowledge of the (existing) difference [in a subject]. For, the conformable and unconformable knowledge proceed when a thing is known to be different from, and unlike Self.

The means conducive of happiness are the conformable, while those of misery are termed the antagonistic or unconformable. Now they do not resemble Self in appearance [for self is substantial while these *means* are not] even admitting happiness to be a substantiality, its means are not so, so that when a thing is determined as something else than substantial, then its 'conformable' and 'unconformable' knowledge can be formed.

Thus to determine all things as different from self,—conformably or unconformably—according to the existing difference in their conditions and in that of self, is the source of both conformable and unconformable knowledge; and so long as this difference-creating knowledge is not put an end of, the conformable and the unconformable remain in-tact. Now this difference-creating knowledge is the result of ignorance, because all objects are centred in ignorance which is present everywhere and in all times; and this is also laid down in the sacred writings.

Thus then, ignorance (of Self) is the source of all kinds of misery, and unless ignorance concerning an object (here Self is meant) is destroyed, its exact knowledge cannot proceed; because when we have known it once, we cannot be ignorant of it: that is to say, ignorance is destroyed by the advent of knowledge. As for instance, ignorance concerning a chord is removed by the knowledge of the unknown chord, and not by anything else; similarly, knowledge of self, by removing the ignorance concerning it, is the destroying cause of all misery, and such knowledge, helps the cognition of *Brahma*, which is eternal, full of bliss,—without any relation to grief (i. e., unconditioned).

And, inasmuch as knowledge of the Real established it as eternal and unconditioned, so far as grief is concerned, and that it is all blissfulness, hence the attainment of such happiness follows as a matter of course. Thus we find that knowledge is the source from which proceed the destruction of ignorance and the attainment of the supreme blissfulness of *Brahma*, and it is necessary to have it.

A person possessing such discrimination is called an enquirer of truth (seeker of Self-knowledge.)

'Emancipated' is one who knows self—different from the gross physical, the subtle-astral and the cause-body—to be the same as *Brahma*. This knowledge is invisible knowledge.* These then are the four varieties of persons.

Moreover, if in a stupid and worldly person, attached to the world, there is an yearning for material comforts; while there may be another of the latter class who is desirous of possessing the supreme bliss, but is ignorant of the means, which help its attainment, yet he desists not, but finds it out by his intelligence (*Boodhi*)

---

* Intelligence marked by invisibility refers to *Brahma*; such intelligence is universal, all-pervading, and omniscient, while Intelligence marked by visibility refers to the *Jiva*. It is parviscient and partial.

and follows it. Because, to determine the means is to follow Truth, and hear the *Shastras* (ascertain their true meaning by hearing the precepts of the sages). But they are not possible for him, hence a stupid and worldly man has no inclination for studying the work, whereby to acquire happiness, but is inclined to hunt after the other means for procuring a cessation of misery, which again, is another cause of dislike for the book. In this way, we see, why stupid and worldly individuals have their dislike for the book. An emancipated individual has also a similar dislike, but his dislike proceeds from quite a different cause. Because, an emancipated individual is a knower of self, and, for such a knower of self, nothing more is necessary to be done (this will be explained hereafter). Even if his desire of release be generated by good actions, then also for him, there need not exist a liking for the work (for the subject, which the work treats of, he has already ascertained, and as one already possessed of knowledge of self, he stands in no need of foreign helps).

Not so, for a seeker of truth; without any yearning for material comforts, but desirous of supreme bliss, and for the entire extreme destruction of misery which can proceed only from knowledge, for such a discriminating person—a follower of truth—the present work is not futile.

Thus is determined a qualified person desirous of release.

Brahma is like a witness. Non-dual, without the smell of any difference between it and *Jiva*; anger and spite are the virtues of the intellect (mind) and not of *Brahma*, [which] a blind person (unacquainted with it) however may admit as residing in the *Brâhma*.

For the presence of anger and spite, which dwell in every individual mind, as has already been said, non-duality cannot be established as the subject of the work. If such a contention be true, then the witness without anger and spite can be determined to be one with *Brahma*; and to consider such witness to be some other agent or instrument than Self, is tantamount to the saying 'a sterile woman's son:' this can never happen and hence untrue (*asat*). For, witness means the agent or instrument (who is the doer, eater, etc.,) only in an emphatic form; without such an admission the agency of the individual is destroyed.

The internal organ is an associate of the one and same intelligence to render it a witness, and the agent or instrument is only a qualifying entity; that is to say, possessing a distinguishing qualification as that of an adjective and substantive.*

What serves as an associate to a thing is called associated.†

An associate is a thing which being placed near another, makes that to be known, while it remains separate. As, according to the *Nyayika*, hearing is said to be the function of the atmospheric air situated inside the ears, so, the site of the ear is the associate of hearing; because wherever the ear is present, it takes cognizance of sound and renders it known, by the help of ether‡ present inside,

---

* Indication of the conditional relation of an adjective and noun can thus be explained:—as in the phrase 'That Devadatta is this,' 'that' refers to Devadatta seen in past time and 'this' refers to the Devadatta of the present time, so that, a relation is created by the exclusion of time which is the only difference subsisting between them; so in the sentence 'That art Thou' is the relation of subject and predicate (same as adjective and noun) between Intelligence distinguished by invisibility,—the indication of the word 'That,' and Intelligence distinguished by visibility indicated by the word 'Thou,' a relation constituted by the exclusion of the difference present in them.

† *Upadhi* ($up + a + dha + e = upadhi$) is a thing which communicates its own property to another situated close to it: as for instance, when a red flower is placed near a crystal, it imparts its red colour to the glass which then appears red; here the flower is the associate of the glass. In the same way, Ignorance (present in all individuals) imparts its property of unconsciousness to Intelligence (*Brahma* which is present close to the *Jiva* in each person) so as to render it separate and twain (dual), hence Ignorance is the associate of Intelligence. In like manner, the associate of a thing is called associated by it. For instance, of Intelligence, the associate is Ignorance, consequently Intelligence is Ignorance-associated.

‡ Ether and atmosphere are convertible terms, so no apprehension needs be entertained from their promiscuous use. Sometimes the reader will find the word space used for it.

while it retains its separate individuality. In the same way, the internal organ, wherever present, renders its indwelling intelligence manifest as a witness, while it remains separate. Hence, the internal organ is the associate of witness. From this, it is established, that the function of the 'internal organ' *(antakarana)*—its indwelling intelligence—is the witness.

Visheshana is a substance which manifests an object along with itself. As for example, "The person with the ear-ring is come." Here, the ear-ring is the qualifying entity (adjective) because it establishes the approach of the person along with it [as the man that is come, has got them in his ears and has not left them behind]. " I have seen a blue pitcher." Here also, 'blue' is the *Visheshana* (adjective) of 'pitcher.' In the same way, the internal organ is the adjective or qualifying substance of Intelligence, which is the agent or instrument (doer etc.,) and same as *Jiva*—inasmuch as the internal organ manifests that Intelligence along with itself in the form of an agent or instrument. Thus the 'internal organ' is the qualifying adjective or the worldly: that is to say, the function of the internal organ, Intelligence, is its subject, and the internal organ is liable to continued births and deaths. This will be particularly explained further on. Now, the passions anger, spite, and the rest exist in the worldly (which entail an individual to future re-births) and do not constitute the condition of the witness (agent or instrument). Then again, the predicate of the worldly is the subject of the internal organ and not that of intelligence, which is the predicate of the internal organ. For, between the predicate of the worldly—intelligence—and the instrument, there is no difference whatever; inasmuch as the same intelligence in company with the internal organ is subjected to future existence, and without such accompaniment of the internal organ, it constitutes, what has been mentioned, a witness; so that there is consequently no difference between the portion which constitutes the predicate of the worldly and the witness. If this predicate be admitted to be the seat of pain, then the witness must alike be subject to it (for they have been determined to be equal and non-different, and hence, pain cannot be present in one without affecting the other in a like way). But such is not a fact as has been said in the *Vedas* "The (internal) witness is free from all sorts of pain." From this it follows, that the predicate of the worldly is also without pain (for their condition of equality) and that all pain resides in its subject viz., the internal organ. With this purpose, anger and spite have been mentioned as properties of the intellect and not that of the *Jiva*. In this way, one with the internal organ is not identical with *Brahma*, but the witness associated with such organ is non-different from *Brahma*; but then it has been before alleged, that such witnesses are several (as many as there are individuals) and *Brahma* is only one, hence, How can many be equal to one ? Therefore such identity is not proved.

Moreover, " the admission of their oneness creates another difficulty, inasmuch as *Brahma* is all-pervading and the (internal) witness must also be possessed with an identical pervasion, and if so, then it must be able to experience the happiness and misery of all individuals which it never does."

Such arguments are useless. No matter about the many and one, they imply an identity. For, as the space appropriated by several pitchers, is different from one another; though they are only fractional units of the infinite space or ether *(mahakas)* from which they are non-different. Similarly, though *Iswara* is one witness and the individual witnesses are many and divisible, yet they are non-different from the all-pervading witness of the *Brahma*; and these divided and separate individual witnesses are but merely fractional units, or the distributive segregate of the one, infinite, and indivisible *Brahma*. And, the previous assertion, that happiness and misery are not subjects of the function of the internal organ, is inconsistent. For, even if happiness and misery are apparent witnesses, and as such witnesses are many, yet they (happiness and misery) are only a modification of the internal organ, its function for the time being, determining or creating them, which the internal witness occupying that function discovers. This is the reason why authors have determined happiness and woe as subjects of the internal witness with function ; and not without it. To illustrate it by reference to a common saying :—Let us suppose the instance of a pitcher. Here as the pitcher has its own ether residing within it, non-different from the great body of it occupying all space; and as it serves as a means of carrying water; but then, the sight of a pitcher (as an associate of ether) establishes the presence of ether as well as its function as a water-carrying medium; in its absence, ether only can be determined which is the same as the great body of ether: so is intelligence the witness, and function, of the internal organ, whose action is to discover and whose associate is the internal organ, determined by the sight of its associate; without the sight of the associate of intelligence—the internal organ—neither can the witness, nor its function of discovering, can be determined, but only Intelligence as *Brahma* is established. Hence *Brahma* and witness are one. Because, without discovering the associate, it cannot be conceived as many and divided, and such witness is the indication of *Jiva* (of which more hereafter.) In this way is considered non-duality of the *Jiva* and *Brahma*, the subject of the present treatise.

> Illusion proceeds from a conception, caused by knowledge
>   of things, similar in form to one another.
> It is immaterial, whether such things are real or unreal.
> Nor is it the invariable source of any defect (in the organ)
>   that causes it,
> Nor is it the product of a given cause; as a cloth is the
>   result of a weaving brush and loom etc.
> Self *(Atmá)* free from similarity;[*] (white) conch (from some
>   defect) appears yellow and sugar bitter (illusion).
> Desire is not always its moving cause, a person possessed
>   of indifference sees silver in a nacre.
> Ether is sometimes mistaken for blue, and pan, for a tent
> Even by persons without defective sight, or jaundice, to
>   account for them.

If bondage be real and permanent, as has been alleged before (by a *Poorbapakshi*) then knowledge cannot destroy it; for what

---

[*] Therefore to say, he is the same as the three upper castes *Brahmana*, *Khshetrya* and *Vaishnava* is illusion.

is false can only be destroyed by it (knowledge). Self is not composed of the substances of bondage which are unreal. Therefore to say, bondage is real, and knowledge cannot remove it, is quite inadmissible. Because it is unreal, and knowledge destroys it, [i. e., Self-knowledge prevents future re-incarnations.]

Moreover, according to a *Poorbapakshi*, it is said, that conception produced by the knowledge of a real substance can only create an illusion, hence its source ; as has already been said, in the instance of a snake in a chord. Here, for such an illusion to arise, one must have knowledge of a real snake ; he must have seen a snake and have an abiding conception of its form in him, wherewith to mistake it in a rope. And one who has never seen a snake, nor knows what it is like, cannot confound it with a rope or string. In the same way, knowledge of bondage establishes its reality [in other words as bondage is admittedly known by all, it must be a real substance.]

"Substances not belonging to Self are unreal. Such an inference is untenable from the premises already advanced. For, illusion has its source in conception produced from the knowledge of a real substance, and as such a condition is absent, bondage is not the attribution of illusion, but real."

But such contention is untenable. For, the conception of illusory attribution is the source, from which, knowledge of things proceeds. It cannot determine the real, hence is not the cause of its knowledge. Now such things are either real or false. And if knowledge of the real thing is alone the cause of illusion, then a person, who has not seen the tree yielding the real Arabian date (*chhoara*) but who has derived its knowledge from the sight of a common date tree (*khejur*) shewn to him, by a performer of magic, and repeatedly described to him, as the real *chhoara*, and he never heard otherwise, is liable to confound the date tree for that other, and becomes the subject of such an illusion. But this should not be ; because he is unacquainted with the real *chhoara* tree, [hence your inference with their premises are wrong. But] from my standpoint, that person's illusion is the result of the false date tree shown to him. Hence, illusion arises from the conception, derived from the knowledge of an existing similarity between the thing mistaken and for what it is mistaken. And, whether a thing is true or false, conception can only proceed from its knowledge, which again is its source. Now such a consideration as to their mutual interdependence, implies no difference; for it signifies knowledge as the cause of conception; and conception that of illusion. So that, it establishes conception produced by knowledge to be the source of an illusion, even if it do not signify that by conception is produced knowledge.

Moreover, knowledge only can never be said to be the source of illusion. For the rule is, that a source or cause must have an unintervening prior existence than its product; as for instance, the turning rod or potter's wheel is the cause of an earthen-pitcher. Here, the rod had an uninterposed prior existence before the production of the pitcher; in the same way, if knowledge be admitted as the source of illusion, it must have an uninterposed existence prior to the production of the illusion; but this is not the case, inasmuch as a man who knows a snake, is apt to confound it with a chord, a month afterwards, and this should not be. Because, if the illusion of snake in a chord is the product of knowing a snake, such knowledge has been destroyed, hence there is no unintervening prior time, but simply past time.

'Unintervening' means without intervention or interposition, and 'intervening' with interposition [so that the one has a signification of immediate and the other mediate; immediate past refers to a close proximity between the cause and its effect; while the mediate past must refer to the distant past, between which time and its product, there intervenes a space of time.]

If it be said, that action must have a cause prior to it, either in the immediate past, or ante-dated to that; and such cause then becomes the source of the immediate past accordingly, then it amounts to a non-admission of 'sanctioned actions' procuring heaven and prohibited works, hell, to which they stand as their respective source, as mentioned in the *Shastras.*

For, mental, oral and bodily works are called 'actions' and from the commencement of their practice, incessant succession ceases; while the abode in heaven follows in another subsequent existence. So that heaven and hell, from sanctioned or prohibited works, do not follow from the immediate past, but are the result of such actions done in the remote past.

In the same way, to say, that the knowledge of a "snake in the immediate past is not the source of its illusion in the chord" is absurd. Because, it virtually leads to the admission of an illusion, from knowledge which has been destroyed, as also the attainment of heaven and hell from works that have ceased; and one may as well argue in the same strain, that a turning-rod which has ceased to exist, and a dead potter must alike turn out a pitcher.

Because, as in the illusion of a snake in a chord, the knowledge of the snake in the mediate past; and for the attainment of heaven or hell, the good and bad actions of the mediate past, are prior conditions, potentially present as their respective sources: so in the instance of the pitcher, the dead potter and the destroyed turning-rod of the mediate or distant past must be looked upon as quite capable of turning it out. But this is plainly impossible. Hence, what exists in the distant past cannot be determined as the source; but something subsequent to it, or the immediate past, is the source; and also, good and bad actions are not the source of bringing forth heaven or hell in a future existence, but that good actions produce, in the immediate future; virtue, and bad, sin.

Now, virtue and sin are subjects of the internal organ (constantly abiding in it) which in their turn, bring heaven and hell in a subsequent time, and thus in their consummation, cease to produce any more effects subsequently. For such a purpose, the *Shastras* describe good and bad actions by their novelty as the productive source of their respective results, and call them virtue and vice. Then again, good and bad works produced from virtue and vice have been sometimes called virtue and vice: in the same way as a man performing a good and meritorious action is said to be doing virtue and *vice versa*. Here, the meritorious action or its reverse, is not the virtue or vice, but is the parent; therefore actions are called virtue and vice, in the same way, as marrow *(ghee)* for instance, is called life in the *Shastras*, because it produces longevity.

Thus is determined, how the immediate past is the productive source; and as there is no knowledge of a snake in the immediate past, i. e., a little prior to the illusion of creating it in a chord, therefore such knowledge is not the source of the illusion; but such source is the conception, derived from knowledge, concerning the reptile.

Similarly, the illusion of silver in a nacre, is due to conception of silver. Thus then, conception is the real source from which all illusions originate. Conception in its turn, is produced from the knowledge of a thing.

As the results of good and bad works,—virtue and vice,—are constantly present in the internal organ, so is conception derived from the knowledge of things present there; and a person unacquainted with a snake, may have conception of other things, which he has a knowledge of, so that, the snake illusion may not occur to him, but other illusions may,—produced by an existing similarity in the condition of the two. Hence similarity, and not dissimilarity, is the determining cause of an illusion. A snake has a similarity in another snake, and not in anything else. One who has never before seen a snake and is perfectly unacquainted with it, but who knows something else, can have no conception of a thing similar to a snake; hence its illusion in a chord, can never happen to him.

'Conception' signifies a subtle condition of knowledge. Thus it is shewn: the source of illusion is conception of previous knowledge, regarding a thing similar to it (illusion); and it is immaterial, that the conception of knowledge of a real only, and not an unreal substance, be the cause of creating an illusion. This has already been explained in the instance of the Arabian Date-tree. So that, the conception of false knowledge, regarding a thing, is alike productive of illusion, and it is likewise applicable to bondage. For 'Egoism' etc., are unlike, self, and bondage is nothing more than their knowledge. It is unlike the illusion of a snake in a chord, which is created only when known, and not otherwise; [because bondage is ever present and requires no previous acquaintance]. Such is the dictum of the *Vedás*. For this cause the non-existence of all things in the state of profound slumber is explained.* As in such a condition, nothing can

---

* When a man sleeps profoundly without being disturbed by any

be ascertained or confused, hence the destruction of the objective world then takes place [relatively of course to the individual who is sleeping soundly and not to the rest of mankind].* It is called the controversy of sight-creation in the *Shastras* and will be explained in the sequel.

Thus is derived a knowledge of Egoism and its endless modifications, as well as their final destruction. Its birth and death is coeval with its knowledge. That is to say, with the springing up of knowledge concerning egoism, egoism arises, and with the destruction of that knowledge, egoism is destroyed.

Egoism etc., and its knowledge, are called 'illusory attribution.' Though Egoism is spoken of as a testifying witness [agent or instrument], (it has already been explained when the Subject was considered) its knowledge is determined in the form of such witness;—and its birth and death therefore are not possible—yet as it discovers the Egoism etc., through the function of the internal organ, though not directly, therefore such function can be said to have a beginning and an end. This is why knowledge of Egoism is said to have an origin and an end. And conception can be established in connection with it in the following wise:—that is to say, the knowledge of false individuality of a prior period of time, evolves the subsequent individualities and so arises its knowledge. Moreover, if it be contended, that the conception of the illusory attribution of the subsequent, is due to the illusion of prior individualities and their conception, then the source of the first individuality and its source in conception, cannot clearly be created. For, if any individuality precedes it, then its knowledge can produce conception, but prior to the first evolution of egoism there cannot be another individuality, in the same way as the illusion concerning a first thing cannot be said to be derived from its conception*

---

dreams, he cuts off all connections from the objective world, which then ceases to exist for him in an objective condition ; and such a condition is a trite example of ascertaining the actual condition of Self who is actionless, undisturbed, passive and full of bliss.

* Conception is an act of memory; knowledge creates an impression

For that can be admissible only if a previous Egoism were present, then for knowledge to follow, and produce conception is an easy and natural inference.

But such a conclusion is mainly attributable to ignorance of the Vedántic doctrine. For the Vedánta holds (1) *Brahma*, (2) *Iswara*, (3) *Jiva*, (4) Ignorance, and (5) its relation to Intelligence (*chaitanya*) and (6) the difference in uncreated (*anadi*) things, as the six entities which are identified to be without an origin. A thing which is not derived as a product of another, is identified as uncreated, or without an origin. These six are not produced, hence they are uncreated (*suroop se anadi*), while egoism is described in the *Sruti*, as having a beginning; hence it is not uncreated, but a derivative product. But for a continuous current, every substance can be called as without a beginning. This continued current (of evolution, in which one succeeds another in the usual course of nature) cannot cease in the eternity of time, nor was there ever a time, when such substances can be said to have had no existence.* [To illustrate by an example] a pitcher is said to be without a beginning, for there never was a time when it was not preceded by another pitcher and so on to the infinity of time, both upwards and downwards; considered in this light, every substance has a chain of continued existence, for which it is called (*anadi*) without a beginning. In (*Pralaya*) cyclic period of destruction of the objective world, all substances are reduced from their objectivity into a subjective state of potentiality, in the same way, as in profound slumber, a man though dead to the

---

in memory which retains it vividly, hence conception is a subsequent act and can only be produced by the certain knowledge of a substance. For conception to follow, there must be present knowledge in a relation of priority, so that conception of a first thing cannot be deemed a source of illusion. But its fallacy will be pointed out in the text further on.

* This is Kapila's doctrine. He denies total destruction of the objective world, but asserts instead, that there was not a time when the world and all it contains was not existing, nor will there ever be a time, when it will cease to exist altogether. Western Evolutionists may take note of this fact.

external world retains conception of it in his memory; such a continuous train of existence is called 'without a beginning;' and it applies to the vast expanse—the world. One who is unacquainted with it, may apprehend the non-applicability of first illusion to its conception, as also that of egoism etc., and illusion concerning them, before all things; as the *Sidhanta* has it. But its source is determined by a prior existence of its predecessor, which precedes such illusion, so that here conception is quite, out of question, incapable to create it.

From such a stand-point, conception produced by a previous knowledge of similarity, can create an illusion of Egoism etc., which serve as bonds for a continued chain of existence hereafter. (The first line of the stanza indicates it.)

Moreover, as the faults or defects which have already been referred to, as giving rise to illusory attribution, cannot be said to be present in bondage, therefore bondage is real, to say so, implies a contradiction, hence it is clearly unmaintainable. Because, if illusion proceeds from defects and not otherwise, then defects are its source. As for instance, the source of cloth is the weaving brush and loom, and in their absence no cloth can be produced; so are defects not the source of illusion. Inasmuch as in the absence of the defect of similarity even, Self is confounded or mistaken as having distinction of caste. A Brahmin or any other casteman, has his caste-distinction in his gross physical body, hence such caste is a creative function of the gross body, and neither self nor the subtle body (astral) has any thing to do with it. For, the same self and the same subtle body rehabilitate another gross body after death, and the caste may be different from what it was before, and the rule does not prevail, that an individual shall retain his original caste in all his subsequent re-births. If such distinctions of caste were due to self or the subtle body, then, the individual would never be subjected to any other caste than the first, in his next journey after death; hence it follows, that it is the function of the gross physical body, and not of self or the subtle body, to determine caste.

"I am a twice-born (*Dvijatee*) Brahmin etc." Such a saying attributes the condition of a *Brahman* to Self, and apparently determines his cognition so; in the same manner, conditions of *Kshetrya* and *Vaiswa* are applicable to Self. Here, the attribution of caste to Self is illusory; just as the projection of a snake in a chord is not real but apparent, (that is to say appears so) hence an illusion, so Self is without any caste ditinction, and what appears, is simply an illusory attribution of caste. Moreover, between Self and caste, there does not exist any similarity, inasmuch as the first is all-pervading, while the second is divisible. Self is internal, while caste is external; Self is the discoverer, while caste is the subject discovered by Self. Thus then things antagonistic to Self are confounded with him. Here the word (*Dvijatee*) twice-born signifies the three upper classes Brahmin, Kshetrya and Vaiswa.

As in the absence of similarity, we have seen illusion to arise concerning Self, so in the absence of the same similarity between Self and bondage, such as Egoism etc., bondage is attributed to him through illusion. The defect of similarity is hence not the cause of illusion, for if such were the case; then he [*Brahma*] could never be confounded with caste: in the same way yellow cannot be attributed to a conch-shell, nor can bitterness be said to exist in sugar-candy. For if a conch is white,—and yellow is an antagonistic color to white, white and yellow have no resemblance of similarity between them. In the same way sweetness and bitterness are directly opposed to each other, they are not similar, but dissimilar. Hence, the presence of similarity of a false thing is not the source of illusory attribution. Similarly temptation, fear, and the other defects in the demonstrator, can be construed as not its source. For, even a man free from temptation and perfectly indifferent to the pleasures of this life or the next, is apt to mistake silver in a nacre. This should not be, if illusion were caused simply from the presence of defect in the see-er or demonstrator. Neither is defect in demonstration its source. For ether possesses no form; yet every one confounds it with the blue [heavens above]. Another instance of such illusion is that of a frying pan with a tent. Likewise it cannot be asserted that from defective sight, such illusion is produced. For, all persons cannot be equally affected in sight as to be the subject of the same illusion. Hence, defect in demonstration is not the source, from which illusion originates.

In regard to the ether, it can be said, there is wanting at least one defect in demonstration, while virtually all the defects are absent; besides, there is wanting presence of similarity too; so that, since in the absence of all defects, ether is confounded with the blue sky, in the same way, in the absence of all defects, Self is confounded as subject to bondage. Here, it cannot be said, that as the necessary defects which create an illusion are wanting, therefore bondage is not illusionary [but real]. For, as already seen, in the absence of all similar defects, a person is apt to mistake the ether, for the blue heavens over-head. Hence it is natural to infer that 'defect' is not the invariable source of illusory attribution. A person not suffering from biliousness or such another malady* is even liable to mistake the ether for blue, and pan for a tent, from a similarity of appearance. Therefore the natural conclusion is, that defect [in demonstration] is not the cause of illusory attribution.

The word '*Kshema*' signifies peace, and the defects in demonstration which destroy it are termed (*akshema*) unpeaceful. The 'organs of sense' through which cognition is derived are termed (*pramana*) demonstrations. Thus is determined illusion uncaused by defect.

In such a consideration, it is not necessary for a defect to be present, to create the illusion of bondage (in Self). Moreover, the abridged edition of *Shariraka Sutras* contains especial reference to it, which for lengthiness I have abstained from entering upon; especially if the facts were true I would then have fully considered defects and their nature, but since it is otherwise, I need not further dwell upon the matter.

Thus is determined the works of illusion.

---

* There is a proverb which with certain restrictions generally holds true. It says that a jaundiced individual sees every thing yellow; hence our author refers to it while explaining away the alleged sources of illusion. But then, there are other classess of persons, who so to speak, are color blind, that is to say, are quite incapable of distinguishing one color from another.

On the sources of Illusion.

In the ordinary manifestation of Intelligence (*chaitanya*) ignorance dwelleth not.

But the Intelligence present in profound slumber is Ignorance.

"Ignorance has been already mentioned as particularly apt to be confounded with reality. But as Self is illuminated by himself he cannot be mistaken with Ignorance; for light and darkness are naturally opposed to each other, (and Ignorance resembles darkness). For instance, as in the broad daylight, the illusion of a snake in a chord never arises, so to Self, the illusion of bondage can never be attributed (for the *Atma* is Self-luminous.)"

Further, this even cannot be said, that if the *Atma* is Self-manifested, his intelligence is not directly opposed to ignorance. For, if such were the case, then in the condition of profound slumber, Self ought to have retained consciousness. But instead, we find a man on rising from his sleep to say "I was sleeping peacefully," "I knew nothing then." Here, the conception of happiness is the subject of ignorance. This happiness and the knowledge of ignorance in the waking condition are not visible,—for we call that knowledge visible, whose subject appears in front, which neither happiness nor ignorance does in the waking condition, hence not visible—but they resemble remembrance; and remembrance concerning a thing unknown, is never possible, it can only proceed from knowledge; so that, the conclusion is, the happiness felt in the condition of profound slumber is the product of ignorance; that is to say, it is due to unconsciousness, which is the normal condition of ignorance. And, as such knowledge of the profound slumbering condition is never, the result of the mind or the senses, for they then cease to carry on their respective functions, it can be determined as proceeding from Self. Knowledge and manifestation have the same signification. Thus is shown, the manifested condition of Self in profound slumber, which manifestation is like happiness itself, and the same as ignorance. If it were otherwise, then the presence of ignorance in sleep cannot be satisfactorily explained; and it certainly ought not to be there. Therefore, the

Atma is self-manifested, or conscious, and between him and ignorance, there is no antagonism present. On the contrary, ignorance helps to determine his likeness of manifestation. For this purpose, the Vedântin, says, ordinary Intelligence is not opposed to ignorance. But such an antagonist is the particular Intelligence. The all-pervading Intelligence is called 'ordinary,' and Intelligence present in the function (of the internal organ) is called 'particular.' As for instance, ordinary fire residing potentially in a piece of wood is not an antagonist of darkness, but the solidified particles of fire present in a candle are so; in the same manner, the all-pervading Intelligence is no enemy of ignorance, but Intelligence residing in the modification of the internal organ, after it has assumed the shape of *Brahma*, is its opponent.*

Thus then, we find pure and simple Intelligence is not an antagonist of ignorance, but function *plus* Intelligence, or Intelligence with function, are directly opposed to it. In the first condition, intelligence destroys ignorance, and function (mental) is its coadjutor. In the second condition, that mental function is the destroyer, while its help-mate is Intelligence. This method of consideration seeks to put a limit and (its supporters are the *Abachhedavadins*) is called therfore the differentiating view. But there is also another view: in which both the ordinary and particular Intelligences are looked upon as not directly opposed to Ignorance, but function illumined

---

* Intelligence is differentiated into two :—invisible and visible. The former refers to *Brahma*, therefore all-knowing; the latter to the *Jiva* therefore parviscient. In the state of profound slumber the latter, though devoid of all the envolpments of ignorance, yet *Jiva* is wrapped in ignorance itself, and this must be got rid of, to be one with Intelligence and blessedness *(Brahma)*. In such a condition, when the modification of the internal organ has assumed the shape of the Impartite *Brahma*, he has no more ignorance left in him, he has merged into *Brahma* and become one with it; then he is Intelligence simply. Hence such Intelligence and ignorance are opposed to each other. The *Sruti* says in reference to the state of profound dreamless slumber :—"For the illumination of Intelligence *Prajna* enjoys felicity."

with the reflection of intelligence, or the reflected intelligence with function are so. In such a view, reflection is admitted hence its supporters are called *Abhasabadins*. In this way, intelligence which is self-manifested is established to be no antagonist of Ignorance, but that the latter is included in, or dependent on, the former. So that, the subject of Self, covered as he is by ignorance, can be easily confounded with Intelligence, and particularly with the subject of ignorance.

Moreover, as Self is unconditioned, *i. e.*, neither ordinary nor particular, as above explained,—therefore neither particular knowledge nor Ignorance can be admitted to be present in him; so that their attribution through mistake is clearly untenable. Such an assertion cannot be maintained. For, everyone admits the existence of the *Atma* which means Self. No one says that "I am not existent," but on the contrary "I am" ["I do," "I eat," "I go"]. All these clearly establish the existence of *Atma*, and an universal belief in such existence. But then, as Intelligence, blissfulness, pervasion, eternal, pure and free, Self cannot be conceived by all. Therefore there are two conditions present; the first which establishes the existence of the *Atma* is knowledge, the second which prevents our conception of intelligence, bliss and the rest, is ignorance. Such an inference is determined by experience, and even analogy cannot destroy it. Of them, the condition of existence is the ordinary, while the perception of Intelligence, bliss etc., derived only from knowledge, is the particular condition. 'Ordinary' signifies that which prevails in many countries, and for a greater portion of time; and 'Particular' is what is known in few countries, and not at all times, but sometimes.

If it be said, since the *Atma* is intelligence, bliss etc., he is present everywhere like truth; and in reference to truth, the prevalence of intelligence, bliss and the rest in a few countries; and in regard to the latter, the pervasion of the former in many countries, imply an inconsistency, therefore to consider truth as constituting its ordinary, while Intelligence, bliss etc., as forming its particular portion is untenable. Then the reply is, as truth *Atma* is essentially known to be existent, by all persons, from their conception of "I am" and similar other phrases; such a conception has nothing to do with ignorance. The advent of knowledge, or its shutting out, cannot reduce it to non-existence. But, so long as knowledge is shut out, a person cannot conceive Self to be intelligence bliss etc., *that* conception is only brought about by knowledge of Self; yet even in such a condition of ignorance, the bliss, intelligence, purity, freedom, etc., are already present there,—only they are not conceived. Hence such experience is called ordinary, and for the matter of that, intelligence, bliss, etc., have been called to prevail only for a short time, and truth for a greater portion of time; though truth and intelligence etc., do not actually limit Self into ordinary and particular conditions. For this reason, the conception of existence (truth or Reality) is called the ordinary portion of Self, as that of intelligence, bliss etc., is his* particular portion. Moreover it does not create any contradiction in what has been termed the unparticular condition. Because, the admission of ordinary and particular can be said to tell against the unparticular condition, and as such an admission is not made here, but reference is only made to ignorance which creates a distinction resembling them.

In this way, to know Self as essentially existent, [truth] and from ignorance not to know that he is intelligent, blissful, eternal, pure and free is to attribute bondage† to him—which he is not, but a mere product of illusion. But such an illusion is destroyed by knowledge, hence is created a necessity for the work in hand.

Also, as has been already told, by discarding the forbidden and optional acts, and recoursing to the practice of the daily and occasional rites and penances,—even in the absence of the forbidden acts, —a man cannot attain the eternal abode. And, in the absence of optional things he cannot attain to the abode of the good, and by abstaining from the daily and occasional rites, what sin is produced

---

* *Atma* is masculine, therefore Self has always been used in that gender, but in English, Spirit is always neuter, and Self is synonymous with it as also with *Brahma* which is neuter. The reader may take note of this, to avoid falling into mistake.

† The attribution of bondage signifies Self to be subject to re-births.

it is destroyed by their adopting into practice; and by ordinary or extraordinary penances are removed the sins committed in this, or in a prior life. In the absence of a desire for the result, his optional works do not procure 'deliverance.' Hence 'deliverance' has no reference to knowledge, but is simply an absence of re-birth. Such an assertion is clearly inadmissible.

For, the daily and occasional rites, produce the desirable abode in heaven as a result, as has been proved by analogy by the commentator [Sankaracharya]; hence, it is clear, that such actions will procure the abode of the good, and not a deliverance from future re-births. Moreover, if it be said that such actions produce no fruit, then it will be tantamount to an admission of the fruitlessness of the Vedâs which propound them:—inasmuch as from your point of view, their non-performance is injurious and sinful, and to say that they bring forth no bad result is to admit that sin will not be engendered from their non-performance. For such non-performance indicates want, while sin indicates existence, in other words an absent or non-existent thing which is the same as nothing, producing sin which is existent or something; and such a statement of nothing producing something, is clearly inadmissible for they are antagonistic of each other. Hence their non-performance cannot be admitted to produce sin as a result. Then again, if it be said, that the non-performance of the daily and occasional rites engender sin, then it amounts to the admission of something being produced from nothing, which is inconsistent as remarked by Bhagvan SreeKrishna [in the second Chapter of *Bhagvad Gita*]. Therefore, the absence of such works which is equal to nothing, cannot produce sin, which is equal to something (harmful). In this way, is determined that sin is produced from other actions besides the non-performance of daily and occasional rites. So that, not to admit the blissful abode of heaven (*svarga*) as a result of their performance, is to reduce them into a condition of unproductiveness, and with them, the Vedâs likewise. Here there is another proof, as to their procuring the desirable result of abode in heaven.

Also, it is similarly inadmissible to look upon the 'optional works' of a prior existence, unactuated by any desire to the enjoyment of fruits thereof, as barren and unproductive. For, the seed of action produces two seedlings which are (1) desire and (2) *Adrista*: of them, *Adrista* signifies virtue and vice or good and bad works. Now 'the good' produces good desires and virtue, while 'the bad' bring forth harmful desires and sin. With the good desire is originated first an inclination for 'good works,' which in turn produce happiness. Similarly bad desires produce an inclination for harmful works, which lead to misery. Thus we see, how the seed of action produces the two seedlings, desire and *Adrista*. Of them, the first has a remedy which causes its destruction; while the second can only cease by producing its usual results, and not otherwise. This is the authoritative assertion of the sacred writings. In other words, the sin engendered by harmful desires can be destroyed by seeking the company of the good, hearing their precepts and similar acts. Then again, virtue, produced by good works, and desires, is sure to bring forth happiness, which in turn is destroyed by keeping the company of bad men and similar other bad acts. It does not end here, but all the desirable results which the *Shastras* say are produced by an inclination for them, are destroyed with their root desire, thus proving desires to be fruitful; but such destruction cannot affect the *Adrista* which is determinately the source of enjoyment [of good and bad alike]. Hence we find that actions must inevitably produce their results, which cannot be removed or destroyed till they have ceased [*i. e.*, till the individual has enjoyed them in full, and the consummation of results have taken place]. Such an assertion of the *Shastras* makes no contradiction, nor does it imply an inconsistency.

Thus then, the inevitable law of 'Karma' entails upon the ignorant an enjoyment of their fruits, which can only cease with their consummation. But to the knower of Self, it is otherwise; for actions and their agent (results) are not derived from the excellent *(Brahma)* but are due to ignorance; and as the two are antagonistic of each other, consequently knowledge destroys ignorance and its results: therefore it is said, that the wise (knower of Self) obtains a respite from the result of works, without enjoying them. As things seen in a dream are destroyed and rendered non-existent in the waking state, so action, agent and result produced by the sleep of ignorance are destroyed by the wakefulness of knowledge. But no destruction proceeds without knowledge.

Moreover to say 'that no enjoyment can proceed in the absence of a desire to enjoy the fruit of action,' is to annihilate the determination of *Iswara*; inasmuch as, it is His determination, that the ignorant should consummate their actions by reaping the results, so that, when a desire is wanting, no result is to be enjoyed; to say so, is to do away with His determination, [and create desire as the true determining source of all actions];—a contradiction of what the *Shastras* teach as to the reality of *Iswar's* determination.

[But it may be asked where is the contradiction? The answer is]—If the optional works will produce no result to one who desires not enjoyment, then by extending it similarly to harmful actions one may as well say, that as such actions bring forth misery as their result, which no one is ever desirous to have for his share, so by shutting up his desire, he goes on performing them without any fear of creating sin, or another equally undesirable result. But such is not the fact. Without knowledge, actions cannot cease to produce results, and as has already been pointed out, according to the conclusions of Vedâs, a person engaged in practising works unactuated by any desire as to their result, is not liable to reap any fruits thereof; in the same way, to say that if the desire be subsequent to the practice, even that will bring forth no enjoyment is quite against the Vedâs; [and untrue]. For, actions done with, or without desire of reaping fruits, must produce their necessary results, and the individual must certainly have to enjoy them. But then the difference in the two is this:—actions originating without a desire for the results, clear the mind and render it pure and faultless; while those with desire, simply bring in their usual results without purifying the internal organ; the first produce knowledge from 'hearing,' the precepts of the wise and thus procure a respite from results. Because it is his knowledge which causes him not to desire for results. But if from want of such 'hearing' or any other cause, he derives no knowledge (of Self,) then for him, actions must continue to produce their usual results, though the desire for their enjoyment may be wanting. This is what the Vedâs conclude. Hence we see that without knowledge, actions cannot cease producing results.

Moreover, what has already been said with regard to penances causing the destruction of bad actions, do not hold true. For, the past misdeeds of all previous births extending to infinity, cannot be possibly destroyed by penances of a single life-time. Hence, the ordinary penances such as bathing in the Ganges, pronouncing *Iswar's* name, and the rest, which cause the destruction of all sorts of sin, are merely so many means for obtaining Self-knowledge, and as such, they are called destroyers of sin, because they bring forth knowledge,—which destroys sin.

Moreover, what has already been said in regard to the pains attending the performance of daily and occasional rites as being produced by the connection of the results of forbidden works; consequently they cannot produce any more result. Such an assertion is untenable for the prohibited acts are infinite in variety, and the results they produce are also infinite, so that the pains accompanying the practice of the daily and occasional rites cannot be looked upon as enough expiation for them.

Moreover, what has already been said in regard to 'optional works,' that their entire accumulated results produce the one physical body. Even this is not possible; inasmuch as the accumulation of such optional works is infinite, hence they cannot determine the subjects to be enjoyed during a single life-time; and so far as an emancipated practicer of *Yoga* is concerned, it may be said, that during one life-time, he may dissipate all his works by enjoying in several bodies; but with regard to the rest of mankind this is impracticable. And furthermore, a *Yogi* already emancipated may attain to extraordinary powers; but without knowledge, he cannot achieve his deliverance from future re-births, as is mentioned in the Vedâs.

Thus then, it is rendered apparent, that by simply abstaining from the optional and forbidden acts and by engaging in the performance of the daily and occasional rites, an ignorant person, for reaping the fruits of the latter works, as also the good and bad actions of a previous life, is subjected to a course of consecutive re-births, extending through the infinity of time, and that he is not emancipated. Hence, for the acquirement of knowledge through the means of the present work [to procure emancipation], its necessity is clearly established.

As things created in a dream turn out false in the wakeful condition, and they are destroyed: so the unreality of bondage can only be removed by the acquisition of knowledge which resembles the waking condition. This will be particularly dwelt upon, on a future occasion. Thus is determined the 'qualified individual,' 'subject,' and 'necessity of the work'; and in their presence the necessary relation is also established. Hence to begin the work is not fruitless.

Such is real bliss, supreme, manifested and kind to the indigent, beyond the range of intellect, non-different from me.

SECTION III.

He, who reads this work, with a full knowledge of its four moving considerations along with his spiritual preceptor, or hears it with a friend, with an earnestness of mind, attains the road to emancipation by deriving knowledge [of Self]. Easy it is, to plant the seeds of knowledge, in the garden of intellect, for which reason, the discourse between a preceptor and his pupil is introduced here.

Now such a discourse between a preceptor and his pupil is termed easy, because the pupil is easily made acquainted with the doctrine which the work treats of, and thus ascertains its drift; hence the work is commenced with the above dialogue.

On the signs of a Spiritual Preceptor.

He who knows well the drift of the Vedas, recognises self as the only Reality, non-different from *Brahma*; who is capable of removing the five differences by analysis and analogical inference; and by clearing Ignorance and other defects, brings *Brahma* vividly into the mental conception of his pupil, as something tangible, and reduces the objective world into its actual condition of non-reality, similar to the illusion of a mirage; and who speaks not of things other than *Brahma*, is a real and unrivalled preceptor;—unlike those who simply cut away the forelock of their pupils' hair, to turn them into their followers.

The above receives further elucidation from the following comments: "who knows well the drift of the Vedas" is made to signify that the *Acharya* or professor is dependent entirely on the Vedas, and has neither the inclination nor the boldness, to misinterpret them. He does not set aside the precepts inculcated there, to replace them with others of his own, but follows them with faith. 'Non-duality' has reference to self-knowledge, and the 'means' helpful to its success. A preceptor is therefore a man, who has achieved success in knowing

Self to be non-different from *Brahma*. A person may be well-read in the Vedas, but devoid of Self-knowledge ; such a one is not a fit preceptor : then again, a man may be thoroughly versed in the practice of Self-knowledge, but is totally ignorant, so far as the Vedâs are concerned, he cannot be called an *Acharya*, though he is one 'emancipated.' For, he cannot clear away the doubts from the mind of his pupils. Such of them, as have already cleared their minds of all blemishes, and whose conceptions (convictions will be more proper) are good, who have passed over the stage, in which doubts distract the mind,—to them, he may indeed become a preceptor. But to the rest (who constitute the great bulk of pupils) he is quite unfit to impart instruction in a manner, as to dispel their doubts.

Hence the real preceptor is one dependent on the Vedas,—a knower of self—capable of dispelling the five sorts of distinctions from the mind of his pupils, by analogy and reasoning.

The distinctions are :—

(1) Between *Jiva* and *Iswara*.
(2) Between one life and another.
(3) Between sentient and insentient.
(4) The distinction present in *Iswara* and insentient (inanimate).
(5) Between one inanimate and another.

'Distinctions' are likewise called sources of apprehension, for which, they ought to be ascertained. Hence, the preceptor is one, who having ascertained the five distinctions, removes them by logical deductions, destroys the ignorance concerning *Brahma*, and establishes Its identity with Self (*Atmâ*) which he renders apparent. Besides this, his lectures destroy the reality of the world (*i. e.,* establish its unreality) ; such an uncommon preceptor is the (*Acharya*) real professor—otherwise, one who simply shaves his head, and causes the removal of the forelock from his pupils' heads, or distinguishes them with the usual signs of the religious order to which he belongs, is no teacher at all. The real teacher is engaged in giving his lectures, that cause a desire of release from bondage ; he never insists on his pupils to dye their clothes red. He is well acquainted with the *Shastras* and is himself free (Buddha).

Give us the signs which distinguish a knower of the *Shastras* ;

let us hear the words of a sage accordingly, so that a pupil may try to be qualified in them.

Here, a Guru's knowledge of the *Shastras* is his distinguishing sign. The means which qualify an individual to read the work, are the signs of a pupil. Therefore the signs of the qualified person already mentioned, constitute the signs of the pupil.

ON LOVE AND REVERENCE FOR A GURU.

The pupil must shew more love and reverence to his professor than he does to *Iswara*, for without them, he may be wise, but yet, without knowledge of self.

Without a Guru, the Vedâs appear a sea full of salt, and emancipation cannot be had; but his arguments *pro* and *con* are nectar.

As a person residing in the seashore, and drinking sea-water conceives its brackish taste, from the brine present in it, and is therefore put to great inconvenience and suffers pain; so he who attempts to ascertain the drift of the Vedas without a Guru, hurls himself in the salt-sea of the Vedas, his mind is distracted with doubts and distinctions, and he is subjected to the pain of birth and death. Hence the interpretation of the Vedâs by Ramânuja, Madhava and others, without the assistance or instruction of a Guru, are full of distinctions, which they had failed to ascertain, or clear; and for such, had been subjected to re-births and its attendant miseries instead of being 'delivered.' But then, it does not mean that Ramanuja and his compeers had nothing to do with a preceptor and they read the Vedâs themselves. What is meant is simply this :—The preceptor who gave them instruction, to enable them to produce the commentaries, as they have done, cannot be called real *Acharyas*. For, we have seen that such a one expounds the non-duality of the *Jiva* and *Brahma*; while *they* have sought to create a difference by expounding duality. Hence the word 'Guru' cannot properly be applied to them. To call so, is unnecessary or unoccasional; as a pupil without an occasion for a Guru calls him preceptor, similarly the men who instructed Ramanuja and others, in the Vedâs, were merely their teachers and not Gurus, for they taught them duality instead of delivering them from it. In the same manner, those who read the Vedâs themselves, or repair for instruction to a person not possessing the qualifications already pointed out, experience the salt of difference, and are subjected to transmigration.

Moreover, the arguments used for and against by a Guru well-versed in the knowledge of *Brahma*, to ascertain non-duality and promote Self-knowledg in his pupil, are more delicious than nectar, and cause him more felicity; as the salt is removed from the sea-water by rain which renders it sweet, so he derives knowledge by his discourse and is released.

A preceptor without Self-knowledge is thus declared:—

The ignorant resemble the leather bags used in drawing or carrying water from a well, while the wise are the clouds that pour forth rain. Both read the Vedâs, but the wise only, for the sake of knowledge are to be selected, leaving the ignorant.

In other words, as in the instance of leather bags employed in carrying water, they cannot cause its excellent taste, and hence not its cause ; so those who draw the water of knowledge from the sea of the Vedâs by repairing to a teacher devoid of Self-knowledge, cannot determine the excellent felicity (which proceeds from it), therefore the ignorant are likened to the leather bags, and the wise to the rain-clouds; of whom the former are to be avoided and the latter selected either for reading, or hearing the Vedas.

But here is the source of a misapprehension. For, if the Vedas are to be read from a wise person, to ascertain non-duality and derive knowledge for being delivered from transmigration, then the necessity for other Sanscrit or vernacular works, as they cannot procure that knowledge, exists not. This is now being removed.

"A knower of *Brahma* is himself a *Brahma*," as is declared in the *Sruti* : and his word is Veda, no matter whether it is in Sanscrit or vernacular; hence it is useless to create a difference between the Vedas and his words. Further to say, that without the former, no knowledge of Self can be derived, (as has just been mentioned in the preceding paragraph) is to admit what is not the inevitable rule. As for instance—the *Ayur Vedas* treat of diseases and their treatment, but a man can have thorough knowledge of medicine from a study of Sanscrit, Vernacular or Persian works of medicine without ever reading the *Ayur Vedas*; so can knowledge of the Universal Self—*Brahma*—be derived from a study of the vernacular and other works. With such a purpose, wise sages have declared the *Smriti, Puran,* and works on History (the *Mahabharat and Ramayana*) as treatises for knowing *Brahma*; so that these books will be perfectly futile, if knowledge is only to be obtained from the Vedas. Hence any work that expounds or treats on Self, can create knowledge, no matter whether it be the Veda, or any other work, or a vernacular treatise.

Serve him whose word is equal to the Veda—when he is pleased, the pupil ascertains the nature of Self.

The words of a spiritual preceptor versed in the knowledge of *Brahma* are like the Vedas. Such a one is to be served by the pupil seeking for knowledge, for, when he is pleased with his services, then he knows what Self is like. In other words, services done to an '*Acharya*' are more valuable than those tendered to *Iswara*; inasmuch as the former bring in both visible and invisible results, while the latter can only bring forth the invisible. The 'invisible' are the results of virtue and vice produced by good and bad actions. The 'visible' produce tangible results independently of good or bad deeds. By serving *Iswara*, is produced virtue, which purifies the mind; consequently the result of such service is 'invisible.' By serving the professor and pleasing him, independently of virtue [produced by such a meritorious action] the pupil obtains the benefit of his instruction, which is a 'visible result,'—and as such service is meritorious, therefore it produces virtue, and purifies the mind—'an invisible result.'

Therefore, as it produces both 'visible' and 'invisible' results, it is superior to serving *Iswara*, (which produces only invisible results), and a pupil ought always to be engaged in doing the different sorts of service to his Guru.

These consist :—(1) In shewing reverence, by falling like a stick before him, kissing the dust of his feet, or besmearing the body and head with it. (2), In giving away [here giving away is equal to dedicating or sacrificing] body, mind, wealth and speech in his service so that the pupil may obtain 'deliverance' from the bondage of future births.

(*a*). 'Dedicating the body' is to perform all menial services which the spiritual preceptor may require at the hands of his pupil and to obey him in everything.

(*b*). 'Dedicating the mind' is to love him, so that he may grant the pupil's wish (impart instruction), being well-pleased with his services, or that he may be well-pleased; and to meditate on him constantly, looking upon him as *Brahma*, Sun, Ganges, or something equally holy, and not to pry into his defects, which should be considered as unreal as dreams are, if the pupil wants his own well-being.

(*c*). 'Dedicating the wealth.' Wealth consists in wife, son, land, animals, maids, servants and other things; 'dedicate' is to relinquish them and take shelter with a Guru. For, the preceptor has relinquished them already, (when he has taken the path of an ascetic) and he will no more accept them, therefore to abandon them, is to follow his example. Hence it is called the 'dedicating of wealth'; or if the teacher be one with family and house, then to dedicate these to him as an offering. This is another variety of dedicating wealth.

But if any apprehension arise as to a man with family and house being a Guru, or teacher of the knowledge of *Brahma*, then the instance of Yagyavalka, Udalak and such other well-known teachers, who kept a family and house as well, ought to remove it. Hence a Guru may be a man with family [as well as an ascetic].

(*d*). The 'dedicating of speech' consists in knowing the utterances of a Guru as full of merit, purity, and free from blemishes; and thus to offer his intellect (so as to ascertain the drift of his speech).

A pupil desirous of his personal benefit, should after dedicating his body, mind, wealth etc., in the manner aforesaid, reside with his Guru wherever he may be, or near him, and support his life by receiving alms; which he presents to his teacher with all respect, never asking for a share, nor going a second round for collecting alms in one day, in the same village, but subsisting on what he receives from his teacher's kindness. And if to test his faith, his preceptor does not give him anything, then not to part company with his profession of begging, but to bring all he receives before him, and present them accordingly. And then, when he finds him well-pleased, and sitting unoccupied with anything, the pupil stands respectfully before his preceptor, and with humility enquires, "May he ask any question"? And on receiving a reply in the affirmative he seeks an answer to his enquiries.

Moreover, if for a preponderance of the good action of his past life, the preceptor imparts instruction to a pupil, who has not served him by dedicating body, mind, and the rest in the usual way, then also he is sure to derive benefit. For, the results of service are two-fold. The first is to please his preceptor; and the second is to purify his mind, both of which results he succeeds in achieving.

Thus a pupil serving his preceptor by making an offering of his body, mind, wealth, and speech, is sure to find the donee, helping him always to the path of knowledge.

SECTION IV.

The discourse of a pupil and *Guru*,
To benefit the young, say I to you.
He who in that manner seeks instruction
Is wise and sound in discrimination.

Three brothers, are sons good
Of a sovereign, who stood
Without any rival
In Heaven, earth and *Patal*.
Of them, the lord was he,
King Suvasantati.
Adored alike by all,
In Heaven earth and *Patal*.
The eldest of sons three
Was call'd Tatwadrishti.
Adrishta was second ;
And Tarkadrishti third.

(Thus says the king.)

"I lost my infancy in play,
Spent youth in sensuality
Amidst women, family and th' rest ;
Thus had I in full, enjoyment.
In Heaven, earth and in *Patal*
To acquire enjoyment, seek all."
The king by his own arms prowess,
Managed the state business.
The father now takes leave,—retires
After due reflection considers :
Self alone is uncreate and bliss,
Things different all are worthless :

For this, the state, he abandons
(To find Self-knowledge) to his sons.
Between whom the kingdom he divides,
Of Heaven, earth, *Patal*, and gives.
Thus did the king resolve in mind,
Asks his sons, the minister to find,
Sends for the citizens to come ;
Speaks of his 'indfference' to them :
Says "take care of the state again.
Let one be the king of Heaven,
Another Patal, and the third take
Benares, his capital to make.
Where dwells the internal knower—
The God Siva or Maheswara ;
Where at death, hearing his precept
With ease, his abode one does get.
Where the renown of the Ganges,
The main theme of discussion is
Among men ; and where for reasons
Many, north-ward her course she runs."
Amongst his sons, divides his states.
Exhorts them to protect subjects.
For, without proper partition,
They cause much pain and dissension.

(Thus Says the King.)

Kingdom and society I relinquish, now that
I know them the source of pain of all 'like
Pain then, is the lot of man and each has
His share ; that is inevitable law.
The rich are ignorant, the poor spirited.
Having found its cause, I leave the world
To find Self, who is eternal blissfulness.
On vari'd topics the father discourses,
Which the brothers with attention listen.
Seated aloof, they weigh and ponder over

His word; and learn, the world is a source of pain:
That, he wants to remove by becoming *Bráhma*,
Encumbering them with worldly concerns.
He is an ocean of intellect, who discards
The world, to extinguish misery and pain.
So leaving their states a source of much pain,
They betake to work for spiritual end. *
Thus after mature consideration,
They leave society and home behind
In quest of an able and proper Guru,
For obtaining emancipation.
Pronounced they, the name of their father
Subhasantati, in its literal sense.†
And took it earnestly for truth.

After much search in countries many,
Apart on the banks of the Sursari,
Amidst trees, branches and leaves,
In the wood, they find a recluse;
Seated under the *ficus Religiosa*,
With fingers intertwined [in prayer].
On the oneness of *Jiva* and *Brahma*
Was this man of merit lecturing to his pupils
Faultless, and intent in mind,—
Dependent on him, like servants, to a king.
Seeing him employ many arguments,
To instill knowledge of non-duality.
They liken him to Sambhu in *Kaylas*
Affording instruction to Sanak &c.

---

* Self-knowledge which is the means for attaining emancipation from future re-births.

† '*Subha*' means good, and 'santati' children. Therefore it would signify one who has good sons. Hence they armed themselves with the faith of their goodness, so as not to be thwarted from their present purpose.

Seeing that, they take protection under him,
Prostrate on the ground like a stick;
Kiss the dust of his feet, and besmear it
On the head and body as something precious.
Six months did they live with him,
In the manner prescribed for pupils:
Amply did they serve him, keeping
The desire of emancipation in mind.
Then was the Guru well-pleased,
And asked he of them in a low voice:
What brings you and your brothers?
Who brought you? And why live here?
At this, Tatwadrishti the eldest,
Makes a sign to his brothers younger
With hands joined as in prayer;
Humbly acquaints the teacher with his desire.

(Says Tatwadrishti.)

Oh Bhagavan! We brothers three
Are sons of king Subhasantati.
Poor, young and ignorant, we want
To find out the distractions many,
That cause so much suffering.
Thou hast commanded me to speak,
Hence I do now ask of thee [for],
Thou art extremely kind to dependents.

Replies the Guru. Hear my words in answer to what you ask, fix in your mind peace and it will destroy doubts. The pupil finding him thus to be very kind and in his own heart yearning for the desired success enquires:—Oh Bhagavan! Thou art a mine of kindness, resembling Mahesa in contentment and art all-knowing; I have placed myself at a distance from the world which is full of pain, with birth, death &c., &c., please instruct me as to the remedy which will procure its destruction, and cause me to acquire the supreme bliss. I had hitherto been always engaged in devotional excercises, and actions. But they have not procured me the desirable result; I have cut myself off from the bondage of the world, please discover that other remedy that I may succeed.

The Guru, finding in his pupil's heart the desire for release which causes the destruction of pain and produces supreme happiness, discourses on the means cited in the Vedas for the purpose. Though the *Shastras* speak differently of knowledge, yet the knowledge leading to the destruction of duality (which creates a difference in the individual and universal intelligence as separate and twain) is determined as the principal means for attaining emancipation. He speaks about it as follows:—Know thou, Oh Pupil! a man desirous of causing cessation of pain, attending a worldly life in the shape of birth and death, and of acquiring the supreme happiness, has the origin of such a desire in mistake. For, since he is supreme happiness himself, how is it possible that he shall get it? A desire can only be for a thing which one has not got. Moreover, Self belongs to him, and in that Self is centred the ineffable bliss, which he seeks for, but that is already present there, hence such a desire is due to mistake. Then again, the world with its births and deaths cannot affect you, if it does, then only is it possible for a desire to cause its destruction to be present. But they are not your subjects (that is Self is not subject to birth and death, for He is eternal, uncreate, all-pervading, and internal knower). Hence in the absence of pain, to seek its destruction is a mistake. Therefore, Pupil! Thou art the Intelligence devoid of birth and death, eternal,—the *Brahma*; and thou shouldst not admit the pain of birth and death as subjects for thine mind.

Says Tatwadrishti. If Self be bliss, it follows then, he ought not to desire any happiness from property and riches. Self is therefore not blissfulness, but his relationship with the world constitutes the subject of happiness.

Guru. A person with an intellect averse to Self, is desirous of property. Its means of enjoyment is called *vishaya* (an object of pursuit). Hence, a desire of such enjoyment induces him to acquire wealth, take a wife, beget children etc., which in turn produces inconstancy of the mind (intellect literally), and prevents from realising blissfulness by an absence of its reflection in *buddhi*. But, on the other hand, when what he is desirous of having (property and enjoyment) comes to him, his intellect [inconstancy of intellect] subsides and becomes the subjective function of the indwelling intelligence, wherein is reflected the blissfulness of Self, and conception of which (reflection) leads him to the error of believing that his happiness is the result of material prosperity.

But such happiness is not inherent in property, riches and the rest ; for then, a man satiated with one variety and seeking for obtaining another, may as well derive happiness from the first, (which had satiated him) but that is never so. From my view, the absence of happiness in that case, is due to the inconstancy of the intellect produced by the fresh desire of possessing a fresh property. Here there is no reflection ; or if happiness is really present in property, then a person ought to feel it always after the first interview with a dear son, or any other equally beloved relation, caused quite by accident,—unexpectedly—after a long absence or separation, is over ; in other words, the happiness produced by the first meeting ought to continue ever afterwards, but that is not so, because the source of happiness—the object of his love (son or any other)—is now near him; hence on the first interview only, happiness is produced: inasmuch as the intellect then becomes constant and fixed, and it blends with the object. Therefore intellect is said to be inconstant and happiness is not inherent in riches and property.

Then again, if it were otherwise, it will be quite impossible to expect any happiness in a state of profound meditation (where the subject, object, and knowledge are all blended in one and their separate existence is reduced to non-being). The same rule may apply to the state of profound slumber ; in such a condition, a person cuts off all connection with the world, (which ceases then to exist relatively to him) and if happiness be an inherent property of riches and wealth, then as his connection with them ceases, he cannot be said to conceive of it. But this is otherwise ; for, the individual experience establishes that happiness always attends in sound sleep ; and a man on rising is apt to say "I was sleeping happily, I knew nothing then," Hence it is established that happiness is not inherent in property, riches and wealth etc., but in the Supreme blissfulness (Self), and can be felt in all things; the mistake arising out of their close proximity with him. Therefore the Vedas say: "From the presence of happiness in Self, everything is said to be full of it." I have thus, Oh Pupil! Made thee acquainted with the felicity discovered by the possession of property and my conclusions thereof. If you have any lurking doubts about them, keep your wits about you and I will reply them accordingly.

Tatwadrishti—Oh Bhagavan! What hast thou hitherto said is in reference to the ignorant only, and does not apply to those who have knowledge (of Self); for thou hast referred (in the beginning) to a 'person with an intellect averse to Self,' and such an aversion can only be present in a man of ignorance and not in the wise; so please say in reference to the wise. Whether knowledge of happiness be due to the desire for material comforts such as wealth etc. or otherwise?

Guru. Pupil, listen to me with attention. What I have said in reference to aversion to Self does not refer to the ignorant alone, but when a wise person's intellect is engaged in the manifested external world, [in its ordinary uses and practices] then he forgets Self; so that, for the time being, he also is equally averse to Self; moreover if the intellect of the wise be always after the modification of Self, then his ordinary* practices as eating and the rest will cease, hence in such a condition he (the wise) can be said to be averse to Self. An ignorant man's intellect is always averse to Self, while during the time when a wise man's intellect is averse to Self, (that is when it has not assumed the shape of Self) his desire for property precludes him from the perception of felicity in Self in common with the ignorant. But then there is this difference between the two :—when [*i. e.*, afterwards] the perception of happiness

---

* There are three kinds of existences from the Vedantin standpoint called respectively (a) *Parmarthika*, (b) *Vyvaharika* and *Prativasika* or true, practical and apparent. Here practices of the *Vyvaharika* are meant by the author.

derived in connection with property accrues to a wise person, he knows that it is non-different from Self; but simply reflected from him *(Atma)*; this the ignorant does not know. Hence in regard to the former, enjoyment of property and its attendant happiness are in its effects similar to that realised in profound meditation. An ignorant person is apt to commit the mistake that the happiness which he feels from property is not a reflection of Self and its relation with wealth and riches etc., is a fact. But this is conceived in error.

Tatwadrishti. Oh Bhagavan! Thou hast said, Self is "felicity" this I know full well; and that "I am not the subject of pains—birth, death and the rest,—hence in that case their destruction cannot be possible;" I have my doubts on this point, for if I am not the subject of birth and death and their attending pains, then they are quite different from myself. Please therefore inform me what is it that is born and subjected to death. So that I may not confound it with Self.

Guru. Pupil, Hear my word, that will clear away your doubts, it is the source of much evil. But you and I are out of it.

Tatwadrishti. Bhagavan! If birth, death etc.,—the miseries of the world—are not my subject, or that of another, then why such pain is cognizable as something apparent and visible. An absent or non-existent thing cannot make itself visible. As for instance, a sterile woman's son; flowers (are not present) in ether; hence they cannot be determined as actualities. In the same way, if the world be not an actuality, it ought then to remain inapparent and invisible. Moreover from birth to death, the world is always tangible, and its miseries are felt and perceived as something real and actual, therefore they cannot be said to be non-existent.

Guru. Like objects seen in a dream, or the illusion of a snake in a chord, or the blue in ether, the objective world is due to illusion, while in truth it is non-existent; birth and death are due to Ignorance concerning Self (or *Brahma*); [knowledge alone can determine their unreality].

Tatwadrishti. As the creation of a snake in a rope is unreal, so you say, the attribution of pain to Self, derived from world and its concerns, is false. But in the first case, without a knowledge of an actual snake (derived from its sight) its creation in a rope is not possible, please determine its production.

Guru. There are four different views in reference to the production of a snake in a rope, silver in a nacre, and the rest.

A Charvaka* calls it pervasion of non-existence [*asatkhyati*]. Kshanika Vijnana Vadi says it to be pervasion of Self [Intelligence] (*Atmakhyati*); † a *Naiyayika*‡ and a *Vaisheshika*§ says it to be a apparent pervasion (*anyatha khyati*); a follower of Kapila¶ and a Prabhakara‖ again refer to another pervasion (*Akhyati*).

---

* A Sunyavadin or Lokayatika asserts the unreality and emptiness of the objective material world, he condemns all ceremonial rites, ridicules the *Sradha* ceremony observed after death, and it is anniversary days and calls the Vedantins "fools, knaves and buffons." Professor Wilson says of them, [works ii p. 87] that they were called Charvaka after one of their teachers the Muni Charvaka, their other designation, Lokayata, expresses their adoption of the tenet, that this being is the *Be-all* of existence; they were the advocates of materialism and atheism. According to Colebrook their principal tenets were (1) the identity of the soul with the body; (2) Akasa is not an element (3) perception is the only means of proof. Professor Cowell says in reference to them, that their doctrines were at one time widely prevalent in the world, for which they assumed the appellation of Lokayata. Wealth and desire are considered the only ends of man and there is no future existence.

† Probably the Yogacharas are meant. They are a sect of the Buddhists, who maintain all is void but intelligence; hence the Kshanika Vijnanavadin's assertion as it admits intelligence only, can be no other than theirs.

‡ A Naiyayika or Tarkika arranges all things under sixteen heads.

§ Vaisheshikas arrange all things under six heads.

¶ Kapila was the author of the Sankhya system of philosophy. His doctrine of *Prakrita* and *Purush* (Matter and Force) accounts for the evolution of the world. He is against a personal creator. His Purush represents the *Atma* of the Vedantins.

‖ Prabhakaras are called after the well-known scholiast of the Purva-Mimansa—Prabhakara. Their doctrine is called Akhyati Vadi.

The Charvaka doctrine is thus explained. A Sunyavadi says, in the province of a rope a snake is unreal and non-existent. Here non-existence implies its actual want. In other words, a snake is never actually present in a rope, though it is apt to be mistaken ; and this is due to a previous knowledge of a snake derived from seeing it, so that a man who has never seen it, can possibly never create it in another object.

The *Kshanika Vijnana Vadi* says, no snake exists outside of *Booddhi* either in a rope or in any other substance ; all objects are cognized by (*Boodhi*) Intellect (and their conception retained in memory) which then assumes the shape of what it cognizes, hence *Boodhi* is transient intelligence ; that is to say, not always present, but apt to come and go, it appears and disappears,—appears with cognition of an object and disappears after it has discovered it,—so that in the case of a snake, intelligence covers it, assumes its shape and produces its discovery so long as the object is in close contiguity or brought near to it, by means of the different organs of sense. Now this Intelligence is the same as *Atma*.

According to the *Naiyayika* and *Vaisheshika*, the sight of a real snake and the presence of a defect in sight, reduces it to cognition, and makes it appear in front as a thing quiet close. Actually a snake is seen in a wood, and its reflection falling upon the eye, remains impressed in it ; but then, the presence of a defect in sight also presupposes the creation of such an illusion along with the impress of its actual image inherent in it. It cannot be urged, that a person whose eye-sight is good, is free from all defects, since he is equally liable to err in the manner above indicated, therefore, the premises advanced are not maintainable. On the contrary, a defect will diminish and not increase the visional powers ; just as the solvent powers of the gastric juice are reduced by the presence of air, bile and mucus in the stomach, all of which are defects. In the same way, the presence of darkness etc., in the eye, (its defects) will diminish its power of vision. Moreover, it has already been said, that the cognition of the snake in the wood is produced along with the inherent defect by its impress on the retina, and that an object can be seen situated externally to the eye ; hence sight is rendered intense by the presence of the defect. It cannot be said, that it is quite unique; for, we find in diseases engendered by bile, the appetite is so morbidly increased that a person suffering from it will consume four times the quantity of his accustomed food* and yet will not feel satiated. In the same way, darkness present in the eye has the faculty of intensifying vision, and rendering a hidden snake visible or manifest. In this way, a snake lurking in the woods, or somewhere else, and its transposition or transfer in the rope present in front of us and called the province of a rope, is spoken of in a different way, which is therefore termed extraneous or something different.

The author of *Chintamuni* expounds it in the following manner :—

If the visibility of a snake living in the wood depends upon the presence of defects in the eyes along with sight, then such a mode of cognition may apply as well to a wall and other substances (which are situated between the sight and the snake) hence sight cannot render visible an object which is concealed. Also the presence of a defect in sight will prevent a person to determine the exact form of a rope, but will make him see a snake in it, hence the rope,—and not a snake,—is reduced to a different substance, and its cognition also becomes different.

An *Akhyativadi* says, to expound it on the principle of non-existence is tantamount to a sterile woman's son, and rabbit's horns; hence it cannot be maintained. Furthermore, if it be due to a modification of intelligence which assumes the shape of a snake, then as it is said to be transient in duration, the cognition ought also to last for a moment and not longer; therefore such a conclusion is also untenable. The same applies to the expounders of extraniety [another *khayti*]. His first method is established faulty by the *Chintamuni Karaka*; in the same way, the method of extraniety may be proved

---

* It is worthy of note that the disease referred to is Diabets mellitus; here the appetite becomes voracious for a time. Recent researches have established the origin of the disease in a faulty action of the liver; the bile secreted by it is not entirely normal, but undergoes some metamorphosis which gives rise to sugar, hence the author is perfectly right to connect it with bile.

to be unsound by the method of Chintamuni. For (they say) knowledge is in accordance to what is known. So that, from a rope that is known, follows the knowledge of a snake; surely this is contradictory. But it can be admitted, that where the illusion of a snake arises in a rope, a relation or connection is established between the rope and eyes, through the medium of their function (sight); in which condition the rope is brought under cognition as exemplified in the instance, " This is ;" and snake is produced from the impression left in the mind after its sight,—an action of memory.—"This is a snake." Here both of them follow and co-exist, the first is an ordinary knowledge of an apparent rope, and "This is a snake" is a knowledge derived form an act of memory. But from the presence of fear (or defect) in the individual (subject to the mistake and who is in the position of its demonstrator) and that of darkness * (a defect) in the eyes (which are the demonstrative proofs), he is unable to distinguish that he has in him both the varieties of the knowledge; he cannot discriminate whether his apparent knowledge of a rope is correct, or that derived from the sight of a real snake in a prior time and left impressed in his memory is correct, so that in the absence of knowledge of both of them, a Sankhya or Prabhakara finds the clue for the mistake, and such absence is present whereever there is a mistake.

The pupil says that of the four different doctrines about the origin of the mistake of snake in a rope thus explained, which am I to entertain? He therefore addresses his preceptor in the following strain :—Kind Guru teach me the best of them.

Guru. There is yet another method beyond the four already explained, it constitutes the fifth. It is called the 'indescribable' [*Anirbachanya Khyati*]. The *Asat*, are expounders of 'nothing ;' the second look upon intelligence and are called the *Atmakhyati*, the third depend upon a cause situated outside of the object and are called *Anyathakhyati* while the fourth are called the *Akhyati*. They base their doctrine on the inability to distinguish between the ordinary

---

*In broad daylight no mistake occurs, but in darkness it is pretty common, hence the defect of darkness is strongly insisted upon.

knowledge of the object (rope) and the impression left in the mind of the absent snake. They are all inconsistent.

As according to the view of an *Akhyati*, the three others are faulty and unsound, so is the case with him too.

For, he says that in "this is" the first knowledge relates to an ordinary acquaintance of it which renders it apparent; and "this is a snake" is the result of an impression left in his memory by the sight of a real snake in a former time; so that memory is admitted while the presence of a snake in the rope lying in front is not taken into consideration; now in such a view, a man ought to feel no fear nor should he run away from the supposed snake; but as the case is otherwise, the presence of the snake in front (in the rope) is fully established, and not the recollection of a snake seen before. Or from a particular acquaintance of a rope, a man may subsequently find that his perception of a snake in it is false; even in such an obstacle (to the creation of a snake) its presence is determined, while the same does not hold true with regard to its recollection: (he does not say that he is subject to the illusion because he recollects to have seen a snake before.)

Moreover when he says "It is a snake" it shows that he is subject of one knowledge only and not two (*i. e.*, snake *plus* rope); besides the internal organ cannot be the subject of two perceptions at one time,—memory and apparent visibility. Therfore the doctrine set up by the *Akhati* is extremely faulty.

All the above four doctrines have been fully explained in *Svarajya sidhi* and other works; and the arguments for and against have been clearly set forth, but as they are difficult of comprehension I have only just briefly described them.

Now for a consideration of the 'indescribable' [*Anirbachaniya*]. When a subject is seen by the eyes, the internal organ asumes its shape, drives away the ignorance which envelopes it and thus renders it visible; without visibility or light, cognition cannot follow. When a rope is mistaken for a snake, the function of the internal organ projected by the eyes establishes a connection with the rope, but the obstacles or defects as they are called *viz*, presence of darkness, do not determine the modification of the internal organ, so as to make it asume the shape of the rope, consequently its envelopement of ignorance remains undestroyed ; since therefore the conditional relation of its function for the destruction of the envelopement having been created, its ignorance remains in tact, how can the rope already situated in such function (intelligence) excite or stimulate ignorance, so as to make it assume the modification of a snake ? And if the action of ignorance - the creation of a snake—be true, then the knowledge of the rope need not be an obstacle to its existence. But it is quite otherwise, for when the actual rope is discovered, then the snake is reduced to an unreality— to non-existence—and if on the contrary, it be non-existent then it is virtually not like a sterile woman's son ; for such a condition is quite impossible, whereas in the rope it is present and continues so long as the mistake is not discovered. Hence (Ignorance) it cannot be non-existent, but quite distinct from it, as also from (*Sat*) existence, or being. Therefore it is described as something indescribable. The production of silver in nacre is in the same manner termed indescribable ; and for these reasons it is called the indescribable mode. As the snake is a modification of ignorance, so is its knowledge a modification of ignorance too, and not of the internal organ. Because, as the knowledge of the rope is an obstacle to a serpent, so is it an obstacle to its knowledge, which should not be, if it were a modification of the internal organ. Hence knowledge is also indescribable, and quite a distinct entity from existence and non-existence, like the snake of ignorance. But the snake is the product of a preponderance of (*Tama*) darkness present in Ignorance along with the associated intelligence of the rope ; and knowledge is a result of a modification of the (*Satwa*) good element of ignorance inherent in the manifesting intelligence; when the ignorance-associated intelligence of the rope assumes the modification of the snake, the ignorance present in the innate intelligence assumes its modification; for the stimulus of excitation which is a proximate cause of the ignorance-associated intelligence of the chord, is also an excitor of the innate intelligence dependent on ignorance. Hence the source of the mistake in regard to a snake-illusion and its knowledge, proceeds in the same time as the knowledge of the presence of the chord blends with that of ignorance.

Thus then, in reference to the production of a snake-illusion its formal or proximate cause is the particle of external ignorance (*vahya avidya*); and the particle of ignorance situated inside the witnessing intelligence and dependent on it, is the proximate cause of its knowledge or perception. And as in the dreaming condition, the particle of darkness (*Tamas*) of ignorance dependent in the witnessing intelligence, assumes the modification of a subject, while its particle of goodness assumes the modification of knowledge or perception. Hence in dreams, the internal ignorance assumes both the modification of subject and perception or knowledge, and that ignorance is their proximate cause, consequently the snake in the external rope, and the internal dream objects are said to be discovered by the witnessing intelligence. In other words, what is discovered by the function of ignorance is called the discoverer [witness.]

The discovering of the mistake of the 'indescribable' snake in the rope called illusion, or illusory attribution, is a modification* of Ignorance; and intelligence is subject to another modification which is called *vivarata*.† Now *parinam* produces a change of form in the same way as does a formal cause; while *vivarata* is possessed of properties antagonistic to what an object has. As the formal cause ignorance is indescribable, so is the snake in a chord and its knowledge equally indescribable. Hence, the last two have equal properties in common with Ignorance. That is to say, Ignorance brings in a change of form, or the semblance of a difference from what it was; it is its modification of change or *parinam*; similarly the predicated intelligence which abides in a rope and distinguishes it from another object is real. But the presence of snake in a rope and its knowledge or perception

---

* Modification stands for *parinam*; therefore it signifies a changed condition. It applies also in the preceeding instances wherever it has been used.

† With reference to causes it has been said that when a cause undergoes a change of form to produce an action it is called *Vikara* or *Parinam*. But when no such actual change of form takes place, it is called *vivarta*—curdled milk is an instance of the first variety and snake in the rope of the second.—(*Dhole's Vedantasara. p. 34.*)

is quite different from what has just been said to be real. Hence the rope with its knowledge, are antagonistic in nature to the abiding consciousness of the snake etc., (inasmuch as the first is real while the last unreal—illusory); call them naturally different, for they are different in form from intelligence. The seat of the unreal snake is not in the chord but in its associate of intelligence, consciousness, or knowledge ; for, like the snake, the rope itself is a designed contrivance and as such, one cannot take possession of, or occupy the other; hence the consciousness associated with the chord (and not the chord) is the seat of the snake. Moreover, if the predicated intelligence of the chord be said to be its seat, even then both the chord and intelligence will be the seat of the snake. But here, to connect the rope with the seat is not possible on account of the obstacle which it introduces, so that the associated intelligence or knowledge of the chord is such seat or occupation itself, and not its predicated intelligence. In the same way, the manifesting or witnessing intelligence is the occupation of the determining knowledge which evolves a snake. According to such a view, the subject and its knowledge in connection with a mistake, on account of the difference of their associates, creates a difference in occupation and such seats are not one. And particularly for the stimulus of Ignorance, the rope is not discovered, therefore it is the material cause, from which springs both the mistake of a snake and the non-discovery of the actual condition of a rope ; similarly its knowledge is the material cause for the destruction of both. If it be said, that knowledge of the rope cannot destroy or remove the snake ; the reply, is the occupation of an unreal substance can be destroyed by the knowledge of its site or occupation. This is the inference of a non-dualist. Or if it is alleged that the site or occupation of the false snake is the associated knowledge of the chord and not the chord itself, so that with the knowledge of the chord the snake cannot be removed. Then the reply is :—The knowledge of a bit of string or another equally insentient substance is derived by the function of the internal organ, so that the enshrouding ignorance concerning the subject is necessary to be removed ; and 'envelopment' is a force of ignorance consequently it is not dependent on the insentiency of the subject, but on its abiding intelligence; hence the function of the internal organ after having assumed the shape of the chord (or another object which it covers to cognize) breaks away the encasement of ignorance from the intelligence present in the chord, and discovers it by the reflection of intelligence residing in it (function). Intelligence is Self-illuminated, it needs not the help of reflection for its discovery. This will be fully discussed further on. Thus with the reflex intelligence of the internal organ, its functional portion acts upon intelligence of the rope and results in the removal of envelopment of ignorance; and the reflex intelligence of its function discovers the rope. Therefore, the subject of such function is not the rope only, but its knowledge as well. Hence it is written in the work *Sidhanta*, that the function of the internal organ forms the subject of *Brahma*. In this way by the removal of the envelopment of ignorance from the chord, the presence of the snake in it, is discovered by the indwelling intelligence or knowledge of the chord; so that the knowledge of the chord is the determining element of the presence of the snake in it, therefore it is quite natural to expect its removal. Now for the objections against such a view. If then the presence of the snake is removed by the knowledge of the rope according to the manner just explained, yet the knowledge of the snake cannot be destroyed. For the snake is present in the knowledge of the chord which is included in and not separated from it, and the individual intelligence is the occupation of the knowledge of the snake. From the first named condition is produced the reflected knowledge of the chord, which is not separate from it, and not the individual perception; so that even with knowledge of the chord, the presence of the snake along with it, is a creation of ignorance present in the individual along with intelligence, which is a function of the mind; and such ignorance cannot be continued nor removed; but knowledge by its occupation can alone so do. Hence the perception of the rope cannot remove the perception of the snake from it. But such a mistake is cleared away in the manner stated below.

Knowledge is dependent on the subject, therefore the snake which is the subject, is removed along with the destruction of the subject; for in its absence, the perception of the snake cannot continue; and if it be said that without the knowledge of the thing actually present, the supposed or fancied contrivance or superimposition of another thing on it cannot be destroyed; in other words, here, the presence of the snake is only a fancied superimposition on the chord, which is clear to the intelligence present in the witness (individual subject to the mistake) and without its knowledge the snake cannot cease to exist in perception; then such an assertion is soon disposed of. Cessation is of two sorts, one is extreme cessation, and the other is its final disappearance into its cause. Of them, the first refers to the removal of the effect together with its cause. All fancied contrivances are due to the inherent ignorance present in objects, which is removed with its effect by the occupation of intelligence. But the second variety does not depend on it. As for instance, the relative destruction of all objects in the condition of profound dreamless slumber, and their actual destruction in *Pralaya*, proceed from ignorance without the occupation of intelligence. Here, in such a destruction, the source of the results which such actions were to have brought about, is destroyed by their want; similarly without the knowledge of the witnessing agent, is removed the perception of the snake. So that, in the absence of the subject of perception—the snake—is the source of the destruction. In this way, the snake is destroyed by the knowledge of the rope, and in the absence of the snake, which is the subject of that knowledge, its knowledge is also destroyed; or both the snake and its perception, are removed by a knowledge of the chord. Because, when it is plainly perceived, the function of the internal organ projected by the eyes, covers the rope, and assumes its shape; then the function associated with intelligence, becomes one with the associated perception of the chord, and there is no more any difference between them.

But why? Consciousness is one, and there is no difference whatever (the actual difference is in the objects which it covers, hence consciousness whether derived from sight, hearing etc., is all one and the same) but that, which is produced by a difference in the associates. The intelligence associated with the function of the internal organ, and that associated with the rope are differentiated by their respective associates,—function and rope; which again as they are divers according to the sites they occupy, thus create a difference therefore in the associated intelligences. Also, when the two associates co-exist, no more difference in the intelligence is possible. It is declared in the commentaries on the Vedanta, that the difference in the associates situated apart, constitutes the difference in their associated consciousness, or intelligence; and when both the associates are present in one place, then there is no more difference between the associates and their associated intelligence. Thus then, during the apparent perception of the rope, its associated intelligence is one with, and non-different from, the associated intelligence of function, which again is the same as the witnessing intelligence. For, the intelligence present in the function of the mind, is its discoverer and called witness.

Thus is determined that during the perception of the rope, its associated intelligence is one with the witnessing intelligence, and that the former as well as the latter, which is non-different from it, proceeds from the knowledge of the rope; and that during the time of such perception along with the knowledge of the witness, the fancied superimposition of the snake is destroyed. Or, as Bidyarana Swami says in reference to a lamp :—The mental function after dispelling the Ignorance (*avarana*) which occupies an unknown jar discovers it or renders it cognisable to the senses, by its indwelling reflex intelligence, like a jar rendered visible by the light of a lamp, which discovers it by dispelling the surrounding darkness. In the case of the jar, the reflex intelligence of the mental function is its knowledge, while the mental cognisor is a discoverer, (*i. e.,*) brings the perception or knowledge that "it is the jar:" in this way, the reflex intelligence of the mental function only discovers the jar. "I know a jar," here, the first personal pronoun is the agent or subject, and jar is the object (of cognition), and its knowledge, are the three constituent elements discovered by the witnessing intelligence. In the same way, all objects have the same three constituent elements in them, which are discovered by the witness. But if the witness be full of ignorance it can discover nothing; hence the knowledge of the three entities enables the witness to discover, and the same knowledge of the witness can remove a snake from a rope according to the previous method. Accordingly, the snake and its occupation by knowledge (its inherent knowledge) have been considered as two and different from one another, and as it is liable to produce similar other misconceptions, I proceed to consider the position where the snake and seat of its knowledge are looked upon as one.

In this view, it is said that the intelligence present externally in the rope (*vahya*) is not one with the snake and the seat of its knowledge; for all knowledge is either dependent on the subject or witness, and the intelligence of the rope situated outside cannot help cognition; similarly, if it be said that the function of the internal organ superimposes it on the rope, that is to say, the associated intelligence of the internal organ—witness—is the seat of the snake and its knowledge, then such a snake ought to be present inside the body,—in the internal organ and not in the rope itself: and if it be said, that at first, the source of the snake is inside the body in the internal organ, whence it is projected on the rope, it will amount to an admission of the doctrine of the expounders of Self. In this way, the associated intelligence of the rope cannot be ascribed to be the seat of intelligence; nor the associated intelligence of the internal organ can be determined as the site of the knowledge of the snake. Hence, though the snake and its knowledge are not the occupation of one intelligence, yet the modification of the internal organ after the shape of the rope, and the ignorance dependent on its function of intelligence, after the modification of the snake, are the respective changes wrought upon them; of which the latter is therefore positively the result of ignorance. Intelligence associated with the function has a particle of ignorance, which for its quality of darkness (*Tamas*) is the formal cause of the snake, whilst its *satwavic* quality is the formal cause of the knowledge of the snake. The snake and its knowledge are the occupation of intelligence associated with function. But as the function is situated external to the chord, its associated intelligence is also similarly placed, hence, it is the site of the snake. In proportion as it resembles the internal organ, so is it identified with the agent or witness. The internal organ situated inside the body, is modified or changed after its function, and as the intelligence associated with it is the witness, therefore it is the seat of knowledge: when the rope is rendered visible, then its intelligence blends, with the associated intelligence of function, so that with the knowledge of the rope the production of a snake and its subsequent removal implies no inconsistency and the sight of one rope creates the mistake of a snake, stick, wreath, or water current to different persons; or, all may equally fancy it to be a snake; so that in such a case, when the person discovers the rope, the superimposition of the snake in the functional intelligence is also destroyed, and who fails to discover the rope, his illusion continues: so here even, the same functional intelligence is the seat of the fancied snake, and not the associated intelligence of the rope, stick and the rest. For if that be the case, then the individual perception of stick, wreath &c., may be equally present in all alike; and from my point of view, a person sees one only, according to the object conceived by his functional intelligence, and not another. Thus then, the seat of the external snake and its knowledge is the functional intelligence which is called agent or witness. Objects seen in a dream and their knowledge have their seat in the associated intelligence of the internal organ, the same witness. Thus the modification (*parinam*) of ignorance which is neither existent nor non-existent and hence 'indescribable' is explained, and for a similar existence and non-existence, (that is, neither the one nor the other, but quite different from them,) the superimposition of the snake, stick &c., &c., on a rope is also called 'indescribable.'

Saith the pupil. Oh Bhagavan! let me hear that instruction which will establish the unreality of the world.

Guru. Your ignorance of Self who is *Brahma*, creates this unreal world as something substantial, hence you are its receptacle as well as its seat, in the same manner as a snake created in a rope has for its receptacle and seat, the rope. Though the site of the snake is said by one to be in the intelligence associated with the function, while another has it in the intelligence associated with the rope, but none determines it in the rope itself; yet in the last case the presence in intelligence of the associate is the rope, so that ordinarily speaking, the rope is said to be the site.

As the site or receptacle of the false snake is the rope, so are you the site and receptacle of the unreal world.—Now this is a common saying. As a rope has twin similarities of which one is ordinary, and the other particular,—and the ordinary resemblance refers to a thing of similar in shape with it, while the particular is the semblance of a snake; here the rope is present along with the snake all the time the illusion lasts, though in a manner non-different from it: therefore the particular resemblance prevents the object being recognised so long as the mistake is present, but when it is discovered once, then the mistake or the fancied resemblance of a particular object is removed at once—so has Self his two semblances, ordinary and particular.

Sat or existence is the ordinary. Unconditioned, Uniform, Eternal Free etc., are the characteristics of the particular. When Self is considered to be bounded or limited by the gross or subtle body, even in such a misconception, he is manifested as non-different from it, and his (marked) reality is the ordinary semblance.

Moreover, in that state, the real nature of Self,—unconditioned, eternal, free—is never discovered, but when that is realised then his finity is removed; therefore infinity, eternity, purity, pervasion, etc., etc., constitute the features of the particular condition. The receptacle is the reality of the ordinary substance which is the source of the illusion, and its connection with the particular is called its occupation. As for instance, the rope for its being the site of the snake is called its receptacle, which is the particular occupation of the rope; in the same way, Self as a receptacle of the phenomenal world, his ordinary condition of existence is the receptacle for this vast expanse, while infinity and the rest are his particular occupation. Hence, there is some difference between receptacle and occupation as has been described by a sage named Surangatama in his work.

Pupil. Who is the seer of the unreal world? Inasmuch as its receptacle and occupation is Self, then there must be some other seer than he; in the same way, as a rope is the receptacle and site (occupation) of a snake, and its seer is a person subject to the illusion.

Guru. When the occupation is that of an insentient object, then something different from it must be its seer; when intelligence itself is occupation then it requires no one else to behold it. As in dreams, the occupation belongs to the witnessing intelligence, which is their seer, so is self the occupation, and as such, he sees the unreal world; so that, as the ordinary sight produces a snake in a rope, does self behold the unreal world. Against such an inference, it is said in the *Sidhanta*, that the presence, occupation or site of the snake is in the witnessing intelligence, which is the seer. Accordingly to look upon the site as what sees, cannot be maintained. In this way, is determined the illusion which subjects self to grief. Self is not the actual sufferer, to consider otherwise is a mistake, but then the destruction or removal of the mistake is not possible, just as through the force of a *mantra*, a performer of magic, creates the enemy of a person, whom no one desires nor prepares himself to destroy.

Pupil. What you have just mentioned about the unreality of the world, and Self as not subject to grief, is true, but instruct me the means which will enable me to recognise Self as not the subject of birth and death with its attendant ills. Moreover, even if it be true, as you said, that for the removal of this mistake, no remedy is needed, yet since such unreality is the source of grief, therefore the unreality is something in a state of actual existence, otherwise why do I realize pain, and suffer birth and death? Hence I want the destruction of the world; with kindness instruct me as to the remedy that will bring it about.

Guru. I have already told you the remedy which will cause the destruction of the unreal world. Firmly ascertain it and you will find Self free from pain and misery. Ignorance attributes to self the pain which attends worldly existence; knowledge can alone establish it otherwise; as the super-imposition of a snake in a rope is known, so does self-knowledge dissipate the belief that Self is subject to grief, birth, and death: because a false thing cannot produce any ill consequence to its site or occupation. For instance, as a mirage cannot moisten the earth, so the cognition of the world as something apparent cannot produce any injury to me. For I am Eternal, Intelligence, and Bliss,—the *Brahma*—and this is what is called knowledge; the one means for the attainment of emancipation. I have already had my say on such knowledge when discoursing with you.

The formal cause of the world is ignorance which is darkness (*Tamas*) itself; with its cessation the world ceases to exist, because after the destruction of the formative cause, its effects can no longer continue to exist. This ignorance can only be destroyed by means of knowledge, and not by actions and devotional excercises. For, ignorance and knowledge are antagonistic of each other, while actions and devotional exercises are not so. As for example, the darkness present inside a room cannot be removed by any act, but only by the introduction of light, so is the darkness of ignorance removed by the light of knowledge and not by any other means. Thus, pupil, have I given you the instruction you asked of me.

Pupil. What you have said Bhagavan, I know to be true, your reference to Ignorance as the cause of the world, and its destruction by knowledge, I am aware of. I know knowledge alone can determine the unreality of the world, and the perception of eternal Intelligence and Bliss by the individual self—non-different from *Brahma*—which is the same as knowledge; but I fail to recognise the two as one, for in my heart I have doubts as to such non-duality which you are expounding.

I am the doer of virtue and vice, and consequently must have my share of enjoyment which they produce, and death, and its many miseries. Moreover, I seek for the destruction of ignorance the creative cause of the world, but since *Brahma* is not the subject of virtue or vice, birth and death, happiness or misery, or any pain whatever, and has no desire for knowledge, hence between my-self and *Brahma* there is seen an antagonism; how then, can you say them to be non-dual? Though it may be alleged that my chief purport is not a worldly existence, and that illusion alone attributes to my-self as being the subject of birth and death, but since *Brahma* is not so subjected, hence the difference between them is clear enough.

I have yet another doubt, I have seen it mentioned in the Veda, that in one tree of Intellect there resides two birds which are equal. That one is the result of past actions, while the other is purity itself, beyond the pale of enjoyment, unconditioned and is the discoverer of him who enjoys; its subject is the *Jiva* who is the agent of such enjoyment; and the other is called the Supreme Self (*Paramatma*). Hence how, can their identity be established? Then again, the Vedas refer to action and devotional exercises of various kinds, which also render such non-duality fruitless. For your non-duality signifies either the subject of *Brahma** is a modification of the *Jiva* or *vice versa*. In the former condition (the first), the qualified person will be wanting, consequently works and devotional exercises will bear no fruit; and in condition the second (when you say the subject of the *jiva* is a modification of *Brahma*) the subject of such devotion becomes one with the worshipper, hence in the absence of the latter, all devotion will be useless; and since the Supreme Self who is to give the desirable results after having become one with the *Jiva* will be incapable of fulfilling the desires of the individual engaged in works, so they are useless too. Then again, what the *Mimansa* says in reference to works that "action is the Lord" cannot be maintained as true, for actions are insentient, and they are wanting in the power of giving the desirable results. Hence from such a view, if the Lord gives the desirable results of an action then that will tell against non-duality of the individual Self and the Supreme Self.

Guru. I will now clear out your doubts. As in one ether there are four distinctions, *viz.*, the ether of a jar; ether of water; ether of cloud; and the great ether; so is one Intelligence divided into four and called separately the uniform (*kutasta*) and Individual (*Jiva*), Iswara and *Brahma*; their mutual distinctions are similar to what has been said about ether; so that when you have come to realise their perceptions, doubts will cease to trouble you, and you will be able to solve them as they arise. For this reason, I am going to give you a description of their likeness, by hearing which you will be free from doubts, and thus having obtained self-knowledge, you will be freed from the trammels of future re-births.

Now then about the ether of a jar:—when a jar is filled with

---

* *Saguna Brahma* (with attributes) is meant by the author.

water, and a portion left empty, the void or vacuum is called by *Pandits* as the ether present in the jar.

Ether in water. The reflection of the sky with its stars &c., in water inside a jar, with the space or ether contained in it, (the two) constitute the watery ether. If any one will say, there can be no reflection of the sky, for it is formless, but that the stars alone have it, then it is removed in the following manner. If the sky can have no reflection, it cannot likewise have any depth of sound, which it does communicate to the human ear by the rushing of a torrent of water ; hence one is obliged to admit the sky as producing its reflection [in water]. Form is not essentially necessary to produce a reflection ; an echo is produced by sound which is formless, and echo is nothing more than the reflection or shadow of sound. Hence it is quite clear that the formless sky can produce a refletion.

The Cloud-Ether. The ether present in clouds as well as its reflection in the water which they contain, constitute the cloud-ether. If any doubts be entertained as to the admission of the reflected shadow of ether in the water of clouds, for without seeing such a condition, one cannot believe it, then they are removed easily. It is indeed true, that no one can see the presence of water in the clouds nor the shadow of the sky, yet by inference it can be known ; inasmuch as clouds produce rain and if it is not present in them, they will be quite powerless to cause rain, and rain is the subject of the clouds : and where there is water, there is a shadow of ether, and there can be no water without such shadow. Therefore the subject of the clouds—rain—is a reflected shadow of ether ; and its inference is a natural conclusion. For this reason, water is termed *Udaka* and *Odaka*. *

That fluid which pervades everywhere, both within and without is called by a *Pandit*, *Mahakasa* (the great body of ether).

Thus has been described the four varieties of ether ; their hearing

---

* 'Odaka' is not a word ; 'Udaka' becomes 'Odaka' when coming after the vowels *a*, or *á* ; by union (sandhi) its *u* is transformed into *o*, as 'Ganga' + 'Udaka' = Gangodaka.

will enable you to distinguish one from the other, and that will yield knowledge as a result.

Intelligence present in each individual unit of Ignorance is called the Uniform or Eternal (*kutasta*) ; but when the *Jiva* is said to be intelligence with *Boodhi* combined, then the site of *Boodhi* (intellect, Spiritual Intelligence or soul) is fixed in the Uniform Intelligence, and when *(Jiva* is looked upon as the distributive segregate of Ignorance with Intelligence combined, then the site or occupation of the distributive unit of ignorance is the Uniform Intelligence. That is to say, the predicate of *Jiva* and its occupation is called the Uniform Intelligence. It is uncreated and without a beginning, unlike the reflex intelligence which is separate from *Brahma* and derived from It. But it is *Brahma*-like. As the ether of a jar is non-different from the infinite ether, but simply its modified likeness; in the same way, the Uniform Intelligence (*kutasta*), is what is indicated by the word Self. It is also called the internal, and constitutes the personality of the individual; and this *Jiva* is the witness.

The reflection of intelligence present in *Boodhi*, which determines or causes a man to be engaged in works and optional acts, is called by the wise *Jiva*; and this reflection only is not the *jiva*. But as the ether of a jar with the reflected shadow of the sky is called the ether of water, so is *Jiva* the reflection of the internal Uniform Intelligence with its reflected shadow of intelligence. Here the conclusion is that the reflex intelligence of *Boodhi*, and its indwelling intelligence, both constitute *Jiva*.

It is to be remarked, from what has just been said in regard to the *Jiva* as being a composition of the Uniform Intelligence with the reflected shadow of intelligence, that it is natural to conclude the reflection of intelligence in *Boodhi* is that of the Uniform Intelligence, and not that of *Brahma* which is external; for reflection can only proceed from a thing that is placed near it, in a position so as to affect it in that way, and such a thing is the internal Uniform Intelligence. As in the instance of a red flower and crystal placed near one another, the flower imparts its red color by the reflection of its shadow, to the crystal, which then assumes a red color;

so *Boodhi* which is dependent on the Uniform Intelligence for its property of discovery, receives its shadow by reflection and becomes illuminated.

As a crystal is very brilliant, so is *Boodhi* very pure, for it is the resulting product of the (*Satwa*) good quality. Hence the spirit of the Uniform Intelligence is called reflex intelligence. As in the water of a jar, there is reflection of the infinite space or ether and not that of its internal space, inasmuch as the depth of water rendered apparent inside a jar is not present in the space inside it, but such depth is merely a shadow of ether, therefore such reflection is that of the ether external to the jar; so is the assertion that the pervasive intelligence can produce no reflection is cleared away. For, if ether which is equally pervading can produce its reflection, then the pervading Intelligence can also produce its reflected shadow. Then again, if it be said that a substance having a form and shape can alone produce its reflected shadow on another which has a form : to such a statement the reply is, that is not essentially necessary; for as has already been pointed out, a sound is formless yet it produces an echo, which is its reflected shadow on the ether. Thus then we find that the reflection of intelligence is admissible.

In this way *Jiva* is determined to be the reflex intelligence of *Boodhi*, with its indwelling intelligence ; and the indication of the word *jivanta* is therefore referrible only to the Uniform Intelligence after the exclusion of the reflected intelligence, the former of which is the indication of 'Thou' (*Twam*). *Aham* also refers to *Jiva*, and it indicates the same Uniform Intelligence.

> In *Boodhi* the reflected intelligence alone enjoys virtue and vice.
> It comes and goes, but connects it not to Intelligence.
> The ether of a jar is by mistake, said to be the cause of inducing many actions.
> Though it is always actionless, and always uniform.

As has already been said, *Jiva* is the sum of reflex intelligence *plus* the uniform Intelligence, and the attributes of the *Jiva* are the subjects of reflected intelligence. That is to say, virtue and vice, with the enjoyment of their results in the next life, or re-birth in another sphere of abode, all these are underwent by the reflex intelligence with *Boodhi*. The Uniform Intelligence is not so subjected, but illusion attributes them to it; and this illusion even in such a condition affects the individual *Boodhi* with its reflex intelligence. For, the Uniform is unconditional and unchangeable, like the anvil which supports a piece of iron and is beaten continually by the hammer; or it is the unassociated spiritual soul centred in the subjects of ignorance and rendered apparent by it. Here its subjects cannot be mistaken, as that is only possible with the reflex intelligence. Moreover if duly considered, it will be found that virtue and vice with their results,—happiness and misery, a future life or re-birth, are all attached to *Boodhi*, and absent in reflex intelligence; but in its combination with *Boodhi* they are so. As a pitcher full of water is inclined, or kept in a straight position, or carried about, by its relation with the reflection of ether present inside, (independently it can do nothing,) so the pitcher of *Boodhi* filled up with the water of 'optional' and 'lawful acts' sustains [that is to say is the holder of] virtue, vice and the rest; and from the relation which the reflex intelligence bears to it, this also is alike their holder. And as the ether of the jar is not subject to any change, which the jar filled up with water is apt to have, so is the Uniform Intelligence unchangeable;—in other words, not affected by any change. So is the case with its knowledge too. Hence the attributes of the *Jiva* are inherent in the reflex intelligence, and ignorance only attributes them to the Uniform Intelligence. Thus then *Jiva* the subject of *Boodhi*, is the Uniform with its reflex intelligence. But such a description is harmful to *Prajna*.* For his conceit of profound slumber, he is called *Prajna*. In that condition, *Boodhi* is entirely absent, so that its reflection cannot be said to exist. Hence it will be antagonistic to those *Shastras* which treat on *Prajna*. For this reason, *jiva* has been defined separately :—

---

* *Prajna* means almost ignorant. Its derivative signification is *pra + ena + Ajna* parviscient. Therefore parviscience differentiates the *Jiva* from *Iswara* who is omniscient.

Or, the reflection of intelligence present in each individual unit of ignorance,
With the inherent Uniform Intelligence is calld *Jiva*.

The individual unit of ignorance* is called its distributive segregate, as its collective totality is called its collective aggregate. The reflection of intelligence present in the first kind of ignorance with its inherent Uniform Intelligence is the signification of the word *Jiva*. It cannot imply any contraindication to *Prajna*. For in profound slumber, ignorance is present along with the reflected shadow of intelligence, which latter assumes the shape of *Boodhi*, and determines the appearance of virtue and vice, and the other phases of a worldly existence both here [and hereafter]. With this view, *Boodhi* has been described in some *Shastras* as an associate of *Jiva*, but on a proper consideration it will be seen, that such associate is Ignorance.

Now for a description of ISWARA.

The reflection of intelligence associated with *Mayá*, with the inherent intelligence,
Like the ether present in clouds, is the Internal Knower, and Free.

---

* Ignorance is used definitely or indefinitely to indicate one or plurality; for instance as a collection of trees constitute a forest, so the collective totality of Ignorance present everywhere in all individuals, in diverse forms, is regarded as one. It is the associate of the excellent Intelligence or consciousness of *Brahma* and is composed chiefly of the pure *Satwa* quality.

Consciousness associated with this totality or collective aggregate of Ignorance is designated the omniscient, the Lord of all, the controller of all, the unspeakable, the internal Ruler, cause of the world and *Iswara*.

As the integral units of a forest signify a variety of several trees, so the distributive segregate of Ignorance is manifold, in no two individuals it is alike, for this difference it is particularized as the individual unit of ignorance, in contradistinction to the original, indivisible and Impartite ignorance centred in *Iswara*, called 'Mahatatwa.' It is the companion of the parviscient finite being. Its composition also differs, for it is

The reflection of intelligence in *Maya* with the inherent intelligence present in it, (the two together) constitute Iswara or Lord. He resembles the cloud-ether. He is the internal knower, for He controls all internally and is always free; for, He is devoid of envelopment, and is therefore not the subject of birth and death; for this reason, He is eternal and free, omniscient, and all-knowing.—Because in him, *Maya* has a preponderance of pure *Satwa* quality, and not *Satwa* overpowered by *Rajas* and *Tamas*; but on the other hand, when the two last are overpowered by the first, it is called pure *Satwa guna*. It is the productive source of knowledge, hence its property is that of discovering or illuminating, for which it is called discoverer. The Intelligence or consciousness of *Maya* for this preponderance of *Satwavic* quality, cannot envelop its subject, or cause another object to be so enveloped by the reflected shadow of its intelligence, therefore it is free and omniscient. The inherent intelligence is not the subject of bondage and release either in *jiva* or Iswara. Like ether it is one fluid, but the reflected intelligence is the portion that is liable to them. The former is apt to be mistaken for the latter, which alone is subject to bondage and release. The difference is this: the envelopment of the reflex intelligence is the subject of bondage, and when the envelopment is wanting, it is free; and as Iswara has it not, therefore He is always free. But in the *jiva*, it is present, hence he is subject to bondage *i. e.*, liable to re-births. For *jiva* is the the reflex intelligence associated with an individual unit of Ignorance, which has naturally the property of concealment. Now *Maya*, *Avidya*, and *Ajnana*, always refer to the same Ignorance, but there is a difference in their composition. For, the first is made chiefly of the pure (*Satwa*) good quality; and the last is derived from a preponderance of the impure good quality; while the second and third are synonymous. When the good quality is overpowered by the active and dark qualities, it is called impure good. Thus then, as *Jiva* has a preponderance of impure

---

made chiefly of the impure Satwa quality. Hence it is but an humble associate, and its consciousness also has limited perception for which it is called Prajna (almost ignorant).

good quality, the reflex intelligence associated with the distributive segregate of Ignorance, is enveloped by it, and makes him the subject of re-births, which *Iswara* is not. The inherent Intelligence associated with *Maya*, together with its reflection, constitute Iswara. That is indicated by the word (*Tat*) 'That' [of the transcendental phrase 'That art Thou']; while its real signification refers only to the inherent intelligence. *Iswara* is the creator, protector and destroyer of the world. This is the unanimous testimony of all *Shastras*. Its purport is this:—Intelligence, is unassociated like the astral light, while its reflected shadow creates the world, protects and destroys it, for which He is omniscient. He likewise delivers those who are desirous of release, from transmigration, through kindness; moreover whatever force of manifestation there is, it is present in Him. The particle of intelligence is uniformly alike and without its illumination, no success can follow in any pursuit.

[We have now to give a description of *Brahma*.]

> Intelligence present in and out, full and entire,
> Like the all-pervading ether, is *Brahma*. It is neither near [you] nor distant.*

The intelligence present in *Brahma's* egg † [universe] both internally and externally and completely pervading it, like the great body of ether is called *Brahma*. It is neither near, nor distant from you, for It is (objectively) different from you, inasmuch as It has neither name, form nor associate (unconditional), while you have all the three—hence It is called distant from you. But (subjectively) It is present everywhere, It is the Self of every individual, and unassociated, hence It is not distant from you. If the signification of the word *Brahma* be that of an associate, as It embraces all objects and

---

* The Vedanta doctrine propounds the contiguity of the Universal Spirit to the Individual. The word *Upanishad* refers to it also, for its etymology *up* + *ni* + *shad* (*up* near, *ni* certain, *shad* to destroy) implies the knowledge which causes the destruction of Ignorance and enables the individual to realize the certain contiguity of *Brahma* to Self.

† I means both the microcosm and the macrocosm.

is all pervading, yet such pervasion is of two kinds :—(1) Dependent and (2) Independent. Now the 'dependent' refers to pervasion depending on a substance or otherwise, as for instance, the pervasion of *Maya* in earth etc. Here *Maya* is not dependent on Intelligence for its pervasion ; [though it is so, as regards the earth and the other elements, hence the definition does not imply a contradiction as at first sight it is apt to create]. The 'independent' refers to a substance that is all-pervading itself. Hence the object of its pervasion is independent. Such is Intelligence, for there is nothing equally pervasive, or more so than it. It is the most pervasive of all, hence it is called 'independent.' A substance possessed of the above two kinds of pervasion, is the signification of the word *Brahma*. They are the subjects of intelligence associated with *Maya* [Illusion]. For the predicate of the subject—*Maya*—depends on it for pervasion, while with reference to Intelligence, it is independently pervasive. Though the subject of *Maya*-associated-Intelligence cannot be all-pervading independently of Intelligence, for it is confined in one province [in the distributive segregate of individuals,—hence the Pure (Unassociated) Intelligence is such independent pervasion—yet really they are non-distinct from one another, and the first is only another form of the second. This necessarily brings the predicate of Intelligence present in the subject (*Maya*,) to the level of independent pervasion, and as such, it may refer literally to signify *Brahma*, while Its real indication is the Pure Intelligence. Thus then the signification of *Iswara* and *Brahma* are equally known by the indications in the manner just cited ; and that there is no different meaning. But even here, there is a marked difference in the indication, and the literal signification of the words, *Brahma* and *Iswara* ; inasmuch as *Brahma* generally expresses the indicative indication of a subject, and at times It only signifies the literal signification ; while *Iswara* on the contrary, denotes the literal signification in most places. For this difference the literal signification of *Brahma* has been ascertained by reference to Indicative Indication. *

---

* Every word or sentence ('pad') must be construed under one of three heads viz., literal ('vachya') indicative ('lakshya') or suggestive

Thus are considered the four varieties of Intelligences.
Of the four Intelligences the *Jiva* is unreal,
He is subjected to enjoy the fruits of merits and demerits;
While the inherent Intelligence is *Shiva*.

Oh, Thou Pupil! Of the four Intelligences already mentioned, the reflected shadow present in the *Jiva* alone enjoys happiness, or suffers misery, for good and bad actions, and their resulting products; and the inherent Uniform Intelligence is designated *Shiva*, because it is beneficial. Thus then, your first doubt in reference to the presence of two birds in the tree of *Boodhi* [Intellect, spiritual soul, or spiritual intelligence] is fully answered; inasmuch as the Supreme Self and Individual Spirit are meant, with this difference in them, that the first is Self-illuminated, while the second is its mere reflection, and the subject of happiness and misery for deeds good and bad; but do not attribute to it as a place of, abode, that wherein reside both *Jiva* and *Paramatma*.

The actor's shadow produces results, without any connection with intelligence;
That portion is one with it; bad people know it to be different.

The reflected intelligence of the *Jiva* (which is identically the

---

(Vyangya). Denotation, Indication and Suggestion or *Abhidha*, *Lakshana*, and Vyanjana are their three functions. Our author uses both the words Vachaya and Lakshya; so that it is necessary to illustrate Indication. This is defined in the *Kavaya Prakasa* 11. 9., as that imposed function which determines the signification of a sentence or word by introducing another meaning as indicated, and doing away with the literal meaning, when it is incompatible. It has its sanction either in usage or in the presence of a motive. As for instance "A herd station on the Ganges." Here the literal meaning of Ganges—a river—is incompatible with the rest of the sentence, for no one can live on it. Hence the bank is indicated; and this meaning is imposed upon the word Ganges in accordance to usage. Besides, there is also a motive in using Ganges, instead of the bank; as the author sought to convey purity, coolness etc., which the latter word cannot strictly signify.

same as *Jiva*) is called shadow, and actor, for he is the doer of actions; such actor's shadow of action which is the reflection of Iswara, is the producer of results. As a row of lamps placed on a wall, lights the north, and other directions; so has the reflected shadow a similar relation to illuminate the past and future, besides something else. Now such shadow is an agent, actor, or doer of actions. It likewise gives or produces results; which means, the reflected intelligence present in *jiva* is the doer of meritorious and bad actions, and reaps their results accordingly; while the reflex intelligence present in Iswara is the producer of such results, *i. e.*, gives good or bad results to the individual, in proportion to his merits and demerits, and subjects him to enjoy happiness or suffer misery; and that, the Intelligence common to them both, is quite aloof, and not in any way connected either with actions, their results, enjoyments or production. In other words, the portion of Intelligence present in the individual, is never subjected to perform actions or reap their results; nor is the same particle of intelligence present in Iswara, a giver or producer of results. They are each quite unconnected either with actions, their results, or their production. And he who connects that intelligence in such a relationship is an illiterate man. Because the Intelligence common to them is unconditional and unrelated (unassociated); identically they are one and non-different. Bad men only know the individual Intelligence and Iswara's intelligence or *vice versa* as distinct. Here 'bad' signifies a person who is a reviler. Thus your second question which tried to render the Vedas fruitless,—as they define actions and enjoin works and devotional exercises,—on account of admitting such non-duality is answered. The particle of intelligence present in the individual as well as in Iswara is one, though their reflections, owing to their different association, are different. Thus both varieties of Intelligences are identical.

Pupil, Thus have I met the questions asked of me.
What you say in regard to one tree inhabited by two birds,
Of which one is an enjoyer and the other undesirous.
Intelligence and its reflection, you make them appear

Distinct ; as you do with reference to ether and its reflection.
Say the agent and giver of results are two [and]
Intelligence reflected in Boodhi is the actor,
And that in Maya is the father (of results) ;
Of them intelligence is alike in Jiva, and Iswara,
Without the trace of distinction; and peerless.
So then know "I am Brahma."
'I' is the inherent Uniform Intelligence, know it means Brahma
Keep in mind its indication, the same as infinite ether.
One who knows not "I am Brahma" is poor and miserable,
and persuaded by fear.

The commentator expounds the verses in the following manner: Thus I have answered your questions in reference to one tree having two birds, of which one is an agent and the other devoid of any desire of enjoyment. It does not establish non-duality ; [for if they were one, same inclination would be present]. I have duly met this objection. Here you are not to accept the doctrine of Jiva and Brahma as one, but to look upon the inherent Uniform Intelligence and its reflection in Boodhi as distinct, like the ether in a jar and the reflected shadow of the sky present in it. Moreover what you said in regard to the agent or doer of actions, and devotional exercises, and the Supreme Self, the giver of results, as distinct and cannot possibly be one. To that even, I have given my reply, Jiva is not such an agent. Nor is Iswara the giver of results ; but the particle of reflex intelligence present in the former is the real agent, while the same reflection in Iswara is the giver of results ; and intelligence common to them both, is non-dual, without even the trace of distinction ; as the distributive particle of ether inside a jar is non-distinct from its collective totality,—the infinite ether. In this way, pupil, you are to determine non-duality, and regard Self, as Brahma and say "I am Brahma." Know then *Aham* (Self or egoism) signifies the Uniform Intelligence, and the word 'Brahma' has a similar indication with that of infinite ether ; their literal signification is separate, but their indicative indication is non-different. Hence so long as you do not perceive "I am Brahma" in reference to yourself, you must admit that you are poor and miserable and your knowledge of Self will only be a source of fear for you. So that you shall know that you are a Brahma.

Tatwadrishti says :—

Oh Bhagavan ! Who has got the knowledge 'I am Brahma' ? I know it not, without your words I am ignorant.

Preceptor, kindly say who possesses the knowledge 'I am Brahma,' without your utterances I know it not. The purport of the pupil, in reference to the perception of such knowledge in the mind, is to determine whether such knowledge is the subject of the Uniform intelligence, or of *Boodhi* with reflex intelligence. If it be said, that it proceeds from Uniform Intelligence, then it will be subject to a modification of change [in that case its uniformity is destroyed] while by connecting it with Boodhi *plus* reflex intelligence there will be a mistake, for Boodhi etc., is not Brahma. Hence one cannot identify it in such a manner as to say "I am Brahma." Because you have already pointed out the oneness of the Uniform Intelligence and Brahma ; while its reflection is quite distinct from it. Hence to know such reflex intelligence which is a distinct entity, to be the same as Brahma, will be an illusion similar to that of a snake in a chord. Thus then the attribution of "I am Brahma" to Boodhi, with its reflex of intelligence, is not real knowledge, but an illusion. Moreover, if the knowledge "I am Brahma" be admitted as unreal, then there will be no cessation of the unreal world, which can only proceed from a knowledge that such perception is real ; in the same way as knowledge of chord destroys the illusion of a snake on it. In this manner, there is no possibility of attributing to the reflex intelligence of Boodhi the perception of 'I am Brahma.'

Saith the Guru.

Hear Pupil ! I speak on the seven conditions of reflex intelligence, which is not the source of Intelligence ; in it is this knowledge.

Pupil, I will now tell you the seven conditions of reflected intelligence, which you (better) hear, they are without the Uniform Intelligence as well as the knowledge "I am Brahma."

They are called (1) ignorance, (2) envelopment, (3) misconception, etc., (4) ordinary knowledge, (5) particular knowledge, (6) destruction of misery, and (7) extreme happiness.

1. Ignorance is such as prevents a person from knowing Brahma and he says I know it not.
2. From '*avarana*' or concealment he says there is no Brahma and it cannot be known.

Oh Pupil, 'I know not Brahma' is an expression due to Ignorance, and he who uses it is ignorant. "There is no Brahma" "It cannot be known" are expressions due to envelopment. [Why?] Because Ignorance is possessed of two powers called respectively *asatwapad* and *avanapad*? (non-existence and want of knowledge). Both of them are called 'envelopment.' Now, argument employed to ascertain the non-existence of an object is known by the first name; while the second has reference to such other arguments as determine its imperception, or want of cognition. Hence, when a person declares, "There is no Brahma;" it is an instance of the first named power present in Ignorance (non-existence); while that other expression "I cannot perceive Brahma" is an instance of (a want of knowledge) the second power. Both non-existence (non-being) and want of knowledge are called by the name of envelopment (concealment.)

3. Misconception, error, or mistake.

To attribute birth, death, the subject of destruction; to acknowledge virtue and vice, weal and woe
To one's Self, and to perceive so, is in the Vedas called mistake.

Here Self refers to Uniform Intelligence; to attribute the ills of an worldly existence to him, and to believe that he is the entity that is subjected to birth and death, to happiness and misery, for good and bad actions is called misconception, error, or mistake. It is likewise called grief.

4 & 5. The two varieties of knowledge
Are the invisible and visible.
"Brahma is" an instance of the first,
"I am Brahma" of the second kind,

The 'invisible' destroys the non-being of Brahma
Visibility destroys all ignorance with its trammels.

The non-being of Brahma, due to 'envelopment,' is destroyed by the knowledge of the 'invisible kind,' which clearly defines Its existence by the expression "There is Brahma." For the two are antagonistic of each other, and cannot co-exist; hence the admission of the existence of Brahma, must do away with Its non-existence or non-being; and as such a perception is dim and vague, (nothing definite) it is called invisible. " I am Brahma" is a definite perception, hence it is called 'visible knowledge' [or knowledge marked by visibility]; and it causes the destruction of Ignorance with its trammels. For this knowledge is antagonistic of that ignorance which says "I know not Brahma," and of that other kind which declares "There is no Brahma." "It cannot be cognized"—varieties of concealment or envelopment as has just been remarked;—and to the declaration "I am not a Brahma," but an agent of virtue and vice, and an instrument for enjoying weal or suffering woe *i. e.,* the same as Jiva ; which is a mistake and these are the trammels or nets of ignorance which cannot exist with the real, definite, and visible perception of Brahma, which is expressed by 'I am Brahma.'

6. Birth and death are not in me, nor is there a trace of weal and woe ;
But I am the Uncreated Uniform Intelligence. To remove a mistake [by this knowledge] is the best (of its kind).

I am neither the subject of birth and death, nor of happiness and misery with the concomitant ills of a worldly phase of existence, but am the Uniform Intelligence, uncreated, and unborn,—eternal). Oh Pupil! in this way to seek the prevention of all mistakes is to know Self, or such a knowledge is the best of its kind. Here the reference of Uniform Intelligence as unborn, stands for all the rest. For creation implies death, happiness and misery, virtue and vice, so that when it is said to be unborn, it is free from birth and the rest, and therefore by calling it uncreated and unborn, the mistake of attributing miseries to it, is removed or prevented, for which it has another name also viz., destruction of grief.

7. Happiness and its nature.

    To be free of doubts as to Self, is unalloyed knowledge.
    Then is produced delight, that you know to be happiness.

Pupil, when you are freed from doubts as to the knowledge of what Self is like, so as to enable you to say "I am Brahma" (free from duality) then you will experience delight, which know then to be happiness.

    I say to you the seven conditions, pupil for you to know.
    To know them of 'reflections' constitutes knowledge
    Who derives knowledge, you asked of me
    That I have replied, now ask what you like.

In other words, the drift of your question is now being rendered apparent (or discovered) by a pupil.

    Bhagavan! 'I am Brahma' is then of reflex Intelligence's
    Thou sayst it so, and I apprehend; yet I have a doubt.
    [For]. 'Reflex' is distinct from Brahma,
    This Thou hast pointed out before.
    How then to know 'I am Brahma,'
    Admit Self to be distinct from Brahma.
    To know otherwise (non-duality) is unreal
    Like a snake created in a rope
    Remove this doubt! Worshipful Guru!
    And with thine reasons let me hear thine utterances.

Bhagavan! Thou hast said the Uniform and reflex Intelligences are one; also the last is distinct from Brahma; in that case how can such reflected intelligence—distinct from Brahma,—be identified with the knowledge and perception of 'I am Bramha'? The inherent Uniform Intelligence occupying me is alone Brahma, to know as such its reflection is only real knowledge. Moreover 'I am Brahma' is not real knowledge. For the first personal pronoun signifying the principle of Egoism, individuality, or Self, is altogether different from the reflex Intelligence, and as Self is same with

Brahma, therefore the reflection of Intelligence is quite distinct from It, hence such a mistake confounding the reflex Intelligence with Brahma is a false perception, similar to that of a snake in a rope. Here false signifies unreal, erroneous perception or knowledge; but it cannot be applied to the knowledge of Brahma [inasmuch as It is real].

> Listen now to the signification of Egoism, Oh ye pupil 'discriminating'
> Listen to non-duality, similar defects (to what you say there are) many.

In plainer terms :—

> Though in reflex there is present the perception 'I am Brahma'
> Yet such conceit is in the Uniform,
> Which is non-different from it, pervasive and causal,
> Manifesting itself as Brahma, in the removal of obstacle.

Pupil. Though the spiritual soul or intelligence (Boodhi) with the reflex is the seat of the perception 'I am Brahma,' and not the Uniform, yet such reflex knows that the Uniform Intelligence and its principle of individuality are the *Atma* indicated by the first personal pronoun 'I' which also is the same as '*Aham*.' Now '*Aham*' establishes the Uniform Intelligence as always non-different from Brahma, as the space covered by a jar is always one with the infinite space from which it cannot be in any way demarcated. Hence the Vedantin describes this mutual relationship of the Uniform with Brahma as '*Mukha Samanadikarana*' (a main predicament or inference in which several things are included.

When a thing is always non-different from another thing, their association is called a *Mukshya Samanadhikarana*. As for instance, the space engrossed by a jar is always non-different from the infinite space which is ever present along with it, therefore the jar-space is the infinite space; and as such, the first has in relation to the last, the condition of a predicament in which it is included with it. In the same manner, the Uniform Intelligence has, in connection with Brahma a similar 'main inclusive predicament,'* because they are always non-different from one another.

Moreover, the reflex intelligence rendered apparent by the first personal pronoun 'I' for including or confining Self in it, is non-distinct from Brahma, just as the reflection of a face is non-distinct from the face and included in it. Hence the Vedant *Shastra* declares the reflex intelligence as an associate of Brahma and included in it. This is called *Vadha samanadhikarana*. It means that condition of mutual relationship, when a thing establishes its non-difference with its companion by lapsing into It. Here the thing is a *Vadha samanadhikarana* to its companion. As for instance, the reflection of a face merges into the face (when the mirror is withdrawn) hence they are non-distinct; the reflection is the face itself and not as something different, and this mutual relationship of the reflection with the face is called (*Vadh samanadhikarana*) 'community of reference by merging.'

Or, as in a person mistaking the stump of a tree for a man, after the tree is known the form of a man disappears and the tree is rendered apparent. Here the person has a community of reference to the tree of the second kind ;

Similarly by the disappearance of the reflected Intelligence, it becomes one with Universal Intelligence, which is one with *Brahma*, hence its reference to 'I' is the same with *Brahma*, and not distinct from it. Such a 'community of reference' the reflex intelligence has with *Brahma*, by merging or disappearing into it.

In this manner pupil, you are to determine the Uniform Intelligence indicated by the word 'I' as without any distinction whatever, and by the merging of the reflex into it, this one is likewise non-different.

Says Tatwadrishti :—

The witness and reflex are recognized in the function of Egoism, say then, whether they are contemporaneous or otherwise.

Bhagavan, you have said that in Egoism both the witness and

---

* Community of reference or mutual relationship is the meaning of *Samanadhikarana*.

reflex are recognized to be present; on this subject I do not understand whether the function of the subject [witness] of that individuality, or Egoism, determines the uniform and reflex intelligence at the same time, or at different times; do explain it so that I may understand.

The utterance of the reverend Guru is as follows:—

Listen attentively to the essence of the reply which I give, that will clear your darkness and bring in the light of perception [help your knowledge].

Pupil, I will now reply to your question; it embraces all the points raised by you, so that if you listen attentively to it, the darkness of ignorance will be destroyed and the light of knowledge will help your perception.

> In one time the witness and reflex are cognised
> Secondly on the subject of intelligence, the first is Self-illuminated.

Pupil, both the witnessing and reflex intelligences are manifested in the principle of individuality at one time; on all subjects, reflex is to be taken as the reflected intelligence along with the internal organ; 'secondly' means the intelligence present in the internal organ with its reflex intelligence and which constitutes what is called a witness, agent, or instrument and recognized, or determined as such, by the function of the internal organ. The witness is self-illuminated, and is not the subject of the function of the internal organ with its reflection of intelligence.

The perception of a jar or another external object takes place in the following manner:—

When the Sensory organs combine with a jar etc., the function of the internal organ issues through the senses, and assumes the shape of the jar; as a melted metal assumes the shape of the mould in which it is cast, so does the function of the internal organ assume the modification of the jar (or other external object which it cognises) but that function is not without reflex intelligence, but with it; for function is only a modification or condition of the internal organ, and is called so. As the internal organ is derived from the *Satwa* or good quality, it is naturally transparent and luminous, consequently the subject of its function is reflex intelligence—and as its function is likewise transparent and luminous and a derivative product of its action, it has also a reflex intelligence. Moreover when the function is excited, it is produced with the reflex intelligence from the internal organ ; even from such a cause, the function is derived from the reflex intelligence, and its subject 'a jar is' the result of *Tamas* or dark quality, hence naturally insentient ; and its subject ignorance is also its envelopment. Here a doubt may arise, that ignorance and its envelopment are also present in the intelligence and not in 'a jar' for similar reasons derived from analogy ; for ignorance is dependent on intelligence, and forms its subject, according to the Vedanta. Moreover as has already been said, while treating of the seven conditions, that ignorance is dependent on the internal organ together with its reflection, so that the predilection for such ignorance as expressed by the declaration "I am ignorant" can only refer to the internal organ with its reflex intelligence. Hence intelligence is said to be the prop or main support of ignorance,—which intelligence represents the internal organ together with reflection, because the internal organ with its reflection of intelligence are an action of ignorance. Now as the action of a thing cannot be its prop or support, therefore intelligence alone is the receptacle or support of ignorance ; also it is the 'subject' of ignorance. What conceals the identity of a thing is spoken of as a subject formed by ignorance ; in connection with insentient objects, ignorance can play no part in concealing their identity or real likeness, for they are naturally covered or enshrouded, [as they are wanting in the light of intelligence] so that the envelopment of ignorance does not apply to them. In this manner, Intelligence is the prop and subject of ignorance, just as the darkness of a room envelops its interior, and forms its environment and not that of a jar (present there).

(Why) ? As ignorance is something quite distinct from intelligence—neither existent, nor non-existent—it is dependent on intelligence. Hence ignorance enshrouds intelligence. In the same way, ignorance which is quite distinct from a jar, though not dependent on it, yet it covers a jar and discovers it as something insentient; hence a jar is always covered by the darkness of ignorance. Because ignorance has a preponderance of darkness and is the productive source of all the elements, and jar is elementary in composition, hence it is derived from ignorance: and as darkness has naturally the property of concealment in it, therefore a jar is naturally devoid of luminosity and is darkblind. Thus is established the natural darkness of a jar which is due to its covering of Ignorance.* Moreover, the Ignorance dependent on the inherent intelligence of a jar covers that intelligence, and endows it with environment which is naturally covered already. Now though a body naturally covered needs not any other covering, yet it is generally known, that in the absence of such necessity like an uncovered object, Ignorance [producing concealment] does cover a body which is already enshrouded, so that a jar with its covering or envelopment of ignorance is only rendered visible by the internal organ with its reflection of intelligence assuming the shape of the jar, its function

---

* Ignorance is explained in quite another way. It is the same as *Mula Prakriti* or the primordial undifferentiated cosmic matter. *Sankhya's Prakriti* (Matter) and the Vedantin's Ignorance and *Maya* are synonymous. It is described as neither existent nor non-existent. Existent since every one says 'I am ignorant,' it is present in all men and animals, in the inanimate world, and everywhere else. Non-existent, because with the advent of knowledge it disappears—for a similar reason it is called indescribable, *i. e.* to say something which cannot be definitely determined. Ignorance is possessed of the three qualities,—*Satwa, Raja* and *Tama*—the good, active and dark. According to Kapila *Prakriti* through the changes wrought upon it from a close contiguity of the *Purusha* or Spirit undergoes a change in its qualities, which disturbs its equillibrium and induces further changes, whereby the objective world and all it contains are produced. In such a view, there is no need of a personal Creator. It is simply evolution brought on by the influence of the physical forces through the change impressed upon them, by the contact of the Spirit, in the same way as a magnet attracts a piece of iron and converts it into a temporary magnet, by imparting its properties.

dispersing the covering of ignorance, while the reflection of intelligence present in such function discovers or renders it visible. Thus then in regard to all external objects, both the function and its reflex intelligence are applied to render them visible. For example, as in a dark room, an earthen or iron vessel covered by an earthen salver, can be uncovered by breaking the salver with a stick; yet without the light of a lamp, the vessel cannot be discovered though its envelopment has been removed; so a jar covered with ignorance, gets its covering removed by the function of the internal organ, but that does not render it visible, because the jar is naturally insentient and wanting in light, which is also the case with function, whose province is only to break the covering, hence the reflex is the discoverer of the jar, *i. e.*, renders it visible to the eyes. In this manner, cognition by means of sight is brought about. The same rule holds with cognition by means of hearing and the rest.

This is called visible knowledge, because the function and jar reside in the same province.

As the function of the internal organ asssumes the shape of a jar, and between it and function, there is no relation, but the latter is quite distinct, therefore this is called the invisible knowledge of a jar. Now such a knowledge can only determine the existence of a jar as 'Jar is,' while the first renders it visible and ascertains it definitely as "This is a jar." These then are the forms of; 'visible' and 'invisible knowledge.'

Though the remembrance of a thing is its 'invisible knowledge' yet such remembrance is due to conception; inference in the same way produces 'invisible knowledge' by analogical proofs, that is the difference in them. While on the subject of proofs I have ascertained their nature. A Charvaka anly admits visible proofs. The followers of Kanada and Suguta admit the proof established by analogy, for by admitting the former, there will be no inclination for enjoyment necessary to the gratification of appetite. The sight of an uneaten dinner can produce no gratification of the appetite; in such a condition the visible proof is inefficient to cause visible knowledge; hence one who has experienced gratification by eating a dinner, and has determined the source of gratification, may equally conceive such gratification to be present in an uneaten dinner, for reaping which, he shows an inclination to eat, thus admitting the proof of an analogical inference; this is the reason why the followers of Kanad and Suguta admit both the visible and analogical proofs. Moreover the followers of Kapila, the author of the *Sankhya* Philosophy admit the proofs derived from sound. They say, visible and analogical proofs ought not to affect a person whose father is absent in a distant country, by the receipt of intelligence that he is dead; for here the death of an absent father in a distant country cannot be rendered visibly clear to the son either by the visible proof or an analogical inference, hence according to Kapila, sound is the third variety of proof; that alone explains the grief which the son suffers on receiving the intelligence of his father's death. The followers of Gautama, the author of *Naya*, admit compassion as the fourth variety of proof. Because, from an admission of the first three proofs, when a person who has never seen a *Gayal*, * but has heard a description from one residing in the woods, that it resembles a cow, goes into a jungle and sees the animal, he recollects the description given of it by a resident of a forest, and from such a recollection, he afterwards recognizes the animal to be a *Gayal*; this should not be. Hence such a distinct knowledge is due to simili, resemblance, or comparison, which is also recognized as a proof.

A Pravakar—follower of the author of Purva Mimansa of the same name (a disciple of Vadia of another country)—cites *arthapati* as a fifth variety of proof. From the sight of plumpness in a man who eats nothing by day time, a person is apt to conceive that he takes his food in the night, as otherwise it is impossible for the body not to lose flesh; under such circumstances night-eating is a promoter of corpulency; hence it is the promoting cause of corpulency which is its effect, therefore the knowledge of the first is called the *arthapati* or denoting cause of the knowledge of corpulency. The knowledge of the effect of night eating is called the

---

* A species of ox, erroneously attributed by Hindu writers to be a deer.

denoting casual proof; and the Vadia followers of Purva Mimansa cite a sixth proof in what is unfelt by experience (*anupalabdhi*). The necessity for it is established in this manner. In a house the absence of a jar is felt, here an object is wanting, yet it produces the knowledge (that it is not present) : now an unperceived object is called an unfelt or unexperienced one, therefore the imperception of a jar, determines its absence. In this way, the source of ascertaining the absence of an object is its imperception, which is called (*anupalabdhi pramana*) or proofs unfelt by experience.

The means of producing true knowledge or perception of an object are called proofs. The instrument which forms the subject of unrestrained signification and different from memory, is called *Prama* or real demonstrator. Knowledge of memory cannot be called true perception or consciousness for that must be dependent on the giver of evidence or *Pramata*,* which memory is not, but dependent on the witnessing intelligence (instead); this is an admitted fact. Moreover misconception and doubts are also admitted as dependent on the same intelligence. For this reason recollection, misconception, and doubts are spoken as forms of Ignorance (*avidya*) with reflection of Intelligence, and not that of the function of the internal organ, so that they are independent of the (*pramata*) senses but dependent on the Uniform Intelligence which is a witness, agent, or instrument. Therefore knowledge which assumes the shape of (*i. e.*, modification of) the function of the internal organ is dependent on the senses, but independent of the witnessing intelligence and what is derived through the senses is called *prama*. Knowledge derived from memory is not a function of the mind, hence independent of the senses ; so is true perception or knowledge hence the indications of true knowledge are necessarily called to be distinct from memory or recollection, knowledge derived from which,

---

* In a former portion of the work the author refers to the sensory organs as giver of evidence, or *pramata*—inasmuch as all knowledge is mainly derived from experience which they are the means of producing, and this fact is corroborated by the Western Metaphysicians too. Hence the 'senses' are used for *pramata*.

though it forms the subject of unrestrained interpretation, yet as such knowledge is not distinct from memory, therefore what produces the true perception, the subject of unrestrained interpretation, is called *prama* (consciousness *). Such an indication is free from defects. Moreover some look upon knowledge derived from memory as true perception (*prama*); we should not say, that in their mind they do not hold the indications of true perception or consciousness as something distinct from memory or recollection; but true perception is that which forms the subject of unrestrained interpretation. A misconception cannot form such a subject, hence the indications of true perception are absent in misconception; and one who in his mind uses knowledge derived from memory as a true perception, such knowledge then becomes a function of his internal organ, and not a function of ignorance independent of the witnessing intelligence, but dependent on (*pramata*) proofs; inasmuch as the protector of the mental function is the one who gives evidence (*pramata*) and not the witnessing intelligence. In this way, knowledge produced from recollection is a function of the internal organ in some persons and thus resembles a true perception, while in others it is only function and hence not such perception.

Moreover, misconception and doubts are the functions of Ignorance in every mind and dependent on the witness. This is universally admitted; also on due consideration it will be found that knowledge derived from memory is equally a function of ignorance, and likewise dependent on the witness, and quite unlike true perception or knowledge. Because the followers of *Vedanta* classify knowledge of proofs under six heads, in which knowledge from memory is not included, hence it is not true knowledge. Then again Madhusudana Swami says it to be dependent on the witness.

Knowledge from proofs is thus classified.

(1) Visible perception † (*prataksha prama*) derived from sight.

---

* Consciousness, true perception or knowledge are synonymously used for *Prama*.

† Or better as follows :—Perception, inference, sound, comparison etc.

(2) Inferred (*anumiti*) derived as a natural inference.
(3) Heard (*savda*) derived from sound.
(4) Similitude (*upamiti*) caused by resemblance.
(5) Denoting cause (*arthapati*)
(6) Negative (*abhav*)

These with the six visible proofs before mentioned, constitute in a consecutive order the instrument or means of action (*karma*).

The instrument or means of true perception is called visible proof (*pramana*).

The extraordinary (or particular) cause is called an instrument, while the general cause of all actions is called the ordinary cause; as virtue and vice for their being the general cause of all actions are called ordinary cause and not an universal cause; but an extraordinary cause is that which produces a certain action,—something definite, as for instance the turning rod of a potter. Here it cannot produce all sorts of actions, but stands as a cause for the production of an earthen jar, or something equally definite, hence its cause. Therefore a turning rod is called an extraordinary cause, as also the cause of a jar, a pitcher, etc.

Similarly Iswara and his will [*i. e.*, volition, consciousness] are the ordinary cause of visible perception, (*i. e.*, the objective world which ever floats before the consciousness of the individual); because all actions are derived from him, and without him nothing is produced. Hence Iswar is the ordinary cause. Then again, the external organs of sense, [eyes, hearing, etc.,] are called the extraordinary cause of visible perception. In this way, the sensory organs,—eyes, hearing and the rest—constitute the visible proofs (*prataksha pramana*), though the Vedanta does not look upon them (sensory organs) as the cause of the perception,* because intelligence is marked by four distinctions.

---

* The senses are the source of illusion, hence they cannot be looked upon as the cause or source of true perception or real knowledge. This is the conclusion of the *Vedanta*. It is worthy of note, that Western Metaphysicians have also been coming round to admit its truth.

These are—
  (1) Intelligence of one who gives evidence (*Pramata*),
  (2) Intelligence of proofs (*pramana*),
  (3) Intelligence of what is proved, or authentic; same as perception (*prama*) and
  (4) Proveable or finite; or subjective Intelligence (*prameya*) as it is also called.

Thus 'perception' is another name for intelligence, which is eternal. It is not derived from the sensory organs, hence they are not its cause. But then, the function of intelligence which accomplishes true perception and determines its uses, is likewise called perception, consciousness, or knowledge. The sensory organs are its instruments or means. The limited or finite intelligence of the internal organ intrinsically situated, is one which gives evidence and called so (*Pramata*). That internal organ issuing out of the body through the respective channels of sight, hearing, and the rest lengthens its size to cover the site occupied by a jar or another object, which it seeks to discover; it then assumes the modification or shape of that jar, by combining with it. As water, confined in a tank, issuing through a tap, or opening, runs into an aqueduct and is then lengthened in size till it reaches the several beds in a garden which it irrigates; and as in its several stages, that water assumes the modification, or shape of the aqueduct, and the beds through which it traverses; so the internal organ issuing through the outlets of the sensory organs, goes to the subject of its discovery (as if its bed); then from the body to the subject of the jar, the elongated size of the internal organ like that of an aqueduct, as in the above instance, is called its function, which for limiting the intelligence is called (*pramana chetan*) demonstrating intelligence, and the functional intelligence or modification of the internal organ is called demonstration (*pramana*).

Like the water running through its beds assuming their shape, the internal organ assumes the shape of the subject it overtakes or covers; in this way, it is modified into a jar or another object, and the limited intelligence is thus called (*prama*) the intelligence which gives evidence. Consciousness which is the subject of a jar etc., and limited by it, is called the subjective intelligence, as also proveable intelligence. Now those versed in the *Vedas* determine their explanation and ascertain the difference between them in the following wise :—

Those who propound the distinguishing feature to consist in the limitedness (*Abuchedavadi*) of the intelligence, assert that the functional intelligence of the internal organ is the demonstration. It is likewise the agent and instrument; and its associate (witness) is its demonstrator or giver of evidence, and therefore the predicate of that demonstrator, while the demonstration is an associate.

A predicate (*visheshan*) is such as enters into the nature of a subject. It is an object capable of covering or surrounding a subject, and, inasmuch as it seeks to differentiate or particularize a thing from another, it is called a *byavartaka* [or encompasser]. As for instance a 'Blue jar'. Here 'blue' is a predicate of its qualifying substantive jar, for it enters into [covers] a jar and differentiates it from a yellow or black etc., jar, hence 'blue' is an 'encompasser,' and is likewise the predicate of jar which is the object covered. That is to say, since, a blue jar is distinct from such another jar that is white, black, yellow, green etc., and since this difference, is manifested or created by the jar itself, it is called covered, or encompassed.

It is likewise the subject or noun. As in the example, "He is a *Dandi* or stick carrying person,"* here the stick is the subject of that person. In the same way, the internal organ is the predicate of the one which gives evidence (*pramata*). Because the subject of such witness is covered or entered into by the internal organ, and establishes it as something distinct and particular from the intelligence concerning a thing to be proved (*prama*), thus constituting what has already been mentioned an 'encompasser.'

---

* A class of religious mendicants who burn the sacred thread, and carry a stick in their hand. They live entirely on alms, not begging twice in the day, nor going to a fourth house after being refused a meal in the first three. They are given entirely to study, and religious works and meditation. In Benares many of them are to be found; of whom very few are real *Dandees*. They dye their clothes with the red *garoa*

A thing that enters not the substance of a subject, but is only an encompasser is called an associate (*upadhi*). As (according to the *Naiyaikas*) the divided ether present in the external meatus of the ear is called the organ of hearing ; here the external meatus is the associate of the hearing organ, for it does not enter into the subject of such hearing [situated outside, it does not cover the internal parts which are concerned in the production of sound] but is simply an 'encompasser'—because it differentiates the ether present in it, as something different from the ether situated outside of it, inasmuch as it hears, which the outer ether cannot.

Likewise in the instance of the ether in a jar, the former gives the latter space enough to contain a maund of food-grains,—here even, the ether is the associate of jar, for the creator of the space to contain the maund of rice etc.,—ether—cannot be entered into by a jar; as it is earthy in composition, it has a void space in it, and cannot be naturally penetrated. Moreover the ether is particularized from the all-pervading ether present everywhere, hence the creator of the space to contain a maund of food-grains—ether—is the associate of jar.

Similarly, the associated intelligence of the internal organ is the associate of witness, for the nature of the witness cannot be penetrated or covered by the internal organ, and it differentiates the intelligence of that which is to be proved, as something distinct from the witness, so that the same internal organ is the associate of witness and the subject of that which gives evidence, and called *pramata chetan*. In this way, intelligence associated with the internal organ is the witness, and the subjective intelligence of the same organ is one that gives evidence. It is the agent or instrument, that is to say, a doer, an eater, and is happy and miserable.

According to the doctrine of *Avasvada* (who propound the reflex intelligence) the internal organ with reflex intelligence is the predicate of *Jiva*, and associate of witness, so that *Jiva* is reflex intelligence with the subjective intelligence of the internal organ, while witness is the same reflection of intelligence with the associated intelligence of the internal organ.

Though in both these views, intelligence with its predicate is

Jiva, who is subjected to an earthly existence, yet that portion which is the subject of the predicate *viz*, intelligence, cannot possibly be a subject of birth and death, happiness and misery, and the usual phases of an earthly existence; hence the predicate alone refers to earthly life, which sometimes appears and is set forth in the subjective intelligence, as in reference to the subjective conditions of virtue, and sometimes as a subject of subjective virtue; while in other places, both as a predicate and subject in the subjective conditions of virtue. As the space or ether; in a jar is destroyed by a stick (which breaks it); here jar is the predicate destroyed by the stick, and not its subject the ether, for it is impossible to destroy it, yet in common parlance, it signifies that the stick destroys the subjective space or ether of that jar.

Moreover, in the instance, "He is the man with the earring"; here 'with the earring' is a predicate, having for its subject 'man.' Now the predicate 'earring' cannot be formed or created by the subject 'man,' but the contrary holds true, and thus 'with the earring' is used to signify a subjective condition,—a condition which constitutes the predicate,—the possession of the earrings in the present case.

Also in the instance, "An armed person has gone to battle"; both arms [of war] and person—the subject—have gone to battle, so that both of them signify the occupation and are used to indicate the constitution of the predicate.

Here an *Avachedavadi* looks upon the internal organ as the predicate, while the expounders of reflex intelligence hold the reflection of the internal organ as predicate, but both of them agree in calling Intelligence as the subject. Now this Intelligence is devoid of birth and death, happiness and misery; but the predicate internal organ or its reflex Intelligence—which is the entity that is subjected to birth and death—is used to signify the subjective intelligence. ('Used' stands for expressing or declaring.)

Thus then is the difference in the doctrine of the two aforesaid sects. According to an *Abhasvadi* the internal organ is said to be made up with reflection of Intelligence, while the doctrine of his rival, (*Avachedvadi*) does not admit of such reflection. Of these two, the former is the best, for the (*Bhashykar*) commentator of the

Vedanta has admitted reflex intelligence as a fact, thus upholding the doctrine of an *Abhashvadi*; while in regard to the *Abuchedradin* Swami Vidyaran says it to be faulty.

If the finite intelligence devoid of reflection of the internal organ be accepted as the one which gives evidence *(pramata)*, then the limited intelligence of a jar may equally be called so. Because the internal organ is a derivative product of the elements; so is a jar equally so. Then again, as the intelligence of the internal organ is limited [distinct]—call it hemmed in, sourrounded or encompassed—so is the intelligence of a jar equally limited. Hence the intelligence constituting the predicate of the internal organ, equally with that constituting the predicate of a jar, may justly be considered as the one which gives evidence; but such defect is easily removed by an admission of the reflex intelligence of the internal organ, inasmuch as the internal organ being derived from the *Satwavic* or good quality present in the elements, [ether and the rest], is luminous and transparent, while a jar is a product of the dark quality of the same elements, therefore not luminous or transparent. A transparent or luminous substance is only capable of reflecting; a dark thing can create it not. For example a (looking) glass and its cover are equally produced from earth, but the former is transparent while the latter is not, hence glass alone is capable of showing the reflection of a person's face. In the same way, the internal organ, being produced from the good quality [of ether and the rest] is transparent, for which intelligence is reflected on it. The gross physical body etc., as well as a jar, and other substances are all products of the dark quality, hence they are not transparent, consequently intelligence is not reflected on them. Thus we find the internal organ to be the seat of two sorts of manifestibility; of which one is the manifestiblity of the all-pervading Intelligence, and the other that of reflection. The first (not the second) is present in the gross body, jar, and other objects. Hence the internal organ for its being endowed with both the intelligences is the *pramata*, while a jar etc., having only one intelligence is not so. Those who do not admit the doctrine of reflection of intelligence in the internal organ, are reduced to the condition of looking upon it as the seat of one intelligence, like that of a jar etc., consequently the same all-pervading intelligence is present both in a jar and the internal organ, so that for the presence of this one intelligence equally everywhere,—in the internal organ, a jar, the gross body, etc.,—all of them equally with the first, must be reckoned as what gives evidence. Accordingly we find, wherein is the difference between the body etc., and the internal organ. That is to say, the internal organ for its being an action of the good quality is transparent ; and the rest, as they are opaque are not endowed with the property of receiving such a reflection. And the internal organ for its capability of receiving a reflection in combination with intelligence, is what is called '*pramata*,' But the body, jar, etc., are not so favourably circumstanced ; they have no property of receiving a reflection, consequently without such reflex, but with only the one pervading Intelligence, they are not '*pramata*.' Thus is determined why the doctrine of reflex is superior to that other the *Avacheda vada* ; and why the latter one is not good.

As the internal organ is possessed with the reflection of intelligence, so is its function endowed with a similar reflection ; this functional reflex intelligence is called the demonstrating (*pramana*) Intelligence. Intelligence over-riding the mental function which assumes the shape of a jar etc., (for the purpose of cognising or discovering it) is called true knowledge, (*prama*). The means for attaining such knowledge,—the external organs of sense—are called (*praman*) proofs, for intelligence which rides over the function that assumes the shape or modification of a subject is called true knowledge. And it may be said, that such intelligence being permanent, it cannot stand in any need of the sensory organs, hence they cannot be called as a means of true knowledge. But as all true knowledge is not attributed to the unassociated intelligence, but to the associated Intelligence of the mental function, after it has assumed the shape of a subject, therefore in regard to intelligence, in the inclination for true knowledge, the associate is the mental function which undergoes the shape of a subject, which is due to the senses, for they are its means.

If the associate of true knowledge—mental function—be due to the sensory organs, then the associated knowledge must alike be due to them, hence they are called the means for true knowledge. Then again, all modifications or changes wrought upon the mind are not called proofs. Hence when the mind situated inside the body, takes for its subject 'a jar' for the purpose of discovering it, and assumes its shape, such a change or modification is alone a proof (*pramana*) and its subjects or the component units of such subject after which the mind is moulded, are called true knowledge (*prama*). From the mind situated inside the body to its subject a jar etc., and its assuming the shape of such subject, is modification of true knowledge, so that there is not much difference between such true knowledge and the function of the internal organ* which is only a form of proof.

Thus then, in the cognition of an external object the mental function issuing out of the body covers such an object,—a jar and the rest,—and assumes a similar shape: in the case, of Self (*Atma*) that function does not issue out, but remaining inside is moulded into the shape of the *Atma*; by the same function, the concealment of Self is driven away, when through his own luminosity he is manifested or discovered in the function. For this reason, it is said, the subject of the mental function, and not that of reflection of intelligence, (a result of that function), is Self. In this way, the witness—Self—is known as Self-manifested. This is clearly established.

Saith Tatwadrishti

> Without relation of the senses, to know 'I am *Brahma*'
> How is rendered visible, Lord, explain it to me.

The visible or apparent knowledge of *Brahma*, destroys all the meshes of ignorance, the invisible cannot effect it, as has already been said; if any doubts arise concerning the visible knowledge of *Brahma*, inasmuch as cognition by the sensory organ can alone render an object visible, which cannot apply to *Brahma*, for the

---

* Mind and internal organ (*antakarana*) are synonymous.

sense of sight is powerless to determine or render It visible; that the image of Rama, Krishna, etc.,—their human shape—are all productions of illusion,—false—and do not represent the *Brahma*; though in the *Purana* Ram, Krishna etc., are said to be incarnations of *Brahma*, yet it does not say that their bodily figures as represented in images are Its representation; what it means is simply this, that the intelligence present or inherent in such bodies is *Brahma*. Now with reference to such intelligence it may be alleged, that its presence in all bodies is *Brahma*; accordingly its presence in the bodies of Ram and Krishna is *Brahma*; so that birds and beasts as well as other creatures having the same inherent intelligence may equally claim to be *Brahma*, and conditionally similar to a Rama or Krishna, so the natural inference is, that the resemblance with *Brahma* is not the inherent intelligence, but to particularize It and the individual, the body is the source. But this is clearly inadmissible. For if the impediment of body constitutes a *Brahma*, in the case of Ram and Krishna, then other creatures have their individual bodies too, they may as well be called *Brahma*. But such is not the case, for bodies having a form and features, with hands and feet, and subject to action, can claim no identity with one which is formless and actionless, and such a one is *Brahma*. Thus we find the bodies of Ram and Krishna are not *Brahma*. Now the difference is this,—the individual's body is dependent on his merits and demerits, and is a product of the elements (ether and the rest). From the force of ignorance, he is apt to connect Self with the unspiritual parts of his body—beginning with the body and ending in the mind *—and

---

* Says the Vedanta Sara :—

An illiterate person considers his son to be his Self. A *Charvaka* says his gross physical body to be his Self; another believes Self to be identical with the senses, a third says his vital airs, Self; there are others again who recognise the mind as Self.

Some Buddhists affirm that *Boodhi* (Intellect or spiritual soul) is the *Atma*.

'mine' and 'thine' are attributions of illusion on the different parts of the body which can only be dispelled by the precepts of a professor.

Now in reference to the body of a Ram or Krishna, virtue and vice plays no part in its production, nor is it derived from an action of elements; but as the time of creation arrives after each cyclic period of destruction, for enabling individuals to enjoy or suffer according to their merits and demerits of a previous birth, *Iswara* though entirely dependent on his own Will, is actuated with a desire to create the world; no sooner he resolves to do it, than the world is created; subsequently he determines to sustain it and he maintains it accordingly. Here 'maintain' signifies allotting to each man his share of happiness and woe according to his merit or demerit. In the midst of such determination to maintain the world by the sheer dint of devotions on the part of his worshippers, he resolves to set forth the images of of Ram, Krishna, and though he is devoid of a particular name and form, yet the image of Krishna, Pitambar, Syam-Soonder, has its origin in his resolution. They are independent of action.

A good man as well as a bad one may equally enjoy happiness or suffer from misery one after the other, by serving a Ram or Krishna; what constitutes the cause of happiness or misery is composed of virtue and vice, hence they are said to be dependent. Thus then, as the incarnated bodies of good and devout persons are produced for enjoying happiness, their bodies are said to be composed entirely of virtue; in the same way, the body of an *Asura* and undevout person is mainly for the suffering of misery—hence it is said to be made of vice, so that it cannot be said that such incarnations are not the products of virtue and vice.

Then again, as the subsequent body is the result of virtue and vice, *i. e.*, of good and bad actions done in a prior state of existence, and happiness or misery which the individual has for his share is an after effect of such works, yet the *Jiva* has a conceit or predilection for his body dependent on his own good and bad actions, which are a source of such weal or woe. Now with regard to Ram and Krishna this does not hold true; their incarnations are not due to virtue or vice, they do not enjoy happiness or suffer misery, hence their bodies are independent of good and bad actions. This is clear enough. In the same way, their bodies are not produced from the elements, or changes wrought in them, but are dependent on Intelligence, and are a modification of pure *Satwavic guna*. If the body of Krishna be a product of quintuplication* of the elements, then the absence of rope or string to serve as bonds, in that body as the *Shastras* say, will be absurd. If the body of an emancipated Yogi, whose composition is elementary, be devoid of bondage † yet it may possibly be present, in which case the practice of his chief purport—*Yoga*—destroys it. In the case of Krishna, there does not exist such a primary object, and hence it may be inferred that his body is of itself free from bonds, consequently its composition is not a modification of the elements.

Anandagiri in his notes on the commentaries of *Mandukya*, says that the body of Ram etc., is a modified form of the elements; this is simply an ordinary view, and further sets forth many bodies like the gross physical body of a man with this object; for, as the commentator of the *Gita* says, "the Supreme Self for his extreme kindness to his creatures assumed human shape in the form of Krishna by the force of *Maya*. He is devoid of birth, hence the attribution of parentage to Basudeva, and Devaki,—is simply an act of the same illusion." In this way, the commentator describes the body of Krishna to be due to illusion, so that his incarnation is not a product of the elements; but its proximate cause (*upadana karana*) is illusion. An individual is forgetful of the real nature of his Self, such is not the case with Ram and Krishna; for the former has his associate in ignorance, abounding in impure goodness; while the associate of the latter is *Maya* abounding in pure

---

* It is thus defined in the *Panchadasi* :—Divide each element into two equal parts, take the first half of each and divide it into four parts, add to it (one eighth each first portion of the other elements.

† Since he is already freed, he has destroyed all bondages; that is to say, for him subjective re-births are no longer possible; he has consumed his actions in his present life by his knowledge of Self. Hence he is emancipated.

goodness. Hence the former is subject to delusion as a result of ignorance, while the latter for *Maya* are all-knowing; an individual for the destruction of the 'envelopment' of ignorance, and that of delusion, has recourse to the instruction of a preceptor concerning the indication of the transcendental phrase 'I am *Brahma*.' 'That art thou' etc., while Ram and Krishna as they are free from such envelopment and delusion, have no necessity for a similar instruction. But like the functional intelligence of the internal organ of a person, the function of *Iswara's Maya* (*i. e.* Self-knowledge) proceeds without any instruction; such knowledge serves no purpose for him; for in the case of the individual, the consciousness of jar etc., breaks through the envelopment of ignorance, and discovers the subject—a jar etc. In regard to *Brahma* the process is exactly similar too—for Self-knowledge destroys the envelopment of ignorance which enshrouds the *Atma*, then as He is Self-manifested and luminous, he is discovered by himself without the assistance of a second substance, though such Self-knowledge cannot discover a subject of cognition. In the same way as the function of *Maya* in *Iswara* realizes the knowledge "I am *Brahma*" and as the subject of that knowledge—his Self (*Atma*)—is free from envelopment and Self-illuminated, it serves him no purpose, either in breaking through the envelopment or discovering his *Atma* to be the same as *Brahma*.

As in the instance of one liberated in life, the uncovered *Atma* stands in no need of the mental function to break asunder the envelopment of ignorance by the consciousness of "I am *Brahma*," so without a similar necessity for breaking through the envelopment, the function of *Maya* determines the consciousness of 'I am *Brahma*, in *Iswara* in spite of any instruction. Thus then, Ram and Krishna are different from a *Jiva*, they resemble *Iswara*, and their bodies are built of *Maya*; but they are not *Brahma* but non-real. The *Maya*-made bodies of their incarnations with features and limbs are subjects of the sense of vision but *Brahma* cannot be seen, hence It is not a subject of sight; the same holds true with regard to touch and its especial sense; the sense of hearing, taste and smell. None of these senses can discover *Brahma*, for It is quite a distinct entity from sound, and the rest of the organs of especial sense, which are puite powerless to bring forth knowledge of *Brahma*.

Moreover, the active organs are not the means of attaining Self-knowledge—but are a mere co-adjutor of speech, for which they can produce no knowledge in a person; thus we find that knowledge of *Brahma* cannot in any way be perceived by the help of senses. Then again, such knowledge is called visible, the same as *Aparoksha*, which cannot apply to *Brahma*. Words alone can produce a knowledge of *Brahma*, and that knowledge is of the invisible type. *

Guru utters :—

> Without the senses no visible knowledge can arise pupil, know it not, to be the rule
> Without them, is rendered visible, as weal and woe.

It is not the rule that for an object to be visible, there must be a relation of the senses with it; for, as in the case of perceiving happiness and misery, no senses are needed to render them visible or apparent, therefore it cannot be said that knowledge derived from the senses is alone to be called visible; on the other hand, when the mental function in relation to a subject assumes its shape, then is produced, what is called visible knowledge. Now such a relationship of the mental function with a subject is brought about sometimes by the senses, at other times without them,—by words, as for example the condition of the 'tenth person.' † Here the tenth person referring to the person counting the others—indicated by the word 'ten' has his mental function modified in the shape of 'ten' by its relationship with it, consequently sound (of ten) is here the means of bringing in that knowledge visibly to himself and the others. Similarly,

---

* Words refer to the transcendental phrase 'That art Thou' etc. 'Invisible knowledge' signifies subjective and not an objective perception, as in the case of idols which can be seen by the eyes and felt by the hands etc.

† *Vide* 2nd note p. 18.

in the perception of happiness or misery to the witness (agent or instrument) his mental function assumes the shape or modification of them, the function creates a relation with such pleasure or pain, hence their knowledge is called visible. After the destruction of previous happiness or misery, when a person subsequently comes to recollect it, his mental function assumes the shape of its subject of recollection, be it either happiness or its reverse; but with the disappearance of such function no relation can be said to exist between it and its subjects; hence such a perception or consciousness cannot be called visible but is (*smriti*) liable to destruction. If the property of the internal organ is to manifest or discover pleasure and pain in the witness, yet by its function after having assumed the shape of pleasure and pain, the witness discovers them. Though witness is an illuminated entity, yet it discovers them through the instrumentality of the mental function. As for instance, the apparent production of silver in nacre. Here, through the force of ignorance, the witness discovers a nacre as silver, but in the discovery of happiness or misery, the mental function is called a co-adjutor of witness, as in the case of false silver in nacre, the function of ignorance is termed co-adjutor. Thus then we find, that in discovering a visible object or producing its cognition, the witness is dependent on mental function, which if produced by the external organs of sense in connection with an external object, then the subject of that function is not illuminated by the witness.

It is said, that the external organs are not the source of producing the subject of happiness and misery to the function of the internal organ, but when they arise, that function (of internal organ) assumes their shape without the agency of any other means; and as the witness overrides such function, it therefore discovers happiness and misery. This is why witness is said to discover them. Moreover in the case of an external object a jar etc., a relation is created by the organs of vision etc., between such jar and the mental function, hence a jar is not discovered by the witness. Similarly when the mental function assumes the shape of Brahma, it is not projected outside the body, but remaining inside creates a relationship with that *Brahma*, so that like the perception of happiness and misery the cognition of *Brahma* is definite and tangible. But then, in the modification of the mental function after happiness or misery there is no interdependence on the external means, so that witness illumines it; while in the modification of the function after the shape of *Brahma*, the external means of hearing the precepts of a spiritual teacher, or the utterances of the *Vedas* are requisite to create a relation between that function, and the cognition, consciousness, or knowledge of *Brahma*. Hence *Brahma* is not illuminated or discovered by the witness.*

In this way, when a relation is established between its subject and the mental function it is called 'visible knowledge.' 'I am a *Brahma*' is a subject of the mental function, and it has a relation with it, hence knowledge of *Brahma* can be classed under 'visible knowledge.' Moreover when a fire is known, or perceived by its smoke, the perception of smoke is visible knowledge and not that of fire. Because by the organs of sight a relation is created between

---

* Witness refers to the Witnessing Intelligence, hence it has been rendered neuter. It is superfluous to say that the several Intelligences known respectively as the 'reflex,' 'witness,' 'uniform,' are all to be regarded as one and non-dual. A difference in associates creates the difference, while virtually the cardinal doctrine of an *Adwaiti* is to admit that identity. But it may be urged that there hardly exists any necessity for creating so many distinctions of the one Intelligence and increase the difficulties of a student struggling for that knowledge. The reply is, no system of philosophy can be complete that does not take note of the possible objections to be raised against it, by the rival schools, hence, more in harmony with the Madhyamika Buddhists these several intelligences had to be satisfactorily accounted for, the more so as they were then firm in the popular belief. Therefore it is to be remembered that the Uniform Intelligence which is changeless is *Brahma* and the reflex *Jiva*; and the two are one and without any distinction whatever, just as water confined in a small tank is non-different from the whole body of it collected in a vast expanse, or the integral units of forest non-different from it. Now the word Intelligence has a very wide signification. You may call it the Soul, Ego, Vitality or Life Principle; or regard it as Spirit, Consciousness, Self, or *Atma*.

the mental function and the smoke, hence its knowledge is called 'visible.' Also by inferences or hypothetical conception, the mental function assumes the shape of, or is moulded into, the form of fire inside the body; but between fire and that function there is no relation whatever, so that knowledge of fire is not apparent or visible. Thus then, when there is created a relation between function and its subject, it is called visible, apparent, or tangible knowledge, perception or consciousness; and when no such relation is established, and the subject is either distant or external, or belongs to a past or future time: then again, when the mental function assumes the form of, or is moulded after, its subject either from inference or the sound of words, that is called invisible knowledge. Knowledge derived from the senses is thus not alone a visible perception. This is not the invariable rule, as for instance, the senses cannot cognize the perception of happiness or misery, yet it is called visible knowledge; and the knowledge of the tenth person derived from sound is also 'visible.' In the same way *Brahma* produced by hearing the instructions of a preceptor on cognition of the transcendental phrase "That art Thou," is called, 'visible knowledge.' This knowledge is derived from the sound of words.

> Hearing such precepts from a Guru, the gifted Tatwadrishti Sees *Brahma* in Self; delusion only created a difference [between the two].

[End] The mental function after having been denuded of its 'envelopment' of ignorance is moulded into "I am *Brahma*"
This I do recognise now, kind Sir.

SECTION V.

KNOWLEDGE of non-duality is apparently produced by hearing the precept of a *Guru* on the utterances of the *Vedas*. But the second pupil, by name Adrishta, raises objections to it in the following wise. If the *Vedas* and *Guru* are both true, then they imply a duality and hence injurious to non-duality; if they are untrue, then the chief aim of human existence (emancipation) cannot be derived from them. Thus in both ways, the *Vedas* and *Guru* are destructive of non-duality.

> If you call the *Vedas* and *Guru* untrue, [world.
> Then they will be powerless to destroy the miseries of the
> As the false perception of water in a sandy waste,
> Is powerless to appease thirst.

Say you, a true *Guru* and *Veda* are two, contrary to the conclusions of Sankaracharya on non-duality; leave such impure ideas which belong only to the *Madhyamika* Buddhists; this is the conclusion of the proposition contained in the first line of the stanza.

> Bhagavan, such doubt arises in my mind, by your kind reply dispel it.
> Says Guru to his pupil, listen to the doctrine of Sankara, it is full of proof [and very convincing].

The four friends (*Madhyamiks*) speak in opposition to the *Vedas*; hear therefore the words of Vyasa which confirm Sankara's doctrine.

> In *Kalu* various are the interpretations put on the *Vedas*.
> Sri Sankara was born to extirpate the Buddhists; the Lord brought forth his image in the Ganges.

As the sun dispels darkness from the world by his light, illumines all objects, discovers them as they are, and removes all doubts and antagonistic ideas;

So Sri Sankara removes the misinterpretation and clears the *Vedas* from it, he has likewise removed all doubts and determined their true signification.

UNREAL DELUSIONS.

If the indication of the *Vedas* be artificial and ungenuine, then why labour in vain ; what Vyas has said in the *Purans*, acknowledge them true. The doctrines of the *Madhyamiks* are unsound and illogical, that I know from the words of Vyas ; and listen to the proofs I adduce, know what Valmika says. Hearing it, Bashishta compiled his work, having non-duality for his doctrine plainly ; Sri Sankara held non-duality only, his doctrine is for this reason excellent.

The words of the sage Valmika are construed as antagonistic to the *Vedas* by the impure-minded only.

Now all this means, what Vyas has said in the *Purans* concerning the delusion as to the real signification of the *Vedas* in the *Kali-yuga*. In such a crisis, the kind-hearted Siva assuming the name of Sri Sankara, will take the form of Budrinath and reincarnate. He will issue out of the holy river (Ganges), fix himself in his usual place, destroy the tenets of the Sankhyas and Buddhists, and interpret the *Vedas* in their true light. According to Vyas, the doctrine of Sri Sankara is an authority, while that of the *Madhyamiks* (who are divided amongst themselves into sects) who hold duality to be true is without an authority. Moreover, though the *Upanishada*, *Gita* and the *Sutras*—these proceed from the *Vedanta*—have been construed according to their own doctrines by the *Madhyamiks*, such interpretation is a forced one, while the version set forth by Sri Sankara, and the utterances of Vyas on the subject are alone real. Then again, the first poet Valmika—all knowing sage as he was—in his *Utara Ramayana*, called *Bashishta*, insists on non-duality, more especially, as its principal doctrine about the six kinds of (*drishti*) observation has been declared in many works on history. Hence according to the words of Valmika, the doctrine of non-duality is authoritative and self-evident ; while the rival doctrine of duality which creates a difference between the individuated Self and *Brahma*, in contradiction to what Valmika says, is unsound and illogical. Thus then, the last mentioned tenet, as it is antagonistic to the confirmed statements of all known sages and devout persons, is for the reason of that, called unsound and illogical. Besides such difference is opposed to natural inference, and sound reasoning. Its fallacy has been exposed in several works by Sri Harsa and others. But as the arguments used are difficult of comprehension, I have abstained from introducing them here. Then again, the utterances of the sage are all directed against the false assumption of difference between an individual Spirit and the Universal, and have completely broken it down; their hearing will likewise establish the unsoundness of the view held by the Buddhists, so that for a qualified person, (who is not an atheist) arguments are no more needed. This is the indication of the three pieces of verse heading the present remarks.

What Sri Harsa has written to break down the difference between a *Jiva* and *Brahma*, and establish non-duality (in his work he has entered largely upon it, and shown that duality does not rest on sound reasoning),

And the works which deal exclusively on the qualification of duality, with the arguments against it; are difficult and the mode of their illustration contains very abstruse arguments which no one minds to study:

So that, what you say about breaking down the doctrine of duality, arguments are not necessary, since it is itself untenable; and you know it to be so already. And as has already been said, even the *Vedas* are opposed to it.

Knowledge of duality produces much pain, it is the source of of death-pangs, hence I drive it away from the mind and show my love for non-duality; for as the *Sruti* says, "duality brings in a recollection of death, which is constantly present in him and he sees it certainly."

Who holds duality in his mind is called in the *Vedas* 'fear'; he sees in the subject of his knowledge and mind something else, and is no better than an animal according to the *Vedas*.

The second is productive of fear, while that other is natural,
The *Vedas* destroy the former as animals are subdued by the
Devas. (*Sruti*.)

[Know then] pupil, that the tenets of the *Madhyamiks* entail a multitude of miseries, and he who entertains the doctrine (utterances) of duality in his mind, so as to perceive the difference as something real and apparent makes non-duality disappear; with the recollection of duality, is removed a former remembrance of perception of its opposite non-duality. This is illustrated in the following manner.

A Raja appoints a person by name Varchhu to manage his estate, his officers and minister grew jealous of him, but failing to do him any injury, as he was a great favorite with the sovereign, they all combined to spread plunder and devastation. The Raja hearing this called all his officers, held a court, sent for his chief ministers and asked them to run in pursuit of and follow the plunderers, but they replied, that as you have always known Varchhu to be your worthy servant, now you are sending us only to die, why not send Varchhu? Then he (Varchhu) said, with hands joined as in prayer, if ordered, I am ready to follow the plunderers and beat them. The Raja granted his prayer and asked him to finish the work. He routs them in the first encounter; when his rivals heard of his success, they spoke to the Raja that Varchhu had been foiled in his attempt to overtake the robbers. On hearing such false accounts, he appoints his chief minister in his place, honours him with a gift of the umbrella and fan as marks of royal favor, who makes his own arrangements for administering the state, and takes special care to keep back all information concerning Varchhu from his royal master. Varchhu hearing this, assumed the garb of an ascetic; for he knew fully that he would never be allowed to have an interview with his master, and that he will lose his life, before he reached the palace gate. He began to contemplate thus:—Till now I have enjoyed everything both corporeal and sensual.

Like a quadruped; with hands strong as an elephant's, heart of a stag; brave and nimble as a lion, and eyes tremulous like those of a horse, and complexion excellent; like a bird enchanted with four fruits and flowers; face resembling those of a flamingo, the throat of pigeon, voice sweet and melodious, surrounded with the plumage of the peacock, face resembling a water-lilly, the chin, a linseed flower indicating the abode of intellect, nose glossy like the sesamum seed containing oil within or having a mole; and color, a beautiful faint yellow like the magnolia. The four fruits:— The upper and the lower lips red like a pomegrante, teeth set like the seeds of the *Bael* fruit, and free like a parrot, and with all the indications of a profound intellect.

Never abstained from using the Ganges water for which all clever persons have an attachment, fate has made another courtezan.* With her beauty, she sits at ease, and is never left alone for a moment by her lover, who supplies her with all sorts of enjoyments, leaving nothing undone that can make her comfortable and happy. A dunce only conceives such to be happiness and its season, existence in the world, Oh rake! Till now you have had enough of sensual enjoyments. Consider where is the beauty in her. She is a temple of impurity, emitting foul odours from the genitals always. Though her thighs resemble the plantain tree in roundness and symmetry, yet adjacent to it is a column of fæces [*i.e.*, the rectum] the sides of which are full of bad smell. You are fondly attached to them, you blind; her mouth filled with saliva, wets your face with her kisses. A bad looking girl—she is fond of the bottle and deprives you of your sense of the clean and unclean. Now, 'bad looking' signifies one whose sight provokes lascivious desires. It is said that the best part of a female's body is her genitals, and this should be spoken of disparagingly; she is formed of artifice, deceit, and poison, that I know to be sure, and am thinking now of discarding her. Of sweets,—curd, rice-pudding, rice, butter, vegetables and other things I have had enough, but am not yet satiated, so that in vain am I engaged in serving another, and hence dependent for a house, orchard, garden, or cave and riches; I have become a slave of the king. By my own powers have I acquired jewellery, beds, and water pots.

Varchhu sitting alone was enjoying felicity; for in
Company no happiness can be enjoyed.

A prince healthy and young, stout and strong, with all sorts of learning is considered by all men to be extremely happy. A king over men and *Gandharvas*, with good qualities, has for his share, happiness. [One ruling over] *Gandharvas* and *Devas* is more blessed in that respect than that other king. The happiness of a *Gandharva* and *Deva*

---

* Tilotoma, the beautiful courtezan of India, from *Til* or mole and *Utama* excellent, *i. e.* beautiful.

proceeding from good qualities, is equally felt by their departed ancestral spirits. Then who knows that his good actions belong to the *Devas* who procure happiness for him ? They in their turn assign their merits to their king Indra who procures happiness to them in turn.

Brihaspati is the Guru of all *Devas*, he derives his happiness from the good actions of Indra ; Prajapati derives his felicity from Brihaspati in turn, from whom comes the fill of *Brahma* ; human existence is full of miseries of diverse kinds, mixed with happiness in the manner aforesaid in following each other (*Taiterya Upanishad*).

From what has been said, Brahmâ takes all his happiness from the Raja who always keeps himself aloof from actions. Where then happiness is to be found ? A fair woman and issue together with riches are always a source of misery.

On the Miseries of keeping Company with a Young and Beautiful Girl.

Say to a young and beautiful damsel, that she is the owner of a mass of excrements. For what sin am I subjected to the punishment of being reckoned as an immoral and unfit person ? Like an ox or she buffalo &c., or like a she-camel her voice is shrill ; she would never have me till the thousandth time.

Guiltless, yet without parting company from you, I cannot be indifferent to wordly enjoyments, but am constantly in the midst of sin, which as it were forms a part of my mind, and brings no end of trouble by day and night, hence daily I know you to be ugly and deformed. Thus a fair damsel with sweet voice is reduced into an ugly creature producing misery, the shining skin is only loved after all, but she is the destroyer of riches, virtue, and emancipation.

On the Wasting of Riches.

By sweet words, or frowns, or quarrels she steals all intellect from her lover, who blinded with lust, sees nothing but her even in dreams, gives her jewels, riches, whatever she desires, and all that he earns from outside ; but keeps his father and mother in poverty, without food and clothes, never once remembering them ; supplies her with sweets and rare fruits, which he offers to her with all homage as if she were a goddess, his attachment and love for her never cease, his very words breathe of affection.

ON THE DESTRUCTION OF VIRTUE.

Like a parrot confined in a cage and taught to speak, unmindful of purity or impurity, the husband treats his revered parents according to the instructions he receives from his wife; as a peacock dances in front of a pea-hen, to show his affection for his partner, so he shews his attachment to his wife by providing her with various suits of wearing apparel and pleases her. When both are actuated with a desire produced by affection, then is awakened the intoxication of lust, and the excesses committed by its delusion are a source of wonder to those who are indifferent to female charms. But this intoxicating passion leads one unmindful of any sense of right and wrong, ending in madness, to commit an act of injury in another's house, bringing on misery by the very act which was thought to produce happiness. Violent are his desires produced from his intoxicating passion, it affects the female likewise, so drinking it both, the male and female are subjected to miseries. Thus then a man's subjection to misery induced by female beauty is to be avoided by dissociation, as insisted upon by sages. Even the charms of beauty inducing love and affection in a male are sure to end in miseries for both. Such is the unanimous testimony of all devout sages. Semen is derived from elaboration of various kinds of food, vitality is dependent on it, in all men. It destroys all mental pain; when a person's mind is affected with the bad effects of distress, and he is perfectly indifferent, then, semen inhabiting the blood induces activity in him, for its action resembles the active (*Raja*) quality; when the mind dwells in semen, then mental distress and its meddlesome activity are alike destroyed; then again a strong man knows it to be indicative of good actions and he is delighted. When the quantity of semen is increased it adds to his personal beauty, and gives him the flush and brightness of health; its waste destroys health both corporeal and mental. But one whose semen is never spent, does not show his body covered with dirt; a devotee by keeping his semen, engages himself in communion by an aerial intertwining of the fingers in worship, holding the coin of semen, and in that way achieves the eight kinds of success (*siddhi*) over natural (occult) forces. Semen is of all worldly things, the excellent, it is snatched by a female in her vagina; her love causes an incessant drain of the vital fluid and thus spoils the man, in the same way as a crusher grinds the sugarcane and squeezes the juice out of it. In the Punjaub the crusher employed in breaking the mounds of earth, is looked upon in connection with cultivation as a *Devta*.

Repeated acts of coition drain away the semen from the system, exhausts its supply, and thus deprives the body of its vitality. I attribute all my evil actions to Krishna, who destroys them, in the same manner, as a flower is deprived of its sweet scent by being dried in contact with oil seeds which then draw the smell. He is handsome and very rich—Sree Krishna—entertains many maids who call him husband, or lord; desirous of being re-united in love, like a clumsy ungallant person he holds her by the hand, whose husband never goes (near) to bed, and is abused in turn. She makes signs by her eyes, and expresses her disapprobation of his act by winks and drawing up her nose, like the essence of a thousand thunder-bolts; the dart strikes his heart of adamant and he is laughed in turn by all sages, who proclaim his love [with Radha]. He, nothing undaunted clasps her in his arms humming a favourite tune of his, and cunning as he is, gratifies his desires and then lets her go. Versed and well-read in the *Vedas*, *Purans*, *Smriti* and the arguments of the *Gita*, made he the last subservient to him, and played he the part of a trickster as one does with a playing monkey.

Mind, dwell upon what has been written there. I consider the arguments, and draw the inferences accordingly; its simple perusal will avail nothing, but shall be only brute-like. Hear it attentively when a *Pandit* reads and explains it. When it is full well remembered, it resembles the *Vedas* in driving away all grief, and the individual is actuated with a desire of relinquishing the world, and retiring, thus causing the destruction of all impermanent things, which in their turn, have brought ruin everywhere since the dawn of day, and like a deadly poison brought death in its trail. A wise man's words are his riches, while a cunning man of the world delights in the acquisition of property which constitute *his riches*; for him, proceeds not that sharp indifference to those material comforts which spoil the intellect over and over, make a slave of ignorant persons, and order others to execute his commands, while he sits at his ease like a lord of men. A man or woman actuated with a thirst after riches, can never have his or her mind straight. Happiness and misery are equally unknown to them, for, they are drowned in forgetfulness. Though money is the central source of all worldly miseries, a woman, a prostitute, and an old hag are equally marked with the signs of hell, whom a man with indifference ever shuns. They make their affections in artifice and deceit, and their love is only verbal.

How Virtue and Emancipation are Ruined by Women.

They are the source of ruin; with all his wits about him, a man shall avoid them knowing it to be a fact; a son is equally the source of much grief; in conception, birth and death, he brings endless troubles. During pregnancy the mother's sufferings are intense, her anxieties, whether she will bring forth a son or daughter are incessant and not removed till the child is born; fear of abortion is another source of anxiety and uneasiness for her. When the morning of the ninth month arrives, both the mother and father feel extremely anxious, and suffer much misery, they cease not to worship the nine planetary deities for a day, while others are engaged to propitiate the Deity by sacrifice and offerings to good folks. Seated alone, the parents are by day and night immersed in thought on the planetary spirits. When from distemper the child refuses the mother's breast, the parents both take up its tending and think of giving alms, as a few months have already been past. During teething and the growth of hair, another source of anxiety for the parents is to see their child getting thin and emaciated; they remove his forelocks and secure them in a good place. The unclean and low dregs as a tanner, a Syud, a Mahomedan saint, and *Dervishes* are, equally with a Brahmin priest, officiating in the ceremony of hair splitting, saluted and homage paid with hands clasped in prayer. Whom a Hindu never shows any reverence for, is now recognised [as a guardian angel] to keep the child in health and guard or protect it from all bad influences. Even the spirits of the infernal regions are invoked, and their aid sought by propitiating sacrifices on the cremation spot. A Dhanaka also receives his share, and without feeling any shame the parents worship him; moreover, charms and amulets are written and duly covered placed round the neck. Worship they in their own line one Achutá, but they tender the child to the care of another line hoping to profit thereby; this is simply a bad practice, and they do not shrink from it. When small pox rages, the parents loose their delight, leave off bathing and assume dirty habits; and make the ass which carries the goddess a subject of their worship, entreats the animal and feeds it with gram while the mother carries in her lap and makes the child ride on it.

In this way, the child is brought up with infinite care and trouble. When he arrives at puberty, the same incessant care is bestowed upon him. If his span of existence be ascertained to be short, numerous are the means adopted to lengthen it; dashing their foreheads against the ground do the parents give vent to their grief, when death overtakes him; they look upon their lot as the most miserable, consider themselves as helpless, and perfectly undone; with cries they rend the air by day and night, and curse their existence repeatedly and thus finish their life. Then again, in the absence of a child the parents experience grief similar to that caused by death in them, who had one living. If he lives he is maintained till youth when he behaves like the *felidae*. Now 'with son' means one whose son is living, and 'without son' or in the absence of a child signifies one who has it not, nor ever had any.

One who had been tended with great care, if thirsty in the night the parents give him no water to drink, lest it may produce sickness; they rock him to sleep in bed, heaping abuse on my head, or getting up in the morning from the bed, a good child looks for the mother and father, who understanding by his stare, approach him and appear in front, while a corrupt and bad one begins his morning speech by commencing to abuse; with tears in his eyes he kicks up a row, ill-treating those who come near and harassing the parents unnecessarily and incessantly. If ever he attains maturity, he never deigns to enquire or look after the maintenance of his father and mother, but is engaged in taking care of his own body. Such a son is a source of constant misery.

Thus then, a person who seeks to derive any happiness from a son is a prince of dunces. For on due consideration, it is to be seen, that he is an unceasing source of trouble to his parents. Cast him off therefore; and he who expects to obtain riches by him ought to be smeared in the face with dust. To accumulate wealth, to preserve it, and spend it not, is the root of misery. Who in this delusion amasses *lacs* fruitlessly, leaving virtue to take care of herself and discarding the usual customs and practices of his line of descent, believing spending to be wasting away, and if without luck such fortune is never amassed, yet its custody, and not to spend it anyhow, are his incessant thoughts, and at last, he dies in the midst of such endless anxiety.

Fie to him, who is ever bent after the pursuit of wealth. A young mother looks upon her son as a mine of wealth, but Varchhu knowing him to be a source of incessant unhappiness has no tender attachment, so leaves him behind.

Varchhu went to the woods alone, and quieted his mind. In his new position he heard everything that had transpired in his absence, and thought within himself, if the king hears him alive, or if he be met by a third person, some mishaps may befall, so to avoid them he becomes a powerful ghost. Having adopted this course, he repairs to the court. All says of him, that he has become a low devil. Besmearing the body with ashes, he enters appearance; no sooner he is seen than some try to drive him away, others attempt to beat him; men in this way abuse him and run away. The king hears the certain news that after death Varchhu has become a ghost, he gets up from his seat, but seeing him soon faints away. A few days after, his majesty went on an hunting excursion. In the mountain woods dwelleth the lion, here was also residing a devotee no other than his own Dewan Varchhu, engaged in the practice of religious austerities. His very sight made the king depart, knowing and believing him to be a ghost, that had produced him uneasiness on a previous occasion. Actuated with fear the king distrusts his eyes, but puts faith in the false reports of Varchhu's being a ghost, and recognises not the living personality simply for the delusion of fear. In the same way, those ignorant persons who believe in duality are led by fear, while a believer of non-duality sees *Brahma* apparently and cognizes it perceptibly in his mind, wherein dwelleth such belief.

When an ignorant person believes in duality, by hearing it, he is ever subjected to suffer miseries, and never can possess knowledge of *Brahma*; and he who hearing it, distinguishes it as non-real, then he becomes acquainted with the indication of the transcendental phrase 'That art Thou.'

Pupil, what you have heard about difference, know it to be untrue, and such untruth is a mark of hell, and those who speak about it are tellers of untruth, and you are right in getting angry with their artifice which seeks to destroy happiness—the end and aim of all right-minded persons; avoid their company and hear not their precepts about duality; if you ever listen to their words, immediately leave them. Look upon them as unclean and leave them. If the *Vedas* and *Guru* are true then how do the precepts taught there destroy the unreal miseries of the objective world ? Hear the replies on the subject. An unreal misery is destroyed by an unreal thing. If the *Vedas* and *Guru* are not untrue, they cannot destroy the unreal worldly miseries. Listen to the illustration which is adduced here, it will remove your doubts.

Like the king of heaven, Indra, there was a mighty brave king ; he had a large number of followers like Bheem, who always used to remain round him, and mount guard on his gate to the number of several thousands. Even in the temple of the inner department they kept a strict watch with drawn swords ; on the balcony of the highest room, was spread the royal bed covered with flowers. A bird even could not get here, how then could any one else to reach ? Now the king sees a dream, that a jackal has got hold of his legs, he wants to unloose them but to no purpose; then he shouts for help to destroy the animal; the sentry who were keeping guard on the door, give him no assistance ; he then takes a stick in his hand and gives a good beating to the animal, when it takes out the teeth from the muscles of his leg. The parts where the teeth stuck fast give pain to the Rajah, he limps with the assistance of the stick like a lame man, and arrives at the house of the gipsy surgeon, asks him to dress his wounds with a plaster as will induce suppuration and bring on granulations at once; the surgeon replies, he has not got ready such a dressing as he requires, but if the king would pay him in advance, he can prepare the necessary remedy. The king then retires, having not a pice with him to give, ponders on the circumstance as he gets out of the house of the gipsy, and says to himself, the fellow ought to have thanked his stars with such a rich customer as myself for a patient, but instead, refused to do me the service, I stand in need of, for even a rich man will welcome my presence in his house. He took me for a man of straw, without occupation and so drove me out of his house, but the fault is not in him; no one does a service for nothing. Mother, father, friend, wife and children, all have their self-interests to serve; if unsuccessful they condescend not to cast any glance or consideration; for interested motives, they share his grief and not leave him alone for a single hour, but when unfortunately he becomes a leper, fingers sloughed away and with flies disturbing constantly, the members of his dear family finding him quite unserviceable to them, desert him and wish that he may die soon. They are disgusted with the sight and sickened. The dearest wife will try to avoid the infection of the disease while fanning him and adjusting his clothes. The parents even shrink from him, and brothers who always embraced him, will speak from behind a screen. In this way the whole world has its motives of interest to serve, which is ever an object of love. Fate has not made me possessed of wealth hence I have been refused a piece of dressing here. With these thoughts in him, he meets with a sage, who gives him a root to apply to his wound. When the king wakes up from sleep, he finds his pain in the wound gone. Pupil, this illustration have I given you in the way of example, see how a false wound is removed by a false remedy. When the Raja was the subject of a false pain, it was a product of the actual condition of society. His (real) wealth &c., were of no service to him. Now the meaning of the above illustration is this. Worldly miseries are non-real, hence for their destruction the *Veda* and *Guru* must alike be false. For what is false cannot require the aid of a true remedy to remove it. Then again, a true remedy cannot procure the destruction of what is non-real and unexisting. As in the instance of the foregoing Raja, he saw in a dream a (false) jackal approach him, without finding any obstruction from the real sentries keeping guard, and when he shouted for help, the animal passed away unhurt by any one; and though he had several weapons with him, yet with a false stick—a creation of his imagination—he kills the animal, and when he received a false wound, he could find no real surgeon or doctor to cure him; but had recourse to a false surgeon, who asks money from him. Really all his treasure was of no avail, for he could not find even a copper pice wherewith to satisfy the (non-existent) doctor and procure a piece of dressing. All the substantial and really existing means were perfectly useless here, to cause a destruction of his pain and wound; but a false sage seen in a dream, gives him a medicine (equally false), to cause the removal of pain along with his wound—which never existed.

A similar dream is the common experience of all men. A substantial thing of the waking condition is not fit to be given to any one in a dream. Similarly the falsity of worldly miseries is removed by the false *Veda* and *Guru*; and a real *Veda* and *Guru* are not needed. As you said, the false impression of water in a sandy waste (mirage) cannot appease thirst, so a false *Veda Guru* cannot procure the destruction of worldly miseries which are not real; for if it were so, then a mirage must equally succeed to satiate thirst. Pupil, your doubts in this respect are settled in the following manner:— If the false waters of a mirage can never remove thirst, yet your instance is an extreme one and I find in it no similarity of condition.

In other words though the perception of false water in a sandy waste can never succeed to appease thirst, and like the cessation of pain by the help of a false *Guru-Veda*, the false water must equally cause thirst to cease, but this never follows, hence in the same way a false *Guru-Veda* can never cause the destruction of the world and reduce it to a non-reality, yet your illustration is an exremely ill-matched one, for between the mirage and thirst, there is a condition of non-similarity; as I find the water in the first mentioned condition to be non-existent, *i.e.*, false, while the feeling of thirst is a reality and fact.

> Your miseries are subject to the same conditions as that of a *Guru and Veda*,
> And are possible to be removed or destroyed by them.
> Between the things where similarity exists,
> I see in such similarity as a means and prevention.

In other words, between your miseries *Guru* and *Vedas* there exists a condition of similarity so that they are quite able to cause a destruction of your woe; where such similarity exists between different things, it serves both as a cause and remedy. That is to say, between a jar and earth there is this condition of similarity, the latter is the means of the former; between a piece of wood and fire the same similarity is present. Here fire is called a prevention. Now means and prevention signify cause and destruction.

Between the false perception of water in a sandy desert and thirst, there is not such conditional similarity present, hence the first cannot destroy the last. Now the purport is :—In intelligence is true existence, and all unrealities which are different from it have two varieties of existence; one is practical existence, and the second apparent or sequential. The first refers to what is destroyed by knowledge of *Brahma* and not otherwise.* As for example *Iswar's* creation,—the objective world &c., &c. For the body together with the sensory and active organs and the vast expanse are the created

---

* The *Vedanta* holds three kinds of existence :—
  (1) *Paramarthika* or true.
  (2) Practical or *Vyvaharika*.
  (3) *Prativashika* or apparent.

Brahma is the sole representative of the first, while *Iswara*, and his created works including individual self, heaven and hell, and all phenomena are really non-existent; but in connection with our daily practice they are all regarded as really existing hence they are called practical: apparent are the things produced by imagination as mirage &c.

works of *Iswara* which are only destroyed* (cease to exist as real) by knowledge of *Brahma*, and not otherwise; but as material, they are open to destruction in the cyclic periods of *pralaya*, hence knowledge of *Brahma* with or without can have no effect then; yet as such knowledge determines their non-reality by an actual connection of cause and effect and the refutation which its contradiction implies, hence it is said, that such knowledge alone can refute their existence. In this connection, *vadh* is defined as the ascertainment of the unreality of a visible substance. Now such an ascertainment in regard to the created works of *Iswara* does not proceed at first in any instance without a knowledge of *Brahma*, but follows subsequent to it, so that the sequential product of the basic unit of primordial Ignorance—the phenomenal world, a creation of *Iswara*—and its use in practice† can easily be regarded as practical existence. That is to say, in connection with birth and death, bondage, and emancipation, which determine such existence practically, *Iswara's* creation must be regarded from a certain standpoint as a practical existence and called so. Where such a refutation is produced in spite of knowledge of *Brahma* it is called 'apparent existence.' As for instance, a mirage, silver mistaken for nacre, or a snake imagined in a rope. In all these conditions [which are simply illusory] water, silver, and snake, are destroyed by knowledge or perception of the actual substance, hence their production was only apparent, in contradistinction to real, and therefore called apparent existence: that is to say, it implies a perception or knowledge of the product of primordial Ignorance—silver, and the rest and creates them apparently, for which from a certain standpoint, they are an apparent existence. When a substance remains unaffected and is not destroyed in the course of time it is called 'true existence.' Now

---

* Here the word destroyed used for *vadh* is not a happy expression. *Vadh* means a refutation by contradiction between cause and effect; but as the commentator had used it as *nasa* or destruction and the reference to the latter word in the concluding sentence, require a little discrimination to distinguish them.

† *Vide* note preceding page.

intelligence can never be destroyed, removed, or refuted, hence it is called truly existent.

Thus then, if the *Vedas*, *Guru* and the usual miseries of life were regarded as equally practically existent, a condition of existing similarity will be established between them, so that from a false *Guru*, *Veda*, the false miseries of the world shall alike be destroyed. And hunger and thirst are simply the attributes of *prana*. Now this (*prana*) vital air with its attribute is only removed by a knowledge of *Brahma*, so that thirst is practically existent. The water of a mirage, is refuted or destroyed without a knowledge of *Brahma*, but simply from a knowlege that it is a false perception of water; hence it is called 'apparent existence.' But thirst and mirage are not subject to conditions of identity of existence; hence a mirage cannot destroy thirst. Thus in the instance cited here for illustration, *Guru* and *Veda* are the destroyers, and worldly miseries are the things to be destroyed. Between 'destroyers' and the 'destroyed' there is an identity of existence, which is not the case with the subjects of the illustration—*i.e.*, between water of a mirage and thirst; for this absence of identity or constitutional difference in their existence, the illustration has been termed an extreme one, and unlike the first portion of it.

(Doubt) Save *Brahma* every thing else is unreal; say it so.
       The cause of their difference has to be said,
       This doubt has overtaken me,
       Lord, now cut it off.

Lord, you have spoken every thing to be unreal save *Brahma*; amongst all such unrealities, the apparent silver in nacre, a snake in a rope, or water in a mirage is refuted or destroyed without knowledge of *Brahma*; while worldly woe is removed subsequent to such knowledge; why maintain such a difference between them, and what is its cause?

    [Reply.] All the products of Ignorance are unreal.
        Pupil, what produces them, that is
        The derivative cause, Ignorance
        Is destroyed by knowledge.

If therefore all the products of Ignorance—phenomenal world— different from *Brahma* are unreal, *i.e.*, subject to destruction and therefore impermanent, then the fabricator which determines their production is alike unreal; but what is produced from Ignorance in the case of an individual, is removed with the advent of knowledge. That is to say, the presence of a snake in a rope, or water in mirage, or silver in nacre, all are conceived in Ignorance, and with the discovery of the mistake caused by knowledge, they cease to exist. Moreover, Ignorance of *Brahma* imputes birth and death, and the usual miseries of existence [to Self] which Its knowledge destroys *i.e.*, discovers to be false and unreal.

Says the pupil:—

Bhagavan, if the world be produced from ignorance of *Brahma,*

How does it take place consecutively, speak unto me.

And the Guru replies in plainer terms:—

Like a dream, the tangibility of phenomenal world is false and unreal, and not derived consecutively from something preceding it, but a mere delusion. If you know it to be gradually produced, it will be similar to wrenching a piece of cloth soaked in mirage water.

In other words, according to the *Upanishads*, the doctrine of evolution of the world implies every thing else to be unreal, save Intelligence. That is to say, if the production of the world has been declared differently in the several *Upanishads*; as for instance, in the *Chhandogya*, it is determined as produced from the Supreme Self who is ever existent—from whom are derived, one after the other, fire, water and earth; and in the *Taitirya Upanishad* ether, air, fire, water, and earth are said to have been produced in a consecutive serial order; thus has been ascertained the origin of the five elements, while elsewhere everything is said to be created by the Supreme *Iswara, i.e.*, without any consecutive seriality; so may these different doctrines in regard to the origin of the Universe signify it to be an unreality. If it were a reality or something substantial, then the *Vedas* would not have determined its origin in different ways. A difference of consideration as to the source of the world signifies the purport of the *Vedas* is to determine only the secondless *Brahma*, and not the Universe; which last it seeks to reduce into the condition of an

unreal non-existence; for its existence is illusory. As for example, for the sake of pastime a paper elephant filled with gunpowder is made to fly in the air, it has ears, tail etc., to straighten which no water is applied; so, to produce a knowledge of non-duality by reducing this vast expanse into a condition of non-existence, the objectivity of the phenomenal has been attributed to illusion; hence there has been no attempt made in the *Vedas* to determine the consecutive formation of the universe in one way, *i.e.*, it has used several methods to account for its origin: thus then we know, why the several doctrines have been introduced; it shows the purport is simply to destroy the existence of the objective universe, and not to ascertain its source of origin. Moreover the commentator as well as the author of the *Sutras* in the second chapter of the *Sruti* text, where the origin of the universe is dealt with, have cleared all antagonisms from it, and followed the doctrine adopted in the *Taitirya Upanishad*, which they say to be the unanimous purport of all the *Upanishads*. Now this has been done simply to satisfy the enquirers of difference. Those who are unacquainted with the purport of the utterances already made in respect to the origin of the world, to such enquirers of difference, the *Upanishads* will appear to imply contradiction, concerning the several views they allege in connection with the subject; to remove this, all of them have been mentioned to support the one doctrine about the evolution of the universe. Also, for those who cannot derive true knowledge by determining the *Brahma*, the consecutive consideration of the origin of the universe has been set forth, so that they may ponder constantly on its destruction (*laya*). The same serial order which has caused the evolution will produce its destruction or disintegration, but quite in a reversed order of downward progression.*
Pondering and reflecting on this subject will make the intellect fix

---

* Matter is eternal hence in '*laya*' it does not cease to exist; therefore disintegration is a better term. It may be remarked that the *Vedanta* doctrine upholds the eternity of matter, its objective condition is destroyed in the cyclic period of destruction, but it exists potentially or subjectively in the *Parabrahma*. Now this is evidently what the Western Scientists maintain alike with the Materialists.

its site on non-duality. How to dwell on *laya*, has been mentioned by the Vartikar Sureswaracharya, while treating quintuplication, in his work on the subject. As the present work is intended for a better qualified person, it does not contain any account as to the origin or destruction of the Cosmos. But it is a veritable ocean, and shows the right way that leads to emancipation. The universe cannot proceed from the *Brahma* alone, for It is unassociated and actionless; but *Iswara* having a preponderance of *Maya* in him is its procreator. Hence (*Maya*) illusion has been explained as something similar to Ignorance.

  Recognize Intelligence to be one with *Jiva* and *Iswara*.
  Admit *Maya* is unborn, uncreated, endful*
  And distinct from being and non-being,
  And called also Ignorance or *Avidya*.   [co-adjutor.
  Intelligence is ordinarily not antagonistic to it and its
  The mental function is antagonistic to
  Ignorance, know this to be a fact.
  The reflex-intelligence, present in *Maya* together with it,
  Constitute the Omniscient (*Iswara*); Whom
  Know to be the Cause of the Universe.

That is to say, *Maya* is dependent on the pure Intelligence which is non-different with *Jiva* and *Iswara*. It is said to be uncreate, or unborn, because it is without a beginning. If it be admitted to be a created product, then that will imply a contradiction; for, before the evolution of this vast expanse it must necessarily be absent, and it cannot proceed from its product (the material world) as that will amount to a son begetting his father. *Maya* must necessarily be admitted to be derived from intelligence. In such a view both *Iswara* and *Jiva* are the results of *Maya*. Without the determination of *Maya*, (its actions) *Iswara* and *Jiva* cannot be established. Hence to say *Maya* is derived from the Intelligence of *Jiva* or that of *Iswara* is absurd and untenable. Moreover the pure intelligence is unassociated, actionless, and subject to no modification or change, therefore, to attribute illusion to be derived from it, will imply its being subject to change, which it is not; besides *Maya* will then be a co-adjutor of

---

  * Impermanent.

emancipation, and the several means cited in the *Shastras* by which emancipation is to be attained will be rendered futile.

These are the reasons why Illusion is called uncreated—without a beginning. 'Endful' implies subject to destruction by means of knowledge; and something distinct from 'being' and 'non-being' is what cannot be definitely classed under either heads of existence or its reverse. 'Being' is eternally existent, and can never be destroyed in the three divisions of time. Intelligence is of this nature. With knowledge is destroyed Illusion, hence it is said to be different from being; 'non-being' is its opposite condition and cannot be recognized any how in any time; like "rabbit's horns," "a sterile woman's son," and "ether flower," it is non-existent. Prior to knowledge (of *Brahma*) the presence of illusion and its action are recognized, so that when a person says in regard to the Cosmos 'I know it not,' 'I am ignorant of *Brahma*' it indicates the presence of illusion.* Then again, the

---

* Says '*Panchadasi*' in reference to *Maya*, Book II., v. 42 and 43. "*Maya* is defined as the inherent force residing in the PARABRAHMA, which is essentially existent and which cannot be differentiated. As the consuming flame of fire imparts an idea of its force, so the potentiality of force present in Self is plainly seen in the objective world. But this *Maya* cannot be said to be one with PARABRAHMA, nor as something distinct, in the same way as the consuming force of fire cannot be said to be the fire itself. Then again if you admit it as a separate entity you cannot by any means describe its separate or independent existence."

It will thus be evident that *Maya* and PARABRAHMA are but another name for Matter and Force. We all know Force cannot exist without Matter as a separate entity, yet to say, that it is the same as matter, is absurd. Hence we find in the text quoted, a non-dualist asking his opponent,—a *Madhyamik* Buddhist—to describe Force as a separate entity. But it may be urged that PARABRAHMA is force and we have seen *Maya* to be also a force; therefore we have force + force or force within force, something equally absurd. But such apparent ambiguity is far from real. For *Maya* is matter in its undifferentiated condition—a condition in which the difference between matter and its indwelling potentiality is minimised to the lowest numerical figure; it is the boundary line of Matter and Force,—where Matter losing its grossness assumes the subtlety of *super-etherial finis* where no Matter is distinguishable as such, but all

subjects of a dream are all produced from illusion which is their proximate cause. The presence of Ignorance in the state of

---

is Spirit or Force. And such an inference is derived from Nature. To quote a familiar illustration, the transition from a mineral to vegetable is so gradual, that it is impossible to distinguish the one from the other. Even at the present moment, science is undecided as to whether certain classes of the lowest vegetables belong to the mineral class, or the last in the scale of the animal series belongs to the vegetable. So much do they resemble each other. If such a view be accepted, the apparent inconsistency is removed : virtually then, the difference between *Mulaprakriti* (Matter in its undifferentiated cosmic condition) and *Purush* (its Spirit or PARABRAHMA) for all practical purposes is nil. * * * * Now *Maya* is described as a force and it is elsewhere defined as something indescribable which is neither existence (*Sat*) nor non-existence (*Asat*) in short it is one with Ignorance, which again, being the chief factor of the grand Cosmos, is the same as *Prakiriti* of Kapila. Therefore *Maya* is nothing less than matter. Now this *Maya* existed potentially in the PARABRAHMA, and if we say, that by an act of volition created He the objective world, we imply no such contradiction, as the Hebrew's account of God's creating the world out of nothing. But then, we may be asked, PARABRAHMA is an impersonality and volition is due to consciousness, which It can lay no claim to. To such of our task masters, we reply, that matter *per se* is unconscious and inert and can bring forth nothing until acted upon by an intelligent co-operation of a force and that the PARABRAHMA is consciousness itself, consequently the impress of change which It produces in the mass of inertia to make it evolve things varied and innumerable is tantamount to the volitional agency of a Personal Creator. Then again, if it be asked that since the PARABRAHMA is a pure Spirit, how can it have any connection with Matter which is Its antagonist ? We have seen that spirit and force are convertible terms, and we have likewise seen that force cannot exist without Matter, hence wherever there is force, there matter must always be ; to sum up then we find, that *Maya* existed in the PARABRAHMA, and it is the same *Maya* which brought forth the universe in a natural order of sequence by undergoing mutations impressed upon it, through its force or PARABRAHMA.—*N. D. Philosophic Inquirer*, Vol. vii. p. 73.

* * * * * * *

profound dreamless slumber is determined in the following manner :—
A man on waking from sleep, says "I was sleeping in peace, I knew nothing then." Now, such a recollection cannot proceed from a thing which one is totally ignorant of [but it implies the presence of a certain consciousness still left to enable him to be cognizant of the fact that he 'knew nothing.' Hence recognition of ignorance in profound slumber is easily established. This ignorance and illusion are identical with one another, and there is no difference between them. Thus the presence of *Maya* is established in the three conditions of time :—waking, dreaming, and profound slumber. Hence is it distinct from 'non-being.' Thus then, as *Maya* is neither 'being' nor 'non-being' its product is also similarly conditioned [for the qualities of a cause-body are transmitted to its products]. From a non-dualist's standpoint, what is neither existent nor non-existent is called unreal and indescribable. Therefore *Maya* and its product cannot establish duality; for that is only possible if, like intelligence, *Maya* and its product were possessed of the property of 'being'; but as they are distinct from 'being' and 'non-being,' that is to say, unreal, such unreality cannot create duality, as things seen in a dream are unreal and cannot produce duality. *Maya* is dependent on the pure Intelligence equally and without any distinction, present in a *Jiva* and *Iswara*, and enshrouds the pure *Brahma* as the darkness inside a room envelopes it. Now such a doctrine is called by the *Shastras* the supporting view of Self—the subject under consideration. Self refers to the pure *Brahma* as the receptacle. It likewise indicates its subject *Brahma* being enveloped in Illusion—*e. g.*, *Maya* envelopes *Brahma*.

The abridged description of *Sariraka Sutras*, *Vedanta Muktavali*, *Adwaita Siddhi*, *Adwaita Dipika*, and similar other works recognize Ignorance as the source* of covering which envelopes *Brahma*. While Vachaspati says "Ignorance is dependent on the *Jiva* for a dwelling, and makes *Brahma* its subject." When a person says "I am ignorant," "I know not *Brahma*." Here the first personal pronoun refers to the individual (*Jiva*), and in connection with the

---

* Source stands for *As'raya*.

subjective perception of ignorance, the expression establishes its source of dependence on him. "I know not *Brahma*" explains the subject of ignorance is *Brahma*. Thus we find, that in both the expressions Ignorance is dependent on the individual for a site or dwelling place. Ignorance makes its subject *Brahma*, that is to say, covers or envelopes It. But this ignorance is not one, but multiform and infinite. If ignorance be admitted to be one, then its destruction by one knowledge will preclude the possibility of its being recognized in others, as also its resulting product,—the objective world. If it be said, up to the present time, no one has acquired knowledge (of Self), so in the same way, it is not very probable that any one will have it in the future. So that, the usual means 'hearing,' 'consideration' and the rest are perfectly useless for the purpose. And as ignorance pervades universally in all beings, it is therefore infinite. But this universal pervasion of ignorance in all beings is a fancied conception. *Iswara* and *Brahmânda** are infinite. With knowledge, ignorance along with *Iswara* and *Brahmânda* are destroyed. And one who has not acquired knowledge is not freed, according to Vachaspati; but that is not true. For to say, that Iswara is a conception of ignorance in *Jiva* is directly antagonistic to what is taught in the *Sruti*, *Smriti* and the *Puranas*. *Iswara* is infinite, and the presence of distinction between one created being, and another is likewise antagonistic. Hence to look upon ignorance† as manifold is unsound, and its admission is untenable.

---

* *Brahmânda* is the egg of *Brahmâ*. He is one of the Hindu triad and different from *Brahma*. The first is masculine, the latter is neuter. It is impersonal.

† The author here adduces the distributive segregate of ignorance and not its collective totality. He rests his arguments mainly on the assumption, that if there are several ignorances present, there will be in company with each unit one *Iswara*, and one world, which is clearly not the case. But the collective totality is made of an infinite number of individual units of ignorance, hence, it can be said to be multiform, manifold, and infinite, but with the distinction mentioned.

Moreover in the admission of manifold ignorance, *Iswara* and creation are untenable. For *Jiva, Iswara,* and the universe are all conceived by ignorance, so that if ignorance be multiform—as many as there are *Jivas*—then with each individual unit of ignorance there must be present one *Iswara* and one world—that is to say, both *Iswara* and the universe will be as many as there are ignorances. For this reason, Vachaspati says "there are an infinite number of *Iswaras* and worlds." But the view which holds ignorance to be one is true, and *that* ignorance is not dependent on the *Jiva*, but on the Pure *Brahma*. Because the condition of *Jiva* is due to ignorance, and its separate existence* is quite unconceivable. It never exists as an independent entity, and from that independent ignorance, no *Jiva* can be produced. In the first place, therefore ignorance must be dependent on something else, and next its product will be the *Jiva*; like the *Jiva, Iswar's* condition is also a product of ignorance which depends on him for its site. But the collective totality of ignorance† is dependent on the Pure *Brahma*. The collective totality of intelligence—uncreate—and the uncreated ignorance have an interconnection with the material world which is also uncreate. From an interconnection of intelligence and ignorance, both *Iswara* and *Jiva* are uncreate; but they are dependent on ignorance, so that 'I am ignorant' is a product of ignorance.

In this way is set forth the dependence of ignorance on *Jiva*. But the collective totality of ignorance which is dependent on the Pure *Brahma* cannot be conceived by the individual to enable him to say "I am ignorant." Moreover *Jiva* is a product of ignorance, hence ignorance cannot be said to be dependent on the *Jiva* for its inherence or site. But the Pure *Brahma* is the *de facto* source on which ignorance is dependent for its site, and this dependent

---

* Matter *per se* cannot possibly be conceived apart from the objects which are found in the world. It existed in the beginning potentially in the PARABRAHMA, by combination they brought forth the evolution of the Cosmos.

† The collective totality of ignorance is without a beginning, it is uncreate.

ignorance enshrouds the *Brahma*. "I am ignorant" is a subsequent product and distinct from it. Thus is *Jiva* a vehicle of ignorance, and ignorance with its vehicle is subject of Self; and as that ignorance is one, it can be destroyed by knowledge. Now the intelligence of the internal organ has a modicum of ignorance, which is removed by knowledge. The internal organ is the seat of knowledge, and all knowledge must proceed from it, so that its knowledge destroys the particle of ignorance situated in it. When this follows in the case of a person, he is called freed. But if the case be otherwise, and no knowledge is produced in the mind, then the particle of ignorance remains in tact, consequently the individual continues to be a subject of bondage. In this manner 'bondage' and 'emancipation' are attributed by the supporters of ignorance.

Moreover, if after Vachaspati, any one will pin his faith with the doctrine of ignorance being many and not one; even that shall be conducive to the knowledge of non-duality, hence there is hardly any necessity for disputing or exposing its fallacies. Any how when an enquirer obtains an insight of non-duality, he should fix it in his mind or intellect.

Maya the vehicle of the Pure *Brahma* and dependent on It, is ignorance, or call it *Avidya* and *Ajnana*. It is called *Maya* (Illusion)—because it is possessed of numerous powers and is only affected by reflection and arguments—hence it is so named. It is destroyed by knowledge (*vidya* hence it is called (*avidya*) *A*-knowledge. It conceals the real nature, hence it is called (*ajnana*) ignorance. *That* intelligence which supports it is not antagonistic to it, but such ordinary intelligence is its supporter, and helps to manifest its presence; on the other hand, intelligence occupying the function of the internal organ or intelligence *plus* function are its antagonists. The first three lines of the verse give a description of the actuality of *Maya*. The fourth line defines the reflection in *Maya* and describes *Iswara*.

Maya abounding in pure goodness, and its occupying intelligence, these three, constitute *Iswara* who is omniscient, and source or cause of the universe.

There are two sorts of causes, one is called proximate, and the other instrumental or material. The first* is defined as that which enters into an effect and without which no effect is produced. As for instance, earth is the proximate cause of a jar; it enters every part of a jar, and without it no jar can be produced. What does not enter into the composition of a substance, but produces an effect situated apart from it, and whose destruction does not affect the effect, is called the instrumental or material cause. As for instance, in the case of the above jar, a potter's revolving wheel, and the turning stick are its instrumental cause. They do not enter into the composition of the jar, but produce it by remaining apart from it. Besides, the death of a potter and the destruction of the revolving wheel and the turning rod subsequent to the production of a jar, cannot affect it in any way. These are the two sorts of causes.

With regard to the world, *Iswara* is both its proximate and instrumental cause. As a spider is said to be a proximate and instrumental cause of its web, so is *Iswara* of the world. If it be alleged, this comparison is not an apt one, for in the case of the spider its insentient body is the proximate, and its intelligence, the instrumental cause of its web, hence one *Iswara* cannot stand for both causes; then the reply is:—like the spider, the insentient body of *Iswara* (*Maya*) is the proximate, and the intelligence present therein is the instrumental cause of the world. Thus is determined both a proximate and instrumental cause, so that the instance of the spider is not an inapt one. But the principal illustration is dream. When the actions of an individual produce no results it is destruction (*pralaya*). When they bring forth results, then creation begins. In this manner, the creation of an individual is dependent on the totality of his actions, good and bad (*karma*). Herein consists what is called the resemblance with a *Jiva*.

---

* *Upadana* means, cleaving to existing objects. At death, when the component units of the human body are dispersed, the actions of the individual—his *karma*—and *upadana* produce a new body in proportion to his merits and demerits.

Reflex intelligence present in ignorance abounding in impure goodness is the *Jiva*, who expects to enjoy the results of action.

Pure goodness is that which overpowers the two other qualities active and dark; but what is overpowered by them is called 'impure goodness.' The reflection of intelligence present along with ignorance abounding in impure goodness, ignorance, and its indwelling Uniform Intelligence—these three—constitute a *Jiva*. He is engaged in action and desires to be benefited by its results. With a view of enabling him to enjoy the fruits of his action in proportion to his merits and demerits, *Iswara* creates; hence *Iswara* cannot be said to be either partial or unkind. If it be alleged, that in the beginning no action was present so as to produce a high or low station in life for an individual, yet *Iswara* did place some in a position of felicity, and others in quite a low situation, to make them suffer, consequently he is partial. But that is not the case. For virtually the world is without a beginning, and the prior action of an individual subject him to a subsequent existence to enjoy or to suffer according to his merits and demerits. There is no first creation, and *Iswara* is therefore faultless.

> Prior to an individual, in proportion to his actions, good and bad, *Iswara* desires to create the world, for him to reap their fruits;
> Creates he accordingly the elements,—ether, air, fire, water and earth.
> Sound, touch, form, taste, and smell, (sing of) qualities.
> The particle of good quality with the five (elements) produces good,
> The particle of the active quality gives rise to *Prana*.
> Each element, with the good quality produces one sensory organ
> While the active, gives origin to the active organs.

When actions are different, to give adequate fruits thereof to individuals, then begins destruction (*pralaya*).—Then all objects in their subtle condition remain potentially in *Maya*, so that the unfinished actions of individuals also continue to exist, but in a subtle form, in the same *Maya*. When such actions are able to bear fruits then *Iswara* is actuated thereby with a desire to create; with this desire *Maya* is overpowered with an abundance of darkness, from which are produced the elements ether, air, fire, water, and earth; gradually they become possessed with the five properties sound, touch, form, taste, and smell.

Ether with its individual property sound, is produced from *Maya*; from the ether—air (air is an action of ether, hence sound is present in it along with its individual property of touch); from air—fire (fire is an active or resulting product of air, which being derived from ether has sound and touch, therefore they are present in fire also along with its individual property form); from fire—water (water contains the sound of ether, touch of air, form of fire, besides its own property of taste); from water—the earth, which has all the four above-mentioned properties, besides that of smell, which is its individual quality.

Sound is present in ether in the form of echo. Air has acquired from ether a whistling noise in it, while its touch is something quite distinct from heat and coldness; and darkness. The sound present in fire resembles that of crackling; its feel or touch is hot, and its form that of light or luminosity. The sound of water is a gurgling noise, its feel or touch is cool, form transparent, taste sweet; when water is brackish or unpleasant in taste, it is due to earth* present in it. Otherwise water is always sweet in taste and hence drunk by all. Its drink after taking things of pungent taste proves it to be sweet. The sound of earth is hard, it is a deal thud, its feel is also hard, its form is color, such as white, blue, yellow, green, etc. Its taste is either sweet, acid, pungent, bitter, astingent, or saltish and has both good and bad smell present in it.

Thus then we find ether has one, air two, fire three, water four, and earth five properties, of which each has an individual quality, while the rest are derived from their causes, therefore all the elements

---

* Modern chemistry traces various salts in water which produce a brackish taste, notably the Chlorides of Sodium, Calcium, Nitrate of Potass, Nitrate of Soda, etc. These are called earthy salts, so our author is not at all incorrect in what he says.

have them in common. *Iswara* is the primal Cause of all. Now both *Maya* and Intelligence are present in him, and as *Maya* is illusion it is false, while Intelligence is real. The first two lines of the verse indicate this.

From the good quality present in ether and the rest, is derived the internal organ. It is the source of knowledge, which has been shown to be a product of the same good quality also. Hence the mind or internal organ is a product of the good qualities present in the elements. Now these five elements have five organs of sense, which are called vehicles, hence the five elements combined with the quality of goodness are said to be the source of the internal organ. It is derived from two words, *Anta* signifying 'internal' and *'Karana'* a means of knowledge. Its combined signification is therefore, what is situated inside the body and which is a means for acquiring knowledge. Moreover, as it is a derivative product of the good quality of ether and the rest it is called *Satwavic, i.e.*, having goodness, or composed of goodness. Its modification or change is called function, which is four in number.

1. Function which determines an object as good or bad. It is called intellect (*Buddhi*).
2. Function marked by determination or its reverse is called mind.
3. Function of thinking is called intelligence (*Chit*).
4. The conceit of ' I am I' determines the function of Egoism (*Ahankara*).

From the particle of active quality (*Raja*) of the five elements, is produced the five vital airs, according to a difference in their site and function :—

1. *Prana.* The air situated in the heart and whose function is to produce hunger and thirst is called *Prana*.
2. *Apana.* The air situated in the anus and whose function is to produce the excrements urine and defæcation is *Apana*.
3. *Samana.* The air situtaed in the navel and which helps the digestion of food is called *Samana*.

4. *Udana.* The air situated in the throat and whose function is respiration is called *Udana.*

5. *Vyana.* The air present in all parts of the body with the power of affording life to the respective portions thereof is called *Vyana.**

Besides the above, some men say there are five more airs which they designate as follows.

(a). *Nág,* causing eructation,
(b). *Kurma,* causing the opening and shutting of the eyelids,
(c). *Krikara,* causing sneezing,
(d). *Devadatta* yawning, and
(e). *Dhananjaya* is the air which continues in the body after death.

Consecutive action in a serial order is explained as follows:— From each of the active qualities inherent in ether and the other elements has been produced the five vital airs *prana* and the rest, one after another as has just been explained. It is not a combined action of all the active qualities present in the elements. But according to the conclusions of the *Vedanta* (which admit it not) it is quintuplication. This is the opinion of Vidyaranya Swami. Sureswaracharya (one of the principal pupils of Shankaracharya) otherwise called Vartikakara, considers the subtle body and the five sheaths are quite unconnected with the five airs *Nag* etc. They do not form any part, or enter into the composition of the *Linga Sharira* or *Panchkosha.* Moreover, he says that the five vital airs *prana* and the rest are derived from the joint action of the active qualities of the elements, so that the doctrine of their separate

---

* The vital airs are respiration (*Prana*), inspiration (*Apana*), flatuousness (*Vyana*), expiration (*Udana*), and digestion (*Samana*). Respiration has an upward motion, and abides in the anus, etc. ; flatuousness moves in all directions, and pervades the whole body ; expiration belongs to the throat, has an upward course and is the ascending air ; digestion is the assimilation of solid and liquid food, on its reaching the stomach.— Jacob's *Hindu Pantheism,* p. 59.

production from each particle of the said quality present in each individual element is clearly unmaintainable. Then again to say, that the subtle body receives the other airs, *Nag, Kurma, Krikar, Devadatta* and *Dhananjaya* is equally untenable. The five vital airs are alone accepted by the subtle body. *Prana* resembles projection which is an attribute of the active quality, hence it is said to be a product of the joint action of the elements. This is meant by the third couplet.

From the good quality present in each of the five elements are derived the five organs of sense. From each particle of the active quality present in them is derived each of the active organs (*i. e.*, organs of action); from the etherial goodness—ears; aerial—the skin; igneous —eyes; aqueous—organ of taste (tongue); earthy—nose or organ of smell. These five organs are means of knowledge for which they are called sensory organs; knowledge is produced from the good quality, hence it is said to be derived from the good qualities of the elements. Ears receive sound, a property of ether, for which they are said to be derived from it. In the same way, each organ is said to be derived from each one element, whose properties are present in it. The organ of speech is derived from the active quality of ether, hands from the same source of air, feet from the active quality of fire, genitals from the active quality of water, while the same property of earth produces the anus; the 'genitals' mean the male and female sexual organs concerned in the enjoyment of felicity derived from coitus. 'Actions' include works. These 'five organs' of action are means for work, for which they are called 'active organs.' Actions arise from the active quality, hence they are said to be derived from the active quality present in the elements.

> Recognise the creative source of the 'subtle' in elementary non-quintuplication.
> From elementary quintuplication are produced all gross bodies.
> The cause, subtle, and gross bodies and the five sacs I know
> With discrimination distinct from the *Atma*. To know him to be one with them is delusion.

Here 'subtle' indicates the mind or internal organ, five vital airs, five organs of sense and the five organs of action; all these are the products of non-quintuplication of the elements. They cannot be known by the sensory organs. The seat of the eyes, nose, etc., is their subject, but the organs situated in those seats are not subject of either the individual or the organs themselves.

Subsequent to the evolution of the subtle [bodies], were the elements quintuplicated by the desire of Iswara, for the creation of the gross. Quintuplication is said to be of two sorts. It is in this wise.

(*a*) Divide each element into two equal parts, and subdivide each part into four [equal] parts, leaving the first half of each of the five elements undisturbed, and keeping separate the sub-division into four parts of each half. After omitting from the major half-part, each share of the individual element add this half, to each part of the elements.

(*b*) The second variety is formed in this way. First is a division of each element into five parts of which one part is made up of four, the other of one part; in this way, one is major and the other a lesser part. Now these major parts are to remain as they are, quite separate and undisturbed. The fifth lesser part is to be subdivided into five parts, and then by adding each of these with each major part of the other four elements, kept separate, and keeping one-fifth with its own major part.

In the first method, four parts of one part remain separate, with each half part is combined each element leaving its first half; but in the second, the smaller part of the fifth remains separate; and with the major fifth part is added each individual part of the elements. In the first quintuplication of the element, to each half of an element is added the half of another element, while in the second, with each twenty-one parts of an individual element is combined the four parts of another element. Therefore the second method is an easier one. Here each element is divided into twenty-five parts, of which twenty-one and four parts remain separate. Then they are added in the same proportion of twenty-one of one element with four of another, leaving its own twenty one apart. These then are the two modes of combination called quintuplication

(*Panchikarana*), which means the combination of five elements with each element. That one, which is subjected to, or produced from it is called quintuplicated (*panchkrita*).

The gross Brahmâ's egg—a subject of the senses—has been derived from quintuplication of the elements. In the Brahmâ's egg are included the several abodes designated Bhur, Bhuvar, Swar, Mahar, Janas, Tapas and Satya, one above the other. They are the higher abodes, while the nether ones placed one below the other are Atala, Sutala, Patala, Vitala, Rasatala, Talatala and Mahatala. These fourteen abodes with the requisite food-grains fit for their inhabitants—Deva, men, animal, etc.,—and their gross physical bodies have all been produced in that manner. Thus have I briefly described the creation of the cosmos. A full description of *Maya* with its resulting product is not even possible with the lifetime of a crore of Brahmâs. This is the dictum of Valmika and Vashishta in all their writings on history. The meaning of the two couplets is thus explained. The third signifies the production of three sorts of bodies and the five sheaths from an action of *Maya*.

Maya in combination with its purely good quality constitutes the cause-body of *Iswara*; while in combination with the impure good quality of ignorance the cause-body of *Jiva* is the product. The gross body is a subsequent result of the subtle body which again owes its origin to the five subtle elements. The subtle astral body is derived from the mind, intellect, thought, egoism, five vital airs five sensory and five active organs. (The collective totality of individual subtle bodies constitute *Iswar's* subtle body known as *Hiranyagarbha*.) *Brahmâ's* egg in its entire grossness constitutes *Iswar's* gross physical body called *Virat*. Now the physical (gross) body of a *Jiva* is too well known [to need any mention]. From these three sources are derived the five sheaths or sacs.

The cause-body is called the blissful sheath (*Ananda-Maya-Kosha*) the cognitional (*Vijnanmaya*), mental (*Manomaya*) and vital (*Pranomaya*) are determined in the subtle body:—The five sensory organs with (*budhi*) intellect—a function of the internal organ—characterised by certitude form the cognitional sac or sheath (*Vinjnanmayakosha*). The five sensory organs with the function of the internal organ represent the mental sheath. The five vital airs with the five active organs indicate the vital sheath. The gross body is called the foodful sheath. Thus then we find that the five sacs are present in the three bodies called cause, astral, and physical [gross]. Now in *Iswar's* bodies are present Iswar's sheaths while a *Jiva's* sheaths are present in his. The meaning of *kosha* is sheath. Because they cover the *Atma* like a sheath, hence the foodful and the rest are called sheaths (or sacs).

Ignorant and unspiritually inclined persons, many in number, mistake their Self with some one of these sheaths, from which they are entirely different, and are debarred from cognizing Him who is the chief witness. Hence the foodful and the rest are said to cover the *Atma*. There are others equally dull in intellect, who after the manner of the *Virochanas* say the gross body—a receptacle of food— is Self; and base their assumption on the ground that "Self is perceived in the intellect as the particle of individuality or egoism represented by the first personal pronoun 'I' and this is clearly the case with the gross body. For, an individual is apt to say 'I am a man.' 'I am a Brahmana.' Such an experience is universal; and the necessary conditions of a human creature, or that of a Brahmana, are present in the gross body; consequently as the gross body is the seat of individuality and perceived so by the intellect it is Self; or Self is that which is a chief object of love. And as a son, wealth, animals, tend to the comfort of the gross-physical body they are objects of love; objects which are not conducive of comfort to that body are not loved. Love for another object is centred in the gross body, hence it is the *Atma*. It derives pleasure from the enjoyment of food and clothing of various sorts." Such is the doctrine of *Asur Swami Virochana.*

---

* A *Charvaka* calls the physical body, derived from the four elements — fire, water, air, and earth his self, and argues thus: the subject of the perception of Egoism is self, "I am a man." "I am fat." "I am lean." "I am a Brahmana," etc. Here the physical body is perceived as the subject of Egoism, and is accordingly taken for a man, or his qualities of corpulence and of Brahman etc. Hence the body is self, or what is the

Then there are others who say the gross body is not Self; but that something whose presence in the physical body constitutes subject of supreme affection is self. In this way as a wife, son and the rest are conducive to the well-being of the body, and it is the seat of the highest affection, consequently the subject of the indications of that extreme love—the body—is self, and the highest aim of humanity consists in feeding that with good things and clothing it with good dress, jewels, etc., and death is emancipation. Now this requires no other proof than what actually follows in every individual and is plainly seen; look for instance at the appearance of a prince with all gold and jewels over, an appearance expressing supreme indications of affection for that body, the care bestowed on its feed and dress, providing all comforts for it, and contrast it with the care-worn and pinched countenance of a raggamuffin,— yet even here, you will find him struggling all day long, for the maintenance of the body which he regards with affection and care. All these are proofs enough and as they are everywhere visible, there can be no contention against their cogency.

But this doctrine of *Charvakas* is clearly untenable. For if the subject of perception of Egoism ('I') would constitute self, in that case, the organs of sense and action would be so; inasmuch as they are also perceived in the same way, as in the expressions "I see." "I hear." "I speak." Thus then the organs are also perceived as the subject of Egoism. Then again, in regard to an individual's affection for his body, it cannot be a subject of Egoism, consequently it is a misapplication, therefore the physical body is not self. Moreover, wealth and riches, wife and son, as they shew good deal of affection for that body, evince a similar feeling for the organs too, consequently in the absence of the highest amount of affection, the gross body is not a subject of supreme affection, and therefore it is not self. Further, as the body is wanting in sentiency or intelligence, it is not self, and if a *Charvaka* were to say, just as a mixture of quicklime with catechu and betel leaf produces the well-known red color, so the body for its being a mixture of the four elements, derives its power of knowledge. But this is clearly impossible, for if a blending of the elements were to produce sentiency, knowledge or intelligence, we may as well expect a 'jar,' which is derived from a blending of the same four elements to possess sentiency or knowledge, but that it has not; besides, in conditions of profound sleep, fainting, and death, the body is as insentient

vitality and with whose departure death follows, and which is quite distinct from it is the *Atma*. Life and death are dependent on the

as a jar consequently insentiency is its normal condition and hence it is not self.

If the physical body were identical with self we would never have fixed our belief in the identity of the body of our manhood, with that of our youth, though they are different from each other; and when a person who had seen us in our boyhood comes to see after an absence of several years, when we have attained manhood, he for the sake of recognition recalls to our memory a few leading incidents of the past, and we exclaim " Indeed that am I." As this is a common incident, therefore the body is not self. Further, since the body is subject to birth and death, prior to its being born or subsequent to death, it is non-existent, consequently self who is eternal cannot be same with it. Because that will imply the acknowledgment of two defects—of destruction of actions done, and the fruition of actions not done, after death; both of them are inapplicable. That is to say, if the actions performed in life, were to produce no result, in the absence of self who is no agent and instrument, a person would then cease to practise works enjoined in the Vedas, and we see the contrary to be fact. Then again, for the existing difference of self of boyhood with that of prime, when a person has read the Vedas in his youth and boyhood, should enjoy no fruits subsequent to that period either in prime or old age; similarly all works done in the present life should yield him no results, thus the admission of destruction of works done already and their unproductiveness is injurious, and in a previous birth from an absence of a do-er or agent no actions could be done, so that in the present life whatever a person has to enjoy or suffer should be equally the case with all, and there shall be no cause of the prevailing difference as to happiness or woe in its various shades, as we actually find to be the case,—one is happy, a second miserable, a third beset with difficulties,—so that, it is impossible to acknowledge the fruition of actions not done, and along with it, the assumption of the body being self.

Now according to *Charvakas* the chief or ulterior aim of humanity consists in eating, dressing, &c., but it is not so, because a desire for a thing constitutes an ulterior aim or supreme purport, and as every one is desirous of acquiring happiness and removing misery, necessarily that desire is the supreme purport of humanity, and the highest of that felicity

organs, so long as they remain in the body, life continues, in their absence vitality cannot continue. And because of the experience "I see," "I hear," "I speak." Thus then, as the organs determine the presence of individuality, they are no other but Self.*

---

and extreme destruction of misery is called 'emancipation' in the *Sidhanta*. But enjoyment cannot be ranked with this ulterior aim, for it is apt to take an extreme turn, and there is no limit for it; neither can death be taken in the light of emancipation.—Dhole's *Panchadasi*, p. 78.

* That is to say, Intelligence being the indication or sign of self, the organs as they shew signs of intelligence can justly be regarded as self. This is what another *Charvaka* says, but it is fallacious, because self is that without which the body cannot last; in the case of the organs of sense and action, we find a person may be blind or deaf yet living; he may be paralysed, his hands and feet deprived of action and progression, he may be dumb, yet living, consequently self is something distinct from the sensory and active organs. They cite in support, the expressions "I hear," "I see," "I am blind," &c. But it is to be remembered, the first person used in connection with that hearing, sight, &c., establishes the possession of the necessary organs with which the several functions are carried on, consequently when it is said "I hear," &c., it means "I have ears to hear," or "I see with my eyes" and not "I am the eye," "I am the ear." Thus then, the perception of (subject of Egoism) 'I' in connection with the organs of sense is quite distinct from them; then again, if their identity be sought to be proved by similar other expressions as "My sight is indifferent," "My hearing is acute" by shewing an attachment of sight, &c., with own self, it is simply a misapplication, for the cogniser is different from cognition, and self being the cogniser, is different from sight, hearing, &c. Moreover in mental abstraction, or absence of mind a person, sees not, neither does he hear, though his sight and hearing are perfect; therefore we may lay down the insentiency of sensory organs, and what is insentient cannot be similar to self. In connection with it, in a dead body the organs of sense and action are all present, yet they are insentient.

Further it may be enquired whether one organ is self, or whether their collective totality is so, or they are so many different selves. The first is quite untenable, for if it be said that a single organ is self, a person should die or be insentient when that is wanting; yet the fact is otherwise; similarly if the collective aggregate of organs be regarded in that light,

A worshipper of *Hiranyagarbha* says that his *Prana* (vital air) is his self. Because in the last moments, when a man is in a death-swoon, his son and relations notice the presence of the respiration; so long as it lasts they take him to be alive, when it ceases, he is dead. Or, because in the absence of sight, or hearing, a man is said to be either blind or deaf, or dumb when he cannot speak, and without the presence of the functions of the several sensory organs, the body continues, but when there is no *Prana* present, life ceases and the body falls.

Then again the expressions "I see," "I hear," establish Self to be distinct and separate from the sensory organs, inasmuch as Self can only be determined one with them if the above expressions will explain "Like the eyes I see," "Like the ears I hear," but that is not so; on the other hand, the meaning which they seek to explain is that with eyes I see, with ears I hear. Hence Self is distinct from the organs of sense, sight, hearing, touch and the rest. Moreover, in profound dreamless slumber, though the function of the senses is absent, but as respiration continues, vitality is present for all practical purposes, so that life and death are quite independent of the senses. It is perfectly clear that so long as respiration goes on life continues; with its separation from the physical body, death follows. Hence life and death are dependent on respiration and that is the *Atma*.*

---

then in the destruction of one single organ, all the rest should equally be destroyed, and there should be neither life nor intelligence; moreover if each of them were so many different selves, then like ten elephants tied to one tree breaking it asunder, the body will be similarly affected by desires originating with each of these selves.—*Ibid.*

* But *Prana* is not self. Because like the absence of motion in the external air, when there is no respiration going on, death does not follow, we find plants do not respire like ourselves, yet they continue to grow, and preserve their vitality; in regard to animated beings, it cannot be said that respiration goes on during or after death, yet there are instances when it is suspended and vitality is seen to continue; moreover in sleep, *Prana* is awake, yet if it were intelligence or self, it should show the usual civilities to a new comer related to a person, when he arrives at his house

Others there are who say, like a jar, respiration* is insentient hence not Self. Bondage and release are dependent on the Mind. Its attachment to material comforts is the source of bondage, while that opposite condition, when the mind is freed from any desire or hankering after wealth, is said to be the cause of release.

---

while sleeping, that it does not, nor does it prevent a thief when he robs him in sleep; hence it is not self, but insentient and unconscious. It is contended by the supporters of *Prana*, that with its exit, death follows, therefore it is self. But this does not hold true. Because with the departure [cessation of the secretion] of gastric juice, a man loses his appetite, wastes and dies, and we may as well call it self. Moreover the superiority of *Prana* mentioned in the Veda is only with a view of producing an inclination in one engaged in devotional exercises. If it be said, there are *Sruti* texts which clearly denote *Prana* to be self, but inasmuch as similar texts are also found in connection with the mental sac, consequently one is contradicted by the other, hence it is not meant so; but it serves to establish the non-difference of the abiding intelligence seated in them, with Brahma.—*Ibid.*

* *Prâna* includes inspiration, expiration, &c., hence it is equivalent to respiration, therefore it need not create any misapprehension. But there are others notably in the ranks of the 'Theosophists' who mistake it with electricity, vital magnetism, and what not. Mr. Sinnett in his *Esoteric Buddhism*, p. 27, says concerning it :—" Vitality thus consists of Matter in its aspect as force, and its affinity for the grosser state of matter is so great that it cannot be separated from any given particle or mass of this except by instantaneous translation to some other particle or mass. When a man's body dies, by desertion of the higher principles which have rendered it a living reality, the second or life principle, [*Prana*], no longer a unity itself, is nevertheless inherent still in the particles of the body as this decomposes, attaching itself to other organisms to which that very process of decomposition gives rise. Bury the body in the earth and its *Jiva* will attach itself to the vegetables which springs above, or the lower animal forms which evolve from its substance. Bury the body and indestructible *Jiva* flies back none the less instantaneously to the body of the planet itself from which it was originally borrowed, entering into some new combination as its affinities may determine." How far this is correct it is for the reader to judge.

And in relation with the mind, the senses are the source of knowledge [perception]. The senses alone without such relation can produce no knowledge, hence for all practical purposes mind is the chief source, and that is the *Atma*. According to a *Kshanika Vijnanavadi Boudha*, the action of the mind is dependent on (*Buddhi*) the Intellect, for mind is a transformation of Intellect, hence this *Buddhi* whose intelligence or consciousness is transitory, is the *Atma* and not mind. What they mean by it is this, all objects are merely forms of consciousness, which has the property of manifestibility; but this consciousness springs up and disappears every moment. A subsequent consciousness, intelligence or perception, arises just in the same way as a prior one; but with the appearance of the latter, the former disappears. In the same way, with the appearance of a third perception, the second disappears, and when a fourth one succeeds, the third has already ceased. Thus then a current of perception resembles the current of a river. Now such a current of perception is twofold; of which one is 'habitual' or 'fixed' and the other 'continuous.' The consciousness of Egoism 'I am I' is called a 'fixed current' of knowledge and Intellect; while the 'continuous' variety is illustrated by the example "This jar," "This body," etc. From the current of fixed consciousness arises the current of continuous consciousness, which latter is present in the mind too. Since therefore, the fixed current of consciousness is due to the action of Intellect, such intellect is said to be no other than Self. These *Buddhists* consider emancipation to be obstruction, or more properly, destruction of the 'continuous current' which is subject to 'fixed current' of consciousness [by knowledge] and the permanance or continuance of the current of a particular transient perception or knowledge. In this manner, a *Vijnanavadi* thinking Intellect to be transient and self-illuminated, says it is his Self.

A *Bhatta** says, Self is unlike the transient flash of lightning but is fixed or constant, insentient and intelligent. Now the

---

Bhattas are followers of Kumarila Bhatta of the Mimânsaka who preceded Sankaracharya by a century.

purport is this—a man on waking from profound slumber says "I was sleeping insensibly" such an expression signifies Self [indicated by the first personal pronoun] to be insentient, and he remembers it when he is awaken; remembrance of an unknown thing never takes place. In the state of profound slumber there are no other means [of knowledge] apart from Self, hence the source of recollection in that state is knowledge, which is nothing else but Self. Therefore like the glowworm, Self is both manifested, and its reverse; manifested because he is like knowledge, and unmanifested because insentient. Now the 'blissful sheath' is in this dual condition of manifestibility and unmanifestibility, because the reflex-intelligence present along with ignorance in the condition of profound dreamless slumber is called the 'blissful sheath.' Here the reflection of intelligence has the powers of manifesting, while ignorance has it not, hence according to a *Bhatta* (and a *Pracakar* too) the 'blissful sheath' is his Self.

A *Sunya-Vadi Buddhist* says Self is not composed of parts, hence one Self cannot be said to be both manifested and unmanifested. As a glowworm has the power of luminosity in its tail which gives light, while its body is not so conditioned, but is dark, hence two opposite qualities are present in two portions of its body, and that need not imply any contradiction: but with Self it is otherwise, for he is devoid of parts, hence the same Self cannot be the possessor of two such opposite qualities like the glowworm, as that of discovering and non-discovering, light and darkness, or illuminating and unilluminating, and such an admission will make him a composite body—a body composed of parts. Now a composite body (as for instance, a jar etc.) is a derivative product and therefore liable to birth and death : so must equally be the case with him too. Moreover, a derivative product must necessarily have no existence prior to its birth and subsequent to death. It is therefore "*asat*" essentially non-existent. Because a body that was non-existent in the beginning (prior to its birth) and will be so after death, cannot be essentially existent in the intervening space, during the time it lasts, but on the other hand, is non-existent even then. And such being the condition of *Atma* [from the present stand point]. He is essentially non-existent. Thus then we find all substances (though different from Self) are subject to birth and destruction equally with him, and they are all of them in their collective totality essentially non-existent (*Asat*). Self and not-Self are, equally characterised by that one condition of non-existence, so that 'nothing' is the highest principle. The doctrine of the *Madhyamik Buddhists*, who for their doctrine of nothing are called Atheists, explains the 'blissful sheath' to be a form of ignorance, because ignorance is determined in that way. Those who are ignorant of the teachings of the *Shastras* which deal on non-duality, take the world, which is merely a modification of ignorance for a reality; while they that are learned in the *Shastras*, consider it to be unreal for it is a derivative product of ignorance, which is different from 'being' and 'non-being' and something indescribable. The wise and those delivered in life, look upon ignorance with its product, as something worthless and un-desirable. Now the words 'un-desirable' 'non-being' and 'nothing' are synonymous. Thus then what is not desired by one delivered in life—ignorance—is an object of fond attachment with a believer of 'nothing' and eagerly sought after, because he is ignorant of the chief purport of life (Self-knowledge), and believes the un-desirable 'blissful sheath' to be his Self.

A *Pravakar* and a *Naiyayika* assert that Self does not resemble 'nothing.' For if a believer of 'nothing' were asked whether he has an experience of nothing or not; and he says no, then that will establish the absence of 'nothing'; but if he says yes, then what is different from his 'nothing' is Self. This is established from his admission of experiencing 'nothing.' Thus Self is determined something distinct from 'nothing,' and cognizable only by the help of the mind, and for this quality of knowledge in him, Self is called by the name of intelligence; naturally Self is insentient, so that the properties, happiness and misery, desire and spite, effort, virtue and vice, etc., are the subjects of Self. According to them the 'blissful sheath' is the *Atma*, and the intellect present in the cognitional sheath is his quality of knowledge. For the intelligence present in the 'blissful sheath' is masked and unperceived by an indiscriminate person. A *Pravakar* or *Naiyayika* considering the *Atma* to be devoid of intelligence in profound dreamless slumber, conclude him to be naturally insentient. Hence the 'blissful sheath' with its masked perception is his Self. Moreover a person does not recognise himself to be eternal intelligence, but on the contrary thinks his intelligence to be transient, which again establishes only the function of the internal organ (*Buddhi*) Intellect. For these reasons a *Pravakara* and *Naiyayika* look upon the 'blissful sheath' as their *Atma* having Intellect for his quality. But this doctrine is not true. For things that are different from Self, (a jar, a cloth, etc.,) are non-eternal, and this difference is marked by the presence or absence of intelligence. Self is intelligence, while a jar, a cloth, etc., are insentient. So that, if Self were devoid of intelligence (*e. g.* insentient) then like a jar, he will be reduced to impermanence and that will render release a futile effort.

In this way, persons unacquainted with the drift of the *Vedantic* utterances mistake Self with some one of the five sacs or sheaths, or their component units, and remain ignorant of his real nature which is that of witness and all-blissfulness; and because such ignorance is brought on by the sheath-like coverings that envelope the *Atma* in a sac, or cover him as a sword is confined in its scabbard. These coverings or sacs are designated sheaths. And as these five sheaths hide the real nature of the individual *viz.*, that of a witness, so do the collective aggregate of *Iswara's* five sheaths cover his real nature, in as much as the indication of the word (*Tat*) 'That' expressive of his real nature, is abandoned by some, while its apparent signification, expressing the internal knower as a predicate of the 'blissful sheath' formed of *Maya*, is looked upon by them as a Supreme Principle or entity; and they are deluded in believing *Hiranyagarbha*, *Vishnu*, *Brahma*, *Ganesa*, *Siva*, *Devi*, *Sun*, etc., as also the Ficus Religiosa, Asclipia Gigantia, Bamboo and an infinite variety of substances to be the Supreme Self. As a fact, He is universally present; and the indication of all objects referring to Him in that way, can be presumed to bear no distinction between the objects and *Parmatma*; yet to connect Him with the respective associates of the objects named above, or of other substances is a delusion. Thus these men are precluded from knowing His true nature covered by the respective sheaths of the *Jiva* and *Iswara*, and mistaking Self with the physical body etc., are engaged in works good and bad, and in the worship of all objects from the internal knower to a bamboo, only that they may enjoy happiness. But the result must be in proportion to the merit of the object worshipped, for in the *Iswara's* body are included the cause, subtle, and gross bodies, so that, according to the nature of the body worshipped, the result must follow. But emancipation can never be acquired without knowledge of *Brahma*; where there is a desire of release, an individual by his discrimination, differentiates *Iswara* from the five sheaths.

For example. As the tender and new fibres of the plant Saccharum Munja are separated from the firmer coat of its old fibres, so does a person by his discrimination, distinguishes or separates the real nature of *Iswara* from the five sheaths. This then is the meaning of the verses.

Now the nature of that discrimination is shewn :—

Cognition of the physical body is absent in a dream, when only Self is known.

Knowledge of the subtle body is absent in profound slumber, when is derived a knowledge of his blis-fulness.

In meditation is manifested Self deprived of his 'envelopment,' when the ignorance of the cause-body is absent.

In the dreaming state, no knowledge of the physical body is present, but there is Self-knowledge; in the same way knowledge of the subtle body is absent in profound slumber; but as Self is blissfulness, and self-illuminated, conception of happiness is always present. If it were otherwise, then a person on waking would never have said "I was sleeping happily" which is a conception due to an act of memory, from the actual perception or knowledge of felicity. Thus, then, in the condition of profound slumber there is present felicity, which is easily known; but as that felicity is not subject to material well-being, but something quite distinct, therefore Self is said to be self-illuminated; and for that property, consciousness of felicity takes place. Now this felicity is in the nature of Self, hence its cognition only explains the presence of *Atma*, who is rendered tangible in that condition of profound slumber. During 'meditation without recognition of subject and object'* a result of (*Vididhyasana*) profound contemplation, the *Atma* is discovered, denuded of his envelopment of ignorance, while the ignorance of the cause-body disappears. Such is the way in which the three bodies stand in the path of cognizing Self and ascertaining his true nature. Self is never absent from one, to manifest himself in a second condition, but is equally present in all the conditions of waking, dreaming and profound slumber, for which, he is said to be all-pervading; and discrimination can determine him to be quite distinct from the gross physical body, which is the same as the food-full sheath; the cause body which is no other but the blissful sheath; and the subtle-body which constitutes the vital, mental and cognitional sheaths; so that from a proper discrimination of these three bodies, the five sheaths are recognized in their true bearings. As the real nature of the individual is distinct from his five sheaths, so is *Iswara's*, from their collective aggregate constituting his five sheaths. And as the indication of *Jiva* and *Iswara* had been fully entered into, and illustrated (by the example of varieties of ether in the fourth section,) and as the subsequent chapter will deal with an explanation of the transcendental phrase, for ascertaining the true knowledge of Self and helping his cognition, hence in this place I have only briefly described 'descrimination of Self.'

Thus 'discrimination of Self' as an entity distinct from the five sheaths, cannot be called a process of repetition or the re-doing of what has already been done, because to ascertain the oneness of the individual spirit with the Absolute, and to rest such knowledge on a firm and sure footing, it is proper for a person to consider and reflect, weigh, and analyze all arguments and reasons adduced in support of non-duality. But the necessity of the process of repetition, which is only another name for want of what is proper to be done, is established by the precepts on the transcendental phrase:—

---

* It is the resting of the Impartite mental function on the Reality *Brahma* without a second, and becoming one with It, by the destruction of the three integral constituents of the Conscious Ego.

Self is distinct from the five sheaths ; by knowing this 'good' I know the nature of *Brahma*.

And to know It distinct, and separate from him is only a mine* of delusion.

And as a sovereign reduced to beggary (in dream) cannot be affected in purse, so the presence of the false delusion cannot affect It in any way.

And the attribution of agent or instrument to one, who is actionless, destroys not his condition of secondlessness.

Oh Pupil ! By knowing Self distinct and separate from the five sheaths, know *Brahma* to be one with him. This is called good (knowledge); but then on this subject doubts may arise that Self is an agent or instrument of virtue and vice ; and that he is subjected after death to enjoy happiness in heaven or suffer misery in hell ; so that he cannot be one with *Brahma*. But they are easily removed in the following manner. The next three lines of the above verse refer to those who regard Self and *Brahma* as twain. Now those who have seen this duality concerning *Brahma* and Self, and have heard so from the *Shastras*, have been led into it by the mistake of heaven and hell, virtue and vice, which is the cause of this perfectly false delusion ; admit it as correct. Moreover a false thing cannot affect possession. As a king reduced to begging (in dream) cannot be said to lose all his wealth, and be a poor man ; or as the false waters of a mirage cannot affect the earth, (moisten it) or as a false snake created in a rope cannot be said to have any poison, so to consider Self or *Brahma* an agent or instrument is perfectly false. Now an agent is one who does a good or bad action ; but Self is actionless, hence he cannot be said to be an agent or instrument, but is without a rival and secondless. That is to say, your Self is one with *Brahma*, and neither separate nor distinct from It ; and to consider him identical with the gross and subtle body, and its good and bad actions, together with their productive results, birth and

---

* 'Kupa' is a well, it may refer to a mine, but here the word used is more appropriate hence allowed to stand instead of well.

death, heaven and hell, are creations of imagination derived from ignorance and they cannot in any way affect your Self. Hence even prior to knowledge, Self is one with *Brahma*; and in the three conditions named Its subject—the body—together with its properties has no relation with It, but Self is eternal, and always free, and there is no difference whatever between him and *Brahma.*

If it be said, Self is eternal and always free like *Brahma.*
Then the necessity for 'hearing' (which is a means of knowledge) will cease.

Now this is cleared :—

Like an ether-flower, this vast expanse and its agent *Iswara*, there are none.

The subjects of witness, and witness, as also a discoverer, and objects of discovery, there are none.

If subject to bondage, then only can emancipation follow ; if there be ignorance, it can be destroyed by knowledge.

And knowing this, leaves of the practice of what is proper; then by becoming firm, attains emancipation.

The meaning is cleared by the commentator in the following words :—

In the sight of one who is 'liberated in life' [wise] ignorance and its product [the material world] are undesirable, and the description of such a person is here given. Pupil, know you then, that like an ether-flower, this material world is really non-existent, consequently it can have no agent—*Iswara.*—[that is to say, when there is no world existing, it can have no creator.] The subjects of a witness ignorance etc., are called *Sachhya*, both of them are wanting ; in the same way, there is neither a discoverer, nor the things that are to be discovered. Therefore in the absence of a body, a jar, a cloth etc., there can be no discoverer. If the inherent Uniform Intelligence be reckoned as a witness, it is impossible not to admit its presence ; but the ordinary acceptation of witness, and in regard to the discovering of all visible objects by an observer, the absence of the first as well as the last, is what is meant here. In the same way 'bondage' is not admitted; hence there is no knowledge required, for this can only be necessary to cause the destruction of ignorance which is the source of bondage; there is no ignorance, consequently knowledge to destroy it, is also wanting. To know this will cause the abandonment of what is proper to be done; for, either the present or the next life, is equally undesirable and proper works are not required for them. Then again, Self is not subject to bondage, so that for emancipation, there is no occasion for doing the proper things. In this way, knowing him to be eternal, free, and *Brahma*, when what is proper has been abandoned, then that individual after the separation of life from his body, attains to *Brahma*, which is actionless. [In other words, as one already freed—freed]. Its purport is:—even if prior to knowledge of Self, He is eternal and free, and one with *Brahma*, yet a person from mistake considers him to be an agent and instrument, and seeks to acquire happiness and destroy misery by having recourse to several means, which in their turn subject him to great inconvenience and pain. If he gets a good teacher, to instruct him into the *Vedantic* utterances, he comes to know then, that his Self is neither an agent nor instrument, but *Brahma*, consequently his Self has nothing proper to do. Such a knowledge is a result of 'hearing' the precepts of the *Vedanta*. Because *Brahma* is none other but Self, hence he is every day acquired.

> He who admits the necessity of doing what is proper is ignorant.
>
> He is a wise man, who has no need for any thing else.

[The meaning is already clearly set forth to require the use of any explanation]. It implies that an ignorant person is always engaged in doing works that are proper, but a wise person stands aloof from them. He has no need of anything.

> There is one Impartite, unrelated,* unborn, formless, unseen and nameless.
>
> It is neither Primordial Ignorance, neither the collective, nor distributive aggregate of gross and subtle bodies

---

* The word '*asanga*' is unconditioned, unassociated, and unrelated.

Neither *Virat*, *Prajna*, *Taijasa*, nor *Viswa*; not a doer neither bound nor free.

The apparent tangibility of the objective world in 'waking state' is a work of *Buddhi*.

The enjoyment of all that is to be enjoyed in dream is its exquisite play too.

What merges in the state of profound slumber; know that to be one with the Real.

The desires created by *Buddhi* are surely the objects discovered by It.

What is called knowledge bright, and *Tama* dark, completely destroyed,

Always unconditioned and one with Self, *Brahma* is Self-illuminated.

To him nothing follows who wishes for enjoying his desires.

He seeks not to destroy them; but a wise person has no such expectation.

Seeing, he hears not; hearing, he sees not; takes all [things at their real worth] but has taste for none.

Touches not even nectar when offered, nor quarrels with any.

Accepts not what is given, abandons what he gets; moves not a step, nor exerts himself.

[The purport is thus explained].

The organs do their respective work, my-Self is not related to them.

Self is different from them, they do form no part of myself. Self is the inherent, uniform, unassociated, [Intelligence].

I abandon enjoyment of material comforts; the senses stand in the same relation to myself, as a cloth scented with camphor.

I know this for certain,—he is neither an agent nor a part.

Oh, ye lover of a body! In this manner, though a professor instructs his pupils on the hidden entity, principle, or essence, yet he is not extremely delighted, and concieves not the Supreme felicity; his teacher finds that the pupil has been unsuccessful, so he offers him further instruction in a grosser way, to enable him to think on (*laya*) destruction.

> As a 'jar' produced from earth, has that earth in all its external parts.
> As a wave, a bubble, froth etc., are all parts of the water that produces them.
> So determine the connection between a cause and its action.
> The cause is present in all its products and is non-different from them.

That is to say, as a thing made of clay, has all its parts, both in and out, made of it, so that, all things produced from earth are earthy, and a froth, bubble etc., represent the water of which they are mere parts (composite); so the cause of an action is non-different from it, and they are one. In the same way, the cause of this vast expanse being *Iswara*, he is non-different from his works and " I am that *Iswara*." In this manner, pupil you should know what destruction [of difference] is and continue to think on it.

Now this 'destruction' is being briefly declared. That is to say, the gross *Brahma's* egg is a product of elementary quintuplication and its earth and water produce actions similarly earthy and aqueous, and a product of one element shews a striking similarity to that element only, so that all this material universe resembles the quintuplicated elements from which they are derived. Then again, as the quintuplicated elements are simply products of non-quintuplicated [subtle] elements, they are non-distinct from one another, but shew the same similarity, identity [or affinity]. Carrying this analysis a step further, we find that the subtle bodies derived from the subtle elements without the fractional combination,—as for instance the internal organ etc.,—must naturally have a resemblance, the product with its cause; and as that internal organ is derived from the good quality of the elements—ether etc.,—it must naturally have a close resemblance with that good quality. Similarly, the products derived from the active quality of the elements (for instance *Prana* and the other airs) must resemble that active quality; and the derivative product of the active quality of earth—the anus—must resemble it in every way, as the organ of smell a product of the good quality of that same element must resemble it. In the same way, the tongue and genitals are like the good and active qualities of water; the eyes and feet, resemble the good and active qualities of heat; skin and the hands—the good and active qualities of air; organ of hearing and speech,—the good and active qualities of ether. Thus, then, the whole of the subtle creation resembles the subtle elements from which they are each derived. While thinking in this way one must reflect on the destruction of these non-quintuplicated elements, in a reversed order of progression.

That is to say, water is the source of earth, hence earth is nothing but water; for its being a product of heat, water and heat are equal; heat is a product of air, hence resembles it, and air a result of ether, is naturally identical with it. Matter abounding in darkness is the cause from which is derived ether, and ether and matter resemble one another. Then again, as matter is only another form of *Maya*, they are naturally identical. The principal names of the same substance are Matter, Illusion, Ignorance, and *A*-knowledge. Here the word 'principal' bears the signification of a substance that absorbs all actions within it, and fixes their destruction like an ascetic. Matter is the name of that entity, which abounds in darkness, and is fit for being used for the purposes of creation. As rare things are produced by magic without the actual products of a country, and reference to consideration of time (here magic is called *Maya* or illusion), so in the secondless, unconditioned, *Brahma*, the presence of desire etc., is rare, and it causes creation [or more properly evolution by impressing change in their attributes of matter, and disturbing its equilibrium], hence it is called *Maya* (illusion); and because it conceals the real nature, it is therefore Ignorance; and because knowledge of *Brahma* destroys such ignorance, it is therefore *A*-knowledge [*Avidya*]; and as it is never independent of intelligence, and cannot live separately, it is called Force also. Such is the constitutional difference of the principal (entity, or principle) in Matter, and why it is called so. Now this 'principal' substance is merely a force derived from the *Brahmaic* Intelligence. And as a person's individual powers cannot live apart from him, hence they are non-different; so the principal form of Force present in Intelligence is non-different from the *Brahmaic* intelligence. Thus then, having ascertained the presence of that Intelligence in all substances not pertaining to Self, the individual must give himself up to thinking that he is non-different from it, and then he declares " I am *Brahma*."

Who from obstruction caused by dullness of intellect are unable even with the precepts contained in the transcendental phrase having been explained to them, to have that knowledge of *Brahma*, characterised by visibility, for them this method of thinking on the blending of *Brahma*, or its fusion with every known object, has been said to be nothing else but meditation (*dhyana*).

Now there subsists a difference in the signification of the two words 'meditation' (*dhyana*) and 'knowledge' (*jnana*). 'Knowledge' is dependent on proofs and proveable, but independent of natural laws and personal desire; and meditation is entirely dependent on nature, (e. g.,) a person's desire and faith; for instance:—In the cognition of a 'jar' when the proofs (eyes) and the subject to be proved (a jar) are brought into a condition of a relationship, it comes to be perceived by the eyes in spite of a person's desire. On the fourth day of the (bright phase) month of *Vadra*, the sight of the moon is interdicted, yet notwithstanding a person's desire not to see it, when from some cause or other the eyes are brought into a relationship with the moon, she is seen by the person who had been trying all the time to avoid it; hence visible perception is dependent on the eyes (proofs) and the subject to be seen, and quite independent of law and personal desire.

Moreover by meditating on the *Saligram* (ammonite) a person enjoys good results. Here, a person knows it to be a form of *Vishnu*, with four hands indicated by the signs of conch, wheel, rod, and lotus as the *Shastras* have it; but visibly by his sight, he knows it to be nothing else than a stone; yet for the injunction of the *Shastras*, faith, and his desire, he believes it to be an image of *Vishnu*; so that the stone is transformed into *Vishnu* by meditation Now this meditation is of various sorts. In some instances, the object meditated is different in shape and form from the substance representing it, as in the instance of the *Saligram* for *Vishnu*. This is called 'meditation by substitute' (*Pratika Dhyana*). The inhabitants of *Baikuntha* meditate on *Vishnu*, with his four hands representing a conch, wheel, etc., and substitute no other substance; here the object meditated resembles typically, and is non-different in form and shape with the subject of worship [as has been pointed out in the first instance]. They have no visible knowledge of *Vishnu*, but have ascertained from the *Shastras*, that form which they adopt in their worship, which assign to him four hands, bearing four different symbols, so that this meditation is according to the nature of the object meditated. Now without law, faith, and desire in a person there can be no meditation, and that is called worship, or devotional exercise; and a faith in the utterances of Him, who has sent him here is called belief; and the inclination of the internal organ to enjoy the fruits of this worship (a product of its active quality) is called desire. These are the three causes of 'meditation' and not of knowledge. Meditation, and not knowledge, is dependent on the individual's continued and persevering effort. For *dhayana* is defined as the continuance of the mental function after it has been moulded into the form of the object meditated, and if any obstacles arise so as to cause a destruction of that function, then his persevering effort stems them away and fixes it firmly in the mind; but in regard to the mental function,—knowledge—this fixing is not needed, for after the enveloping case of ignorance has been destroyed, the function is full of light, and subject to no destruction either for the present or hereafter, to render it necessary for the function to be fixed and unwavering. Therefore persevering effort is not necessary to knowledge.

The meditation of 'I am *Brahma*' is similar to the meditation of the four handed *Vishnu* by the people of *Baikuntha*. That is to say, it is not that in which one thing is substituted for another, but the object of meditation is typical of the object meditated. It has a separate name, and is called Self-meditation, which means reflecting on the oneness of the object meditated and Self. A person whose knowledge of *Brahma* is not characterised by visibility, but having a belief in the injunctions laid down in the *Vedas*, with a persevering effort, continually fixes his mental function, and moulds it into the shape of *Brahma*, so as to impress, it with the image of 'I am *Brahma*,' and thus by means of 'Self-meditation' he becomes the possessor of knowledge, ultimately to be released from the chain of consecutive re-births, and emancipated.

> Self-meditation has been spoken of in other ways, besides the above.
>
> According to Sureswar Muni meditating on '*Om*' is Self-meditation.
>
> Hold in your mind the mystic word *Brahma* to be non-distinct from your Self.
>
> No other meditation resembles this; and ascertain it from quintuplication treated by him.
>
> Who devotes himself to the exercise of this meditation is freed.

Pupil! According to the *Munduka Upanishad*, and other works Sureswar Acharya has spoken on the subject of Self-meditation by pronouncing the mystic word '*Om*,' and reflecting that to be the same as *Brahma i. e.*, non-different from Self. This you should practise. I will just give you a brief description of it. '*Om*' is *Brahma*, and you should look upon its alphabets, representing the Supreme *Brahma*, to be non-different from yourself, and have your mental function so moulded after it, that it may remain fixed or impressed there. No other meditation can equal this, and in his work on 'Quintuplication,' Sureswar has particularly dealt on it. (The fourth line is thus explained.) Though many of the *Upanishads* treat on *Pranab*, yet the *Mundaka* has particular reference to it : and from the annotations of the commentator as well as those of Anandagiri the subject has been clearly explained. The Vartikakar* [Sureswar Acharya] has also adopted the same method in his work on

---

* The Impersonal and personal worship had therefore been derived from the *Vedas*; but the question is how can idolatry be discountenanced if personal worship rests on so very high authority ?

'Quintuplication.' But such men whose intellects are unable to comprehend or follow the arguments used in the works already cited, may derive the requisite information from the present work, for it is purposely written for their benefit.

Meditating on the mystic '*Om*' can be done in two ways according to the *Upanishads*; one is to identify it with the Supreme *Brahma*, and thus to reflect and meditate profoundly on that abstract condition of Impersonaity which is devoid of qualities. The other is to meditate on *Brahma* with qualities (personal). Now the impersonal *Brahma* is called the Supreme *Brahma*, while that other is called the (personal) *Brahma* with qualities; and one engaged in the first sort of devotion obtains 'release' while to the follower of the second method can accrue the abode of *Brahma*. Thus then, we find meditation of '*Om*,' from a difference in the method, and subject of worship, is divided into two sorts, of which the Impersonal alone will be considered here.

For, the worshippers of the personal creator are actuated with a desire of enjoying the fruit of their devotion, and this they get by inheriting the blissful abode of *Brahma*. And as that very desire stands an obstacle in the way of impersonal devotion; they are prevented from acquiring the necessary knowledge, and therefore subjected to bondage, and never freed. Now, while enjoining the blissful abode of *Brahma*, and sharing all enjoyments equally with *Hiranyagarbha*, if the individual acquires knowledge, he may yet be freed. But those who have no desire of inheriting the *Brahmaloka*, acquire knowledge here and are freed. Thus then, the results of the personal worship are included in the Impersonal, that is the reason, why this only has been treated here.

From whatever cause an action is produced, that cause has an affinity with '*Om*,' with which it is non-distinct. Hence it follows that '*Om*' is present everywhere in diverse forms. But each object has a name and form. Now the part representing form is not distinct from its counterpart—name—but the first resembles the second; for the form of an object is its shape, for which it receives a name, so as to render it fit either for accepting or discarding, with a name and caste. Simple shape cannot determine its practical use; hence name is essential. Then again, when form is destroyed its name continues in the end. As for instance after a 'jar' is broken, the earth from which it was produced continues; and that earth is not a separate substance from the jar, but the two are evidently the same. Similarly, after the destruction of form, continuance of name, like the earth in a jar is not a separate substance from form; but they are one. Or, as the earth is included in a 'jar' and saucer etc., (*i. e.*, their essentiality), they are merely the transformed products of earth, hence they are unreal; while its essentiality, the earth, is real; so in the diverse forms of a 'jar' and other objects, there is only one essentiality—the mystic syllable '*Om*'; and their different shapes are merely transformations, therefore unreal: while the one name, which every one has in common is real, and the two are not separate. Thus then we find that the shape of all substances though differing from each other is not different, and separate from the name, but the form is after name.

Because an expletive or expressive word is called name, and in the *Sruti* it is said, that all words are derived from '*Om*.' Hence for this natural relation of cause and effect, all words expressing the quality etc., of a substance, and therefore its name and form, derived as they are from the cause '*Om*,' of which they are mere products are non-distinct from it. Therefore the part which constitutes shape is one with the name of a thing, and all names are identical with '*Om*,' hence it is identical with all forms. Or '*Om*' is expressive of *Brahma*, therefore the word signifies *Brahma*; as between the signifier and signified there is no difference, so there is none whatever between '*Om*' and *Brahma*; [the first word is the signifier of *Brahma*, which is signified by it].

On mature consideration it will be found that the 'super-imposition' of *Brahma* on the word '*Om*,' and its presence there, are non-different;* that is to say, between presence, and super-imposition there can be no distinction. Hence from such a standpoint '*Om*' is

---

* As in the superimposition of a snake in a chord, and the presence of the snake in the chord are identically one.

Brahma; so that if '*Om*' is meditated for *Brahma*, then, for the virtual non-difference between It and Self, it will amount to a meditation of Self. For the *Atma* is essentially non-different from *Brahma*, and as It has four parts, so has the *Atma*; *Virat*, *Hiranya-garbha*, *Iswara*, and the indicative indication of 'That'—*Iswara*, as Witness. Now the four parts of Brahma are:—*Vishnu*, *Taijasa*, *Prajna*, and the indicative indication of 'Thou'—*Jiva* as witness. These are the four parts of Self.

    The witnessing Intelligence of the *Jiva*, is the fourth and called *Turya*.

    Intelligence associated with the collective totality of gross bodies is *Virat*, while the association of intelligence with its distributive segregate is *Viswa*.

    Both the associates of *Virat* and *Viswa* are gross.

    They are therefore non-different; and *Virat* is *Viswa*.

Now the *Virat* form of *Viswa*, has seven features. Its head is the *Swarga*, the Sun is its eye, air its respiration (*Prana*), ether its body, the oceanic waters are its urine, earth its feet, and the fire to whom offerings are given is its mouth. The *Mandukya* does not say anything about the blissful abode of heaven forming a feature or part of *Viswa*, but as it does form a part of *Virat*, and the two are non-different, hence it can be said to belong also to *Viswa*. In the same way, the *Virat* form of *Viswa* can be said to have nineteen mouths—five vital airs, five active organs, five sensory organs, and four internal organs.—They are called mouths, because as the mouth is the means through which food is enjoyed, so these nineteen features constitute the several means of enjoyment in the state of waking by the practical use of words and their accustomed functions. Hence the *Virat* form of *Viswa* is said to be an enjoyer of gross, an agent, and in short, instrument for external function, that is to say, of the waking condition.

Of these nineteen features constituting so many means for enjoyment, the active and sensory organs (ear and the rest) together with the four internal organs altogether fourteen, require the assistance of their individual subjects, and their presiding Devas; without them simply, from the organs etc., no enjoyment can be had. For this reason, *Viswa* and *Virat* are said to have nineteen mouths. Now all these features are collectively called *Triputi*;* because the organ of hearing is spiritual, and its subject, sound is super-material. A deity presiding over the quarters, and having conceit for them is called a Supreme deity (*Adhideva*). The 'organs,' for their giving rise to action, and, for the production of knowledge by the internal organ, are accordingly called spiritual. Their subjects are super-material [that of which the presence involves eventual dissolution], and presiding deities are called Superior Devas. The seat of touch—skin—is also spiritual; its subject, touch, is similarly super-material; and its presiding deity is the air which has a conceit for it. The organ of vision is spiritual too, and form is its super-material, with the sun its presiding superior deity. Tongue is spiritual; its taste is super-material with Varana for a presiding Deva. The organ of smell is spiritual, its smell is super-material guarded or controlled by Aswani-koomar, but according to Sureswar Acharya, by the Deva having a conceit for the earth. Even this is maintainable. For smell is derived from the earth, hence earth can be said to be the tutelary deity of smell. But as the Aswanis are derived from the nose of the sun, they can therefore be said to be the guardian Deva of the organ of smell. The organ of speech is spiritual, 'what is to be said' super-material, and fire its presiding deity. Hands are spiritual; prehension is super-material guarded by Indra its tutelary divinity. Organs of locomotion—the feet are spiritual, progression super-material, controlled by Vishnu its presiding deity. The anus spiritual, defæcation super-material, with Yama as its controlling divinity. The sexual organ is super-natural, emission super-material, controlled by its tutelary divinity Prajapati. The mind is spiritual; subjects of consideration are super-material guarded by the Moon. Intellect is spiritual, that which is to be cleared by it is super-material, with Vrihaspati for a presiding Deva. Subjects of knowledge

---

* *Triputi* is three and sac; literally thrice covered.

are called objects that are clearly determined by Intellect; Egoism is spiritual; its subject super-material, having Rudra for a presiding deity. Thinking is spiritual, having 'thought' as its subject which is super-material guarded by the (*Kshetrajna*) witness. These fourteen together with the five vital airs, altogether nineteen, constitute the mouth of the *Virat* form of *Viswa*. As there is no difference between *Virat* and *Viswa*, so the first alphabet '*A*' of the syllable '*Om*' is non-different from the *Virat* form of *Viswa*, because the first part of the *Brahma* is *Virat* [this has already been explained]; and of his four parts, the first part of Self is *Viswa*. In the same way, the first alphabet of '*Om*,' representing the first of its four parts, being identical in property with the first part of *Virat* and *Viswa*, '*A*' is non-different from both of them; and this is to be reflected upon while meditating on '*Om*.' Then again, as *Viswa* has seven parts, and nineteen mouths, so has *Taijasa* an equal number of them; and it is proper that they should be known. But there is this difference between them, that the seven parts and nineteen mouths of *Viswa* are created by *Iswara*, while those of *Taijasa* represented by its organs, controlled by their especial deities, are sac-like [inasmuch as they constitute the sheaths,—vital etc.,] while its mouth* etc., is the mental sheath. *Taijasa* has the 'subtle' for its enjoyment. It may be said, 'enjoyment' refers to the fruition of happiness or woe, and that can have no connection either with the subtle or gross, but the reply is, external subjects, such as, sound and the rest, by their connection or relation make happiness or misery perceptible—therefore called gross—while the relation created in connection with mental desire causing similar enjoyments, either of happiness or its reverse is said to be subtle. Therefore the *Sruti* says "*Viswa* enjoys the gross, while *Taijasa* has for its enjoyment the subtle." For the enjoyable sound etc., of *Taijasa* is mental, therefore subtle; while those of *Viswa* are relatively gross. *Viswa* is the external *Prajna*, while *Taijasa* is the internal. For

---

* For the sake of clearness 'mouth' has been used for the Sanskrit word 'murdha' which signifies the head, or its upper part.

the mental function of the former—its *prajna* is projected out, which is not the case with *Taijasa*. And as *Viswa* and *Virat* are non-different, so is *Taijasa* one with *Hiranyagarbha*, because of their associates which are subtle in both; and this oneness constitutes the second alphabet '*U*' of the syllable '*Om*,'* and their non-difference must be meditated upon. For of his four parts, the second of Self is *Taijasa*; of the four parts of *Brahma*, its second is *Hiranyagarbha*, of the alphabet '*Om*' '*U*' is the second. The condition of the second in all three have equal properties, therefore the three must be considered as one, and non-different, and *Prajna* must be looked upon as *Iswara*. For both of them have for an associate the cause-body.

Iswara and *Prajna* form the third part; the third part or alphabet of '*Om*' is '*M*.' The condition of the third is equal in all the three with similar properties, by which their identity or oneness is established. Now the wealth of this *Prajna* is (*prajnana*) knowledge. Because the knowledge present in the conditions of waking, and dreaming, constitutes what is called the 'wealth' in dreamless profound slumber, and it is virtually one with *A*-knowledge into which it merges then. Hence knowledge is called wealth (*dhana*), and bliss is called *Prajna* in the *Sruti*; for the bliss-covered by *A*-knowledge is enjoyed by *Prajna*. As the enjoyments of *Viswa* and *Taijasa* are determined or caused by these three sacs or sheaths, so is the enjoyment of *Prajna* equally saccular.

Reflection of intelligence constituting the function of *A*-knowledge is called the individuated spirit (*Adhyatma*). The mental bliss-covered by Ignorance is called elementary, or super-material (*Adhibhuta*). And *Iswara* is the Supreme deity. From such a standpoint *Iswara* is the external and *Taijasa* the internal *Prajna*,† and knowledge is his wealth. Now this constitutional difference in

---

* This word is spelt with *A U* and *M* but in English with *O* and *M*; it is apt to create a misapprehension as to the source of *A* and *U*. But $O = A + U$. Therefore $Om = A + U + M$.

† *Prajna* = *Pra* + *Ajna* = almost ignorant; hence parviscient.

the three is due to their respective associates. *Viswa* has all the three associates of gross, subtle and ignorance; and *Prajna* one, to wit, ignorance. Thus then, we find their actual difference is according to the number of associates which each has but in reality their nature is identical, and they are non-different from one another. The intelligence contained in them, when viewed in its true light is unassociated. The 'fourth' is present in the associates of all three. But the two *Prajnas* and *Prajna*-wealth are not it. This fourth is also neither a subject of the active, and sensory organs, nor that of intellect and the subtle elements—ether and the rest. It should be known as the fourth part of the Supreme Self, *Iswara* witness and pure *Brahma*. In this manner, Self is used in two modes of which one is true, and the other untrue. The three parts are untrue, and the fourth (*Turya*) is alone the true part. As Self has two resemblances, so has '*Om*.' *A*, *U*, and *M*, representing the three alphabets are unreal, while the all-pervading existence '*Om*' occupying them in the shape of intelligence is real; and this reality is called in the *Sruti* a word without alphabet. For what constitutes reality cannot be said to have any parts, hence it is said to be without parts (alphabets). Thus then the syllable '*Om*' with its two forms must be recognized as non-different from the Self which also has two forms.

Viswa is non-different from the distributive segregate of '*Om*,' and Virat from its collective totality; Viswa is the primal base of the parts which compose the Atma, as '*A*' is the root of the syllable '*Om*.' Hence they are one. Taijasa is an aggregate of the subtle expanse, and another form of Hiranyagarbha. It is identical with the second alphabet '*U*' of the syllable '*Om*,' hence none other but the second; and as '*U*' is also second, therefore the two are one. The associated intelligence of the cause-body *Iswara* is non-different from the third alphabet '*M*' and as this *Iswara* and Prajna are one, therefore the third form of *Iswara* Prajna is one with '*M*' the third part of '*Om*.' The condition of the fourth intelligence (Ecstasy) is included in all the three, and the only true one. Similarly in the three alphabets of '*Om*' are included the true signification of that syllable, for which they are non-distinct. That is to say, as

Viswa, and the rest are included in *Turya*, so in its three alphabets their exclusion from 'OM' is the real signification which is equally included, and it and *Turya* are one. Thus having ascertained the non-difference between the several component parts of the *Atma*, and those of 'OM,' a person is continually to reflect on it for the purpose of thinking about 'destruction'* or fusion, which is described in the following manner.

Viswa and '*A*,' as also Taijasa and '*U*' are non-different, but only another form of '*U*.' Such a consideration is called 'considering on destruction.' The same applies to the other alphabets too. That is to say, what is called the destruction of 'A' in '*U*' follows in this manner.—Taijasa which is another form of '*U*' is destroyed by '*M*' representing the Prajna, which again in its turn merges into the condition of the fourth (Ecstasy). Prajna being another form of '*M*,' its condition of the fourth is the true signification of 'OM' by the exclusion of its alphabets, and these two are merged into one. For, the source and destruction of the gross are the subtle, hence the 'A' form of Viswa merges into '*M*' which is only another form of Taijasa. Moreover the cause-body is the source and destruction of the subtle. Hence the '*U*' of Taijasa whose cause is the Prajna represented by '*M*' of 'OM' can be said to merge, the first into the last. Here regarding Virat, as a collective totality of Viswa etc.; with their respective three sacs, all these constituting the '*M*' of Prajna are destroyed by '*U*' and the fourth condition of '*M*' merges into the true signification of 'OM' which is without any parts and constitutes the Impartite form [of 'OM']. For the true signification of 'OM' is non-different from the *Turya*; and *Turya* is BRAHMA and pure, while Iswara and Prajna are contrived. A fancied, or contrived representation of a subject is its resemblance; hence Prajna with Iswara, as they are only another form of '*M*' can be said to merge into it, and that Impartite '*M*' wherein merges everything, and which constitutes its reality 'I am I.' The mind must unceasingly

---

* Destruction of difference will be identical with the fusion of the component units of the Viswa, Virat, etc., and Self '*Om*' etc.

think on it, and have it firmly fixed after having been intent on it.

The unassociated, secondless, free, eternal, pure, and fearless BRAHMA comprised in the true signification of 'OM' together with, 'A' representing the fixed vegetable, inanimate, and insentient objects all comprised in that 'OM,'—"That am I." This method of (non-dual) consideration is a source of knowledge, and knowledge is the source of emancipation, hence the devotional exercise of 'OM,' excluding as it does, the attributes of a personal creator, leads to release; and this impersonal meditation is the best of all its kinds. One who knows the signification of 'OM' as in the manner just explained is a sage; but who knows it not, is not a sage. For, a person bent on consideration is called a sage, and thinking on 'OM' is a form of consideration, so that, he who does not think it in the manner prescribed is not a sage. Thus have I briefly treated 'OM' in all its bearings according to the method of the 'Mandukya Upanishad.' In the 'Nrisinha and Tapni Upanishad' this has been explained in a different manner; consideration of 'OM' is a fit wealth for a 'Paramhansa,' and dunces are not qualified for it; but the extremely 'indifferent' individuals are. A family man has no qualification for it; but one without the company of a wife, son, wealth, etc., has. Emancipation results from knowledge produced by meditating on 'OM' in the manner prescribed. But if a person bent after the enjoyment of material comforts in this life, or of inheriting the abode of BRAHMA in the next, and in whom that acute indifference to worldly enjoyments is absent, violently restrains his desire of enjoyment, discards family, abandons them, and wealth, and comes to meditate on 'OM' after being instructed by a 'Paramhansa Guru' on the subject, then as his desire of enjoying (the fruits) stands as an obstacle to knowledge he can have no knowledge, and after death is subjected to another existence in another body; but if he has had restrained desires left in him while practising meditation, after death, he is sure to be born into the pure family of an holy ascetic, where he enjoys the fruits of his previous desires, and from the force of previous habits of meditation, he begets an inclination again for discrimination and meditation, so that ultimately after having derived knowledge, he is freed. Then again, if he has restrained his desire of inheriting the abode of *Brahma*, while absorbed in meditating on 'OM,' after death he inherits it, there to enjoy the rare, and set apart bliss, of the abode of our ancestors and Devas, and acquires all the supernatural powers of Hiranyagarbha, conceived in truth (*i. e.,*) virtually and in fact,—according to his determination.

The way to the 'Brahmaloka' is gradual and takes place in the manner described below. When a person, always given to the worship of *Brahma*, dies, with his internal organ, the sensory and the active organs overpowered in a swoon, so that no consciousness is left, the angel of death comes not unto him to take away his astral body, but the presiding deity of fire with a conceit for it, gets out of the body at death, and takes him to his own abode, thence he is transferred to his own abode by the presiding deity of day, to be re-transferred by the deity presiding over the bright phase of the Moon to his own abode, thence to be carried to his own abode by the deity who has a conceit for the six months of the sun's path on the north of the equator, thence to be taken away by the divinity presiding over year, next by the Sun, Moon, and the divinity presiding over lightning, who carries him to his own abode; there, appears in front of him by the command of Hiranyagarbha a fine person resembling Hiranyagarbha in appearance, to take him away from the electrical abode of lightning to Varunloka. In his passage, he is accompanied by the presiding divinity of electricity (lightning) to the next abode, that of Indra, and keeps company with the inhabitant of the abode of Hiranyagarbha who is accompanying the worshipper's subtle body. The next stage is the abode of Prajapati up to which place Indra accompanies them; but Prajapati is unable to enter the abode of *Brahma*, so he arrives here in company of the fine or excellent person. The King of the abode of *Brahma* is Hiranyagarbha, who is called so, because he is the collective aggregate of intelligence of all gross bodies and for the conceit that he is so. His action is known by the designation of *Brahma*, and the abode of that active (*Karya*) *Brahma* is called 'Brahmaloka.'

Now from what has been mentioned before, it would appear that from the meditation of 'OM' which is a form of impersonal worship of the pure *Brahma*, the person practising it, must have as a necessary result attained that pure impersonality of the *Brahma*; yet as this is only acquired by means of knowledge, and in whom a desire of enjoying the fruits of his worship is present, it must prevent the acquisition of knowledge, so that, he attains that emancipation which is typified in *Karya* Brahma*; and the worshipper who acquires the abode of *Brahma*, is virtually adorned with the glory or supernatural powers of Hiranyagarbha, so that he gets whatever body he is desirous of having, and whatever he wishes to enjoy, he gets by a mere effort of thought. In this way, if he wishes for enjoyments by dwelling in a thousand bodies, immediately with his desire a thousand bodies are produced with their separate enjoyments; in short, whatever he resolves is fulfilled; with the exception of the creation, preservation and destruction of the world his powers equal those of Iswara. This is called *Shayugya Moksha*.

Thus having been blessed with the powers of Hiranyagarbha he enjoys them for a long time, and through them whatever enjoyments, he fixes his mind upon, however rare they may be, till the time for cyclic destruction,† arrives when that Hiranyagarbha's place of abode (Hiranyagarbhaloka) is destroyed, and with it his body is separated

---

* That is the active or Personal God.

† The text requires explanation. The progressive grades of ascent typified in what is called the " Road to Brahmaloka" which falls to the lot of a devout worshipper of Anthrapomorphism after death, cover a vast extent of time. For we find a passing reference to *pralaya* or cylic period of destruction. Now this *pralaya* does not occur except in the night time of Brahmá. With us day is the period of waking and night of rest; with Brahmá day begins with creation and night ushers in destruction, of the objective world. But Brahmá's night comes once after fourteen Manus, a period embracing a thousand Yugas. Each Manu is equal to seventy one Yugas, therefore for one thousand Yugas Brahmá is engaged in creating. The twilights of Brahmá are called the intervals of Manu or Sandhi. To enable our readers to form a correct idea of the subject we subjoin the following table.

by the acquirement of knowledge, to enable him to enter into emancipation, and he is freed.

- 71 Mahayugas=1 Manantvara or Manu.
- 14 Manus or 1000 Human Yugas=1 Brahmá's day,
- 14 Manus=1 Brahmá's night.

But what is a Mahayuga? One solar year constitutes a day and night for a Deva and Asur. The Sun's passage in the north of equator is the daytime of a Deva and night of an Asur, while its passage in the south of the equator is the night of a Deva and day of an Asur, hence it will appear that 360 of our years will form a Deva's year, and 12,000 such years will be equal to one Mahayuga.

Therefore $12000 \times 360 = 43,12,000$ i. e., 43 lacs and 20,000 years go to make up a Mahayuga; of which

The Satya has 4800 years of a Deva.

Treta	3600	,,	,,	,,
Dvapara	2400	,,	,,	,,
Kali	1200	,,	,,	,,

Giving us a total of 12,000 Deva years.

Now a single Brahmá's day has fifteen periods of intervals otherwise called Sandhi. In the beginning of the first day of Brahmá there was an interval, hence there are fifteen intervals between the appearance of the Manus, each of which has a duration of 4000 Deva years.

According to the *Surya Sidhanta*, Brahmá took 47,400 Deva years to collect the materials of creation, and as one Deva year is equal to 360 solar years it will give us a period of 16,464,000 ordinary years during which the earth underwent changes ultimately to fit it for the reception of organic life.

Brahmá has a life time of 100 years. That is to say, 28 Manus multiplied by 360 days constituting a year, and one hundred such years is his span. That gives a period of 1,008,000, half of which must necessarily be night or the cyclic periods of destruction (*pralaya*).

He is now in the fifty first year of his age; six Manantwaras have already been over and the Kali of the 28th Yuga is now passing over. It is very near his noon.

As a follower of the impersonal form of worship ('OM' form of *Brahma*) attains to emancipation by inheriting the abode of *Brahma* so is that worship of 'OM' laid down in the *Upanishads* as *de facto* worship of *Brahma*, and it yields these results. But then without recourse being had to the method called 'Ahamgriha' worship, the abode of *Brahma* cannot be acquired; this doctrine is laid down by the author of the *Sutras* and the commentator, in the fourth chapter; as for instance " Siva and Vishnu have been attributed in a Nerbudesswar* and Saligram (ammonite) respectively, and the worshipper has to meditate on the former while worshipping the latter," for which this method is called 'substitution.'

It applies also where the mind and sun are substituted for *Brahma* in worship. These are not the forms of 'Ahamgriha.' From substitution, its worshipper can never attain the abode of *Brahma*. Meditating on the personal or the impersonal Brahma and considering it to be one with self is called the 'Ahamgriha' method of worship. Its followers attain the Brahmaloka.

The names of the several Manus are :—

1. Sayambhu
2. Swaroichisha
3. Utamaja
4. Tamas
5. Raibata
6. Chakshuha
7. Vaivasuta.

Brahma's night comes once after 14 Manus, when there is a *pralaya*. But as a Manu is equal to 71 Yugas therefore during 1000 Mahayugas Brahma is engaged in creating and there is a similar period of night when every thing is destroyed. But he is not affected by these *pralayas*; when his hundred years are over, there is one *mahapralaya* and he too is destroyed, leaving the ONE ETERNAL REALITY quite unaffected.

* Little oval stones found in the bed of the river Nerbuda.

The way to that abode already described is termed the *Utaranna* or *Devamarga*,* and a worshipper going by that way is never subjected to an earthly existence thereafter, but acquires knowledge and is emancipated with the separation of his body. There the precepts or instructions of a Guru as a means of knowledge are not needed, but it follows as a matter of course, in spite of them; because in that abode of *Brahma*, there is neither darkness nor the active quality, but it abounds in goodness. In the absence of darkness, it can have no insentiency and lassitude, and as the active particle is also wanting desire and passions,—product of that quality are wanting too, and there is consequently no distinction, and for its abounding in goodness, it has the faculty of knowledge—a resulting product of that quality; which abounds there—consequently it has the property of illuminating like light.

What has already been said in connection with the 'OM' form of *Brahma* worship and the signification of its alphabets is (reproduced here) being considered in this manner. That is to say, the indication of '*A*' is the associated intelligence of the gross Virat and Viswa; the associated intelligence of the subtle Hiranyagarbha and Taijasa is the indication of '*U*' and the associated intelligence of the cause-body Iswara and Prajna are indicated by '*M*.' One who has continually dwelt in his mind on the above significations during his sojourn in the earth, and while engaged in this worship, recollects them after death in the abode of *Brahma*, and from the preponderance of goodness

---

* Devamarga or Devajana as it is also called, has its analogue in Devachan of Buddhistic Philosophy. It is a state, not a locality; a state of mere subjective enjoyment in proportion to the merit and spirituality of the earth life last past. So long as the soul inhabits it, there is no requital of evil deeds, for that an objective existence in a fresh incarnation is to follow after the Devachanic bliss has been consummated. But it does not necessarily follow that the evil *Karma* only patiently waits for the re-birth, and all good works are exhausted in Devachan. That would surely be disastrous in its effect, but the re-birth is adjusted by both the merit and demerit of the previous earth life. It would thus appear that "the place of punishment for most of our sins is the earth, its birth place and play ground."

there, he considers that for the collective or distributive associates of gross and subtle, intelligence is differentiated into Virat and Viswa, Hiranyagarbha and Taijasa; and that if the respective associates of gross and subtle are abandoned together with their collective and distributive indications, there remains only the one intelligence, equal in all the conditions of the gross and subtle, both in their collective and distributive forms; and that apart from such associates of gross in their collective and distributive form, there can neither be a Virat nor a Viswa. In the same way, without the collective or distributive associates of intelligence in subtle, there can be neither a Hiranyagarbha nor a Taijasa. Now the indication of 'U' is the associated intelligence of Hiranyagarbha, this cannot exist apart from its associate. Similarly in the indication of 'M' Iswara and Prajna are established as representing the intelligence associated with the collective totality and distributive units of ignorance, and apart from their respective associates of ignorance, there can be determined neither Iswara nor Prajna.

When the subject of a thing is explained in connection with another substance, that subject is not determined in its true bearing; and when without such reference to another, it is being explained, that is its true signification. As for instance, in the sight of a father, a son is a son, in the sight of another he is a grandson, husband, brother etc., now this is not the true signification of a Son. For the body constitutes sonship, that is the real end of a son, so in consideration along with the associates of the gross, subtle, and cause-bodies, what is explained constituting Virat, Viswa etc., and so recognised, is false and unreal, intelligence alone is real; and that intelligence is undifferentiated, for the difference of associates constitutes their difference, so that the collective associate of the gross is Virat while its distributive aggregate is the Viswa, and naturally they are non-different. Similarly the difference between Hiranyagarbha and Taijasa is the difference in associates: the first is a collective, while the last is a distributive aggregate of intelligence associated with subtle bodies; and naturally they are not different. In the same way, Iswara and Prajna, are one, as are Hiranyagarbha and Taijasa, Viswa and Virat.

Thus then, there is no difference in those constituting the associates, for by abandoning the associates, the remaining intelligence is alike in all the conditions, and bears no marks of difference. Moreover, intelligence is non-different from bodies or substances which are not Self; for they [body, organs, etc.,] that are not-Self continue to exist so long as A-knowledge ($Avidya$) lasts, and if considered in their true bearing, will appear non-different (in the manner aforesaid.)

Now this undifferentiated, unassociated, unchangeable, eternal, free *Brahma*, resembling self, the indicative indication of 'OM,' is Self-illuminated. The worshippers of 'OM' discover him with the characterising traits just mentioned, so that an inhabitant of the abode of Hiranyagarbha is subjected to no more earthly existences.

Knowledge cannot accrue to an individual without discrimination of the right interpretation of the transcendental phrase (That art Thou), but the ascertainment of the proper bearings of 'OM' is tantamount to a proper discrimination of the transcendental phrase. Inasmuch as equally with it, the alphabets of the syllable 'OM' have two indications each, expressive and indicated. They are now being declared.

The associated intelligence of the gross is the expressive indication of 'A' but its indicative indication is intelligence only, without the associate. Similarly the expressive indication of 'U' is the associated intelligence of subtle bodies, and its indicative indication is that intelligence after the associates have been abandoned; and the associated intelligence of the cause is the expressive indication of 'M' as its indicative indication is that intelligence without the associate. Thus then, the expressive indication of the alphabets 'A' 'U' 'M' is the associated intelligences of Viswa and the rest, while the unassociated intelligence is that which is indicated. In the same way, name and form associated with intelligence is the signification expressed by the syllable 'OM' while intelligence unassociated with name and form etc., is what is indicated by it. From such a standpoint the syllable 'OM' has the same meaning with the transcendental phrase. Hence from a discrimination of 'OM' knowledge of non-duality is produced.

Having received instruction in the manner aforesaid, the second pupil Adrishti undertook devotional exercises, and by means of knowledge, obtained the supreme and real end of existence,—emancipation. The word '*Kartabaya*' which occurs in the last mentioned verse bears reference to one unqualified for impersonal method and worship. That is to say, for him it is imperative, that he should be engaged in all proper actions, and it is right that he should practise them ; for actions clear the internal organ of all blemishes, and pave the way to knowledge, which is the only means for creating a desire for release

- If one cannot undertake the impersonal meditation, he should then fix his mind on the personal worship.
- If that has not been done, he should avoid all actions springing from a desire of enjoying fruits, and worship Rama.
- In their absence, let him take to actions good and optional.
- If he cannot do them, he must die over and over, again.
- Adrishti considered himself successful with finding the indication of 'OM.' He who reads this section, him the author of this work looks with kindness.
- Thus ends the discourse of the 'second qualified person' with his Guru.

SECTION VI.

Victory be to Rama.

Not Intelligence is not-Self,
Every thing unreal like a dream,
Hearing this, says the third
Pupil, Tarkadrishti the intelligent.

THE fourth section contains the method of instruction required for the best qualified, and the fifth has particular bearing to one who, though qualified, is said to be the second best. The present one will deal the subject with special reference to the third or youngest pupil. One who is filled with very many doubts, inspite of a sharp intellect, is called the youngest qualified. Now this section abounds in reasons and arguments, hence it is particularly adapted for men prone to controversy and ill-matched arguments. The youngest qualified is generally fond of using bad arguments, and shows a good deal of controversial spirit, but he will find suitable instruction in the following pages, particularly intended [for his benefit]. In a previous portion of the work, before treating the method of meditating on '*Om*', and the evolution of the universe, it has been said, ignorance is quite distinct from intelligence, and the products of ignorance (the phenomenal world) are not-Self, but like objects seen in a dream they are unreal. At this, the youngest of the three brothers Tarkadrishti, finding his brothers raising no question against it, asks of his teacher:—

Objects known at a prior date are remembered in dreams.
The waking condition is one of extreme ignorance, consequently none sees [then.]

An unknown object can never be remembered in a dream, but what is experienced in the waking condition, can only be reproduced by knowledge in memory then, so that the subjects of recollection must be real, as they depend on objects seen in the waking condition, which are real; hence objects of the 'waking' cannot be said to be unreal by instituting a comparison with those seen in a dream.

The subjects of a dream are ascertained by a different method as real; for instance, where

> The subtle, leaving the gross body,
> Goes out to see
> A mountain, ocean, etc.,
> That cannot be false.

That is to say, the subtle body gets out of the physical body in the dreaming condition, to see a mountain, or ocean or another object which it wants to cognize, hence the subject of a dream (objects seen then) cannot be false. [But this assumption is incorrect.]

The answer is :—

> "This elephant is standing in front."
> Such a knowledge
> In dream, is like recollection.
> Know then, how is it produced.

Knowledge of objects seen in a prior period of time is called remembrance. As when an elephant seen previously, is reproduced in memory by the sight of another animal in a subsequent period, and the new one is recognised from 'that elephant,' it is called remembrance. But "This elephant standing in front" is called 'visible knowledge,' and not remembrance. Moreover in a dream there can be such perception as "This elephant standing in front." This is a mountain." "That is a river." Hence it cannot be said, that the sight of an object seen in the waking condition is reproduced in memory, while a person is dreaming in sleep, and a dream is virtually the result of remembrance, but it is visible knowledge of an elephant or other object. Then again, if it be contended, that an object seen while awake can only be known in a dream, and an unknown object is never seen then, consequently the impression of an object previously seen, while awake, produces its reappearance in a dream, and that impression is nothing else but an act of reproduction by the help of memory, so that knowledge of the dreaming condition is due to recollection; that cannot be maintained. For visible knowledge is of two sorts. One is in the form of ascertainment; and the other of recognition. Of them, the first is that knowledge which is produced by the relation of an object with the senses. As, by means of the eyes, an elephant is rendered visible, so as to enable us to say, "This is an elephant"; while the perception produced by the impression of previous knowledge and by the relationship of the senses is called recognition, as when an elephant seen in a prior period of time is expressed. "That elephant is this." Now in the second instance (that of recognition), the impression of an elephant previously seen, coming in relation with the eyes produces the recognition of that elephant visibly. The second is the source of perception. Hence knowledge produced by impression is not necessarily in the form of recollection. That cannot be the invariable rule, but the visible knowledge of the second variety is due to impression. To be more explicit, the difference here between the second form of knowledge and remembrance is this, that the former has, in addition to impression, to depend on a relationship being created with the senses, which the latter does not require. It is only knowledge produced by impression.

The knowledge of an elephant in a dream is not due to impression only, but like the elephant, the senses are contrived to be present too; consequently it is the result of the senses. Though the objects of a dream are ascertained or discovered by witness and are not subjects of knowledge for the senses, yet for persons wanting in discrimination, the knowledge or perception in the dreaming condition has been said to proceed from the senses. Thus then, such perception is not a *single* remembrance of a thing seen while awake; and a person on waking from his sleep says, "I was seeing elephants etc., in a dream." Now if it were due to an act of memory, he would have expressed himself in quite another way and said, "I was recollecting *an* elephant in a dream." But as no one says so, that is an additional testimony as to such perception not being produced by recollection.

Moreover, it generally follows that an object seen with the senses wide awake, is apt to be reproduced in a dream. This is not the inflexible rule, because there are occasions when a person dreams of things which he has neither seen nor heard, so that even unknown things can be the subject of a dream, and recollection of a thing unknown is possible, hence that perception is not due to it. [But it may be argued in reply] the impression derived from the knowledge of a thing in this life only does not constitute recollection, but it embraces all impressions of previous existences; for an inclination is produced by knowledge of friendliness and there can be no inclination without it, so that the first inclination for a child to suck its mother's breast is caused by the knowledge of the child that it will support it, and is favorable to it. Here the experience of such sucking being favorable to it, has been a result of previous sucking in prior existences and from its conception (the impression left in the mind) a child is enabled to remember the experience from its first inclination to suck, that it is favorable. Thus then, from the conception or impression of previous knowledge of prior existences even recollection can follow. In the same way, unknown substances of the present life may be the result of impression of knowledge of previous existences, and it is possible that they may be recollected in a dream. Notwithstanding all this, it may be laid down as a broad fact, that at times, things are seen in a dream, which it is impossible for one to see in all his journeys throughout, in the waking condition. As for instance, the beheading of one's own head, seen by his eyes in dream. Now here, it is clearly impossible for a man to see with his eyes, his own beheading, while awake, hence his dreaming it, cannot be a product of memory, so that the subjects of a dream are not the impression of things seen in the waking state reproduced by an act of memory. Various are the arguments used by authors in their works to do away with the view which holds dreams to be due to recollection of things previously seen in the waking condition. In such an admission, the faults already cited are too strong for refutal. The subjects of knowledge produced from recollection can never appear in front, but an elephant seen in a dream, appears so, during the time of dreaming; thus proving such perception to be quite independent of recollection. [To say] the subtle body issuing out of the physical, beholds a real ocean, river etc., [is also faulty] and—refuted in the following way :—

If the subtle body were to get out, that will be (ruinous) fearful to the physical.

It takes the beauty with *prana* ; for the subtle is composed of it [besides the other features].

If issuing out of the physical body, the subtle astral body were to behold a real mountain, ocean, or river, then as in death-struggle a body assumes a fearful aspect, so the exit of the subtle in the dreaming state ought to make the physical body (lagging behind) assume a hideous aspect ; and without respiration too, it must resemble death. But this is never the case ; in that condition of dreaming, respiration continues to be carried on, and the body preserves its beauty in the same manner as while awake, so that the exit of the subtle, from the gross body can never be said to take place. Moreover, if it be said, that *prana* does not go away, but the senses and the internal organ leave the body to repair to a mountain or another object, for seeing and for the continuance of *prana*, the physical body does not become so hideous as in death ; and there is no necessity for the exit of *prana* ; because, the power of knowledge or perception (consciousness) does not reside in it, it has its function only, hence that which has consciousness for enabling it to determine the cognition of a thing, goes out. Consciousness resides in the internal organ and the sensory organs. The organs of action resemble *prana* in this respect, they have no consciousness, but are capable of action. These active organs and *prana* therefore do not get out, but reside in the physical body to prevent its being destroyed, or death taking place ; the internal and sensory organs issue out of it, to see a real mountain or such other object, and afterwards return near the *prana* and active organs. Even this cannot be admitted ; *prana* dominates over the gross and subtle bodies, it is so to speak, the lord, and the physical body cannot live even for a moment without it. When respiration ceases, the body is not allowed to remain a single moment in the house but is removed outside and burnt [or buried]; it cannot be touched with impunity, the person so doing must bathe immediately after ; hence we find, the essence of the physical body is its *prana*. This likewise applies to the subtle body ; for *prana* is here the chief [entity or substance]. *Prana* and the organs quarrelled amongst themselves to ascertain who among them was the chief. They went to Prajapati and asked him to point out who of them was superior to the rest. Bhagvana replied, each of you must enter a physical body and get out of it, one by one, so that when with the exit of a particular one, the body assumes a cadaverous aspect, and falls down (as if dead), he shall be called your chief. They followed his directions and the result was, in the absence of each organ of sense a person was seen to live *minus* that, —deaf and so forth, but when *prana* left the body, it fell down. It was thus ascertained that *prana* was the chief and superior to the rest, and they acknowledged it to be their lord. Hence so long as *prana* lasts they continue to reside; with its exit, they take their departure too. Thus then, like a sovereign of a country *prana* is a chief; without its departure the internal and the sensory organs do not take their leave. Or the internal and sensory organs are the products of the good quality of the elements,—ether and the rest—they have consciousness, but no power of action, which last resides only in the *prana*. By its force, the subtle body leaves the physical at death, and goes to another abode. During life, the function of the internal organ projected by the sensory organs, comes in close contiguity to 'a jar' or other object which it seeks to discover, by the same force of *prana*; without such an assistance from *prana* it is next to impossible for the internal and sensory organs to be so projected out of the body. Hence it is mentioned in the *Yoga Shastras* that "the mind can never be restrained without restraining the breath *(prana)*": so that a person desirous of Rajyoga must practise the method used by the followers of Hathayoga for controlling the breath; with the activity of respiration mental activity keeps pace, and with its restraint, the mind is adequately controlled. Here even, the issuing or projection of the internal organ is subject to respiration, and until it departs, they continue to carry on their functions. Hence, as in the condition of dreaming, the continuance of respiration is ascertained in the physical body; so the mind and senses cannot go out of it to discover a real object. Or that a person having met one of his relations in a dream, if he happens to see him the next morning, does not say that I saw you the night before, and had a conversation on such and such subjects. But according to the view of the opposite* party, if their issuing out of the body or projection, were correct, the relative ought also to be aware of the interview and to know that he had some conversation (or other dealings practically) with him. The proper conclusion of the Siddhant *(Vedas)* is, that the interview in a dream is a creation of the fancy internally. Or if it gets out to see a real substance, then a person in his sleep at night dreams that he is basking in the midday sun at Hurdwar, and sees its site in the east of the Ganges, and that the Nilgiris are on the west. Now, no sun can be seen in night time, nor is Hurdwar situated in the east and the Nilgiris on the west of the Ganges ; so that there is no possibility of seeing an actuality in dream. For in that case, the person in question would never have dreamt of basking in the sun etc., as night is not the time for the sun ; hence in dream it cannot be said, that from the sight of a real or actual substance by means of the projection of the internal and sensory organs, there proceeds consciousness of things seen in a dream, and that it is a result of recollection concerning things seen during the waking hours. Both these doctrines have been disposed of by a Siddhanti thus :—

On this ; are internally produced the three and all the rest.
Says the *Veda*, "Of all doctrines know this means a crown."

Recollection of things seen in the hours of wakefulness, and the projection of the subtle body are not possible [cause of vision or things seen in a dream] ; but then the presence of the three :—knower, knowledge and object—is explained in the dreaming condition as in that of wakefulness. All things therefore take their origin from the arteries or vessels of the throat. Of all the authoritative proofs, those of the *Vedas* are the crown. There it is said (the *Upanishads* mention it) "The objects of the waking state cannot be determined in dreams, but whatever is then seen—a mountain, ocean, river, wood,

---

* *Purbapakshi* and *Sidhanti* (questions and answers) are introduced in the *Vedant* writings for the solution of questions which are apt to arise in the discussion of a subject. In such a consideration, the extreme oppositionists also find their doctrines reviewed and analyzed critically.

village, house, sun, moon, a conveyance drawn by horse and passing the streets with a person seated inside, all—are new productions. Whatever is then seen, arises for the first time, (is newly born) and if such things were not actually present in a dream, they could not be seen; but since they are seen, therefore they are present visibly. Because visibility is produced by the relation of the sense of sight with the function of the internal organ. Hence for the cognition or conscious preception of a mountain and other objects, it must be naturally inferred, the means are either the senses or the mental function creating them internally. If the objects seen in a dream were only discovered by the witnessing intelligence, as in the case of silver in nacre, and had no interdependence on the mental function and the sensory organs,—so that their (objects) origin in dream may properly be admitted, but a knower and knowledge need not be admitted,—yet as dream-objects,—mountain and the rest—are established, so is the continuance of the sensory and internal organs with respiration determined in the physical body, in that state of slumber, consequently they cannot but be admitted; otherwise the visual perception of objects, which takes place then, by means of the usual eyes shedding their reflection on those objects will be undone; for things existing at the same time and equal to one another promote knowledge and *vice versa*. (This has already been explained in the fifth section). Thus then, the usual organs—eyes etc.,—for their extremely opposite qualities with knowledge, cannot create the perception of objects seen in a dream, so that the organs in daily and hourly use are incapable to carry on their individual functions by leaving their seats. Moreover the seats of the active organs—hands feet, and the rest—in that condition of dreaming are fixed and seen by other persons in waking condition and yet the person dreaming bawls out and runs after an object while the object itself is enclosed in his hands; all these considerations as a matter of course, create a necessity for admitting the origin, source or birth of the organs in dreaming slumber.

Similarly happiness and misery, and their conscious perception, that is to say, the resort of that conscious perception of happiness and misery *viz*, the individual, or the internal organ together with intelligence and its reflex, is determined in the dreaming state, but an absent thing can never be determined, so that every thing else besides, equally take their origin in dream.

The supporters of the 'indescribable method' explain this phenomena in quite a different manner. They say, mistake or delusion of an object (*i.e.*, its subject) procures its origin in a manner which cannot be definitely described—indescribable. It is an established doctrine which cannot be gainsaid, that there can be no knowledge without a subject; according to the other *Shastras* a delusion is said to be the knowledge of an object different from what it is. According to the *Sidhanta*, knowledge is determined by the nature of a thing, [accordingly as it is good or bad, so is the knowledge produced thereof], so that a subject must be born to produce a mistake. Now with reference to the second mode which broadly lays down, there can be no knowledge without a subject, the explanation of the three, [knower, knowledge, and known] produce an association of all things. But doubts may arise on this point, that by an admission of the origin of the objects of a dream, they must necessarily be real like the objects of the wakeful condition, as has been explained by alluding to the example of dream-objects and drawing the natural inferences of objects in the wakeful state. For, what are produced as objects seen in the waking condition are necessarily real, hence for this similarity of production, dream-objects must equally be so. But then, if their birth or origin be not admitted, then the fault is done away with. Because objects of the waking state are virtually born, while those of dreams are determined without such production, so that without a subject being present, its knowledge in a dream amounts to a delusion. Now the doubt about the impropriety of admitting their production is thus cleared away :—

What are produced without the means of production are false.

When a thing is not derived from a substance, it is unreal.

Substances not derived from the usual means or causes of production, in connection with place, time etc., are said to be unreal; and dream-objects, such as elephants etc., have neither the requisite place nor time, where they can take their birth; they take a long time to be born, and many are the countries of their nativity, so that their production in a moment's time in the subtle region of the throat cannot be any thing else, but false. Though in a dream, length of time or variety of place may be determined, yet they are simply reflex products of an indescribable nature; for without a subject, no tangible knowledge can arise, and yet in dream, there is present perception of length of time and variety of place—while in practice, such time and place are confined within the narrowest limits—consequently they are reflex products. Then again, these products of reflected time and place are not the source from which proceed the objects, elephant and the rest. For a cause must have a priority of existence in regard to its resulting product,—which is not the case in a dream-object, as the time, place and elephant etc., are all produced at one time and they are co-eval or co-existent, consequently they have no relation of cause and effect. Moreover time and place are practically confined within such narrow limits as are insufficient and unfit for the dream-objects, elephant, etc., consequently they take their origin within the substances time and place, for which reason they are said to be false. And the other requisite cause-substances, such as mother to elephant and the rest, are not present in dreaming slumber. Though the parents of living creatures may be perceived in a dream, yet such parents are not the cause from which their issues derive origin, inasmuch as both parents and children are born at one time. Hence there does not exist between them the relation of cause and effect.

Now the source of dream-objects is A-knowledge (*Avidya*); which is a creator of the fatherhood, motherhood and sonship, all alike in an equal manner; thus then beyond it, there is not another substance which serves as a source of dream-objects; but this A-knowledge is accompanied with the defect (sleep) in its condition of relative cause, and their combined product resembles silver in nacre and is equally false, hence dream-objects are never real, but unreal. Their material cause is the internal organ or A-knowledge with the defect sleep directly.

According to the first view, the witnessing intelligence is said to be the presiding cause of a dream, while in the second, the uniform intelligence is said to be its abiding source. According to the first, dream is a modification or changed condition of either the internal organs or knowledge. According to the second view, the uniform or *Brahma* intelligence is the abiding, and A-knowledge, the material cause of dream; here it may be apprehended whether the abiding is contrived in knowledge or removed by it ? Moreover as *Brahma* abides in dream, without Its knowledge, an ignorant person should be unable to keep away dreams by wakefulness. There is yet another misapprehension in connection with this doctrine. Since *Brahma* is the abiding Intelligence and A-knowledge the material cause of dreams, in the same way the *Vedanta* upholds the usual objects of the waking condition being occupied by the uniform intelligence of *Brahma* and their material cause, A-knowledge. These constitute the practical use of objects in general in that condition; but in dreams they are merely apparent or reflex. There should not be such a difference. Inasmuch as both of them are occupied by the same Brahmaic intelligence and have for their material cause *Avidya*, hence in both the conditions, objects seen, ought in common fairness, to come into their accustomed daily use, or both may equally be products of apparency or reflection; in that case only, doubts and misapprehensions shall cease. But there need not arise such disputes. The first is solved thus. There are two sorts of destruction or removal; (as have already been pointed out in connection with *Kshyati*) (1) Destruction of a product along with its cause, or, as it is called 'extreme destruction.' This can never take place without knowledge of *Brahma* on waking from dreaming slumber. But as in the case of a jar being broken or destroyed by a stick (which is one of its causes) so by the destruction of the defect of sleep, which is the source of a dream, or by wakefulness which is antagonistic to it, dream is destroyed, and it merges into *Avidya* without Brahmaic knowledge. Now about that other misapprehension which seeks to establish an equality between wakefulness and dreaming slumber, but which is virtually not a fact, it remains to be said, that in the first mentioned condition of wakefulness, the material cause of the body and every thing else is the primordial Ignorance, which is uncreated, and without other defects; and in the dreaming state, the pure and simple defect of sleep is also a promoter of that Ignorance, so that for an absence of other defects from ignorance, it is the determining source of their being turned into practical use ; it is called 'practical'; while for the presence of that simple defect of sleep in the same ignorance in dreaming slumber, it is called an apparent product ; hence dream-objects are mere apparent reflection and unpractical, while those of the opposite condition are practical (*i.e.*, usable). Therein consists their difference. But then, these three varieties of admission concerning existence, have been explained from an ordinary view. On analysis, it will be found to be quite impracticable to maintain the three existences, and also a difference between waking and dreaming ; though the *Vedanta Paribakha* and other works deal on the practical and apparent products and have admitted their difference, and the three existences, in the manner aforesaid, and Vidyarana Swami has also admitted the three varieties of existence likewise, for he has written on the subject, that there are two sorts of bodies etc., of which one is external created by *Iswara*, while the other mental, and a product of the *Jiva's* determination ; it is internal. Of these two, the product of *Jiva's* determination and which is internal, and mental, is discovered by the witnessing intelligence. While the products of *Iswar's* creation (external) are subjects of cognition for the individual. The internal, mental bodies are the productive sources of his happiness and misery ; not so, the products of *Iswar's* creation which are external. Hence one desirous of release must have the former removed or destroyed ; for the latter are quite unconnected in their production, so that, their removal is not an imperative necessity. As for instance, if two persons having two sons both living at a distance from home, of whom one is dead, and the other alive ; now if the living son having amassed a fortune and acquired reputation sends intelligence of his success in life and the decease of that other son to his father by a third person, who deceives that father by informing the death of his son, and the father of the dead son, that his son is in health and has acquired wealth and reputation and that he will soon be coming back riding on an elephant, so that the father of the living son is drowned in extreme grief, while that of the dead son is elated with joy. In the same manner, the son created by *Iswara* (*Jiva*) residing at a distance,—

situated externally to one's body—can cause no pang ; but that mentally produced son situated internally, is the source of grief when it fares ill with him. To be more explicit, all the creatures created by *Iswara* cannot affect a person when he hears bad news concerning them, but the son produced by the mind creates a relationship of sonship and fatherhood between him and his parent, so that when the father receives the sad news of his death, he is extremely affected with anguish ; whereas in the first condition, the mind does not create such a relationship, hence he is quite indifferent as to whether they live and die. Therefore it is said, that the mental creations of the *Jiva's*, for their close relationship, produce pleasure or pain while *Iswara's* creation can have no effect at all, inasmuch as no one feels for another, as if the same had happened to himself. In this manner has Vidyarana Swami divided all objects into two classes *viz.*, creation of *Iswara* and creation of *Jiva*, for reasons just explained. Of them, the former are practical, the latter reflex. There are other authors, who likewise maintain existence to be of three different sorts ; for true knowledge, consciousness, is one of them, while all insentient objects have two, practical and reflex. Things which are derived from the desire of *Iswara*, in the beginning of creation, and are elementary in composition, a product of Ignorance (matter) only, are called practically existent, but those derived from ignorance with defects, as objects of a dream, and the apparent production of silver in nacre are called apparent existence. In this way, though objects of the waking state are called practically existent, while those of dreaming slumber are existent apparently, for which they are said to be apparent existence, yet bodies or substances, which are not-Self are classed among the apparent. Hence there are two existences, of which, that relating to consciousness is called true existence, while that concerning substances unresembling it, is called apparent ; and there cannot be established any existing difference between waking and dream-objects.

This conclusion is the best, and has been explained as follows :—

    When a thing is not derived from another,
    It is false, like what is created in dreams.

Without any trace of time and place,
When the objective world takes its source, then
Know it to be unreal, as a dream;
Without a trace of reality.
Like a dream, in wakefulness
It resembles, not wakefulness in dream.

All dream-objects are derived without any connection of time and place, which are called the substances or source of production, as has already been illustrated, while treating on the creation of elephant, mountain etc., hence they are called unreal. Similarly the objective world, with the elements, ether etc., have been derived from *Brahma*, which is perfectly unsubjected to time and place (for It is unconditional). Now dream-objects,—an elephant mountain, etc.,—have already been shown to have some slight dependence on time and place, even that is wanting in the production of the elements, inasmuch as their author the Supreme Self is said to be without the condition of time and place, for which reason the *Taiterya Upanishada* describes the evolution of the elements in a consecutive serial order [and not creation]. Moreover the author of the *Sutras*, and the commentator, have equally been silent on the creation of time and place. Creation implies a derivated product (hence liable to destruction, which they do not admit); for they say, elements have been produced independently of time and place. Therfore, the elements are as unreal as are dreams, [for the existing similarity of condition]. Though Madhusudana Swami has said in reference to time and place, that they are due to ignorance, so that they are anterior to the Supreme self potentially existing in *Maya*, of which *Maya* or matter they are mere modification, and the evolution of the elements are subsequent to them; consequently for the production of the elements there did not then exist suitable condition of time and place, yet his purport is not that time and place are the first evolved and the elements followed them. For, the first productions are called excellent, and the future, subsequent, hence if it be said, that time and place are first productions, while the elements are of later origin, and subsequent, it will be tantamount to saying prior to the period of production of the elements, the Supreme Self was associated with place and time and was abiding in them; consequently there will be established a prior time and place antecedent to the time, when time and place were created; this is contradictory and cannot be maintained; for it will imply the existence of time and place, prior to their production, creation, or origin, which is clearly impossible and absurd.

But such was not intended to be conveyed by what Madhusoodana Swami says. His meaning is, that like the elements and elementary products, time and place have been existent from the beginning (but subject to the cyclic destruction); but they are non-eternal for with the exception of Self, every thing is subject to decline and death. Then again, they are also derivated products like the elements, for the existence of a thing cannot be established from nothing; and as they are existent, therefore they are derived; and as they are derived, therefore they are open to destruction; for things which are derived from some source are non-eternal. Now time and place are derived from a modification or transformation of matter, and a disomorphic modification of intelligence (*Vivarta*).*

Now a disomorphic modification cannot stand as a cause; hence, in reference to time and place and the material elements, this intelligence modified into time and place cannot be reckoned as the source from which the elements have sprung; or, as the cause must

---

* With reference to causes it has been said there are two forms of change, one of which is called *Vikara* or an actual change of form; and the other *Vivarata*, or only an apparent change of form. The formation of an earring from gold, or a jar from clay, are instances of the first. Here, there is both change of form and name; but not of the substance— gold and clay, while the transformation of milk into curds is an instance of the second. Here there is change of name and form and the substance too.

The drift of the foregoing passage is to establish the phenomenal world as an illusory effect of *Brahma* the secondless reality, which is its illusory material cause. The relation between *Brahma* and the objective world is similar to the creation of a snake in a rope—an illusion. *Vikar* or *parinam* includes a real change of name and form. The substance remains unaffected.

precede an action, a result, product, or effect, and, as it cannot be said, that time and place were anterior to the elements, hence from both considerations, time and place cannot be established as a source of the elements; but like the co-existence of father and son in a dream, these elements with time and place have sprung up from the Supreme Self inherent in *Maya*. Moreover some substances are produced in one place and at one time, there are others which are not there produced nor in that time, hence in cyclic destruction they are not produced, but only during the period of creation. The connection of time and place with production of objects is determinable in this way, so that when the vast expanse is created with time and place, from *Maya*, that *Maya* is the cause, whose products are other elementary substances, and time and place are not the cause.

In connection with this subject, it may be said, the existence of a thing cannot be determined without it, but this is not admitted in the *Sidhant*. Such an admission of 'nothing' producing every thing will virtually turn you into an advocate of 'nothing'; and a sterile woman's son, and rabbits' horns will be quite possible. But as they are not to be found in nature, hence the doctrine of 'nothing' cannot explain the production of the phenomenal world; consequently if time and place are not the source, but the force of *Maya* is the source of all products of time and place, will be equally inconsistent. Then again, cause is explained by time and place, therefore they are the source of all products. Moreover as *Brahma* is said by the Sidhanti to be the cause of all phenomena, it is natural to assign causation to *Brahma* in time and place, and not to consider them as the source. For as *Brahma* is the abiding entity in time and place, so is It present everywhere in all objects; and in time and place the causation of *Brahma* is equally present and not outside of them. There can be no cause for saying this, consequently if the occupation of *Brahma* be determined as a source of time and place, then as it is present everywhere in all objects that must necessarily be the cause of all, and it is absurd to connect It, with cause in some, and as a resulting product in others; so that time and place are not the source, but *Brahma* is, and as the all powerful cause *Brahma* can be established, that will virtually be admitting such causation in another, according to the view of the *Anyatha Kshyati*. Because to look upon another substance in a different light is termed *Anyatha Kshyati*. Now time and place are not the cause. This expression signifies another object to be uncaused, and resting on the back ground of this cause, and not to look upon them in the light of cause will establish that source in another substance, and thus necessitate the admission of the view of the *Anatha Kshyati*. But the *Sidhanta* does not admit it, and the admission of such a view will render futile that admission of the *Sidhanta*, which indescribably produces silver in nacre. Because of these doctrinaires *Anyatha Kshyati* have two methods to account for what they say :—

(1) A substance situated in another region and its explanation in a different way is called *Anyatha Kshyati*. As for example, silver seen in the hands of a wife mistaken in a nacre lying in front, and placed in quite a different region from the silver itself; or the different determination of a different thing, as the determination of nacre itself to be silver. All cases of mistake or delusion can be satisfactorily explained by the above methods. To speak about ignorance and attribute the causation to it, in a manner that cannot be described, will be out of place. Then again the doctrine of the Sidhanti lays stress upon resemblance of the subject with the form of the object of illusion, and its cognition; and the knowledge of a different thing in a different manner is impossible,* so that the subject of consciousness—the appearance of silver—is the cause from which proceeds that indefinable silver. In such an inference of the supporters of non-duality, time and place are different from cause; and hence to connect *Brahma* with them as cause is untenable, so that, the assumption of cause in time and place, without their being so,

---

* It is worthy of note that 'a different thing' here means, what is created on the real substance, as for instance nacre is present in front, the apparent production of silver is a different thing, so that the first thing is nacre and the different thing is silver; then again for silver to be found in a different place, other than in a box, family house, or amongst jewels, as in that nacre, is to know it differently from what is usually the case. Now *Anyatha* means different; *Kshyati* signifies knowledge; therefore the two words would signify different knowledge; and its supporters may be called 'The upholders of difference of perception.'

or to fix that causation in *Brahma*, and to recognize that as a cause, does not follow. But causation of *Brahma* is present in time and place, and so it is perceived; in the same way, to say that the elements were derived from the causation of time and place will be inconsistent. As a crystal placed near a red flower receives the reflection of that redness, and appears so by such relationship, and the really abiding intelligence of the individual is transferred in dream to unreal objects created there, (elephant, mountain, &c.,) for being perceived. Now in the first instance of the crystal, the appearance of the redness imparted by the flower, does not necessarily create that colour in the crystal, therefore the perception of the white crystal as red, establishes a difference of perception; similarly on the subject of unreal objects produced in dream, and their perception as something real, to say, they are caused by indescribable truth is just as consistent as the expression "truly false." Then again, a non-existent thing cannot be known, but the truth of the abiding intelligence of the dream condition is perceived or known in the falsity of objects created in dreams, so that false objects are known as real ones, consequently there is a different perception of truth than what it naturally is, similar to the perception of *Brahma* in time and place. Moreover, if it be said, that an admission of this difference of perception here, will require such difference being recognized as the source of all illusions. But there need not be any such apprehension. For in the admission of difference of perception of silver in nacre, the fault is said to be in the absence of distinct knowledge of the subject, and in the perception of redness in crystal the association of the red flower with that crystal, imparts its own redness to the glass; because when the function of the internal organ assumes the shape of that red flower, the subject of the function—the red flower—is said to stand in relationship with the crystal, for which the crystal is perceived red; and in the case of nacre, it is quite impossible for it to have naturally a perception of silver, for its province is situated in the 'indescribable,' where there is no ordinary silver present (according to another view) but only nacre; and in relation with that nacre, the original nacre can only modify the function of the internal organ so as to make it assume the shape of nacre, and not of silver; consequently the indescribable silver, a modification of ignorance, and a transformation of the name and form along with the substance of intelligence, and its perception are both produced; and in the instance of the crystal, the relationship of the function with the crystal and red flower produces its apparent redness. In relation with the red flower, the function assumes its red color, and it has likewise a relation with the crystal consequently its redness is merely a reflected shadow; hence the red property of the flower in the crystal becomes the subject of the mental function. Thus there is a probable relation of two substances and the perception of the property of one in another is probable, therefore the probability of difference of perception is likely to follow. Where there is no relationship of two substances, there cannot be a difference of perception, but it is an indescribable perception, as the association of the flower with the crystal makes that redness known. In the same way the dream-objects—elephant and mountain—are related with the inherent or abiding intelligence, hence, as the faculty of intelligence—truth—is perceived in the associates of that intelligence, *viz.*, an elephant, mountain, etc., therefore it is 'difference of perception'; and as the faculty of that abiding intelligence is causation, it is perceived in its relations, time and place.

Moreover, in connection with the doubt first cited, that as the abiding intelligence is related with the whole of this vast expanse, and as the same relationship determines a difference of perception, it is necessary that the causation of that intelligence in the phenomenal be acknowledged; but there is no occasion for it. For as in the case of a father and son created in a dream, there are two bodies produced at the same time, and both these bodies have a relationship with the abiding intelligence of the dreaming condition, but their causation is known only in the father's and not the son's body, for the father is the parent of the son; so is action determined in the son's body similarly.

In the same way, though the abiding intelligence is related with all bodies, yet the faculty of intelligence determines causation in time and place, and elsewhere its resulting product, effect or action, so that the abiding intelligence being associated, it is not the true cause of anything, though such cause may be attributed to the reflection in

Maya; yet the reflection is unreal, and what is itself false cannot be the cause of another; consequently in reference to the Supreme Self the attribution of causation to the material world, and attributing time and place are due to illusion. Because the Supreme Self is uncaused; He is without the condition of time and place, unassociated—the absolute, and it is absurd to speak of Him as being caused by time and place. But *Maya* creates the indescribable time place, and indescribably assigns causation to them; but virtually and in fact they are not the cause. As one having no son sees both a son and grandson in a dream, here the bodies of such son and grandson are indescribable; and the causation of that grandson's body in that of the son is equally indescribable; and as the true condition of cause and effect between a son and grandson is non-existent, so are time and place recognized as indescribable cause; literally between elements—the phenomenal world—and between time and place there is no relation of cause and effect. In this way the objective world of the waking condition is derived without the causation of time and place, and both wakefulness and dream are equally unreal, and as a dream-created wife or child are sources of pleasure and pain in the dreaming condition only, and absent in wakefulness, so are the objects of the waking state absent in dream. Now both are similar.

Moreover, if it be said, the dreaming slumber follows the waking condition, and *vice versa*; and the objects of the first state of wakefulness continue in the next condition of waking separated by the interval of sleep from the first, and that the objects of a first dream do not continue in the second, hence there is a difference between the objects of the two states; now such an assertion can be made by persons ignorant of *Sidhanta*. Because according to their sight, the current of the universe is without a beginning, and *Jiva* is subject to the three conditions of waking, dreaming and profound slumber. The two last are destroyed in the state of wakefulness, the first and third are kept away in dreams, and the first and the second are destroyed in the third condition. But in dreams and profound slumber, an individual's wealth, son, animals etc., which he had been the possessor of, in his waking condition, are never destroyed, they continue as before; only the perception or knowledge of them is removed, so that when he wakes from sleep, he is the same master as before, of his wealth etc. Such a consideration is only due to ignorance. The *Sidhanta* explains it by alluding to a transformation of intelligence (*vivarta*)—a simple modification of ignorance; so that like silver in nacre, whatever object is produced then, the vehicle of ignorance of the abiding intelligence undergoes two modifications; the particle of darkness of that ignorance assumes the shape of the object it seeks to cognize,—a jar etc.,—while its good quality assumes the likeness of knowledge. Though intelligence is said to be knowledge, so that to say, the modification of the good quality is knowledge, is improper; yet that knowledge is not all-pervading and consciousness over-riding the worldly function is called knowledge, hence the accomplisher of the use of knowledge in consciousness is function. Thus then, function is like an associate of consciousness, and the word 'knowledge' is used to indicate it as a subject of consciousness. As for instance, in the common expressions "Knowledge of a jar has been produced." " Knowledge of a jar is destroyed," here the functional intelligence cannot be said to arise and go away; but function is produced and destroyed, and knowledge is produced and destroyed; hence the word 'knowledge' is used to signify function ; and that knowledge, a form of function, is a modification of the good quality, (this can possibly be said) and intelligence is reflected in that modification of the function, but not in the modification of the subject, a jar etc. Because, though subject and function are modifications of ignorance, yet the first is only a modification of the dark quality of ignorance, therefore impure; no reflection can take place in it; while the second is a modification of the good quality, therefore transparent, and can receive reflection. Thus then, for the function being adapted to receive the reflection (of intelligence) the limited intelligence of the function is called knowledge and witness. And as the subject (jar etc.,) is not fit to receive reflection, the limited intelligence of the subject is neither knowledge nor witness. Therefore the objects of the waking condition and their perception, are both produced and destroyed at one time (such is the firm conclusion of the *Vedas*), hence to say, that they continue **to remain in the next wakefulness after sleep,** and so on, is inadmissible.

Though a person on rising from his dreaming slumber, considers that things continue just as they were, before he went to sleep, so that his knowledge of those things are not produced and destroyed at the same time, but through knowledge they are first rendered visible, and continue to exist even after the destruction of knowledge, yet as dream-objects are produced at the same time, and a person perceives that this mountain and ocean must have a beginning prior to my birth, so that the objects produced then and there (in dreams) are considered to have been produced in the distant past, an illusion—a result of ignorance. Now the same ignorance which creates a false mountain or another object in a dream creates also the conception of time (indescribable) during which dream-objects are existent or not; in the same way, objects of the waking state are not more durable and lasting; but through force of ignorance, a false durability is produced along with the production of those objects at the same time, and thus causing them to be perceived. But if it be said, that dream-objects are a direct modification of ignorance, and those of the waking condition are not so, and like a jar produced by a potter, his wheel and stick, every such object has its own cause from which it is produced, and ignorance has no direct concern in its creation, inasmuch as the consecutive evolution of the elements and their quintuplication, giving birth to Brahmâ's egg as mentioned in the *Sruti* will then be inconsistent; therefore the objects of the waking condition—creation of *Iswara*—are only a modification of their individual material agents, and not a modification of ignorance; all dream-objects are productions of modified ignorance and their formative material is the same ignorance; hence their creation and perception by the same ignorance being produced at one time, is quite possible. But as objects in the waking condition (the objective world) have their own individual sources of production, distinct from one another, and a priority and sequence of time, for the cause must precede the result, and the result destroyed in the cause, consequently before the production of a jar and subsequent to its destruction, a lump of clay still continues to exist. Thus then, some objects exist for a short time and others have a longer duration in that relationship of cause and effect, and it cannot be said, that the same is not applicable to dream-objects. Because, like the objects of wakefulness, dream-objects can be shown to be influenced equally by causes producing them in their turn, as results or effects in a natural order of sequence.

As, for instance, when a man dreams that his cow has given a calf, or that his wife has given birth to a son, the cow and wife are the cause of their respective issue; and such perception may be as lasting as the calf and son—actions of the cause—or it may be short-lived, or the cause and effect may be coetaneous; that is to say, ignorance is the material cause of production, and the cow and wife are no more so in regard to their calf and son. We find the same thing in objects of wakefulness : a cause lasting for a greater period of time, or an action lasting for a shorter period, or there is no relationship of a prior cause and its determining action, result, or effect as in dream, but a direct result of ignorance. Then again, the consecutive evolution of the elements and the rest, as laid down in the *Sruti*, is intended not to give an account of cosmogony, but for expounding non-duality and to attribute everything to the All cause—the Supreme Self—hence that is only a transformation of Him.

Now, a transformed product is nothing else but a prototype of the thing transformed, therefore the objective world with their individual names and forms is not distinct from *Brahma*, but is *Brahma* (actually). To explain this non-duality, has an account of creation been given in the *Sruti*, and there was no other necessity for it. The consecutive evolution therein described is for enabling one, ordinarily to know, how destruction takes place in a consecutive reversed order, equally necessary for the determination or ascertainment of that non-distinction of *Brahma* and the phenomenal world ; so that there was present no necessity for a description of cosmogony. There is no consecutive seriality in creation, but all products have one determining source, ignorance (or call it matter, if you like) ; between the two, matter and creation, there is a relative condition of cause and effect ; and the perception of priority and sequence, is produced by ignorance, a false condition resembling a dream. But the reason for the *Sruti* account of consecutive seriality, or priority and sequence, is only for considering destruction. For consideration, meditation, or reflection, there is no rule, that it will be after the natural appearance or form of an object, consequently objects of the waking condition have no mutual relationship of cause and effect, but are derivative products of ignorance, like the silver in nacre, or a dream-object, discovered by the witness associated with function of ignorance. Hence all objects are discovered by the witnessing intelligence, and their modifications of knowledge and ignorance are produced and destroyed coetaneously, so that when the object is perceived, it then becomes the subject of that perception, and not in any other period of time. To see in this light is called *Drishti-Sirishti-Vad.* This doctrine upholds the presence of knowledge in objects only and does not admit the existence of ignorance [or in other words the knower creates the known and the latter is non-existent in the absence of the former.] In the light of non-duality it is conclusive. Here there are two and not three, existences. Because objects which are not Self (*Anatma*) are apparent like dream-objects; and beyond the time of their perception they are non-existent, hence the third or practical existence [*Vyvaharika*] is done away with, in this method. The witness is their discoverer and there are no subjects for the internal organ or its function to take cognition of. Because the internal organ and the senses, and a jar, all three, and their conscious perception are produced coetaneously in what happens in a dream; consequently there cannot be said to exist the condition of subject and predicate. If the subject a jar, the sensory or jars eyes etc., and the internal organ were existing first, before this perception, then perception or knowledge, *i.e.*, function of the internal organ is caused by the organs, eyes, etc., the proofs—but that internal organ, subject of the senses, all three, are not present before knowledge; they are produced simultaneously like a dream, hence the three are not the determining source of knowledge. Still in the matter of knowledge, the causation of the three in determining its production, like what follows in dream-objects is known, and therefore the objective world is said to be discovered by the witness, and the subject of knowledge is independent of proofs. Here also it is equally false with a dream ; or several objects are determined in a different light from what they naturally are, and appear false in wakefulness, while others are produced as realities, existing in all times, of which some are destroyed giving place to others in their turn.

There can never be any divergence from the rule just laid down about the evolution of elements ; a person may be in possession of knowledge, yet about cosmogony he may be perfectly ignorant ; while there are others who know all its particulars. According to a knower of Self, the world has no existence, but the reverse is the case with persons devoid of knowledge. A preceptor and the *Vedas* are the means of knowledge ; through them the highest truth is known ; such a knowledge is only to be produced in the condition of wakefulness. Thus the falsity of some substance, destruction of others, and origin of a third is determined, the supreme truth—the end and aim of human existence,—is then brought about by the Guru and his precepts on the *Vedas*; the derivative products of ignorance are reduced into their actual condition of nihility like an object in dream. In *Vashishta*, have been given innumerable historical accounts confirmatory of what we have hitherto been considering ; a moment's dream covers a good length of time, during which several personages appear in, and disappear from, the scene of action, as if it were all a dream, but when the accounts are read, they appear like living personages, as what actually takes place in our condition of wakefulness, all given to enjoy long periods of life, so that hardly any marked distinction can be found between waking and dreaming slumber ; but beyond the one reality—Self—everything else is unreal, this is amply proved.

Says the pupil—

 Of the hundreds of thousands and thousand *Kalpas*,
 This produced the world,
 So that a man of knowledge is alone liberated.
 Ignorance is bondage, whose number is thousand.
 If unreal like dream, are moments, hours, minutes, and seconds.
 Who is then bound and who is liberated ? Of what use are 'hearing' and the rest ?

In the infinity of time, Iswar's creation is without a beginning, hence the liberation of the wise and the bondage of the ignorant is dream-like; that is to say, as a dream lasts an hour, a moment, or for several hours, so does the world continue to live, or say it may last for a still greater length of time. If, therefore, the duration of the world be so limited, how can a person be subjected to bondage through infinity of time? And there will hardly be a necessity for the destruction of that bondage, and to be liberated by having recourse to the means 'hearing' and the rest.

Now in this view, bondage, desire for release, *Vedas* and *Guru* are not admitted, but intelligence is looked upon as eternal and free; that various transformations take place in the modification of ignorance—intelligence—which cannot effect the *Atma* injuriously; that self is ever unassociated, and unchangeable; that nobody has been delivered up to the present time; nor is there any chance in the future, but intelligence is eternal and free, without any relation with ignorance or its modification in any period of time, hence a *Veda Guru*, 'hearing' 'consideration' and the other means 'meditation,' are not at all requisite: to consider otherwise is a creation of ignorance and as true as a dream (*i. e.*, false) and its lengthened duration is also due to ignorance; yet one unacquainted with the *Sidhanta* is apt to question in this manner from an ordinary view.

Says the Guru—

As the Deva Agradha created a delusion in dream; in that manner

Pupil, is your knowledge of bondage and release produced in wakefulness.

As a dream is produced, from the defect of sleep, as a teacher is a known source of study, and as from study of the *Vedas*, *Puran*, and *Dharma Shastras*, a student comes to know of actions and their effects, and is deluded with a belief as to their reality; so like dream-objects, these objects of the wakeful state are false, and to consider them real is only a mistake. The verse refers to 'bondage' and 'emancipation'; they include all things which are not Self. As you know me to be your Guru, a learned man is taught the signification of the *Vedas*, which you know to be false; as to an Agradha Deva appears the *Vedas*, Guru, etc., indescribably unreal, like the subjects of a dream, so your subjects of knowledge beginning with one to everything else, all are indescribably false, and that is exactly what happened to an Agradha Deva in a dream. Agradha Deva had been sleeping for a very long time, and dreaming that he was a *Chandal* (pariah) and very poor; his mouth was filled with bones, flesh, marrow, blood, fascia, skin and semen; that he was roaming in a wilderness filled with dreadful snakes and wild elephants. In the course of his travel he sees several places; in one spot he finds fearful creatures ravaging the wood in quest of prey; he finds a second spot filled with blood, where were creatures loudly venting forth their agony; in another spot he finds a red hot iron pillar, to which several individuals were chained; one of the roads was sandy and the sand so very hot, that the unfortunate people who were compelled to walk on it were writhing in pain; their miseries did not cease then, for they were guarded by an officer of law, with an iron rod in his hand, to thrash those who lagged behind; this fearful spectacle appeared in his dream, and he fancied lest he shall be one of them and subjected to a similar treatment. He was very much alarmed indeed. There were some delightful spots too. Here a Deva was sitting at ease with all the good things to enjoy; sight of nectar brings forth satiety, and he knows not what hunger and thirst are; another Deva with a tangible body devoid of excrements—urine and fæces, seated on a good conveyance, was enjoying a drive, and that conveyance was propelled at the desire of the Deva occupying it; a third spot was enlivened with the dance of Panava, Urbasi, and the other *danseuse* of heaven. Incomparably beautiful, without any defect of person, and with all feminine charms, they had lavishly poured on their bodies sweet scented perfume, which inflamed desire. Here and there, a few Devas were keeping company with the girls and enjoying a walk; now he fancied himself amongst one of the party of these Devas, and was taking precious care to protract his stay indefinitely. Sometimes he thought he was accompanying a girl in a pleasant walk. In the midst of his rambles, he was accidently led to a spot filled with ordure and offal, and he had to clean them; one spot was occupied by their king attended by his servants, who were standing in front to serve his commands. To many persons, the king and his servants appeared to resemble the moon, others conceived great dread for them. The inhabitants of the wood were rewarded or punished according to the measure of their good and bad works.

In this manner, was the Deva Agradha by name, visiting several places of that wood in his dream. (The scene was varied, wild, and interesting.) For instance, in one place Brahmans were recanting the *Vedas*; in the sacrificial altar good actions were being done; here was flowing an excellent river, in which people were bathing for the sake of virtue; there a wise preceptor was giving lessons to his pupils on Self-knowledge, who having finished their course, were getting out of the wilderness. In the course of a very short time was the Deva Agradha astonished with what he saw in his dream; he thought within himself, that the wood had been existing from remote ages, and knew no destruction; that he also had been living through all the time; the gardener *Brahmá* with four heads had on rare occasions, to sow the seeds from his mouths, water and protect them; sometimes he laughs so violently that fire would come out and devour the forest in flames; that with the birth of the wood, he (Agradha) was born and died with it; after the wood was consumed the gardener alone remained alive; the seeds of the wood existed (potentially) in *Brahmá's* body (for raising it up again); and that he was subjected to birth and death repeatedly. This he learned from hearing the *Vedas* in his dream.

Having heard of his repeated sojourn in life, he commenced to reflect as to the means of getting out and improving his condition, even if he were to stop there. He thought, if he would succeed in getting out of the place, his condition of a pariah will be removed, and he will attain to a Deva. But there were no other means save and beyond that knowledge of *Brahma*, on which the professor was engaged in his course of instruction to his pupils; they did get out of the wood by its means. With these thoughts, he repairs to a professor (in dream) and receives that instruction, in the manner prescribed, from books written in the language of the Devas. Now the imaginary professor gives instruction by imaginary works, written in the Sanscrit, to an unreal pupil, who exists no where. He translates the works in vernacular. For such translation of Sanscrit works he begins with the usual (valedictory) propitious introduction. For that enables a writer to get rid of the usual obstacles (sin and demerits) that prevents its completion. Sin prevents a good action being finished, and a propitious action by causing its destruction, carries a person through it. Even if a person be faultless and without sin, yet he must begin his work with the propitiatory stanza. For in its absence an author may be taken for an atheist, and there will be no inclination for his writings.

Now this propitious action is of three varieties—

(1) The ascertainment of Reality, *Vastu*.
(2) In the form of salutation,
(3) In the form of blessing.

'*Vastu*' means the Supreme-Self *Brahma*, with or without attributes. 'Ascertainment' indicates singing; praying for the desired object either by the preceptor or his pupil is called 'invoking a blessing.' That object of desire has been expressed plainly in the fourth piece of poetry. The fifth verse exp'ains an object desired by the pupil. Ganesa and Devi are spoken of as Iswara in the *Purans*, hence when mention is made of them, it cannot indicate ungodliness.

The *Purans* contain an account of Ganesa's birth; but the source of that birth is not dependent on actions, like what happens to humanity in general; on the other hand, like Ram, Krishna and others his birth was for bestowing favors on his ardent followers. He was an incarnation of the Supreme-Self, according to Vyas. Now its purport is this:—In the light of truth, the Supreme-Self is non-different from the individual Self; but the illusory attribution of bonds, birth and death, to the Self (*Atma*) which constitutes (*Jivaship*) individuality, is never known to a Ganesa or Deva, hence they are not individuals, but Iswara; and it is but proper, that in the opening passage, a work must contain their consideration. Different methods of speaking about Iswara have been adopted only to make him shine the more, and attachment to him and to a preceptor (spiritual) can only be produced by knowledge, which is the principal means to that end.

For rendering this interpretation more plain the following verse on the ascertainment of the Reality and the good it produces is being produced.

> That Lord who is truth and light, and discoverer of the Sun and Moon
> I am ; a witness of his intelligence purity and bliss.

ON THE PERSONAL REALITY.

> Destroys sin with root, the name of Ganesa.
> Without meditating on him no serviceable action to a Deva can be done (vide *Tripurabadh*.)*

MODE OF SALUTATION.

> My salutation to Siva, husband of Lakshmi, and Parbati who destroyed the giants,
> Whom the devotees are constantly engaged in praying to.

MODE OF PRAYING FOR AN ACCOMPLISHMENT OF DESIRE.

> Let that force† by which Iswara created this world.
> Sit on my tongue, so that the work in hand may be successfully finished.

INVOKING A BLESSING.‡

> [Thine work] destroys bondage, awakes a desire of release, kind preceptor.
> Who reads, or hears it, for him all wordly rubbish cease.

---

* It is a work containing an account of the slaying of Tripur by Mahadeva.

† *Sakti* is another name for the goddess of Force, *Durga*.

‡ Or the mode of a pupil's prayer for fulfilment of desire.

SALUTATION TO A PROFESSOR OF *Vedanta.*

The *Vedic* tree pierces through the forest contending against the air and gives a good shake to disperse the thorns of action over-spreading it,

Tears again an honest and successful pupil;

Who returns again and again to this world of thorns, which the traveller, Bhagavan, knowing it should not be, takes him up, assuming the form of Vyas,

Makes of the *Sutras* a net, and divides the thorny world. Salutes he them, knowing them to be true and unchangeable.

[The commentator explains it in the following wise].

As a storm overtaking a forest, shakes the trees, and by stretching the thorns, tears the beautiful flowers of the water lily (lotus) and scatters them adrift, or fixes them there, so that a traveller is led to believe that the flowers are actual productions of the spot where found; but on reflection he finds that cannot be: for the place is unfit for them; thus meditating he picks them up, and thinks of finding out a remedy that will prevent such a mishap in the future, when wind and storm with thorns will be unable to affect them in any way or tear and scatter them; so he takes a net made of thread and covers the thorny tree in a manner to prevent its thorns getting out by the force of wind to pierce the flower, and having done thus, prevents the lotus to enter into the thorny tree by the artificial partition of the net. Similarly the spiritual preceptor of duality is the wind in the *Vedic* forest, filled with thorny trees of contradictory disputes as to their signification; these excite the performance of acts done with a motive of reward, in a man of integrity, artless and faultless, without any passions, a pupil resembling the lotus in purity and beauty, is thus driven from his proper sphere of meditation, and found in the midst of thorns of works by the traveller, all-pervading Vishnu, who thought such a pure individual is not fit for this place, but his proper sphere is to attain me. He therefore assumes the garb and form of Vyas, and fixes him in the bosom of instruction. As a flower fixed in a person's bosom cannot be driven away by wind, so one seated firmly on the course of instruction offered by a professor, intent on *Brahma*, can never be misled by the random talk of a dualist, hence that instruction is fit for his heart. Vyas did not desist here, but pointed out that even to one who admits the individual and universal spirits are two separate entities, the thorn-like actions are the source which will cause him ever to travel on, so that the remedy must be found that will put an end to his journey. With such an object, he separates the utterances of the *Vedic* tree by the net of the *Sutras*. As in a forest, there are trees with thorns, and trees without thorns, and a net separates them, to prevent the flowers from entering into the thorns, so the *Vedas* contain two different sorts of utterances, one lauds actions and a person undesirous of them, is enticed or induced to perform them, while the other expounds the effect of actions to be shortlived and transient and thus removes a person from their pale. Vyasa divided them. By the *Sutras* he intended to show all the utterances of the *Vedas* have for their purport, the destruction of and not the incentive for, actions. Such of the utterances as determined the incentive for an action were over-ruled by forbidden and natural works, thus they have been completely done away with. Now lawful acts purify the mind, but a person who is intent on knowledge must abstain from them. Hence destruction of actions is the chief purport. Then again, what effects of actions have been explained in the utterances, in reference to the indication, amount to a sugar-coated pill. [Treacle in the tongue is an indication signifying administration of nauseous pills to a cow and horse, disguised in treacle. So does a sugar-coated pill, hence it has been used for treacle in the tongue.] Their purport is not to ascertain such effect. In his *Sutras*, Vyas has sought to establish what we have just been saying, so that a person acquainted with them may abstain from all works. As the thread net prevented the entrance of flowers into the thorns by enveloping those trees which bore them, in the foregoing example, so by Vyas *Sutras*, a person is obstructed from having recourse to actions with a motive of enjoying their fruits in this, or the next life. Therefore the resemblance to a net is mentioned.

Another's pupil takes protection of a generous minded Guru, With hands clasped and head bent at his feet, he asks: Oh Bhagvan! Who am I? Is the world created or evoluted? What is the source of emancipated, let me know them, besides actions and devotions.

Bhagvan! Who am I? Whether my Self is the body, or different from it? I am a man and have a body, both these I know. I have my doubts on the subject. If you say my Self to be different from the physical body, then am I an agent (instrument) or actionless? If the latter, am I a subject of all bodies collectively or of several distributively? The first part of the question has this purport. Then again what is the source of creation? Is it created or evoluted? If it has a creator whether such agent is a *Jiva* or Iswara? If Iswara be its author, whether he is limited in one region, or all-pervading? If he is all-pervading, then, as *Jiva* is different from the all-pervading ether, so is he different from Iswara, or whether the two Iswara and *Jiva* are one. Whether the source of emancipation is knowledge or works; or devotional exercises, or both? If both, 'actions' will be equal either to knowledge or devotional exercises.

To this the Guru replies:—

Everlasting, intelligence, and Bliss, art thou,
One with *Brahma*, unborn and unassociated.

The first question which the pupil had asked is now being replied to. "Thou art eternal, intelligence and Bliss"; now such an expression will signify a difference with the physical body, for that is (*Asat*) 'not being' [and open to destruction]. It is insentient and miserable, and not an agent. For an agent is one who has recourse to actions for the destruction of misery and acquirement of happiness; but in reference to your self, there is no misery (Self cannot be affected by it); hence there is no agent to destroy or remove it by performing actions. Thus then your self is blissfull and it is equally true in connection with the acquirement of happiness. For as he is blissfull, he cannot have any necessity for its acquisition, for which, he is not an agent for good works though he is recognized in that way, in the gross and subtle bodies. Thus then Self is neither an agent, nor an instrument for good and bad works; nor is he liable to enjoy or suffer their results, happiness and misery, but he is the witness in the gross and subtle body; hence he is one and not many. If self were an agent, necessarily he must be more than one; for happiness or misery felt by one individual, does not so affect the rest of human kind, but instead, we find some to be happy, while others are miserable, therefore the number of agents are many; but since self is not an agent, he is therefore one. Though *Sankhya* does not admit the agency of self, yet he recognizes the number of selves to be many. But this is an extremely antagonistic view, for he says, when the three attributes are in an exact equipoise, it is called *Pradhan* or *Prakriti*, and not change or modification *Vikriti*; now modification is a transformed product of *Prakriti*, which is the natural source of *Mahatatwa*, hence it is Matter [*Prakriti*]; and as it is uncreated, it is therefore changeless.

Now *Mahatatwa*, Egoism, and the five *Tanmatras* are therefore called the transformed products or modifications of Matter;* each of the preceeding one is a material cause of the subsequent product, for the productive cause of a result is called *Prakriti*. The *Tanmatras* are the material cause of the elements, hence these seven are modifications of *Prakriti*, as are also the five elements, five active organs, five sensory organs and the mind. These sixteen are not *Prakriti*; moreover Matter and Spirit are not modifications of one another. Because the cause of a thing is called *Prakriti*, and its product (*Vikriti*) modification. But as the (*Purusha*) Spirit is not a cause of any thing, therfore He is not one with *Prakriti*; and as He is neither an effect nor product, he is therefore not *Vikriti*. Thus then he is unassociated. We have therefore twentyfive (*Tatwas*)

---

* To enable our readers to have a correct view of Evolution we should refer to the Introductory Memoir in *Dhole's Vedantasara*, where the whole subject has been carefully explained. In this place we can produce only the classification, but in this connection it is proper to say that what the authors means is this :—The *Mahatatwa* gave birth to egoism. Egoism to the *Tanmatras* and so on.

entities or substances in the *Saṅkhya Philosophy*; which does not acknowledge an Iswara, or Personal Creator for the causation of the universe.

Prakriti requires no help, but is alone its sole cause.* It likewise acts as an exciter for inducing men either to enjoy happiness or misery, or attain emancipation. Spirit is quite unconnected.

---

* Prior to the evolution of the world, matter was in a passive condition it could then produce nothing till acted upon by the influence of its spirit or better still, force. It is impossible to conceive that condition now, what we now have experience of, is matter in its highest state of activity or matter and force. The instrumentality of the spirit in evolution depends only in inducing change, it disturbs the equipoise, the three *Gunas* or forces which matter is endowed with, lose their equilibrium and go on producing the phenomena we know as natural laws. But the very term law is a misnomer, inasmuch as it presupposes a law-giver. This is all very elaborately cleared out, which it is impossible to condense into the compass of a note, and which the reader may find in the Introductory Memoir attached to *Dhole's Vedantasara*.

Now for the classification—

1	*Prakriti*	Primordial cosmic matter.
2	*Prakriti, Vikriti*	1 Viswa
	Matter in a condition	2 Ahamtatwa
	of change	3 Fiery ⎫
		4 Auqœous ⎬ Subtle
		5 Earthy and ⎭ Atoms
		6 Aerial
3	*Niravichinna Vikriti*	⎫ Eleven organs of sense and action and
	Only change	⎭ the five gross elements.
4	*Anuvaya Sarupa*	
	Neither matter nor change...*Atma* (the 7th Principle).	

Prakriti alone can do nothing. The undifferentiated cosmic condition of matter is called *Prakriti*. The contact of the *Purusha* (Spirit, Self or *Atma*) induces a change which disturbs the equilibrium of its three forces, or qualities or *Gunas* and then evolution begins.

Prakriti procures enjoyment by being transformed or modified into material prosperity, and by intellect it is further subjected to a change which is called discrimination. This is also called emancipation. This is another of the means by which enjoyment is derived.

Literally the Spirit or Self is unconditioned and unassociated and can therefore have no concern either with enjoyments or emancipation, but their knowledge, pleasure and pain, the passions, anger and the rest, are all modifications of intellect, which for the *Atma*, acquires discrimination, or not: the attribution of bondage and emancipation to Self is not true to those who have discrimination in their intellect, but to them who have it not, the attribution of enjoyment to Self turns him into an agent according to *Sankhya*. But in its true bearing Self is not an agent (*Buddhi*) intellect is the agent. 'Discrimination' is to know intellect as something different from Self. The absence of such knowledge is called indiscrimination. For these reasons *Sankhya* calls the *Atma* unconditioned, un-related, or un-associated ; and pleasure and happiness are merely modifications of intellect, so that they are the properties of *Buddhi*. Self is not one, but as many as there are individuals, each person having separate Self. Now this statement is very much opposed to reason (or what the *Vedas* say). For,

If pleasure and pain were the attributes of Self, then as each individual is affected quite separately from the rest, one may be in grief while his brother or neighbour is in the height of felicity, and as that distinction is created by the body, consequently Self is divided into as many, as there are bodies. But since pleasure and pain are not the attributes of Self, but they belong to intellect whose properties they are, consequently their distinct perception separately by men will create only a division of *Buddhi* intellect and not of Self.

As the one pervading ether is recognized severally on account of a difference of its associates, by one wanting in proper discrimination of the associate and ether—who knows them to be distinct though they are one—so the attribution to one pervading *Atma* of properties belonging to several intellects, shews an absence of discrimination in the person who so regards it. *Sankhya* ought to admit what we have just said, and not to content with saying "Self is unconditioned, and divisible." For divisibility reduces him to the position of many, and then the first admission is rendered fruitless by the second. Moreover to divide the Self and regard him as many, according to his bondage in some, or emancipation in others, is clearly untenable, for unless the *Atma*, be subject to, or included in, bondage and emancipation, his division cannot be maintained; and as that attribution of bondage and emancipation to Self proceeds only from want of discrimination in the intellect; and as according to the *Sankhyakar*, they are the properties of the intellect only, therefore to regard the *Atma* as divided into many and not one whole, is opposed to reason and sense. Then again what proceeds from 'indiscrimination' is false, as a snake in rope. This is removed by discrimination (and knowledge.) From indiscrimination in the intellect, Self is regarded to be subject to bondage, but discrimination removes such erroneous notions, hence bondage is unreal. In the same way, his emancipation is unreal too. One who is subject to bondage can be said, to have a desire for release; therefore bondage and emancipation must be equally true at the same time; that is to say, where there is bondage, there must emancipation ever be real. But as in regard to Self, bondage is unreal, so must emancipation be like-wise. In this way bondage and emancipation which are unreal, can be shown like the other, to apply to *one* Self; and to divide him into many according to the division of bondage, and emancipation cannot be a reasonable deduction; hence the *Sankhya* view of the *Atma* is unsound, and illogical. The *Naiyaikos* also admit a similar division of the *Atma*, for which this doctrine must be alike unsound and illogical. They say, happiness and misery, knowledge, envy, desire, endeavour, virtue and vice, conceptions of knowledge, number, proportion, separation, addition, and division are the fourteen qualities of the individuated Self. They are his subjects. *Iswar* has eight qualities *viz.*, number, proportion or measure, separation or distinction, addition, division, knowledge, desire, and endeavour. But then:—the difference is this: Iswar's knowledge, desire and endeavour are eternal, while the individual's are manifold, and transient. Iswar is all-pervading and eternal, while the individual is manifold, completely pervading and eternal, and his knowledge is short in duration ; so that when the quality of knowledge is present, then only the individual, intelligence is manifested, and when the first is destroyed, he is reduced to insentiency. Like the *Jiva* and Iswar, void (*Akas*), time, quaters, and mind are eternal.

Moreover, the subtle atoms (*Paramanu*) of earth, water, fire, and air are eternal. A *Paramanu* is an atom. It is the sixth part of the subtle dust perceived in a ray of sunbeam.

Atoms are eternal like the *Atma*. There are other substances besides what have been mentioned, which are considered by the followers of *Goutma* to be eternal, as for instance, caste, species etc., but as they are all opposed to the conclusions of the *Vedas*. An enquirer after truth, can have no necessity for them, hence I will desist from their further discussion. " I am a man" " I am a *Brahman*" are expressions that clearly fix Self in the physical body,— a delusion and mistake—exciting anger and envy, which in turn produce an inclination for good and bad works, that lead to the enjoyment of happiness, or suffering of misery by being connected with a physical body. Thus then we find here, that a mistaken knowledge is the source, which procures for the *Atma* an objective existence.

This mistaken knowledge is removeable by a knowledge of the true nature of things,* Self is quite a distinct entity from all other substances, a body and the rest. To ascertain this by knowledge is called *Tatwa Jnana*. Now such knowledge removes the mistake of attributing or confounding the physical body with the *Atma*, as in the expression "I am a *Brahman*," "I am a man." With the removal of mistake or delusion, anger and spite are destroyed ; in their absence, inclination for merits and demerits cease to excite a person. Where there is no inclination, there can be no connection with a body—no more birth—to enjoy or suffer hereafter, but the consummation of actions already begun, cease only with the destruction of their effects by enjoyment. From a want of bodily connection

---

* *Tatwa Jnana.*

twenty one [sorts of] miseries are destroyed; and destruction of misery is another name for emancipation in *Nyaya*.

They are :—the body ; ear, eye, skin, tongue, nose and mind, constituting the six organs, six subjects of these organs ; and their knowledge which is another six ; together with happiness and misery. They are the parent of misery, hence are called miseries. Then again, after destroying the happiness derived from a residence in heaven, or another equally desirable abode, they bring on misery by producing fear, for which also, they are called miseries. Though according to *Nyaya* the ears and mind are regarded eternal, and therefore not liable to destruction ; but the way in which they cause misery, is open to it. By producing a knowledge of things, they cause misery. But in the time of emancipation, neither the ears nor the mind do produce that knowledge of substance ; because the ether situated inside the aural cavity—the site of hearing—is the organ of hearing, and as the ear is absent during emancipation, the ether just mentioned—the virtual organ—must alike be absent. However in the absence of the site of hearing, no knowledge is to follow, hence the parent of knowledge, the ear or something else resembling it, is the cause of misery ; and *that* is open to destruction.

Knowledge follows from a connection of the mind with the *Atma*, and this connection, according to the *Nyaya*, is either due to the action of one or both of them. As a hawk alights on a tree by its own action, and as two rams in a fight are moved by both their actions, so in the Lord that is self, there can be no action by contact. Moreover, during the time of emancipation, as there can be no action present in the mind, therefore the mind which is endowed with the faculty of connection is then said to be absent. Then again, the connection of the mind is called the source of knowledge by some ; but the contact of the *Atma* is not so called. In the state of profound slumber, the mind enters the vessel *Purita*; it has no connection with the skin, hence there can be no knowledge then. According to them, the mind itself, for its close connection with the skin, and for its being the source of misery by knowledge, is misery. But independently of such connection it is not. During emancipation the sensation of touch is destroyed; hence there can be no connection then, for which there can be no knowledge in it. The mind remains in the period of emancipation, but that sense of touch, which is the parent of knowledge or conscious perception of misery by its contact, or connection with the mind, is destroyed, and with this destruction of contact, it is itself destroyed.

In this way, during emancipation, for his difference with the Supreme Self, devoid of misery, the pervasive *Atma* is reduced to insentiency, and continues so. Because the quality of intelligence in the *Atma* is like light, and discovers every thing; but in the individual, all perceptions are derived from the senses, for which they are transient; and during emancipation the consciousness produced by the organs of sensation is all destroyed, hence without the power of discovering, but like an insentient substance, the *Atma* continues to remain during emancipation. This is the conclusion of the *Naiyaikas*. They further assert that, the *Atma* is subject to grief and happiness, bondage or emancipation, in the manner above referred, hence he is manifold, and completely pervasive; now by pervasion they mean to signify the indication of his presence every where, or of a connection, with the smallest substances. Want of similarity and dissimilarity, or the inherent distinctions, do not constitute the indications of pervasion. Because they say, the *Atma* is without features, shape, and form, hence he cannot be the subject of inherent or individual distinctions; but the distinctions crated by isomorphism and disomorphism are not wanting in him, that is to say another *Atma* is similar to him.*

---

* The three expletives 'one' 'secondless,' and 'existence,' are used to differentiate It (PARABRAHMA) from bodies similar and dissimilar. That is to say, as a tree has its brances, leaves, flowers, and fruits, differing from each other, a leaf resembles not a flower, nor does a flower its fruit, nor either a branch, thus constituting its distinguishing individuality or its segregate units, for though the tree is one, yet it has its composite units different; and such a tree is recognized from another of a different class by its family characteristics, a difference in its leaf, flower, growth, bark

Moreover, he is different from other substances as a jar etc., (distinction created by dissimilarity with other objects), therefore, an absence of the characterising traits of individuality, similarity, and dissimilarity does not constitute the indications of pervasion, but such indication is comprised in the contact or connection with all other substances. Now on this subject doubts are apt to arise that like self, ether, time and quarters are also regarded as pervading, according to the doctrine set up by the *Naiyaikos*; and as atoms are subtle and formless, hence there can be no connection with them, and pervasive substances; because, if these atoms were formed bodies, then between them and Self, there can be said to exist a connection; they are formless, and very subtle—no connection can take place between them, and an all-pervading entity in the same place.—Because that place is filled by the connection of one substance, other substances cannot again create a connection (from want of place), hence the pervasion of diverse substances is quite unmaintainable; but pervasion of *one* substance is alone tenable. Such an expression is absurd. In the connection of a formed substance there is an impediment to the connection of another substance; as in the contact or connection of a hand with a portion of the earth, the feet cannot have any connection with the same spot of earth, but there can be no obstruction for a formless body to be so brought in contact, therefore such obstruction cannot mean to include all substances; this is evident enough, as in the contact of ether in the region of a jar, there is connection of time and quarters too, and if the region of any jar be external to

---

and stone (its family characteristics;)—and as it is easily known from other things as stone etc., it has therefore a third characteristic, which serves to distinguish it from bodies dissimilar. (This may be termed contrast).

So in the case of the secondless Reality, no such apprehension needs be entertained as to the presence of the three aforesaid characterising traits *Dhole's Panchadasi* p. 20.

The words 'inherent' 'isomorphic' and 'disomorphic' refer to the characteristics of individuality, similarity, and dissimilarity, and are explained in the illustration above quoted.

ether, time and quarters, there can be no connection in that place of ether, time and quarters; but there is no such external region; on the other hand, all the regions occupied by substances have a connection with ether, time, and quarters; similarly in connection with atoms it can be said, that in the region of atoms, there is connection with them and different formless substances, and there is no fault in such an assertion. Hence Self is manifold, and completely pervading, and is the medium of connection of all substances with each other. But this inference of *Nyaya* is not correct. Because if Self be admitted to be manifold and all-pervading, then a connection of all Selves in all bodies must also be admitted; so that it will be impossible to ascertain whose body is which, but each Self must have all the bodies. It cannot be said that each Self has his individual body—the one produced as a result of actions,—because, previous to the agency of the body to produce actions, there existed the connection of all Selves, so that actions necessarily will be connected with all Selves, and not one Self. Then again, if it be said, Self has a body in connection with the mind, and the mind is his body; it cannot stand, inasmuch as the mind has a similar connection with all Selves like the body, and it is impossible to ascertain, which mind is the body of a particular Self; but for all Selves all mind will be necessary. In the same way, the organs will also be the subjects of all Selves. In reference to all external objects, to say, 'this is mine' 'that another his' and similar other expressions in common use with men to express their connection with individual bodies, will be entirely done away with, and all bodies belonging to all Selves will necessarily come in practical use; likewise all external objects must be attributed to all Selves instead of that one to whom they belong severally. Further, if it be said that a body with which the *Atma* is connected by the establishment of a relation with the intellect, so as to indicate such body by the epithets 'I' and 'mine' 'that body is his,' then the reply is that 'I' and 'mine' (perceptions of the intellect) are one, and cannot include all souls, but they are one property or faculty, and are equally present in their own subjects. That is to say, it is impossible for 'I' to remain, when there is no 'mine' and *vice versa*. Therefore the *Atma* has only one body, and that body's relative (corresponding) mind, organs of senses and external objects are his. This does not preclude an admission of several *Atmas*, having pervasion for one of his properties. It is impossible to say so, because if the consciousness of 'I' can only affect one Self in one region, yet from the *Naiyaika* doctrine this deduction cannot be formed, but that all selves must have the perception of 'I' in one place. For knowledge is another name for *Buddhi** (intellect) in *Nyaya*, and this knowledge can only proceed from a connection of the mind with Self, and such a connection with the mind all *Atmas* have; consequently as each individual *Atma* has a consciousness of 'I' by his connection with the mind, so in one place (i. e., in one body) all *Atmas* ought to have a similar perception of 'I.' If the reply to the question be, that there is a connection between the mind and all *Atmas*, but where the source of consciousness in an *Atma* is invisible (*Adrishta*), there only the perception of 'I' follows; yet we maintain that the perception ought to affect all *Atmas*, and not one. For, with the admission of the manifoldness and pervasion of *Atma*, it must necessarily follow that the good and bad actions of one individual body, must equally affect the manifold *Atmas* situated in it, in an invisible way; hence the presence of happiness or misery in one body must equally be known and felt by all, for the *Atmas* are manifold, and are all residents of the same place and have the property of pervasion, as we had occasion to say in a previous part of the present treatise. Thus then we find that what the *Naiyaikas* assert about the *Atma* being manifold, and pervading, and agent is not correct.

According to our (*Vedanta*) *Sidhanta*, the internal organ is an agent, it is manifold, and neither pervading, nor atomic, but equal (to the body in size); like the light of a lamp it, can gain access in large bodies, and then discover them by expansion, while in smaller bodies it contracts, as has been explained by Madhusudan Swami in his work styled the *Sidhanta Bindu*.† The internal organ,

---

* I have used consciousness, perception etc., for *Buddhi* which is intellect in the *Vedanta*, but knowledge in *Nyaya*.

† Literally it means a drop, a circle or zero.

by its connection with its own body, becomes the enjoyer or agent. But the pervasion of the internal organ is of that nature, as necessarily to indicate, that it is capable of enjoying, or suffering from its seat in one body, all that goes on in the collective totality of bodies, either in the shape of happiness or that of misery; hence there is no fault in saying it to be possessed of pervasion. (The pervasion of the internal organ is medium sized, it can expand and contract, and thus gain access in a large as well a small body to discover it). If the internal organ be regarded as atomic in size, it must have a definite place to reside inside the body, which is clearly impossible, inasmuch as when a thorn pierces the fleshy parts of the head and feet at one time, pain is felt simultaneously in both the parts: this should not be, if it were an atom confined in one part of the body, there only pain should be perceived, and not elsewhere, —in a part distant from it, and where it is not situated as in the present instance. But since we find the contrary to be true, we therefore hold that it is not an atom, but equal in size to the body, for which, wherever there is pain, it is instantly felt. What is neither an atom, nor pervading is called medium sized.

A new sect of the *Naiyaikas* say, Self is manifold, he is an agent or instrument for enjoying, but is not pervading, hence he is not mixed with enjoyments of other bodies; and as he is not an atom, there can be no impossibility for him to feel pain in two (different) parts of the body simultaneously. But as the internal organ is regarded in the *Vedanta* to be medium sized, so is the *Atma* medium sized too, having fourteen qualities. This even is not correct. For, if the *Atma* were to have the properties of contractility and expansiveness, then like the light of a lamp, he will be reduced to the condition of, and subjected to change, and open to destruction; thus rendering the *Shastras*, which deal on Emancipation, and their 'means' perfectly useless. And if such contraction and expansion are not attributed to him, it is impossible to ascertain, which body he actually resembles in size. If it be said that he resembles the human body, in size, then when he occupies the body of an elephant, he will be unable completely to fill it up, so that the part unoccupied by him shall feel no pain, when hurt. If you say that he resembles an elephat in size, he shall not be able completely to fill up the body of an animal larger in size than an elephant, and the unoccupied part shall have no perception of pain ; then again, as all bodies are large in a scale of comparative gradation, and there is not that which is the largest of all, you cannot say that the *Atma* resembles the largest body in size. Now the body of *Virat* is largest of all, and as that includes all bodies, therefore, an admission of the *Atma's* equality in size with the body of *Virat*, will render it necessary for that *Atma's* connection with collective aggregate of *Atmas* occupying the collective totality of bodies comprised in the *Virat's* body, but such an inference has already been determined to be faulty. Then again, the rule is, a medium sized body (substance) is open to destruction, and is non-eternal like the physical body, so that Self will also be non-eternal. And as we hold the destruction of the internal organ to be caused only by knowledge, hence it is non-eternal, therefore to say that it is medium sized is not open to any objection ; in this manner the doctrine of the novel School of *Tarkikas* is incorrect.

Moreover, those who assert Self is manifold and atomic, say what is faulty and objectionable. Because if self were a doer, an agent or instrument, then the objections already cited, when the atomic view was discussed will equally be applicable here ; and if he is not admitted as an agent, then the necessity for his manifoldness will be entirely done away with. If he is considered secondless, one, pervading in all bodies, unconditioned, unassociated, that indeed is the proper way of regarding Self; but then the non-admission of his agent-ship, or instrumentality as a doer etc., will cause him to abandon his own *Sidhanta*. For the expounders of the atomic view say, knowledge, virtue and vice, happiness and misery, etc., etc., are so many faculties belonging to the *Atma*, so that if he resembles an atom in size, it is impossible for him to occupy all parts of the body, and the parts that are unoccupied by him, will have no perception of pain, when injured, like a dead-body. Then again, if it be said the *Atma*, may be placed in one region of the body, but like the diffusibility of musk his knowledge is scattered in all parts of the body, so that in the matter of all parts of the body, the conformable and adverse relations produce that experience of pain. But this is open to objection. For the rule is, a substance having a property, occupying a region can only fill its province with that quality, and quality does not reside outside, but inside the substance which has that property. [As for instance the scent of the rose is situated in the flower, and not outside of it, in the stalk, stem, or its branches etc., similarly the scent of a rose will diffuse in the place where it is kept, in a room, a flower-pot etc., and not outside in the court-yard, or in the house of a second person]. As for instance, outside of a jar its form is not present, so knowledge cannot reside outside of the *Atma*. Moreover, wherever the subtle atoms of musk are diffused, there its peculiar smell is sure to be felt, though the particles of the musk so diffused are not visible, hence it cannot be maintained that the *Atma* is an atom.

In some part of the *Sruti*, where the *Atma* is described as finer than an atom, or the atom of an atom, it simply means that as the finest particle of a substance or its atom cannot be seen by a short-sighted person, so one who is deprived of knowledge, can have no consciousness of the *Atma*, hence it is said to be equal to an atom. The *Sruti* does not mean to convey the idea of his resemblance to an atom, or that he is an atom virtually, for the *Vedas* have in many places explained the pervasion of the *Atma*. Thus then he is not an atom. In this way it is impossible to maintain either the pervasion, medium size, atomic or manifoldness of Self. To conclude then, there is one pervasion, that is the *Atma*; and if virtue and vice, happiness and misery, bondage and emancipation, are regarded as his subjects, and they belong to him, practically the perception or presence of happiness, in some and misery in others, or that one man is subjected to the bondage of re-birth while another is freed, will cease. Hence virtue and the rest belong to intellect. Though it can be said, as intellect is insentient consequently the perception of happiness and the rest cannot naturally belong to it, yet this has been said only to point out emphatically that virtue and the rest do not belong to the *Atma* but to the intellect, whose faculties they are. Such an assertion does not amount to an admission that intellect along with its properties or faculties, (happiness and the rest) are all comprised in Self.

When a substance is substituted for, or erroneously attributed to another, that does not form a true condition of an object, as a snake in a rope; here no real snake is present. In the same way, neither *Buddhi* nor happiness and the rest are present in Self. Moreover, a substituted substance can never be the vehicle of another substance, hence intellect cannot be the vehicle of happiness etc. But ignorance is substituted for pure intelligence, and the internal organ is similarly transferred to the associate of ignorance, while to the associate of that organ, virtue and vice, happiness and misery, bondage and emancipation are erroneously attributed. Thus then, the situation of virtue and the rest in Self is the associate of the internal organ, for which, they are called its faculties. It is absurd to speak of virtue and the rest, with which the internal function is endowed, its subjects—an attribution due to error.—For the subject is formed with the predicate, and if the internal organ be regarded as a predicate of the *Atma*—the site of virtue and vice etc.,—it will also be reduced to a conditional similarity, and be a seat for virtue and vice, happiness and misery, bondage and emancipation. But this is clearly impossible. For an unreal substance cannot abide in a place, consequently the internal organ is not the predicate for the erroneous attribution of virtue etc. to Self, but it is an associate. Now it is the nature of an associate to discover a thing, placed in the same region with it, while it remains distinct;* while the predicate has the faculty of discovering an object along with itself, when such object is situated in the same spot with it. One having distinctive property is called the subject of a predicate.† That which forms the associate is called associated. Therefore, when

---

* '*Tatasha*' is that property which is distinct from the nature of a thing, yet is the faculty by which it is known.

† '*Visheshana*' is a predicate, an adjective, attribute etc., '*Visheshya*' is the subject or object of the predicate, noun, name. Both are derived from the roots ' *Vi* ' before ' *Shish* ' to distinguish by attributes.

virtue and vice etc., are erroneously attributed to the internal organ as its distinguishing properties, the intelligence of the parts occupied by the internal organ together with that organ, (the two) abide in the attribution, and the organ itself is substituted. Here there can be no occupation. For this purpose, virtue and the rest are said to be substituted in the associated internal organ; so that in the local intelligence of regions occupied by the internal organ alone resides the occupancy and not in the organ itself, is an expression that can be allowed. In the same way, the internal organ is substituted for associated ignorance, and not in the distiguishing properties (or subject of the predicate) of ignorance. In this manner, the substitutes, virtue etc., have their site in Self, and the internal organ is the associate of that occupation, where such erroneous attribution is transferred or substituted, for which they are said to be the faculties or attributes of the intellect; and both the internal organ and Self are, from indiscrimation, regarded as their subjects, for which the subject of the internal organ—the abiding intelligence, demonstrator or *Pramata* is said to have them for its properties. No matter whether they are the properties of the internal organ, or of its subjective attribute (*Pramata*), or like a snake in a chord, or objects created in a dream, like the blue etherial town of a Gandharba, they can never belong to Self as his attributes. Though they are erroneously transferred on the *Atma*, yet when an object is transferred thus, it does not truly constitute that substance. Now a transfer or substitution is a creation of fancy or imagination, consequently Self who is pervading and devoid of anger, spite, virtue, and vice, happiness and misery, bondage and emancipation is 'real.' What is destroyed by knowledge is called 'unreal.' What can never be destroyed in any period of time (waking, dreaming and profound slumber) is called 'real,' and 'existence' or 'being' (*Sat*). Now the site of destruction for all objects is Self, so that if he were to be destroyed, then they must have another site wherein to rest [or merge]. Because they cannot rest on 'nothing' or void (in vaccuo). Hence if self were also destroyed along with the rest, they must have a resting place, and that another *ad infinitum*, thus it will create the defect known by the name of *Anavasta* or carrying an argument *ad infinitum*. Moreover, it may be asked in reply to those who hold destruction of Self, whether any body has ever an experience of such destruction, or not ? If the reply be in the affirmative, then it is an impossibility ; for he who is to experience it, is the *Atma*; and to experience his Self-destruction will be similar to the sight of having one's head beheaded,—and he saw it ; hence it is impossible to experience the destruction of one-self, and it never takes place. Then again if it be asserted, destruction of Self does take place, but it is not experienced by any one ; it will establish his non-destruction, because what is never experienced by any one amounts to what is conveyed by the expression " A sterile woman's son." Thus then the *Atma* is never destroyed, but is ever existent and intelligence. Knowledge, resembling light in its power of discovery, is called intelligence (*Chit*). If the fact were otherwise, and Self had no power of discovery, the insentient world would never be discovered. The internal organ and the senses cannot be credited with powers of discovery ; for they are finite, hence products. Substances that are finite are results, or actions, as for instance a jar ; and as the internal and sensory organs are also finite, they are therefore resulting products or derivative actions. Now ' finite' are those which are destroyed by time and place, and 'actions' or 'resulting products' are those which are insentient [inanimate ?] Hence the internal and sensory organs have no power of discovery, for they are actions, consequently the discoverer of all things, Self, is light-like or self-illuminated. If it be said, self has no power of discovery, but is insentient, and that for the faculty of knowledge, which is his quality, he discerns all objects, it may be asked, Whether such quality of knowledge which self has, is eternal or transient ? If the former, then that will establish self to be knowledge itself. For the rule is, what is different from self is transient; and if knowledge be regarded as a distinct substance from self, it will be non-eternal, so that to speak of knowledge as eternal, and yet to say it distinct from self will be clearly absurd, as that will imply the presence of antagonistic properties,

—of eternal and non-eternal duration co-existing in the same substance; if the latter (knowledge is transient) then it will virtually be reduced to the condition of the jar and other objects; it will be insentient, and devoid of intelligence. When a thing is non-eternal, it is always insentient, hence it cannot be said, that knowledge is non-eternal; it is on the other hand eternal, and in the matter of that, resembles the *Atma*; besides such a consideration, will make the *Atma* sometimes conscious and at other times unconscious, so that consciousness or knowledge will be something distinct from him; on the other hand by regarding knowledge as eternal, the distinction of a separate entity is removed. The quality of a substance may or may not be present in it: as for instance, the yellow or blue colour of a thing may or may not be present all along [it may be removed by washing, or it appears afterwards in a subsequent stage of development as in flowers and fruits] hence a quality is of short duration i.e., transient, while knowledge for its eternal duration, is not transient. Therefore its resemblance with Self is complete. It cannot be said, that knowledge is non-eternal and derived by the senses or the internal organ. For we find in the state of profound slumber, the senses etc., are inactive and at rest, and do not carry on their respective functions, yet there is a conscious perception of happiness as evinced by the experience of a person on waking " I was sleeping happily, I knew nothing then." This should not be, if there were no happiness present along with such sleep, and he ought not to remember it. A. known thing never crosses the memory, consequently the perception of happiness in profound slumber must be taken for an act of remembrance due to the actual perception of such happiness, without any connectio with the organs, sensory or internal; for, they were at rest, inactive and doing nothing. Hence knowledge is eternal. Self never exists without knowledge, hence they are one: as for instance, fire never continues without heat, so that heat is identical with fire, similarly knowledge is identical with Self. What is transitory in duration is always a quality, but as heat and knowledge are not transitory, therefore they are not qualities of, but identical with fire and self. Now when a thing may or may not be present, it is called transient or transitory. The function of the internal organ is subject to birth and death, not so is knowledge. Knowledge which resembles Self is not a cause of particular practice, but either knowledge with function, or knowledge domineering over function is the cause of practice. So says the *Avacheda vadi*.

The supporters of the reflex theory (*Avasvadi*) hold reflection of intelligence with the function, for practical purposes; either by the reflex or by direct function [which is incorrect]. Knowledge identically the same with Self is the means by which practically all things are done and never otherwise. Thus then the all-discoverer, knowledge, is Self. Therefore, as a discoverer of all things, he is called (*Chit*) intelligence and bliss. If there be no blissfulness in self, there will be no conscious perception of happiness in connection with a subject. Happiness does not actually exist in a subject, wealth, etc., (this has already been mentioned). If such were a fact, then all would have equally felt it, but we do not find that to be the case, inasmuch as the same thing may produce happiness in one and pain in another. As for instance, from the touch of fire, insects and from the sight of a he-snake and lion, a she-snake and lioness, are respectively delighted, but the touch of the same fire or the sight of the deadly snake and lion gives pain to others, which should not be. It will simply be an anomaly, if happiness were connected with any subject. According to the *Sidhanta*, the conclusion is, when a fire-insect is actuated with a desire of touching fire, it can derive no pleasure, as the intellect is not then in a condition of steadiness, but is rather fickle and changeable; by the relative connection of fire, that desire is removed for a short time, when the intellect loses its fickleness and comes to realize the perception of happiness; other persons have no desire for fire, but are desirous of other objects, which desire is not removed by the relative connection with fire, consequently the unsteady internal organ has no perception of felicity from the connection with fire.

But in connection with this subject it may be argued, the function of the internal organ in the shape of desire ceases when the object of that desire is fulfilled, and as there is no instrumental cause for another function, it cannot originate, and without a function there is no perception of actual felicity, therefore happiness must necessarily be present in a subject. But this is quite untenable; for though the function of the internal organ in the shape of desire is wanting, and even with the birth of such a desire there is no happiness experienced, for desire is produced by lust, while the perception of happiness proceeds only from the good quality (*Satwavic*) of function, yet for the purpose of accomplishing that desire, and making it its subject, the function of the internal organ in the shape of knowledge or conscious perception is due to the quality of goodness. For knowledge proceeds only from that good quality. This is the rule; and the resulting happiness is due to that quality. But this functional knowledge is externally placed, and the associated intelligence of the internal organ in the form of happiness, situated behind that knowledge, is not received into the function, hence the associated intelligence of the subject is perceived in happiness, and that associated intelligence of the subject is non-different from Self; and Self is said to be the subject of perceptive happiness. As regards that functional knowledge, the instrument is a relationship of the subject with the sensory organs. Or the external functional knowledge produces another function which is internal to it, whose subject the associated intelligence of the internal organ is recognized as felicity. This is a good conclusion. In that function, absence of desire etc., is the instrumental cause. As a devotee residing in a secluded and lonely place, bereft of all desires, has no function like external knowledge, but feels pleasure, so that in the absence of the instrumental cause, desire, the internally directed function is the knower of that happiness; so after its gratification when there is no more desire left, the internally directed function follows subsequent to knowledge, by which happiness associated with the internal organ is perceived. Now between the perception of actual happiness, and subjective knowledge there is no interval, or inter-space, for which men are deluded into the belief of experiencing happiness from wealth or other subjects. This view is superior to the first one. Because, from the subjective knowledge in the form of function, perception of happiness associating the internal organ is not possible; so that if felicity associating a subject were to be realized, the cognition of a tree on the road side must also be due to the good quality. Here too, intelligence associated with the tree representing felicity, ought also to be perceived; in the same way from knowledge, the associated intelligence of all known objects, happiness ought also to be perceived, so that from knowledge of all other objects which do not resemble Self, a form of the externally directed function, there cannot proceed happiness resembling the associated intelligence of known objects. In this manner, from a relationship with material felicity, happiness, a semblance of Self is perceived. If Self were not blissfulness, there would follow no happiness in connection with wealth etc. Thus then Self is happiness. Moreover the things related to Self also excite our love, and the things quite close to him are better loved than the rest. Under such circumstances, external objects will be the least loved, while the most internal will be the best loved; because the former are distantly placed than the latter, which are quite close to him. Thus there is a scale of gradation. What love we have for the friend of a son, is less than the affection for that son. Then again, love for the gross and subtle body is greater than an affection for a son; and of the two bodies, affection for the subtle is greater than that of the gross; of them the last mentioned are in closer proximity than those first mentioned. The subtle body also contains the reflection of Self. That reflection is not to be found anywhere else, so that Self is connected with the subtle body by his reflection, and not with anything else. The subtle body has a relationship with the gross physical, therefore the relation which Self has for the gross body is created by the subtle, and a son is connected by the gross body, as a son's friend by that son. In this way, what are situated in close proximity to Self are better loved than those placed at a distance. Since affection proceeds from a close relationship with self, it must necessarily follow that Self is the source or fountain of affection, and other objects have nothing of it. As an affection for a son's friend is due to the affection which one bears for his son, consequently it can be said, affection is present in the son, and not in the friend of that son; similarly what are nearest to Self are seats of greater affection; hence every one has an affection for his Self, and that affection results in happiness and absence of misery, and not otherwise. What affection is produced for other objects is for the sake of happiness and want of grief, so that beyond happiness and absence of grief, there is not another substance which has affection; hence the *Atma* who is subject of all affections is blissfulness, and without any grief whatever. The absence of an imaginary contrivance is nothing less than what is called presence of site (*adhishtana*). For instance, as in the absence of the imaginary snake, the rope alone remains, so is self in a want of fancied grief. Thus is established the blissfulness of Self. What the *Nyayaikas* hold about blissfulness being a quality of Self is not true. For, if the quality of blissfulness be regarded as eternal, the defect of *ad infinitum* will not affect it, and Self will be established as blissfulness. Moreover bliss is not held to be eternal in *Nyaya*. If it be said to be non-eternal, its friendly subject, and the sensory organs, by their connection, must be admitted to produce happiness; that will preclude the perception of happiness in the profound slumbering condition; for then, between the senses and subject, there exists no relation, consequently happiness is not a quality of Self, but he is himself happiness. Thus then, it would appear that Self is eternal, intelligence and bliss. They are non-different from each other, but are identically the same. If they would have been his qualities, there must naturally be a difference between them, but as they are his semblance, consequently they are not distinct from, but one with him. The same Self is indestructible, hence eternal; quite the opposite of insentiency, hence intelligence; and the very reverse of misery, therefore the subject of happiness and affection. As heat is manifested in fire, so is eternal intelligence and bliss discovered in Self. And as *Brahma* is defined in the *Shastras* to be eternal, intelligence and bliss, so Self is *Brahma*. Then again, *Brahma* signifies pervasion i.e., what cannot be confined or limited by any region, hence infinite. If Self were distinct from It, he would be finite; but that is not the case. What cannot be limited by a region, must also be infinite in regard to time. (This is the rule), so that if Self were distinct from *Brahma* then he will not only be finite, but also non-eternal: for what is confined in one place, has his duration of existence also bounded. Hence *Brahma* and Self are non-distinct from each other. Moreover if this difference were allowed, It* will be reduced to not-self and insentiency, like that of a jar etc. Hence It is not distinct from Self, but Self is *Brahma*. The one intelligence abides in the whole of this vast expanse and in *Maya* (matter), for which It is called *Brahma,*and for its presence in Ignorance and distributive segregate or individual units of bodies is called *Atma* (Self). The indication of 'That'† (*Tat*) is *Brahma,* and 'Thou' (*Twam*) *Atma.* Iswar, witness, is indicated by 'That' while the witnessing intelligence of the individual is the indication of 'Thou.' Intelligence associated with the distributive segregate is called *Jiva* ; Intelligence associated with the collective aggregate is Iswara ; for this difference of associates Iswara and *Jiva* are distinct and separate, but without them, they are one. As a jar placed in a temple, has their individual spaces distinct from one another, but if the jar and temple (associate) are left out of consideration, the space occupied by them respectively appear one, undistinct, whole, similarly without their associates *Brahma* and *Jiva* are one. They are the same entity. And Self the semblance of *Brahma,* is said to be unborn (without a beginning); for birth signifies destruction. If Self were said to have been born he must have a natural death also. But those who believe in a future state of existence do not regard Self to be non-eternal, because in that case, the first birth would be independent of actions done in a previous state of objective existence, and happiness or misery will result not according to an individual's merits or demerits. Besides, the result of good actions already performed will be destroyed without any proportionate benefit. Hence they have no faith in the birth of Self. For in that case, even the admission of Self as a doer, or agent will mainly be in reference to the body. Then again, there must be cause for the birth of a substance ; but in regard to Self it is impossible to find out such a cause ; for in assigning that cause, it will be distinct from Self, and

---

* *Brahma* is neuter. *Brahmā* masculine ; Self masculine.

† 'That art thou' (*Tat Twam Asi*) is here referred.

that distinction from self is entirely contained in him, consequently there is no cause for Self. As for instance, in respect to the rope-snake, the latter cannot be a cause of the former, so a fancied substance is not a cause of Self. As in the same rope, different illusions may happen to different persons:—to a second, a snake; to a third, furrow in earth, or a piece of water; so here, there are two parts; one of which is called the ordinary (*edam*) or 'this' and the other particular (*vishesha*) or snake etc. The first part pervades in the particular portion which constitutes a snake. 'This is a snake.' 'This is a stick.' 'This is a furrow on the ground.' 'This is a piece of water.' In these particular instances, the ordinary portion 'this' pervades a snake and the rest everywhere, and that pervasion represented by the ordinary part 'this' represents the rope : and the knowledge of that ordinary portion for the illusion is called the ordinary knowledge of rope. That ordinary portion ('This') is true, inasmuch as even subsequent to the knowledge of a rope, it continues. As for instance, in the illusion 'This is a snake,' along with the snake 'this' continues to be present, so after the illusion has been destroyed 'this' appears with the rope, as for example 'This is a rope.' Thus then 'this' accompanies both the conditions,—in the illusion, and after it has been destroyed; if it were false and unreal, it ought not to have appeared after the destruction of the illusory snake, hence the all-pervading 'this' is true and real, and the site is rope ; and their mutual change of condition, the snake, is a fancied contrivance. So in the case of all objects there are five parts, *viz.*, name, form, existence, manifestibility or tangibility, and affection (*Priya*). When we say a *Ghat*, we use a name formed of two alphabets,* its form is circular, its round shape

---

† To persons who are unacquainted with the Sanskrit or any of the Indian vernaculars it will rather prove harassing to find a word evidently made with four alphabets, yet said to have only two, as in the word used *Ghat*. Here the first alphabet of the word is represented by the combination of the two English alphabets, the third 'a' is distinctly pronounced after it, but not used, hence there are only two.

establishes its existence "This is a jar"; and what is thus established is its tangibility or manifestibility. Besides this, a jar is a dearly loved article, and one that excites pleasure or happiness. A he-snake is dear to his mate, a female snake. In this way, every known object has (a relative connection or concatenation of) five parts. Of them, 'existence' 'tangibility' and 'affection' pervade all objects, while name and form are a matter of changed condition i. e., inconstant. What may or may not be present in all conditions or circumstances is said to be 'inconstant,' it may be present in some and absent in other conditions. The name 'jar' and its round shape do not apply to a piece of cloth. Similarly as the name and shape of the latter do not apply to the former, so for their want of applicability in all conditions and under all circumstances, in the manner above indicated, they are said to be inconstant. But 'existence' 'tangibility' and 'affection' are included in all things, as if they are attached, so to speak. As in the case of " A snake" " A stick" the word 'this' attached to them is true, and abides in them; so 'existence,' 'manifestibility' and 'affection' attached to all objects are real, and abiding; and like the snake and stick, name and form are mere contrivances of fancy or imagination, and are inconstant. But the other three *viz.*, existence, tangibility and affection are resemblances of eternal intelligence and bliss, consequently they are like the *Atma*. Thus then, eternal intelligence and bliss belong to Self and are real; while the whole of this material objective world is simply a creation or contrivance of fancy, and that cannot by any show of plausibility be ascribed as a parent of Self. Hence the Spirit or *Atma* is said to be unborn—without a birth or beginning. A substance that is born is subject to five modifications *viz.*, creation or birth, growth, change, decline, or waste, and annihilation or death. But as Self is unborn, he is independent of the above modifications, and they cannot affect him either anteriorly or posteriorly. This is why, he is said to be without the six conditions beginning with birth and ending in death; and he is called 'existence' and 'manifested'; while a jar is the very reverse of that,— for it is destructible. And such self is unconditioned, that is to say, unrelated to any thing or sustance, having neither family, dissimilar, nor individual characteristics. To be more explicit, the relation of one jar with another is called by the name of family or similar characteristic, its difference from a cloth is termed the dissimilar, while its individuality is made up by its features. Now the relation which a cloth has with the weaving loom is said to be that of individual relation—a relation set apart and kept within itself. If Self were two and both of them infinite, then there could be said to exist the relationship of similarity caused by the characteristic of the family or genus, but as Self is one, consequently there can be no such family relationship of similarity. Then again, not-Self is dissimilar from Self, but that is a mere creation of fancy like mirage water, and with such an illusory unreality, Self can have no possible similarity, that is plain enough. As with mirage water, the earth (or spot of ground where it takes place) has no relation, inasmuch as the locality is not moistened with that water; so is Self unrelated with not-Self, because the latter are unreal, for they are products or contrivances of fancy and illusion; hence between them, the relation even of dissimilarity does not exist. If Self were endowed with any features, there must naturally belong to him the individual characteristics, but he is eternal, therefore without any form or feature, hence the relation of individuality does not belong to him. Thus are shewn the conditional relations of similarity, dissimilarity, and individuality not to belong to Self, for which he is said to be unconditioned or unrelated, or better still, unassociated. And that eternal intelligence and bliss, unborn and unchangeable, indestructible and unconditioned Self, Pupil, art thou. In this way the tutor replies to the question set forth by the pupil in the first-half of the rhyme. In reply to the query, Who is author of universe? the following half stanza is being given.

> *Maya* subservient to the pervasive intelligence, creates the world and breaks [evolutes].

Intelligence, that is all-pervading has a dependent, which forms that intelligence its subject, and that is *Maya* which is neither 'being' nor 'non-being' but distinct from both. It is an unnatural force of ignorance (matter), from which the evolution of the world is broken. The words 'evolution' and 'broken' have reference to what exists, from which is established, Iswara is Intelligence with *Maya*. He is the creator, protector, and destroyer of the universe; or that it is produced naturally i. e., evoluted.

In reply to the question, Whether it is creation or evolution ? Or whether it is created by a *Jiva* or Iswara ? The reply is, Iswara is the creator; and it is not naturally produced. If an action can proceed without a cause, then a jar can be produced without a potter. Therefore it is reasonable to look upon a creator, who is omniscient, for he who wants to be the agent or doer of an action must have a knowledge of what he is about, and of the formative material with which he is to work; hence we conclude that the creator of the world has built this world with a thorough knowledge of it and its material; and for that knowledge of them, He is called omniscient and omnipotent,—because *Jiva* is parvipotent, and cannot even conceive the vastness of the universe. Therefore this secondless universe must have a cause whose power is secondless i. e., omnipotent. Then again, He is separate and distinct, for a parvipotent being must be dependent on some one who is more powerful, but an Omnipotent Being is independent, hence He is said to be distinct and separate; and this being is called by the name of Iswara (Lord), while a parviscient, parvipotent and dependent being is called *Jiva*.

In its true acceptation, *Jiva* is not parviscient [for he is one with *Brahma*] yet Ignorance is apt to attribute it to him, so that the illusion of parviscience in the *Jiva*, a result of ignorance, is called the [normal] condition of the individual. But a similar illusion of parviscience in Iswara, there is none; on the other hand, he is made of *Maya* and Omniscient. This I will speak of particularly in a subsequent portion of the work.

Thus then Iswara, and not *Jiva*, is the creator of the world. He is not confined in one region, but equally pervades everywhere. If his limited pervasion be admitted, He will be liable to destruction; for what is finite in regard to place, is so in regard to time also. Moreover his liability to be destroyed, will introduce the admission of a creator for him, who must be eternal, for all created products are open to destruction; but it does not apply to Iswara that He created himself, for such a consideration is regarded defective and called (*Atmasrayi*), "self-dependent for existence." It means that He is himself the doer of an action, and is the object of that action; or to illustrate by an example, as a potter is the doer of a jar, a pot, so the agent and the action or the potter and jar etc., are different and not one, and to regard them as one is defective and known by the name of "self-dependence." A defect is defined in the following manner:—

'*Karma*' means an action; what is antagonistic of action is called defect, and as self-dependence is antagonistic of action, it is a defect; consequently the cause of Iswara must be found elsewhere, external to himself, who again must have a prior cause, and that another, which again is defective, and known by the name of 'interdependence;' that will imply the admission of a third Iswara as an agent of creation, and the admission of the second of that third creator, will be subject to the defect of self-dependence, while the first be a characteristic of the defect of circling round in the manner of the revolution of a wheel.

That is to say, the first, second, and third Iswaras arranged in a circle, like so many pokes of a wheel, by revolving produce the one subsequent to him, and thus the third is also an agent of the first, as the first is that of the second. Therefore causation and effect will be performing a circuit establishing no one as the primary agent, but showing their mutual dependence. Moreover in the variety known by the name of 'interdependent' the presence of two, and their mutual dependence on each other are needed. But without the establishment of one, another cannot be ascertained, like the cause of a potter, his father, and not himself; so that there must be a prior cause for the first Iswara; and as the potter's father cannot descend from his son, but had his father prior to him from whom he was born, and not from any or another father, which latter must be relatively non-existent so far as he is concerned, yet such a father must pass for his parent; carrying this to a stage higher, we find that the grand-parent of this potter cannot take his birth either from his son or grandson, but had his own father prior to him, whom we may call for convenience sake as the fourth in the line of ascent, so the third cannot descend from the first, and second potter, hence he must claim his origin from a fourth, who again must have an ancestor in the fifth, and so on *ad infinitum.*

Now this *ad infinitum* defect implies a current of continuity without resting any where in the back ground. If, therefore, a chain of creators be admitted, which of them is the actual creator cannot be determined. There is no reason why one should regard the creator of this universe as one and not many, and the absence of the reason is called separation without going away; and if this 'chain' [of consecutive causation] would rest anywhere, then the final resting spot occupied by a creator must be *the* creator, and he is fit to be so recognized, but all his predecessors are reduced into nothingness, so far as creation is concerned. This is called 'antecedent privation.' It reduces the succeeding ones into a conditional want or absence. Thus then, if Iswara be the finality, He must be the source of creation, and such a consideration will convey the six defects of self-dependence and the rest, hence Iswara is not finite but pervading and eternal, and between him, and the *Jiva* there is no difference whatever, except in their respective associates. Because in the eyes of those [*Avachedi Vadis*] who seek to distinguish them for peculiar properties, Iswara is defined as the predicate of intelligence in *Maya*, while a *Jiva* is the predicate of intelligence in Ignorance.* According to the expounders of the reflex theory, Iswara is the predicate of both the *Maya* and reflex-intelligence, and *Jiva* is the predicate of both the intelligences of ignorance and the reflex. They consider both the intelligences to be one, and non-distinct; what they insist is, the difference in the two condition of *Iswara* and *Jiva* consists in the *Maya* of the former

---

* Ignorance stands for *Avidya*, it should be *A*-knowledge, though in the matter of that they are all one, as they refer to matter. Kapila's matter and the *Vedantin's* Ignorance, *Ajnana* or *Avidya* are all one. It is enough to remember this.

and Ignorance *plus* reflection of the latter. In the same way, the supporters of the distinguishing view (*Avached Vadi*) regard Ignorance and *Maya* as distinct from each other, but no distinction in the intelligence, and that the *Jiva* is a reflection of intelligence in (*Ajnana*) Ignorance,* while Iswara is the light itself.† Here also, there is no distinction in intelligence naturally; but both Iswaraship and *Jivaship* are attributed to that one intelligence; the how and wherefore will be explained in the sequel.

Thus then the creator of the world is the omniscient, omnipotent, distinct, Iswara, who is all-pervading; between whom and *Jiva*, there is only a difference in the predicate, and not in the nature of them. This is the reply to the second question. Whether knowledge is the means for emancipation; or works or devotional exercises, as has been asked in the verse is now being determined.

> The cause of emancipation is one, and that is knowledge, neither works, nor contemplation.
>
> The destruction of the snake in a rope follows only, when that rope is fully known in all its parts.

For emancipation, neither contemplation nor devotional exercises are enough, but knowledge is the only means which accomplish it; for if bondage in reference to the *Atma* be true, it cannot then be destroyed by knowledge, but works and devotion will be necessary for release, but as self is not really subject to bondage, which is unreal like the snake in a rope, and which unreality can only be destroyed by the abiding knowledge, and not by means of works or devotional

---

* *Avidya* and *Ajnana* can only be represented by the same word Ignorance,—though elsewhere I have tried to particularize them by coining A-knowledge for *Avidya*, and allowing Ignorance to do its duty for *Ajnana*. The reader will keep this distinction in mind for following the text closely.

† '*Bimba*' means disc of the Sun, also reflection. I have adopted 'light,' for the creator of the Sun, cannot be compared to the sun's disc, an anomaly.

exercises, in the same manner as the snake cannot be removed from the rope by any action, but only by knowing all parts of the rope thoroughly, so the attribution of bondage to Self is due entirely to ignorance, and that ignorance-created-bondage in Self is destroyed only by a thorough knowledge of Self. If emancipation were to proceed from works as their result, then it will be non-eternal. The rice produced from cultivation is non-eternal. Likewise the blissful abode in Heaven, as a result of sacrificial offering is of short duration.* Since therefore the result of good and meritorious actions are short-lived, if emancipation were to follow from them, it must also be short-lived. Hence it is not a result of works. Similarly if emancipation were to result from devotional exercises, it will be non-eternal, for they are mental actions produced with a desire, and the result of action is always temporary ; hence it is not a result of devotion.

A person engaged in action or work receives for his share, in return, five varieties of results viz., the origin or destruction of a substance, or the attainment of a certain object, or its modification, in the same way, conception in the form of another substance is called 'modification.' Now conception is of two kinds, the removal of a dirt or defect, and the origin of quality. These five are the natural and adequate products derivable from works. None of them apply to one, who is desirous of release, hence emancipation is only attainable by means of knowledge. These means are 'hearing' 'consideration' and the rest already described in an early part of the present work. They produce a desire for acquiring knowledge

---

* Actions are non-eternal, hence their results are likewise so, for the properties of a cause are transmitted to its products. In this way after the consummation of the result, no matter, whether in a higher or lower sphere, the individual is subjected to re-birth. For this reason, it is emphatically laid down to abstain from all works, and be passive. That alone is enough to stop the future birth, though not immediately after, but in a subsequent stage ; for the unfinished results of prior works must have to be consummated by inheriting one or more bodies, as the case may be.

of Self, which actions can never bring about. As a potter can by his act turn out a pot or jar etc., so a person desirous of release cannot by any action or work procure his emancipation. Because the cessation of fruitless pursuits, and attainment of supreme felicity is emancipation, and that destruction of fruitlessness* from Self is always effected as the removal of a snake is effected from a rope; and as Self is the resort of supreme felicity, the attainment of that happiness is always effected. Hence the naturally effected emancipation can never proceed from works.

What cannot be effected by a substance previously, can never be produced by works, and an effected substance never originates. Moreover 'hearing' the *Vedanta* has not been mentioned as a source of emancipation. But Self is free and eternal, and he has not even the semblance of a trace of what is proper to be done. To know this, requires the assistance of 'hearing,' so that the individual ceases to be deluded with what is proper for him to do. If after hearing the utterances of *Vedanta*, any one has an inclination still left in him as to what is proper, he has not learnt the first principle, or primitive truth.† For this reason, the constant removal of the useless, and which answers no purpose, and acquirement of felicity, that is constantly got as a result of hearing the *Vedanta*, is mentioned by the Deva Guru‡ in *Niskarma Siddhi*.§ So that to one desirous of release, actions are inadequate for procuring

---

* Such as are useless and answer no purpose (*Anartha*).

† '*Tatwa*' is first principle, the elements are so many *Tatwas*, it is likewise the primitive truth.

‡ Sureswara the reputed disciple of Shankara Acharya, and author of *Niskarmya Siddhi* disapproved of acting with impunity. The *Panchadasi* uses it to support its assertion, that an enlightened or wise man should avoid evil. Otherwise it will destroy his knowledge, and if he throws of all restraint and acts with impunity, where is the difference between him and a dog ?

§ This word means literally an effecting of absolving one-self from actions in their totality, natural calls of course excepted.

emancipation. In the manner of a stick used for breaking a pot (where a stick is a fit instrument for the purpose), one desirous of release has no fit substance which he must seek to destroy for emancipating him from future re-births, because he has not another desired object save that 'release.' If it be said, destruction of bondage is a fit object for removal; but as Self is not subject to it, it is an illusion to think him to be a subject of re-birth, and a false belief cannot be destroyed by any action whatever. From true knowledge of Self, the cessation of that false belief is naturally to follow, hence for such an individual who is desirous of being freed, there is no other adequate substance, which he has any necessity for removing by means of works. As by walking, a man arrives at a destined village, so by works no emancipation is attainable; because if Self be eternal and free, he cannot have any desire of being freed; who is subjected to bondage, can only have a desire of release, and in Self there is no knowledge, consequently the adequacy of actions to procure emancipation to one desirous of release does not apply. As by cooking, rice is converted into food suited to digestion, so by undertaking works, a person desirous of release, cannot so convert them, as to produce the suitable emancipation, for there is no other change. If on the other hand, Self be admitted in the first, to be subject to the bondage of re-birth, and in emancipation, the acquirement of the distinction of the four hands of *Vishnu* be likewise admitted, then that person, desirous of release, may be transformed into some other shape, that is quite possible; but in Self the acquisition of any other shape is never allowed. Hence by the conversion of actions, adequate emancipation can never accrue to a person desirous of release. As by a cloth sieve, dust and dirt are removed, so a person desirous of release has no conception of removing his dirt or defect, by recourse to adequate actions; because he desires not the destruction of any other defect, consequently the defect must imply Self to be full of dirt, and the destruction will apply to his defects; but that Self is eternal and pure, he is free from defects, fault, or impurities, consequently the conception of destruction, or removal of such impurities is not possible. Moreover as regards sin which is an impurity of the internal organ, and to say that which is to be so destroyed by adequate works is indeed true, but the pure minded person, bent after release has no demerit, or sin in his internal organ, consequently the conception of destruction of the impurity of sin does not apply to him. Then again, if ignorance be regarded as an impurity, that is sure enough present in Self, but no action can destroy it; for knowledge, and not action, is opposed to it, consequently the conception of the removal of impurity by adequate acts does not hold good in his case.

As by the act of rubbing a cloth with safflower, it is dyed red, and a suitable conception of that color is also produced, so in the case of a person desirous of release, conception as to the production of a quality by suitable works, never takes place.

Because in regard to Self, the origin of any quality does not apply, as he is devoid of qualities; consequently conception as to the origin of that quality does not apply to a person desirous of release, and he has no adequate necessity for practising actions which mean results.

Actions produce five, and not more results; but none of them, apply to a person desirous of being freed from future re-births; so that by abstaining from them, he has an inclination for hearing, which is a means of knowledge. Devotion is also a mental act; hence I need not adduce separate arguments to do away with it. [But what has been said in reference to actions apply to it as well]. Thus then either devotion or works alone are barely sufficient to procure emancipation. Knowledge stands alone in the matter of that release as its source.

There are some, who admit works and devotion, with knowledge, as the source of emancipation, and support it by arguments and examples in the following manner :—As a bird cannot fly in the air by a single wing, but by using both its wings, so by the single wing of knowledge, a person cannot arrive at the abode of the freed; but of that other wing, which is represented by actions *plus* devotion besides the one of knowledge,—of that, devotion is a mental act, consequently there is virtually but one wing. Now for another illustration; as the sight of the bridge known as *Setbund Rameswar* causes the destruction of sin, the sight itself is visible knowledge, but with faith and reverence, or love, one should move on; this is the absolute rule, following which, causes sin to be destroyed, and a man without any faith as to the efficacy of the bridge in that way, will derive no fruit. As the visible knowledge of that bridge, faith, and the other rules, must be regarded as necessities for the production of its specific effect, so a knowledge of *Brahma*, in regard to the result, emancipation, must have needs for works and devotion. And if release be admitted as a product of knowledge, even the source of that knowledge is to be regarded as made up by acts and devotion.

In a pure and unwavering mind (internal organ), there can only follow knowledge; and purity of that internal organ can only arise from good works, as its unwavering firmness, from devotion: thus then by the purity, and unwavering firmness of the internal organ, works and devotion have been regarded as the source of knowledge. As the source of knowledge is comprised in actions and devotion, so the effect of that knowledge is fit to be considered as an adequate source of emancipation. For example. As watering a plant is the source of its growth, and also a source of its fruit, though in a case of a woody forest, the trees there, do bear fruits, and grow to maturity without any irrigation, yet underneath the ground, there is moisture [which it absorbs by the roots and rootlets]; and without a connection with water, a tree dries up and yields no fruits; so are works and devotion, a source for the growth of knowledge, and also that of emancipation, which is its fruit. In this manner works, devotion and knowledge are established as the source of emancipation, consequently a man with knowledge is also engaged in performing works; or works and devotion, are a protecting source of knowledge, because if he abandons them both, the knowledge already sprung is apt to be dried up like the tree without irrigation of water: for knowledge only accrues to a pure internal organ, and if good works are abandoned by a wise person, it will be sinful for him, and by abandoning devotion, the mind will return to its pristine condition of wavering unsteadiness, and in that impure and unsteady mind, no knowledge can remain, as a tree springing up in a dry and dried land cannot long subsist without water.

Another example. As a purified spot is selected by a reader of the *Vedas* or *Bramachari* for his habitation, but if for any reason it is defiled or rendered impure, the spot is abandoned; so by abandoning works, impurity, and from devotion, unsteadiness are respectively produced, and then the internal organ will not retain knowledge; for which reason, works and devotion are called the protecting sources of knowledge. In this way, works, devotion and knowledge, (all three) are regarded as sources of emancipation. In such a consideration, knowledge is said to be protected by works and devotion ; while knowledge alone is being regarded the source of emancipation; even then a wise man must find it proper for him to do works and devotion. This is called the expression of the *Samuchaya Vadi*.* But this view is not correct, because those who do not know Self as a distinct entity from the physical body, that can never perform actions, because actions are done for the fruition of a subsequent existence, and a body is consumed by fire, consequently it cannot enjoy the fruits of actions in a subsequent objective existence, hence the consciousness of Self, as distinct from the body is the source of action, and such distinction is the perception of Self as an agent and instrument, which is source of works. " I am the instrument of merit and demerit, or good and bad works, and their effects I am to enjoy or suffer." One who knows this, is a doer of works. But a wise person has no knowledge of Self in that way, he is devoid of virtue and vice, of happiness and misery, unconditioned, like *Brahma*, his Self is. This he ascertains from the teachings of the *Vedanta*, and this knowledge is not a source or cause of works, but on the other hand, opposed to them; hence no works are undertaken by the wise. Moreover, the consciousness of the distinction of an instrument and works, and their result, is the source of works; but a wise person knows not Self to be distinct from either the instrument or works, and their effects, but regards them completely as a perfect resemblance of the *Atma* ; so that, by this also, knowledge produces no actions. Then again, the commentator has

---

* The word means assemblage.

established in several ways the absence of works in a wise* person.

Works and results of knowledge are opposed to each other, hence an assemblage of actions cannot produce knowledge. The result of actions is a short existence, while that of knowledge is eternal release, and the mistaken attribution of caste, state of life, and condition to Self is the cause of works; because different works produce a difference in the conditional castes and state of life, which an individual is to inherit in a subsequent existence; hence the mistaken attribution originates in actions. If they belonged to the body as its property, and for works, there resided not in the body the intellect in Self, but Self is perceived as quite a different instrument of work from the body (this has already been mentioned), consequently the perception of caste, state of life and condition in Self does not follow even to a person, who is a doer of action; yet that person has not a visible or tangible consciousness of Self, as a distinct entity from the physical body, but has only a dim imperceptible knowledge derived from the *Shastras*, and the knowledge of Self in the body is visible. If Self is perceptibly known to be distinct from the body, the visible perception of Self, in the body, will then be opposed to it, and as the invisible and visible knowledge are not opposed to each other, the cognition of a separate instrument from the body, knowledge of Self, and the intelligent perception of Self *in* the body, both can apply to one person. For example, in the *Shastras* knowledge of Iswara in an image is called invisible, while the stone is the visible; between the two there is no antagonism; both of them are perceived by the same individual. Then again, one who has a visible knowledge of distinction between a snake and rope, to him the illusion of a visible snake is destroyed or removed; from this is established the rule of a visible illusion being opposed to or antagonistic of visible, and not invisible knowledge; so that the invisible knowledge of Self as separate from the physical body, and

---

* Wise has been made to stand for a man of knowledge which is a literal translation, of the word (*Jnanavana*) used in the text. It may as well mean a theosophist.

the visible knowledge of that body is possible, and both of them are originated by works. Cognition of Self as an instrument separate from the body, is the source of works, and that knowledge of Self, as an instrument, is illusory, which illusion can never affect a wise person, hence he is not entitled to works. Further, when the visible intelligence of Self follows from the body, the properties of that body—caste, state of life and condition, are determined, but such a regard of Self in the body, a wise man never entertains, who knows him to be *Brahma*, and thus has a visible knowledge of Self; consequently in the the absence of the mistaken attribution of caste, and the rest, to Self, in the case of a wise person, he is not entitled to works.

As for devotion, " I am the worshipper, and Deva is the object of my worship," which originates from the intellect, the wise are free from them; for the condition of a worshipper, and the object worshipped are never known to them; they look upon the constitution of their and Deva's bodies, as contrivances of fancy,—as unreal as objects seen in a dream, and they know to a certainty, intelligence to be one, hence knowledge is opposed to worship.* Also the example of a bird flying in the air with one wing is inapplicable. For a bird has both its wings at the same time, which are not opposed to one another, while knowledge and works as well as devotion are so opposed, they cannot therefore co-exist. The example of the bridge is equally inapplicable, because the sight of a bridge is not a source of visible, but invisible result. Now a visible result is such as is tangibly perceived. As satiety is the result of eating a good dinner, here eating is the source of the visible result satiety; but from the sight of a bridge, no such visible effect is perceived. From the *Shastras*, it is known only that destruction of sin is the result which follows; hence it is an invisible result, not tangibly perceived but known from the statement of the *Shastras*. Thus then, as from

---

* The *Panchadasi* says in reference to worship. Any kind of god, a demigod, or any substance either in the animal, vegetable, or mineral kingdom may be properly worshipped as a part of Iswara, with the expectation of deriving benefit, in proportion to the dignity of the object worshipped. (*Vide* Book VI. *Verse* 206-209).

sacrificial offerings or works are produced the invisible result of an abode in heaven hereafter, so the sight of a bridge also produces the invisible result of removal of sin. What serve as a source for invisible results, and ascertained in the *Shastras*, as an adjunct for all such results, are also comprised in such source of productive results, and not alone; therefore faith, and the observance of rules etc., must be combined in seeing a bridge ere the necessary result of destruction of sin is to follow:—Without them, no sin is removed by the sight alone of a bridge, because such sight yields no perceptible result, but only known from the *Shastras*, that it does produce that result of destruction of sin, and the *Shastras* insist seeing with faith; and there are no proofs whatever, of simple sight proving adequate for the destruction of sin. Hence in reference to the sight of a bridge, faith and reverence are required. Excepting *Brahma*, works and worship stand in need of nothing else to produce their respective effects; because if knowledge of *Brahma* were to produce invisible results of especial abodes like heaven, such particular abodes resulting from *Brahmaic* knowledge, have not been explained in the *Shastras*; but if in connection with works, and worship they had been explained, then the *Brahmaic* knowledge would also resemble the sight of a bridge in producing its usual effects, and will stand in need of devotion and works. But that knowledge of *Brahma* produces release or emancipation, and resembles not the abode in heaven, in setting up particular abodes,—in other words, invisible effects are not the results it produces, but on the contrary, eternal emancipation.

Bondage is set up in him through mistake, and the destruction of that mistake is the result produced by knowledge of *Brahma*, which is visible to me; knowledge of a rope destroys the snake from it, a visible result equally perceived by all; therefore the resulting product of abiding knowledge is the removal of mistake, a visible effect. Substances that are known to produce visible results are called their source, as a cloth is visibly the result of the weaving loom and brush, consequently they are its source; and as from eating is produced satiety, an equally visible result, so that eating is the source of satiety; similarly by the abiding knowledge is removed all illusions or mistakes,—a visible result, hence that knowledge is the source or cause of destruction of illusion. As in the removal of the snake illusion, a knowledge of all the parts of a rope waits not for anything else to bring it about; so the seat of the illusion of bondage in the eternal free 'Self is removed by his knowledge without waiting for the help of works and devotion or worship.

Moreover, if the effect of knowledge, emancipation, be regarded as an invisible result resembling particular abodes like those of heaven, it will be directly opposed to what the *Vedas* say; besides the admission of particular abodes like heaven will render emancipation non-eternal, hence emancipation is not any particular form of abode, and those who do consider emancipation in that way, can only regard it, so far that knowledge leads to it, because the meaning of what the *Shastras* have to say on this subject is that knowledge alone is called emancipation, consequently knowledge is the source of emancipation, and not the three collectively *viz*., knowledge, works and worship, or devotion. The example of the tree does not apply here, for if irrigation be regarded as the source of the growth, and vitality of a tree, yet it is not the cause of its fruit. An old tree continues to live if properly irrigated or watered, but it will bear no fruits, therefore simple watering does not constitute a source of fruit. Similarly works and devotion are practised for the production of knowledge and not emancipation; and before the advent of knowledge as they make the mind pure and faultless, and unwavering or fixed, they are not a cause of emancipation, which follows subsequent to knowledge, and that is why, they are not then undertaken. Prior to knowledge, whatever blemishes or impurities remained in the internal organ, these were all cleared by works, and devotion reduces the mind to a condition of unswerving fixedness, then a seeker of truth has no more necessity for them, he abandons all works and worship wholly and altogether,* opposed as they are to hearing.

---

* *Vide Panchadasi* IV. 43-46. In the same way "as a man extinguishes a torch, when he arrives at the door of his house, or as the husk is thrown away after the grain has been gathered.

Blemishes and impurities refer to sin, which is a cause of hurtful desire ; so long as impurities last there is room for such injurious desires, and when they are absent, the mind is then ascertained to be pure. Eagerness and quickness of the internal organ are established by experience. Hence to a good seeker of truth, and theosophist, knowledge of works and worship are futile, and to say that, they serve to protect knowledge, as has been mentioned before, does not apply. As a tree produced by watering its roots is protected by constant watering, so that if it be stopped, it dries and withers, in the same manner knowledge produced by works and worship is protected by them ; and if a man of knowledge will abandon them, his mind will again be impure and distracted or unfixed and quick : and like the withered tree of an unirrigated or dry land, the impure and active internal organ will be deprived of knowledge, hence it is necessary even for the wise to undertake works and worship. But that is contraindicated. For the function of the internal organ, modified into the shape of " I am the unconditioned *Brahma*" with reflection of intelligence or intelligence, is the resulting knowledge, a fruit of the *Vedanta*, and to say, that it will be destroyed by a discontinuance of actions and devotion, or that the knowledge resembling intelligence will be destroyed, is clearly impossible ; inasmuch as such knowledge of the natural condition of the *Jiva* and *Brahma*—their oneness—is eternal, and it is neither liable to destruction, nor needs any protecting care.

But the fruit of the *Vedanta*—knowledge of *Brahma*,—is never produced by works and worship, consequently it can never be destroyed by discontinuing them, nor are they needed for maintaining that knowledge already acquired. For, when the mind has once been so modified as to assume the shape of *Brahma*, from that period, ignorance and illusion have ceased to exist there, and after the destruction of ignorance and illusion, that function does not require to be any more protected. Then again, it is clearly impossible for the function of the internal organ to be protected by works and worship, for when they are practised, then the function will form a knowledge of the substances, which compose those works and worship, and have no knowledge of *Brahma* ; besides, in the forming of the function, then, it has been not existing from the first; hence works and worship stand in relation to the production of knowledge as reciprocal causes, but are opposed to an already produced function, for which knowledge is not protected by works and worship; and the previous assertion of a wise man's abandoning works and worship, procuring sin for him is also unmaintainable. For the abandoning of good actions can never produce sin. 'Forbidden works' are only a source of sin when practised. This has been explained fully by the commentator. Thus then, the discontinuance of action is not a source of sin, besides it is impossible that a wise man should be ever actuated with any desire to commit sin, inasmuch as virtue and vice, and their receptacle, the internal organ, are not truly existent, but simply are the product of A-knowledge (*Avidya*), and are illusory. Now these false illusions do not exist for a man of knowledge, hence if he abandons good works, or practises bad, they can bring him no demerit or sin. This is the conclusion here.

'Indifferent' and 'firm' are the two forms of knowledge. Knowledge characterised with doubts is called 'indifferent,' while the 'firm' is free from them; a person who has 'firm knowledge' stands in not the slightest need of what is proper [to be done]. The mental function after having once been formed into the shape of knowledge, bereft of all doubts, drives ignorance away, and though that knowledge is also destroyed, yet it leaves no room for any more illusion to creep in and affect the *Atma* again: because the cause of illusion is ignorance, which had once sprung up and been destroyed in knowledge already; consequently in the absence of ignorance, and illusion or mistake, there is nothing left to enshroud the functional knowledge. Moreover, if for the sake of perception of felicity by a person liberated in life, there is occasion for an enforcement, continuance or protection of the function, then by repeated consideration, pondering and reflection on the true signification of the *Vedanta* precepts, the function repeatedly assumes the shape of the *Brahma*; but this never flows from either works or worship, because they cause the destruction of all blemishes and render the mind faultless and pure, and fixed, and pave the way to knowledge, and not by any other method. Then again, the mind of the wise is free from sin and quickness. Sin is produced from anger and spite, and quickness is produced by ignorance. But that ignorance has already been destroyed by knowledge, hence in the case of the wise, from an absence of sin and quickness, there is no occasion for works and worship. And, if it ever be said, that anger and spite are the natural virtues of the internal organ, and so long as the mind lasts, they continue to remain, and cannot possibly be destroyed even by the wise, and from them, his mind becomes quick and unfixed, for removing which, he must have to perform devotional exercises; that though the admission of quickness of the mind does not affect his emancipation which is to take place after death, yet it will prevent his cognition of true felicity, hence quickness is opposed to deliverance in life. Therefore one delivered in life, should undertake worship [if for no other reason yet] for destroying that quickness or unfixedness of the mind. But that is not applicable. For, if to one who has got firm knowledge in his mind, profound meditation and destruction are equal, hence he does not make any attempt to quiet or fix his mind, yet effort or no effort, is dependent on actions that have commenced to bear fruit. Now 'fructescent actions'* are different, in different individuals; with some men of knowledge they produce enjoyments like that of Janak (father of Sita and King of Mithilla), with others, they remove all such enjoyments like Sukhdeva and Bamdeva. In instance the first, there will be a proportionate effort for the desire and means of procuring enjoyments, while in the latter, when all such enjoyments are destroyed by the fructescent actions, the man of knowledge desires for the felicity of the liberated in life ; and one averse to enjoyment, but desirous of the felicity of deliverance in life,

---

* There are three kinds of works mentioned in the Systems. These are the accumulated (*Sanchita*) fructescent or (*Prarabdha*) and current (or *Kriyamana*). The first are the works of former births, that have not yet commenced to bear fruit, the second are those which have produced the present life, and are already therefore bearing fruit, the third are being done in the present life, and will bear fruit in a subsequent existence after death.

has occasion to protect and continue the function after it has assumed the shape of *Brahma*, for which he reflects on the true interpretation of the *Vedanta*, but never worships; for by the quieting of the mind only, *Brahmaic* felicity cannot be particularly perceived; that can only be done by the function moulded into the shape of the *Brahma*; and that modification of the function after *Brahma* is caused by reflecting on the *Vedanta*, and not by worship. Moreover, reflecting on the *Vedanta* removes the mental disquiet, or quickness in the wise, consequently there is no effort to worship, for bringing on quietness of the mind. In this manner, one whose intellect has become firm, there is no inclination in him for works and worship; and the man of indifferent intellect, also keeps himself aloof from consideration, and profound contemplation (*Nididhiyasana*) as also from works and worship, for in fact, he is a good seeker of truth; and for that good seeker of truth, beyond consideration, and profound contemplation, there is not another proper thing to do.✻

Such is the meaning of all the *Sutras* on *Karma* and the commentator. Then again, for a wise person, consideration and profound contemplation are also not required; if for the conscious perception of felicity of the liberated in life, he does endeavour to engage himself with them, that endeavour proceeds from his desire, while duty or what is proper to be done is marked by something like this: " If I do not obey the commands of the *Vedas*, I will be subjected to re-birth." Thus then, the performance of consideration, and profound contemplation by the wise, proceed as they do, from his desire, are not duties for him. And neither the 'indifferent' nor the 'fixed' both have equally any occasion for works and worship. But for those whose

---

✻ If so, why is he not to practise profound contemplation and consideration. He may do away with works and worship, but not with the former, hence the text is contradictory. It should be therefore " engaged in" instead of 'aloof from' in the above passage, but there is no such fear, as the learned author points out and explains away the apparent inconsistency very elaborately.

intellects have not been formed in either of the above ways, but have simply a keen desire to know Self, and are not bent after the pursuit of enjoyments (their internal organs are faultless and pure, hence they also are good enquirers) for them, 'hearing' and the rest, not works and worship, are laid down as the things which are proper to do, in order to help their intellect in the perception of Self. Because, the effects of works and worship they have already acquired, and by the ordinary desire for knowledge, when there is an inclination for 'hearing,' and the mind is inclined to enjoy,—such a one is an indifferent enquirer,—even he does not abandon that hearing to re-engage himself in works and worship; for the usual effects of works and worship are to render the mind pure and fixed, these he succeeds in achieving by means of repeated 'hearing,' and he is enabled to acquire knowledge, either subjectively in this life, or about the next, or about the abode of *Brahma*. If that hearing be abandoned or discontinued to occupy one-self with works and worship, that is called falling from an elevated position.*

In this manner, the wise man of knowledge, and the good enquirer, have no concern with works and worship; likewise an indifferent enquirer, who has already been engaged in hearing the *Vedanta* precepts, stands in no need of them. Then again, one who has a desire for knowledge, but whose intellect is fond of engagement, hence has no inclination for 'hearing,' for him, worship and works are necessary to be performed without any motive or desire [of meriting reward]; and those whose inclination for enjoyment is

---

* '*Arudha patita*' is a composed of two words; of which the first '*Arudha*' means ascended, and the second '*Patita*' signifies falling down, the two conjointly would signify:—by 'hearing,' the person has already elevated himself into a superior position above the level of ordinary humanity in the path of knowledge, so if he does away with it, he descends low, and returns to the point whence he started, works and worship are the common lot of humanity, quite powerless to lead him forward except by the dint of persevering struggles.

strong, but have no desire for knowledge, such impious persons should always perform works of the 'optional kind'; consequently the wise are not qualified for works and worship, as they are opposed to knowledge. Then again, they produce tranquility and fixedness of the mind, thus paving the way, as it were, to knowledge, hence subsequent to knowledge where is the necessity for them ? They are then injurious as they destroy the indifferent knowledge already acquired; therefore they are opposed to and not conducive of it. For "I am doing" and "sacrificial works are proper for me" "as they procure the blissful abode in heaven." Actions are performed with such distinction in Intellect. "I am the worshipper" and "the object of my worship is a *Deva*." This sort of worship also proceeds from a distinction in intellect. Now both these varieties of intellect are removed by the consciousness of "All is *Brahma*."* In this way is explained the antagonism of knowledge to works and worship.† In spite of such antagonism, a theosophist is still bound

---

* "*Sarva khulu Edam Brahma.*" All this is indeed *Brahma.* Such a conception is beneficial to the intellect, it does away with distinction, and removes the particularization of *Brahma* with this or that. Polytheists have here an authority to worship any substance, they may fix their choice upon: for everything is pervaded by *Brahma*, and as has already been pointed out, the resulting merit is in proportion to the dignity of the object worshipped.

† On the subject of works and worship, a wide difference of opinion prevails. We have seen Surveswara putting a restraint on a theosophist and telling him not to act with impunity; but there are others who reverse this, and lay down axiomatically, that for a knower of *Brahma*, there is no further restraint; or he may act as he desires with impunity without fear of being injured. Gough in his article in the *Calcutta Review* says—" The theosophist liberated from metempsychosis, but still in the body is untouched by merit and demerit, absolved from all works good and bad, unsoiled by sinful works; uninjured by what he has done, and by what he has left undone *(Vide Brihadaryanuk Upanishad, 4, 4, 23).*

to perform the natural acts, eating etc., or if he be placed in the situation of a king, he carries on the administration of his State like the King Janak of old, only as a matter of form and habit or practice, as he used to do before the knowledge, that his Self is unconditional blissfulness has arisen; and such practice is not detrimental to his knowledge, for he knows Self to be unconditional, and has nothing to do with his practice, therefore it is not injurious. It can only be so, if he were to know that the usual acts which he had been accustomed by practice to perform are all done by Self, but he knows it not. On the other hand, he attributes their practice to their proper source, the physical body, on which it is dependent; and Self has no relation or concern with the body in the matter of practice, and that intellect is the source of practice. For this purpose effort or no-effort, or inclination and disinclination of the wise has been mentioned.*

Thus then, as these practices are not detrimental to knowledge, so to an impious person to be engaged in the performance of works, and worship with the knowledge that the *Atma* is unconditional, and that actions are dependent on the body and the internal organ, will not prove injurious to his knowledge. Because if that Self who is known by a sage to be unassociated, unconditioned and unrelated [Absolute] were regarded as the agent and instrument [a doer of works etc.,] and with such knowledge, if he were to undertake works and worship, then they will be injurious to knowledge. But that unassociated condition or nature of Self is a matter of firm belief in

---

* *Sankaracharya* in his incentives to the *Svetasvatura* says,—Gnosis once arisen, requires nothing further for the realisation of its result, it needs the usual adjuncts, that it may arise and these adjuncts are :—Works and worship in the beginning for the purpose of tranquilizing and fixing the mind. When that has arisen the seeker of truth begets an inclination for hearing the precepts of the *Vedanta*, which produce, as a result, knowledge. Therefore subsequent to the rising of knowledge, the necessity for works and worship ceases.

the mind of a sage, and works and worship cannot either affect or remove it; hence the reflex acts and worship are also not antagonistic to that firm knowledge. This is why King Janak, and others like him, practised the reflex works.

'Reflex works' are those good actions performed by a sage knowing Self to be unconditioned, and like practice, actions are virtues of the physical body. They are not opposed to knowledge. And what the commentator says about the hurtful effects of works and worship to knowledge, refer to those who regard Self as an agent, and who believe that he is the doer of actions and a worshipper too. Actions done in that light are injurious, but the reflex works from an absence of such an imputation to Self are not antagonistic to knowledge.

To a person of dull intellect, even reflex works and reflex worship prove detrimental and are inimical to knowledge; for, the presence of doubts make him dull or indifferent; if he doubts as to the unconditional nature of Self, that is to say, he sometimes believes it to be correct, and at other times holds the opposite belief, and regards the *Atma* as a doer, an agent or instrument, for him repeated reflections on the unassociated nature of Self, and that there is nothing proper for him to do, will dispel his doubts and make his belief firm; but if on the other hand, he will have recourse to works or worship, they will revive his already dispelled belief as to Self being an agent, or doer of works and worshipper, thus a contrary belief will be confirmed; hence it is, that a person of dull intellect performs actions, and worship, before knowledge has arisen, and not subsequent to it, and if he continues them after knowledge has arisen, the formed belief will be destroyed.

For example, as a bird serves his young ones before their wings have been fully fledged, and as the young ones lose their rudimentary wings, when just come out of the egg from the action of water, so before knowledge has arisen, one must serve works and worship, but their subsequent continuance will destroy, as the wings of the young birds, are destroyed by continued water, the differentiating knowledge [that firmly sets-forth the unconditioned nature of Self]; and as the parent bird suffers no injury for his relation with his young ones, so the firm belief* is not injured, and like that old bird, the man with firm belief or perception has no fitting necessity for works and worship.

In this way is explained why a sage has nothing proper for him to do, on being emancipated. It is an answer to the third question, after the manner of *Vedas* given by the professor to his pupil, consequently it is correct. Therefore it is said.

Pupil thus have I told you the essence of all the *Vedas*,
That destroys metempsychosis without any pain.

Pupil, thus have I mentioned to you the essence of all the *Vedas* put your faith in it, and believe it, for by knowing it, your chain of successive re-births will be easily, i.e., without any pain, cut away. Though the destruction of pain is an illusion, and its absence is called 'easy,' yet for the sake of cadence (and rhyme) the word is maintainable. In the vernacular, for the sake of cadence and rhyme the use of the long in the place of the short and *vice versa*† is allowable and so to read them, implies no fault. Moreover in the place of 'emancipation' the condition of the emancipated is read, because it is a traditional doctrine in the vernacular.

For, metre and cadence the long is pronounced short and *vice versa*.
Ru is used for '*aru*' and '*v*' for '*av*.'
The two, 'Kh' 'Ksh' are pronounced Sh and Chh.
Nor are there in the vernacular the alphabets
N of the T series,
'Ri' 'Li' and and the palatal S'.

---

* The word belief is doing duty for '*bodh*,' and it includes consciousness, perception and understanding.

† '*Laghu*' and '*Guru*' in cadence denote the short or long. As verses are all read in tune, where a short tune is substituted for a long one, that is allowable. The author therefore maintains his position sanctioned by usage and the commentator explains it on that principle, but it is quite immaterial. Had it not been for the fact that as a *Vedantin* he is habituated to find fault with the signification of a misplaced or misused word—nowhere in the world are critics more searching than our Vedantists. The 'short' are the vowels a, e, i, o, (short) that is to say our *Rhasa* vowels, while our *Dhirga* (long) vowels are long.

These alphabets are wanting in the Vernacular and if any one were to use them, it will be ungrammatical, and a poet will say it faulty. For Ksh is substituted Chh, and S for Kh, for the nasal half sound represented by the alphabet N is used the full N, and ri and li are used respectively for Ri and Li, and S´ is used for sh. It is not improper to write the alphabets in the manner just pointed out: all this is allowable in the vernacular.

Iswara is the author of the universe, and he is non-different from you. You are *Brahma*, therefore eternal intelligence and bliss. This the professor has said again in reference to actions.

Casting aside your poverty, look upon your self
As the pure *Brahma*, unborn, the discoverer of phenomena.
With your ignorance, you create the world, destroy them all
    and be eternal yourself.
Looking at the unreal world, why bring misery in your Self
You are a *Deva* of *Devas*, and a mass of felicity,
Jiva, the phenomenal world, and Iswara are all
Creations of illusion (*Maya*); you are glory itself.
As shines silver in a nacre, and snake in a rope.

Passion, and scurrility, and temptation destroy; remove envy
    and lust, and break the chain that fastens you to re-births,
    and mirage-like tempts you over and over.
Bring in the sun of knowledge to dispel the darkness of dark-
    like ignorance, and avoid duality by trusting in the writings
    of the *Vedas* and abandoning the indication of a part.
Ponder well on what the *Vedas* say (intelligence), hold yourself
    carefully, discard friends, servants, and the ties of kinship,
Do away with desire and cast not a lingering look on them,
Your self is fixed. Motion, body, organs, etc., are destructible,
    the tree is false,
They all, like the mistake of ether for the blue heavens, and
    a frying pan for tent [are false].

The means of knowledge are being mentioned in his discourse with a pupil by the professor. 'Passion' means fond desire for an object; destroy it, knowing it to be bad and a source of temptation.

Destroy envy, spite and lust. The acceptance of passion, temptation, spite, lust, includes all the good and bad qualities formed by the second or active, and third or dark *gunas*, therefore destroy all the products created by the two aforesaid qualities, for they are inimical to knowledge. And without their destruction no knowledge can arise. Hence their destruction is absolutely needed for an enquirer of truth. Of the four 'means,' 'discrimination,' 'indifference,' 'quiescence,' etc.,—the six substances—and 'emancipation,' the first or discrimination is the principal means of knowledge.* For discrimination gives birth to indifference to enjoyment and the rest, hence the teacher lectures on it. Know this phenomenal world to be unreal like a mirage water, that tempts a deer to run after it for drink. The world is called finite or bounded by its banks, while Self or *Atma* is infinite for he has no boundaries. The finite is also another name for the unreal, consequently its opposite, the infinite, must be regarded as the reality. This is explained in the following manner :—As in a magic show, a father says to his son, "mind my son, from this mangoe tree to every thing else what that performer of magic has brought forth, all are false." But that does not signify the performer of the show is also unreal or non-existent, on the other hand, he is real. Similarly the unreality is applied to the world, to bring out prominently the Reality of the *Atma*. For this purpose, the professor has said the finite is unreal. In this way, is the unreality of the world to be regarded, and Self looked upon as Reality. Such then is the lesson imparted to the pupil by his preceptor on 'discrimination,' from which arise the other

---

* The four means are :—
(1) Discrimination between real and unreal.
(2) Indifference to the enjoyment of reward in this or the next life.
(3) Quiescence, self-restraint, abstinence, endurance, contemplative concentration and faith.
(4) Desire for release or emancipation.
    The author refers to the six substances beginning with quiescence and ending in faith ; they are included in the third and considered as one and not so many distinct means.

means by themselves, as a natural consequence, so to speak. Hence by referring to discrimination, the other means are also explained. They are the external means of knowledge. 'Hearing' is called an internal one. Pupil, by bringing in the sun of knowledge (in other words, by the aid of 'hearing' the precepts of the *Vedas*) dispel the darkness of ignorance; both ignorance and darkness are referred to by the word *Tama* [the third quality of matter]. Darkness is *simile* and ignorance comparable [or capable of being illustrated by comparison or similitude. The first *Tama* is an indication of comparable, while the second is the quality itself [but in the English rendering it has been reversed, instead of dark-like darkness of ignorance, we have used the darkness of dark-like ignorance.]

What is illustrated by comparison or similitude is called comparable.

With what it is compared is comparison or *simile*.

In other Systems, knowledge has been admitted to be of several sorts, but here that will be described in especial reference to what is set forth in the transcendental phrase. Pupil, between the *Jiva* and *Iswara*, the difference created by *A*-knowledge and *Maya* (Matter or Illusion) should be removed; know them to be one and same. Know the intelligence common to them both, as is said in the *Vedas*, to be one and non-different. It means that they are to be recognised one, by abandoning* the indication of a part of the meaning of the transcendental phrase. [For Shiva read Siva]. The third

---

* Abandoning the indication of a part (*Bhaga Lakshana*) from the signification of 'That art Thou' establishes non-duality as pointed out in the *Vedantasara*. Here, "That" indicates invisible or unmanifested consciousness, and 'Thou' manifested or visible consciousness; hence the literal meaning creates a difficulty in taking cognizance of a consciousness marked by such conflicting attributes, consequently the relation of a predicate and subject is inadmissible. Nor can it be maintained that the qualifying adjectives 'visible and invisible' serve to differentiate the consciousness from consciousness of dissimilar character or establish an identity with consciousness of similar character. For the unseen consciousness is universal, all-knowing, omniscient; while the visible

stanza is illustrated thus. The fourth line is a brief repetition of what has been already expressed. Pupil, your self is not the physical body, organs of sense etc., which are subject to death, but he is the indestructible *Brahma*, and this world resembling a tree is unreal. 'Fixed and motion' refer to the two words indestructible and destructible, Self and not-self. The tree is worldly existence, society etc.; all that is false, like the mistake of blue for ether, and frying pan for a tent, formless; a like mistake is to take place in not-self for self. Existence has been described in the *Sruti* and *Smriti* as a tree, hence the word tree [which means literally wavering leaf] has been used here to indicate worldly existence.

Knowledge is the means for emancipation. This has been described in another way in the following verse :—

> The house of bondage and emancipation is in the conceit for the body and wise,
> With the banners of passion and indifference unfurled.
> Illusion of subject, and illusion of intellect like the wind, brother,
> Shakes, by day and night, nor leaves a moment alone,
> The unclean and pure images of the subjects of the witness, along with him.
> Seeing this, man of anger avoids desire and wants the abode, *Jnanloka*.
> The 'quick' and unfixed look their own likeness in their illusions, a mine of affliction,
> The 'fixed' look the likeness of *Brahma* in their selves, which is that of felicity.

---

consciousness is partial, little knowing, or parviscient." Hence by "omitting the invisibility and visibility from 'That art Thou' there remains the one consciousness common to both, and signified by the characteristic signs of invisibility and its reverse, expressed by 'That' and 'Thou.' Such a rendering is called the '*Bhagatyaglakshana*' or indication abiding in one part of the expressed meaning whilst another part of it is abandoned."

DHOLE's *Vedantasara*, p. 38-39.

Pupil, those who have a conceit for their body are ignorant. Now the ignorant and wise are the respective seats of bondage and emancipation; that is to say, ignorance is the abode of bondage, while in the sage, abides a desire for release. Their banners are passion and their want. As a banner is the sign of a royal city, so are passions (desire) and indifference, the respective standards by which they are known. The ignorant are marked by desires, while the sage is marked with 'indifference.' Hence their difference is called indiscrimination. Brother, the word subject refers to a variety of subjects. It includes material well-being. An illusion consists in looking upon it as something real. Then again, illusion of intellect signifies those who regard all material comforts to be illusions, as unreal as a snake in a rope. Such firm intellected persons are liable to be shaken by the wind of desire and indifference. In other words, as a banner is moved to and fro, constantly by the wind, so those who look upon prosperity as something real, and those who have a regard that all material comforts are illusory and unreal,—both of them move desire and indifference, and do not allow them to rest; the first remove the fixedness of desire (i. e., put desire into motion, or excite it) while the second or those who regard subjects to be unreal, put indifference into motion. But all these subjects are unreal, hence in the light of those who consider them real, they are illusions. To render this apparent in the verse, true illusion has been mentioned, and not true intellect.

Illusory or mistaken knowledge, and the false substance which is the subject of that knowledge, both of them, are called illusions. Thus a difference is created between the indifference of the ignorant and the wise; for the indifference of the ignorant does not arise from a knowledge that the subject of his desire is unreal and false. He has no such knowledge as to its unreality, hence he is called dull. Though according to the arguments used in the *Shastras*, ignorant means a person with false knowledge, or one whose knowledge is unreal, yet subjects are false and unreal, and can only be so perceived by a person of good intellect and not an ignorant one, consequently the invisible false perception of a dull person in regard to subjects, cannot remove the visible reality of truth caused by illusion. In this manner, when a dull person shows an indifference to property, wealth, etc., there arises his invisible, unreal perception, but then, in regard to that invisible false perception, the real visible perception is the strongest, hence the cause of difference in the dull is that false invisible perception; and the stronger real perception only intensifies a desire [of acquisition]; and when indifference arises, that does not proceed from the false perception, but from the observation of defects in the subject. A sage knows all this material expanse to be visibly false, and from visible false perception is removed the visible true perception; hence he has no desire for material comforts and has no true perception in them; for the sake of difference, he regards them all false, and if ever he evinces a desire, or shows any true regard for them, his indifference is then removed; but when a thing is visibly known to be false, it never can be looked otherwise, i.e., true. As for instance : when a snake created in a rope is once known to be visibly false, it can never afterwards be again taken for a real snake. Similarly, a wise man never reconceives a thing to be real after it has been once discovered to be unreal. In this manner, a wise man can never have any desire originated in him, or have his indifference destroyed, hence his indifference is said to be firm. Then again, the indifference produced in the ignorant by an observance of defects, is apt to be removed; for when a thing is regarded faulty at one time, it may in a subsequent period be regarded in a better light. As for instance, after coitus one feels inclined to attribute defects to a female [and shows his aversion], but in a subsequent period all that is gone away, and he has the same attachment as before. In the same way, when the faults are removed from his sight, an ignorant person returns back to his desire, and his indifference ceases, for which, an ignorant person's indifference is never firm. In this manner, the signs of the ignorant and wise, *viz.*, desire and indifference are described. There are other signs too. As the top of a house [door] is decorated with the image of an elephant or some other thing, so the residence of bondage and emancipation, the internal organ, of the ignorant and wise* have their respective images, *viz.*, of

---

* A sage, a theosophist (not the so-called members of that society in Madras who are at best would-be theosophists.) The Himalayan brothers are real theosophists or adepts.

evidence and the witness. In the ignorant mind, the image of evidence is unclean and impure; in the mind of the theosophist, the image is that of witness and pure. Now the subject of the witness *viz.*, this material expanse or phenomena are called evidence. The meaning is cleared in the sequel. The quick and unfixed look upon their Self, through illusion, as a mine of affliction, while those whose intellects are fixed, look upon their Self as non-different from *Brahma*, and enjoy true felicity. These stand in the relative order of cause and effect. Abandoning a part of the indication, has been particularly dwelt upon in the verse, and for describing the source of that subject, the difference in the indication is now being described.

> The three indications are now being said by the poet of great intellect:
> '*Jahti*,' '*Ajahati*' and *Bhagtyag lachhana* are the three indications.
> The first does not apply to the transcendental phrase, know this Pupil.
> Abandon the part represented by your self, as non-different from *Brahma* and know them to be non-dual.
> (Says the pupil.) Lord, to whom, art thou speaking of indications now, I am not acquainted with them;
> Explain the three indications first, and then establish their difference particularly.

Subsequent to ordinary knowledge, arises particular knowledge. As for instance, the ordinary knowledge of a Brahman is to know him so, but when it is ascertained that he belongs to particular sect or class of them (say Sarwasut), [that he has a house in such a place and his name is so and so] then arises his particular knowledge. Similarly, though indications may produce only ordinary, yet particular knowledge follows from the three signs of the indication, metonomy and the rest; and without the first, the second variety or particular knowledge never arises. With this object the pupil speaks to his preceptor in the verse under comment: "Lord, to whom are you speaking about indications, I know them not; therefore first, speak of them in their ordinary or common form, and subsequently point out their particular signification"—the difference of metonomy and the rest. Give a separate description of the three. For the sake of metre, the word 'lord' has not been used in the case of address, though it should be read so; and according to the traditional usage of the vernacular, the word *lachhan* is used for *lakshana*.

Replies the Guru :—

> With one intent, concentrate your intelligence and hear my word,
> If you want to know the difference between 'indication' and 'what is indicated.'
> Know then, there are two sorts of expositions of which one is force (*sakti*),
> And the other is indication (*lakshana*), listen with discrimination.

The relationship of a word with two meanings is called its exposition; it is of two sorts, one of which is called (*sakti*) force [or signification of words] and the other, indicative exposition: hear with discrimination, *i.e.* with indicative signs. Force is thus described—

> The meaning of a word when rendered apparent by immediately hearing it,
> Such a desire of that word to signify its meaning is termed its force according to the usage of *Nyaya*.

For instance, the word jar expresses a pitcher, its very utterance brings that signification in the mind of all persons. Such a desire of *Iswara* is called Force in the *Nyaya Philosophy*.

ON THE SIGNS OF *Svariti* FORCE.

> Know the strength of a word to be its force, according to the *Vedas*.
> As you ascertain the consuming force of a fire in it.

For creating the knowledge of a jar, as a resemblance of pitcher, the strength that resides in the word 'jar' is called its force. Similarly there resides a strength in the word 'cloth,' which helps to grasp what it signifies, and that is its force. This holds true with all words. As for instance, when a piece of wood is thrown into fire, it conflagrates, so that, fire has the force of consuming a substance when brought in contact with it; similarly when a word conveys its meaning by coming in contact with the organ of hearing, through its own strength, it is called its force. Another name for it is energy, or prowess. Like the energy of fire, conflagration, there resides in water serveral forces :—Moistening, quenching thirst, forming a lump [of rice or other offering given to a departed parent etc., after death and repeated yearly at the death anniversary]. These are its energies. Thus every substance has the strength to perform its individual act, which is its energy or force. This is the conclusion of the *Vedas*; ascertain them, and abandon the method of *Nyaya* for it is fit to be set aside.

Says the pupil—

In fire, I doubt, whether there is any other force besides itself,
Because what consumes, is the fire itself.
Similarly, beyond the alphabets of a word there is no other force,
Hence I recognize the strength of *Iswara's* desire.

The separate existence of energy or force in fire cannot be determined, I have my doubts about it, and what you have pointed out before, that the consuming force in the fire is the energy of the fire itself, does not hold true. For the cause, source, or authorship of conflagration resides only in fire, and there is no necessity for the acknowledging of an unknown force, and ascertaining its source, by discarding the known source of that fire. As in the aforesaid example, it is said, there is no possibility of a force being present, so in the case of words, beyond the alphabets which go to form them, there is not another separate force, nor is there any necessity for it; for this reason, the Will force of *Iswara* according to the doctrine of the *Naiyayikas* is perceived by my intellect.

Guru replies.

The separate existence of consuming force in fire is not manifested for the obstacle :
The addition of an exciter destroys that obstacle, and burns or kindles the fire, to consume the substance placed near it.
The cause that is present in fire, consumes all time.
That is the source of its force, from which fire is engendered.

You lover of the body. From the presence of an obstacle, fire is said to want its power of consuming; but if any thing, that will excite or animate it, be placed near, it will kindle the flame, and be consumed in spite of the presence of that obstacle. If without force, fire had the property of consuming, then it would necessarily possess that property in all times, *i. e.*, to say in the presence of the obstacle along with an exciter, and in the condition in which that obstacle is wanting, and when the exciter is wanting, but the obstacle is present; because the cause of combustion is present in all the conditions. Now from my standpoint, such a defect or anomaly is easily removed; for we hold the force of fire or force with fire to be the cause of combustion, and not fire alone. When there is an obstacle, though the fire is not destroyed by the stoppage of the wind, yet the force of that fire is destroyed by it, consequently from a want of the igniting force or of that force along with fire, there does not follow any ignition or combustion; and where an exciter is present near the obstacle, it destroys the force of the fire and stops the wind, but the exciter rekindles or engenders the force again. Hence the influence of the exciter being greater than that of the obstacle, it creates the force of ignition, or kindles the fire along with force, for causing the act of burning. The literal meaning of the fourth stanza is this: You boy, when an unknown element is destroyed any how, that is its obstacle; what engenders it is called an exciter, and that exciting force is the cause of ignition. An obstacle is inimical to an act, but what excites action, notwithstanding that obstacle, is called an exciter. In regard to fire, a gem or jewel, *Mantra* and medicinal substances are said to be its obstacle and exciter. When any gem, *Mantra* or medicine placed in a proximate position to fire prevents its burning, that is its obstacle; and when in spite of that obstacle, a gem, *Mantra*, or remedial agent kindles the fire and imparts to it burning properties, such a gem etc., is called its exciter.

 Pupil, know this to be the matter with all things and recognize force in that.

 Without force nothing is done, no action proceeds without it, know it for certain.

 Pupil, as in fire, so in water and all other substances, there are present their respective forces, without which no action is produced, hence force is the only source of an action or resulting product. In the following verse, its necessity is established. What a pupil had said, "that fire and its consuming force cannot be established or recognized as two distinct entities," is done away with; and the experience of their distinct character is being proved now in the half couplet following :—

  This does not contain any force, that force engendered is different.

 Where can this force be really experienced and what is its site?

 According to the method of the *Sidhanta*, the nature of force is determined 1 its proof ascertained. At the same time the doctrines of other systems regarding force are done away with.

 The will force of *Iswara* does not apply to words:

  This doctrine of *Nyaya* is unsound, its doctrine of current of force is false.

 It cannot be said, that the force of words resembles the will-force of *Iswara*, for *Iswara's* will is his property or attribute, consequently it resides in him, and for that force to affect words is impossible. If force were a [natural] property or attribute of words, then force of words can be admitted. Consequently it will then amount to the strength of words, and represent that strength adequately. *Iswara's* will-force therefore does hold good to words, and it is improper to say that it constitutes the force of a word. Accordingly the rule is false.

 Now the rule of grammar is being given :—

 The adequate meaning which is imparted by a word is its force,

 This is said in the '*Vyakaran Vushan*' by Hari in his *Karika*.

 The meaning which a word seeks to convey is produced by its force according to Hari, who mentions it in his *Karika* of '*Vyakarana Vushana*.' As for instance a jar signifies a pitcher. To impart the idea of a pitcher by a jar is caused by its force, *i.e.*, force enables a word adequately to represent its meaning, and render that meaning cognizable. The word *Vyakarana Vushan*, may yet have another meaning; besides being a work of that name, it may signify the best of grammars; that of which Hari wrote the Karika (commentaries and exposition of the text).

Guru utters.

> Listen pupil, according to Grammar, there is a strong defect.
> Whether there is, or there is not in words? Asks a man of discrimination.
> When a force is manifest, that I acknowledge, and it is known amongst men too,
> If it were not proper, it is fit to say there is no force.
> And that not-force will impart an inadequate signification and create discord.
> If you want more defects to find, *vide* the work *Darpan*.

If the adequacy of a word to convey a proper meaning be recognized as a force, one who so regards it is asked by a person of discrimination :—According to your standpoint, a word may or may not have force. If you say yes, then it establishes what I have been contending for ; *viz.,* that the strength of a word is its force (this is spoken in the third line). "The manifestation of a force" and the next line are in the situation of cause and effect. It says, when a force is apparent so as to be known to all men, that I do acknowledge and recognize ; in other words there is real strength in words, as say the grammarians—strength as is generally known to men—I admit such strength, but I do not recognize the force which is said to convey its proper meaning ; that is to say, when the strength of a word has already been admitted, it is not proper to regard 'force' as a distinct something which produces its proper signification. I contend force is only a form of strength ; this I acknowledge, and it is proper that I should do, for strength, might, power, and force are synonymous. These four words impart the same meaning ; a powerless man is called wanting in strength ; and he has no force. In reference to food or cooked grains, it is said, they have no germinating power in them, and they will produce no corn, they are wanting in force, vigor and energy. Thus then, people regard power and the three other words to bear one and the same meaning. In fire even, its strength constitutes its force, hence it is proper to regard force in the light of strength ; in other words to admit their duality, to acknowledge them as distinct, and both of them existing at the same time will be fruitless, not to speak of its being against the common practice in men. It is simply against common usage and that is its fruit. If it be said, strength is a fit force to convey its proper meaning, that will establish my point. Then again, if it be asserted since I admit strength, force in the form of strength can possibly be applied to words. But, if that strength be not acknowledged, the force which causes the construction of a word properly, will be wanting, and words at least will convey discordant meanings and not the recognized indications proper to them; the reply is, whether the want of strength refers only to words, or it is equally applicable to all substances, fire included. If the latter be maintained, then the arguments already adduced, when the force of fire was being established will do away with it. In the first view, though the defects of the other view do not apply, inasmuch as in fire there is force resembling strength, but for the presence of obstacle, the burning properties are not constant—(remain latent till excited)—they are absent; but with reference to words, beyond the strength to convey an adequate meaning they have no other force, that strength which establishes their proper signification is alone present, this is according to the first method. Here the defect of obstacle which prevents a fire to consume or conflagrate of itself is wanting, yet like the strength in fire, a similar strength must be admitted in words: this is explained in the two lines of the stanza. The third line signifies, if no such strength be admitted in words, yet to say, they are capable of conveying their proper significance from not-strength imply a contradiction, because words are wanting in power, yet the meanings they convey are said to be proper, and significance is the father of knowledge : to say so, is as sound as to speak of the infalliable powers of procreating possessed by a hermaphrodite. For they are opposed to each other, hence words have strength or power. And they are called powerful. 'Powerful' indicates the possession of power, and 'unpowerful' is its reverse or want of power. From want of power no construction results, that every one knows; hence want of power cannot bring forth the action of knowledge, which words convey by their significance, consequently it is fit to admit their strength ; and after the admission of strength, to acknowledge the presence of force in the form of strength is nothing improper.

Thus then, though force is wanting in words to impart knowledge by their several indications, yet there is present another form of it which is called strength. If you want to find other faults which the method of the grammarians imply, consult the work *Darpan* where force has been ascertained. It is painful to enter into the faults of others, hence I have not introduced them as mentioned in the '*Darpan.*'

ON THE INDICATION OF FORCE ACCORDING TO THE METHOD OF BHATTA.

> According to *Veda*, a word is related to its meaning by its own force,
>
> Bhatta says, look there for distinction and non-distinction.

The relation which a word has to its meaning is called force, according to Bhatta; this you should know. But that implies a distinction which it is the purport of Bhatta to expound. Between the meaning of fire and charcoal there is not extreme difference; if it were so, then like water, which is extremely different from fire, inasmuch as it quenches and reduces it into non-tangibility, charcoal would have never been present in the region of fire; an extremely different indication cannot be established by a word; as between a word and its signification there is no extreme difference, so there is not even extreme non-distinction; if the predicate were to express the extreme non-distinction of the object, then the predicate of fire, charcoal, would possess the property of burning the tongue, in the same way, as the subject of charcoal, fire, does; its pronounciation ought to burn a mouth too. But that it does not, hence there is no extreme non-distinction, but with the meaning of fire in the form of charcoal, there is non-distinction along with distinction. Distinction, because it does not possess the property of burning; and non-distinction, because, unlike water and similar other substances, it is possible for charcoal to produce a tangible cognition of fire. As the word fire is non-distinct from charcoal along with a distinction; in the same way the words water, wood, mud, and life are non-distinct from the signification of water along with a difference. If there were extreme distinction, then as between fire and water there is that extreme difference by which water cannot establish the presence of fire and *vice versa*, so the several words, water, wood and the rest, ought not to establish the significance or existence of water, hence it is said, there is no extreme difference, neither is there a want of that extreme distinction; for if such were the case, then as water brings a cooling sensation in the mouth, so the pronounciation of the word 'water' ought to produce a similar sensation, but that it never does, hence there is no extreme non-difference, but for distinction along with non-difference, both defects are absent. Thus then, every where between the predicate and subject of a word, there is difference along with non-distinction which the followers of Bhatta designate the identical relationship of a word with its meaning, (*Tadatmya Sambandha*) and also distinction and agreement. Now this distinction and agreement is nothing but a form of individual relationship; all words have the force of their individual meanings and beyond this individual relationship, there is not any separate force,

Now the arguments in support of distinction and agreement with their proofs are being declared according to Bhatta Acharya.

OM is *Brahma*, when the *Veda* says it is non-distinct.

Again externally to sound a word and its signification appears different.

In the *Mandukya Upanishad*, OM is described as *Brahma*, grammatically 'Om' would then signify to be the protector of all. But *Brahma* is such a protector, hence 'Om' is subject of *Brahma*, and *Brahma* is predicate; if their were extreme difference between a subject and predicate, then 'Om' would not have been mentioned in *Mandukya* and other *Vedic* treatises as non-distinct from *Brahma*, as between the syllable and the word, there is that relation of subject and predicate. Moreover 'Om' is *Brahma*, hence it has been said to be non-different from It; consequently by the absence of distinction between a predicate and its subject, the word of the *Veda* is proved. To all men the difference of predicate and subject is well known. Because fire and similar other words reside in the sound, while its signification, charcoal etc., resides outside the sound,—in the furance or hearth ; similarly 'Om' resides in sound, and its signification *Brahma*, is not there, but outside of the sound, in its own dignity. Though *Brahma* is all-pervading, hence It cannot be absent from sound, yet in *Brahma* there is sound, but in sound there is no *Brahma*. In this way all men know, in the sound of a word and external to the sound of its signification, their reciprocal differences, which establish a difference between a word and its meaning ; for this reason, all persons have the proofs of their individual experience as to the existing difference between a predicate and its subject ; but in regard to their agreement or non-distinction there is the testimony of the *Vedas*, hence the distinction or agreement between its meaning and the word is not a proof of their individual relationship, but proofs are self-evident. In another portion of the treatise has been shewn that distinction and agreement in the form of individual relation of a word and its signification.

> Quality and the body endowed with it, caste and person,
> action and actor, their connection and disagreement ;
> With that connection and its reverse, know the situation of
> cause and effect.

Form, taste, smell etc., are qualities. Where they are present, that is said to be endowed with qualities; as, for the presence of form etc., in the earth, it is said to be endowed with qualities ; many qualities may be present in one body or substance ; but the presence of a single quality, virtue or attribute is called caste, genus, or species, as in the bodies of all Brahmans the office of a Brahman. In all beautiful objects, beauty is present. And as vitality is present in life, and in an individual his procreating power ; as the quality of a jar is present along with it,—(its function of carrying water) and what men designate by the several attributive qualities,— *e. g.*, of the office of a Brahman, beauty, vitality, manhood, water carrying function of a jar,—these constitute the caste of a Brahman etc.: and the receptacle or seat of that caste is termed individuality (*bykti*). Progression, locomotion etc., are called actions, and one having those attributes, that is to say, the receptacle of action has a relation with the signification of the word. This is to be known ; and cause and action refer to the reconciliation of quality with its possessor. That is to say, like quality and the body endowed with it, there is a relation between cause and effect. In the same way, between action and the person abounding in works there is that similar individual relationship ; between caste and the person there subsists the aforesaid relation too.

Now this 'identical relationship' (*tadatmya samandha*) indicates a 'connection with distinction and agreement.' Between an instrumental cause and its action or resulting product, there is no connection of distinction and agreement, but there is extreme difference. Between a proximate or immediate cause, and its resulting action there is that connection of distinction and agreement. As for instance, the material or instrumental cause of a jar, a potter, wheel and the turning rod, are extremely different from the jar which is an act of that cause ; but with its proximate cause, a lump of clay, and its product, a jar, there is an agreement along with distinction. For, if there be extreme difference between them, then a lump of clay may as well produce oil, which is also an extremely different substance from it ; and since no oil can be produced from clay, a jar also would never result from it. Then again, if between the proximate cause and its resulting product there be extreme agreement (non-difference) no jar will be produced from clay : for nothing can be produced from a thing identified with it. Hence between such cause and its product, there is said to prevail agreement with distinction ; and that agreement does not indicate any fault in the difference, nor the consideration of distinction implies any defect to non-distinction. In this manner, the expression that there exists, between a proximate cause and its product, distinction and agreement, is based on sound reasons. Knowledge also establishes it likewise. As 'this is a lump of clay,' 'that is a jar,' the difference is here plainly recognized, and with eyes of discrimination their oneness is palpable enough ; for the external and internal parts of the jar are all made with clay, beyond which there is not another substance in it, so that their oneness is proved. In this manner, the distinction and agreement formed by the individual relationship of a proximate cause with its effect is proved. Similarly between quality and the body endowed with it, there is the same distinction and agreement.

If the form of jar be extremely different from that jar, then as there exists a similar extreme difference between a jar and cloth, and yet the cloth is not dependent on the jar, but they are distinct from each other, similarly the form of the jar will not be dependent on the jar itself. Then again, if there be extreme agreement or non-difference between quality and its receptacle, the form will not be dependent in the jar, for it cannot be its own receptacle; hence it is said, there prevails between them agreement and distinction, a form of individual relationship. The same rule applies to caste and person, as also to action and the person performing it (agent). That is to say, there is the same agreement and distinction. As there is not much necessity for mentioning all the arguments adduced against this view, I refrain from it.

Arguments against the Doctrine of Bhatta.

> In one substance for distinction and agreement (to be co-eval) is opposed (to reason).
> To say that it is based on reason, is absurd, all such views are incorrect.

The purport is:—If there is non-difference or agreement in a jar with itself, and difference with another jar, yet what is non-different has no distinction, and what is different has no agreement. With this object, the presence of distinction and agreement has been said (in one substance) to be contrary to reason. Hence that one substance, a jar, is non-different from itself, and distinct from another jar; but what is non-different has no distinction, and what is distinct has no agreement, hence it is said to be opposed to reason, for they are naturally opposed to each other. The same substance cannot have an agreement with what is different from it, nor can there be a difference with what is non-distinct from it; hence between the predicate and its subject,—quality and its receptacle, caste and person, action and agent, proximate cause and its result—the admission of individual relationship of agreement and disagreement is inaccurate; the proofs adduced in support of that distinction and agreement between a predicate and subject—in sound, subject; and externally, predicate—*i.e.*, their difference, and the non-distinction of *Brahma* with Om, according to the authority of the *Sruti* i. e., agreement, identity or non-distinction is cleared in the following wise :—

Between 'Om' and *Brahma* the assertion of distinction and agreement,

Says not Bhatta the common saying; there is mystery in it.

'Om' is called '*Pranava*;' with it and *Brahma*, the assertion of non-difference according to the *Vedas*, is made not for the purpose of shewing the non-distinction between a predicate and its subject, but it has an occult signification, which is called mystery, which Bhatta has not penetrated. When 'Om' is spoken of as *Brahma*, its purport is not that they are non-different, but ' Om' is to be worshipped like *Brahma*. What has been ruled to be worshipped is not necessarily identified with the object worshipped, but such worship has been declared in quite another way. As for instance, in the worship of *Salgram* and *Nervudessara* as representations of *Vishnu* and *Siva* respectively. Now the indicative signs of conch, wheel, rod and lotus belonging to *Vishnu* are absent in the (stone) *Salgram* [ammonite], nor does it possess the four hands of *Vishnu*; neither are the signs of *Siva*—his Ganges adorned matter hair, tiger skin, peculiar hourglass shaped musical instrument, with the fingers intertwined in meditation, giving his course of instruction on Self without the three attributes of *Satwa*, *Raja* and *Tama* to such of his followers as are dependant on him,—present in the little pebble found in the bed of the Nerbudda and called Nervudessara. Now both of them are stones, yet for the injunction of the Sacred Scriptures one must remove from his mind the impression of stone apt to be created by their sight, and regard them as representing *Vishnu* and *Siva* respectively, and so worship them : but since they do not represent *Vishnu* and *Siva* in their forms or signs, consequently it is said, worship is not dependent on the nature of the object worshipped, but on the injunctions of the *Shastras*. As worship is done by carrying out the orders and rules which the *Shastras* have laid down, for example, the *Chhândogya Upanishad* in the Chapter *Punchagni Vidya*, (knowledge of five fires) lays down the worship of Heaven, cloud, earth, male and female as so many forms of fire, with especial offerings in the shape of faith, nectar*, [Bael patra] rain, food-grains, and (seminal fluid) virility. It needs hardly being pointed out that neither Heaven etc., are so many fires, nor are (*Sradhâ*) faith and the rest can be called offerings in the usual acceptation of the term, still for the injunction of the *Vedas* they are worshipped as so many forms of fire with their respective offerings, faith and the rest. In the same manner, the worship of 'Om' as a form of *Brahma* is there laid down, so that the syllable 'Om' is not *Brahma*; yet to worship it as *Brahma* is maintainable on the ground that the utterances of the *Vedas* point to it. In the word 'worship' it is not necessary that there should be non-difference with a thing, but a different thing can be worshipped holding it to be non-different with the object of worship. Moreover, on proper consideration it will be found that the word 'Om,' the subject of *Brahma*—can be maintained to be non-distinct from its predicate *Brahma*, but such agreement exists not with a 'jar' or other insentient substance : [for they, jar, etc., indicate insentiency, and insentiency cannot possibly be connected with Intelligence—they are naturally opposed to each other]. (The reason of maintaining this non-distinction is) because name and form are all contrived or supposed to exist in *Brahma*,—It abides everywhere in all such names and forms. 'Om' is a name of *Brahma*, hence it is contrived in *Brahma*, and a contrivance is non-distinct from the site, where it abides, but is only another form of it; [as for instance, in the contrivance or supposed existence of a snake in a rope, the snake is the contrivance and rope its site, they are non-different; for the snake cannot possibly exist out of that rope, where it has been projected

---

* 'Soma' juice is a favorite beverage with the Gods ; it has no resemblance with the various liquors of the present time as so many Orientalists have tried to establish. It is an acid plant (the Asclepias Acida or Sarcostema Viminalis) the juice of which was given as an offering after the usual worship, according to prescribed order. Another preparation, of which the secret now no longer exists, was also then known, and it would appear that even the priest who officiated in such worships and sages and Rishis used to partake of it on especial occasions.

through illusion]. Hence 'Om' is identified with *Brahma*; and the meaning of 'jar,' insentiency, is not the site, but with its predicate, 'jar,' is only contrived in *Brahma*, and *Brahma* is its site; consequently the agreement of *Brahma* with all objects is quite possible. But that agreement or non-distinction does not hold true in the predicated signification of the word 'jar' *i. e.*, insentiency, by any stretch of plausibility; hence the doctrine of Bhatta which maintains the non-distinction between a predicate and its subject is untenable. Then again, if their difference only, be admitted, that also is faulty as has been pointed out by Bhatta. If the predicate of the word 'jar' be extremely different from that jar, then as the word 'jar' cannot establish a meaning extremely different from it, so from the word 'jar,' an extremely different substance, a pitcher* cannot be ascertained to be indicated by it. Also if the predicate of the word 'jar' by regarding it as extremely distinct from it, be determined to signify it, then, a pitcher an extremely different article from a jar, can be meant by it; but it may be asserted that as cloth is also an extremely different substance from that 'jar' the word 'jar' may as well signify a cloth. This, (a defect) applies to them, who do not recognize strength in the form of will-force in words; and not to them who support that doctrine. For the predicate of 'jar,' a pitcher, and the unindicated signification of that 'jar,' a cloth, are both distinct from jar; but it has the strength to indicate a pitcher as its meaning, and has no strength to indicate another meaning, hence from the word 'jar' nothing can be understood except a pitcher. In this way, the indicated signification which a word has the strength to express, is only made known by it, and not another meaning, for which it is said there is no defect in regarding the existence of an extreme distinction between a predicate and subject :—Between them cannot be said to lie that individual relationship marked by agreement along with

---

* A jar and pitcher are extremely different. How? The reader may ask. A jar is a small thing, a pitcher is a big one, a jar may be circular or square shaped; but a pitcher, a 'kulus' equivalent to a 'kulsa' or *matka* is circular, though it may have a long or short neck, or none at all. The difference is in the form and size of the two.

difference. Distinction and its reverse are naturally opposed to each other, similarly between a proximate cause and its product, there is no agreement along with distinction, but only distinction; and the faults, which the regarding of difference only imply, do not apply to what the *Naiyayikas* and supporters of the theory of force maintain: for to look upon the presence of extreme difference between a cause and effect is faulty, inasmuch as if between a lump of clay and its product, a jar, there exists such a difference; then as oil is also extremely different from that clay, it may as well produce the oil, and if no oil be produced, then a jar cannot also be caused by that clay. But this fault does not apply to the view of the *Naiyayikas*; because they hold prior existence (*pragabhav*) to be the cause from which all objects are produced. As, for example, the prior existence of earth is necessary for the production of a jar, so that 'prior existence' is its cause, similarly for the production of all substances 'prior existence' is their cause; and the proximate cause of 'jar,' a lump of clay, resides in that prior existence, as the oil resides in its prior condition,—the seeds which bear it [sesamum, linseed, mustard, castor-seed, olive, etc.,] and not in anything else. As prior conditions of all effects or products reside in their respective proximate cause, and their presence in a substance determines the production of that and not another substance; as the prior condition of a jar, is included in a lump of clay, for which a jar is produced from it, and not oil; and the prior condition of oil is present in the oil seed, for which, the seed produces oil, and not a jar; so in every other instance, all products owe their origin to this prior condition. Hence to regard an extreme distinction between a cause, and its product according to the *Naiyayika's* view etc., is not faulty. The supporters of the theory of strength are free from faults too. Because a lump of clay has the strength only to produce a jar and no oil, and an oil seed (sesamum etc.,) has only the strength to produce oil and no jar, hence clay produces only a jar. To regard a proximate cause as extremely different from its product in this way, is not at all faulty. Difference and non-difference; or agreement and disagreement are naturally opposed, and their presence in a spot or substance at the same time is untenable. The faults in connection with difference or agreement adduced by Bhatta, both of them, apply to the view he advocates; for he maintains non-distinction, from which is established that between a cause and effect, there is difference as well non-difference or agreement: for that difference, the faults connected with difference, and for non-difference, the faults pointed out in connection with non-difference —both of them—are applicable. As for instance, if in the same individual the faults of stealing, and squandering are present, he is said to have both faults in him, that of a thief and spendthrift. Similarly in admitting a distinction, and its reverse, between a quality and its receptacle, the respective faults of difference, and non-difference will be established. But from the standpoint of strength, there is no such fault; for quality has the strength to hold that which is endowed with quality, and not anything else. Hence what has been said about faults in difference—as the form and other properties of a jar are different from it, so are jars different from one another, and like form etc., a cloth ought to remain in a jar, or as that cloth does not exist in a jar, form should also not be there,—the supporters of the theory of strength do not admit to be implied by their doctrine. Even simply to regard the presence of difference, according to the expounders of the strength hypothesis, is also not faulty; on the contrary, the above example illustrates the faults of maintaining both difference and non-difference, according to Bhatta. Then again, there is that other defect called 'impossible,' in such admission of antagonism, as is implied by difference and its reverse. In the same way, though there is only difference between caste and person, action and actor, yet as a person has the strength to hold caste in him, and an actor, action, and not the strength to hold anything else, therefore, to regard the presence of non-distinction along with difference in proximate cause, and its resulting product constituting their individual relationship is untenable. And to say, that all substances have in them a distinction, is faulty, (according to Bhatta) —such an assertion—is swallowed up by the hypothesis of strength.

According to the *Vedantic* (*Sidhanta*) conclusion though it is said, there is an individual relationship, and no extreme difference between an action and actor, quality and its receptacle, caste and person, yet it does not maintain that relation to be characterised by difference and agreement;—on the other hand it is distinct from difference and is agreement neither, a condition that cannot be defined, hence 'indescribable.' When it is said to be separate from distinction, the faults of difference cannot apply, and as it is likewise distinct from agreement, the faults of non-difference also do not apply. Thus then in this way, the relation is said to be distinct from difference and agreement—in short, something indescribable. This form of individual relationship exists between them. And as the attribution of distinction and agreement has already been shown to be unsound, consequently the relation of predicate and subject, constituting the individual relationship between a word and its expressed indication is nothing else but its force. Now this distinction of Bhatta is incorrect.

The meaning which a word coveys at its first pronunciation is due to its force, or call it strength. The second force in it, is the force of ascertainment. Knowledge of indication is adequate to produce a possible interpretation of a word; for a 'possible relation' between a word and its meaning is identical with its indication. Without a knowledge of the possible meaning of a term, no knowledge of indication in the form of that 'possible relation' is produced, hence the 'possible' is termed indicated.

> The strength of a word to impart its meaning is termed 'possible.'
> The predicated signification is now being said again, know it to be the expressed signification of a word.

That is to say, the strength of a word to convey its meaning, (that meaning) is the 'attributive signification' of the word, and what a word may possibly mean is called also its 'attributive signification.' As, for instance, the word 'fire' has the strength to convey charcoal as its meaning, hence charcoal is the 'possible' and 'attributive signification' of fire, and the attributive signification ought to be made known by a word is called 'declaratory.'

ON INDICATION AND ITS DIFFERENT FORMS. *Jahati* ETC.

The relation of the 'possible' that is known to be identical with indication.

Know that to be an indication, which indicates or distinguishes a word.

Whenever there is a relation of a predicate, abandon the 'attributive signification.'

Thus is known what is called *Jahati*.*

When the attributive signification is made known with its relation;

Then the indication of *Ajahati* is established.

When a part of the expressed meaning is abandoned, it is *Bhagtiag lakshana*.

Another name is *Jahati-Ajahati*† and proved thus.

Now 'possible' signifies the reconciliation or union of the relation of attributive (expressed) signification, it is same as indication; and when a word has not the strength to express a meaning,

---

* Indication in which a word abandons its own meaning to express what is suppressed.

† The *Bhagtiag lakshana* is a combination of Inclusive Indication and Indicative Indication, and is therefore otherwise called *Jahati-Ajahati lakshana*. As an example of the first may be mentioned :—" The white is galloping." Here literally a white cannot run, but a white horse can, hence the introduction of horse without abandoning the signification of white, clears the meaning. It is called sometimes *Ajahati Swartha* or *Ajahat lakhshana*. It is an indication in which there is the introduction of a suppressed meaning of a word—a part for a whole, without abandoning its sense. Indicative Indication is that, in which there is use of a word with the abandonment of its meaning. As in the example already given " A village in the Ganges." Here the literal signification of the Ganges, a river—is abandoned for that cannot be the site of a village, but it is made to signify its banks—part for a whole (metonomy)—and there it is easy for a village to be situated.

but that meaning is made known by the signs of indication, it is called its indicated signification; in one line of the stanza it is said to be identical with indication. Now the difference in the three varieties of indication is being defined in so many lines. When the expressed meaning is completely abandoned by the predicate etc., to make known its attributive signification, that is called the indication of *Jahati*. As for example in the expression "A village in the Ganges," 'Ganges' indicates the banks of the river, for it is impossible that in the current of the river Ganges, there can be any village situated, consequently the expressed indication of the sentence is completely abadoned, and the suppressed signification of the word 'Ganges,' its banks, are introduced to render the expression intelligible. This is *Jahati*. The third line of the stanza defines the *Ajahati lakshana*. Here there is no abandonment of the sense of a word, but the use of a word is kept along with its attributive indication, as in the expression "The red is running." The literal sense is impossible, for no red can run; but if we introduce the word horse and indicate it by the word red, then the meaning is cleared; therefore the attributive signification of red is incapable of running, but if the suppressed horse be said to be what is indicated by red, according to the canons of 'Inclusive indication' *(Ajahati lakshana)* that incapability is removed, and the indicated signification is established without abandoning the signification of 'red.' It includes a larger sense. For which it is called *Ajahati*.

The fourth line describes the *Bhagtiag lakshana* [Indication abiding in one part of the meaning, while the other part of it is abandoned.] It is otherwise called *Jahati-Ajahati* or *Ahadajahat lakshana*; as for instance, when a thing seen in a prior period is found subsequently in another place, a person is apt to say. "That is this." It is an illustration of the *Bhagtiag lakshana*. Because 'that' refers to a thing seen in the past time and in another place, and 'this' conveys the sense of the present time, and indicates a thing seen in the present moment; hence the two adjective pronouns referring to the past and present respectively, imply contradiction: for the same thing cannot be equally present in both the aforesaid conditions.

Therefore by abandoning the indications of 'that' and 'this' the apparent inconsistency is removed, and as both of them refer to the same substance, that is what is meant;* their equality is identity.

> Now the indication of 'That' and 'Thou' in the phrase,
> 'That art Thou' is being set forth.
> The omnipotent, omniscient, pervasive Iswara, distinct and invisible.
> On whom is *Maya* dependent, is the indication of 'That,' neither bound nor free.

Omnipotent signifies one who has all the requisite strength [for creation, preservation and destruction.] He is called omniscient, because he knows all things; pervasive means all-pervading. 'Is,' a contraction of Iswara refers to his causative powers. He sends every one here and controls them. He is said to be distinct, because he is free and independent; and invisible, because not a subject of visibility; for a *Jiva*, cannot see him. *Maya* is dependent or subject to him, who is without bondage, or emancipation. He who is subject to bondage can be said to be subject to emancipation also, but as Iswara is never a subject of re-birth, he cannot be said to be free from its chain. Iswara's intelligence marked with the above attributes is the indicated signification of the word 'That.'

---

* This view of the matter may be illustrated algebracally. Not being able to admit as an equation the expression 'Devadatta + past time = Devadatta + present time,' we reflect that the conception of time is not essential to the conception of *Devadatta's* nature; and we strike it out of both sides of the equation which then gives *Devadatta = Devadatta*, the equality being that of identity. In the same way, not being able to admit as an equation the expression 'Soul + invisibility = Soul + visibility. We reflect that the visibility, etc., are but the modifications of Ignorance, which we are told is no reality. Deleting the unessential portion of each side of the expression, we find Soul=Soul, the equality being here also that of identity. BALLANTYNE'S *Lecture on the Vedanta.*

On the indication of 'Thou.'

The attributes antagonistic to what has been mentioned in regard to Iswara,

Constitute the Individual Intelligence and that is indicated by 'Thou'

Jiva has properties or attributes opposed to those of Iswara, and his intelligence is indicated by Thou; that is to say, he is parvipotent, parviscient, finite and without a lord or superior, dependent on action, enchanted or entranced in ignorance, and subject to bondage and emancipation and visible. Since the nature of a person cannot be unknown to him, or since his identity is a subject of his visible perception, he is called therefore 'visible.' In the same manner, it may be said of Iswara that he knows himself visibly, but such a visible knowledge of Iswara, no *Jiva* or individual has got; hence he is invisible to all men; but the identity of a *Jiva* is known to a *Jiva* as well as to Iswara, hence the individual is called visible. The indication of 'That' bears reference to that individual intelligence marked by the properties or attributes cited above.

In the transcendental phrase the identity of 'That' and 'Thou' are established,

And their indication does not apply.

In the *Chhandogya Upanishad* of the *Sam Veda*, the sage, Udalaka refering to the creation of the world by Iswara, said to his son, Svetaketu, the indicative signification of 'That art Thou' is, 'That' refers to the author of the Universe—Iswara, who is omnipotent omniscient etc., and 'Thou' refers to the parvipotent and parviscient etc., *Jiva*.—'Thou art that' such an expression makes known the identity or oneness of the Universal and individual Intelligences. But that indication cannot be maintained. Because that will amount to look upon properties which each have and marked by very contrary characteristics as identical. To be more explicit. The attributes of Iswara are characterised by omnipotence, omniscience, pervasion, infinitude, independence, invisibility and the subserviency of *Maya*, while the attributes of the being, are marked by the very opposite distinctions of parvipotence, parviscience, finitude, dependence to actions, visibility and entranced in *Maya*. Under such circumstances how can they be regarded to be identically the same ? To say that they are one is tantamount to the expression " fire is cold." Therefore, Oh you good intellectual! Know the indication of the indicated and recognize the antagonism created by their expressed signification.

> The two first do not apply to the construction of ' That art Thou'
>
> Abandon a part of the Indication, and that is their indicated signification.

Oh child! in the construction of 'That art Thou' the first two *viz.*, Indicative Indication and Inclusive Indication cannot be applied, hence it is to be construed by the canons of Indication abiding in one part of the meaning, whilst another part of it is abandoned; that will remove all antagonism from their signification and create union.

ON THE INAPPLICABILITY OF INDICATIVE INDICATION.

(This is being explained):—

> *Brahma* Intelligence, the object of knowledge is included in the predicate.
>
> If Indicative Indication be acknowledged, it will create another object of knowledge.

The conclusion of the *Vedanta*, in reference to the signification of 'That' and 'Thou' established the non-duality or identity of the Witnessing Intelligence with the Universal or *Brahma* Intelligence. That is to say, the object to be known, witnessing intelligence is the Universal or *Brahma* Intelligence, and both of them are included in the signification of 'That' and 'Thou.' And where Indicative Indication is applied in construing a sentence, their expressed signification is completely abandoned, and another object is introduced as what is to be known, it is related to that expressed meaning or predicate. Hence if Indicative Indication be acknowledged in 'That art Thou' then another object will be set up as what is to be known, different from the Intelligence expressed by the predicate. Now a substance differing from intelligence must of necessity be marked with insentiency or inanimation, non-being, or non-existence (*asat*), [for intelligence is (*sat*) being or existence] and pain or misery, knowledge of which can never procure emancipation—the supreme aim and end of existence; consequently the Indicative Indication or Indication simply is not to be found in the transcendental phrase of the *Vedas*.

On Inclusive Indication and its Inapplicability Explained.

An inclusive indication is present along with the expressed signification. Oh friend.

But the expressed signification entails contradiction with 'indication' simply and 'inclusive indication;' that is their rule

Friend. Where there is 'Inclusive Indication' all the expressed significations are present, and by that, a wider range of the meaning is accepted or implied. If the Inclusive Indication be applied in construing the transcendental phrase, or its application allowed or acknowledged to be faultless, then the expressed literal signification will be established, but such signification is contradictory.*

---

* We do not recollect to have read a more lucid description of these several indications, with illustrations than in the *Vedantasara*. Though a few the examples have been produced in the text, the facility for explaining is wanting, hence it is hoped these notes may, to a great extent, help the reader. We begin with the beginning. 'That art Thou' cannot be construed like "the lotus is blue." The literal sense is not suitable in the meaning of the transcendental phrase. Because in the example of the flower, the lotus being the thing we call blue, and the 'blue' thing being what we call lotus, they both serve to differentiate them from such other substances as have opposite qualities as 'white' and 'cloth' hence they are mutually connected as a noun and adjective or subject and predicate whereas in 'That art Thou,' Intelligence is marked by very opposite

For removing the contradictions the necessity of, 'indication' is introduced, but that 'inclusive indication' will not remove them hence it is inapplicable.

ON BHAGTIAG LAKSHANA.

By abandoning the antagonistic attributes, Intelligence is [established] pure and unassociated.

I see indication in that; good intellected [son] of abandoning a part.

Oh Ye lover of the body! The expressed signification of 'That' is Iswara and of 'Thou,' *Jiva*; by abandoning the antagonism which exists in their individual attributes, to regard the pure and unassociated Intelligence as what is indicated is indication of *Bhagtiag lakshana*. Here the inference is that non-duality of Iswara and *Jiva* explained in several works of *Adwaita* philosophy. In the work *Vibarana*, *Jiva* is defined as a reflection and Iswara light [subject of reflection]. According to the doctrine of Vidyarana Swami, Iswara is the reflection of Intelligence in *Maya* abounding in pure goodness and *Jiva* a reflection of intelligence in *Avidya* abounding in impure goodness which is a proximate cause of the internal organ. Though in the *Panchadasi*, Vidyarana Swami mentions *Jiva* to be a reflection in the internal organ, and as that internal organ is not present in the profound slumbering condition, consequently, then there should be no *Jiva* also; but as *Prajna*, almost ignorant—a form of *Jiva*—continues in dreamless profound slumber, therefore what the Swami purports to mean—is the particle of ignorance modified or changed into the form of the internal organ, and intelligence reflected therein is called *Jiva*, and that ignorance is never wanting in profound slumber, consequently *Prajna* also is not wanting then. Moreover the reflection of intelligence alone does not

---

qualities of invisibility (denoted by the term "That") and visibility (denoted by "Thou") hence there cannot be the relation of a subject and predicate, nor can it be said, that the two words are identical; for we have the evidence of our sense against its acceptance. Hence the literal meaning is not inapplicable.

constitute either a *Jiva* or *Iswara*, but intelligence abiding in *Maya*, and the reflex intelligence with *Maya* constitute Iswara; and intelligence abiding in ignorance, and the reflex intelligence with the particle of ignorance constitute *Jiva*. In the associate of Iswara, there is pure goodness, for which he is omnipotent, omniscient etc., while the associate of *Jiva* is composed of impure goodness, hence he is parviscient, parvipotent and the rest. This is said by the supporters of the Reflex Theory.

The associates of *Jiva* and *Iswara* are identical according to the view of the author of *Vivarana*, who connects them with Ignorance. In such a consideration, both Iswara and *Jiva* must be parviscient. But it is not so; because it is the nature of a thing in which there is a reflection, to impart its defects to the reflection, and not to the image: as for instance, when a face is reflected in a mirror (its associate) the defects belonging to the mirror will prevent a faithful reproduction of the face itself. Hence the defects, though present in the mirror, are not cognized or rendered visible till the face is reflected in a mirror, for which it is said, reflection determines defects.* Similarly in the reflection of the *Jiva* in the mirror of ignorance, are produced the defects caused by it, such as parviscience etc., while Iswara (in the form of image of pure Intelligence) who is the visage has none of them, for which He is omniscient. This is the cause of His omnipotence, omniscience etc., and the parvipotence and parviscience of a 'being.' Now between the respective doctrines set up by these supporters of reflection and reflected image, the difference is this.—A reflection is false, but a reflected

---

*To be more explicit, defects or faults are the natural accompaniments of a reflected image; for we all know, there are few glasses which will give a faithful representation of a face. On the other hand, all of them would invariably make it either long or pointed, or square shaped, short etc., though naturally they are wanting in that face. In the same way, the reflection of the *Jiva* in the glass or mirror produces the defect of parviscience, which naturally does not belong to him (for he is one with *Brahma*); while Iswara, who is the face has not got it, but is on the contrary, omniscient.

image is true, and not false. For the expounders of reflected image conclude as a natural inference that the reflected image of the face in a mirror, is not a shadow of that face, inasmuch as a shadow is situated in the same site, where its original is placed; but in the case of a face reflected in a mirror, it is always placed in front, or exactly opposite to the original, hence a reflected image is not a shadow in a looking glass. But for making a subject of the mirror, the function of the internal organ, projected by the organ of sight makes that mirror its subject; at the same time, it ceases or retreats from that mirror, and makes the face situated on the neck, its subject. As quick playing (*Bunite*) makes the wheel of a firebrand perceived, while actually it has no wheel, so the velocity of mental function for making a subject of the mirror and face, produces the perception of that face in the glass as situated in it; while actually it is placed on the region of the neck, and not in the glass, and is not a shadow: and by the velocity of the mental function, the knowledge of a face in a glass is reflection. In this manner, from the connection of the associated mirror, the face placed on the region of the neck appears both as a visage and its reflection. Moreover, on due reflection, it is to be found, there is no reflection. Similarly by the close connection of the associate formed by Ignorance, the site of visage in the unassociated Intelligence is known Iswara, and its reflection, *Jiva*. And there are no separate conditions of *Iswara* and *Jiva*.

The perception of a *Jiva* in Intelligence, from Ignorance is called its reflection in Ignorance; so that, both the considerations of visage and its reflection, are unreal, while actually they are true; for the site of their actuality is the face and its reflection in a mirror; and in the subject of the illustration—Intelligence—that face and Intelligence are true. According to this view, as a reflection proceeds from the original, it is consequently true; and a reflected shadow, for its being the shadow, is untrue. This then is the difference between the expressions 'reflection' and 'reflected shadow.'

Moreover in several other works, Iswara is said to be the predicate of Intelligence in *Maya* abounding in pure goodness; and the particle of Intelligence inherent in Ignorance forming the proximate cause of the internal organ, abounding in impure goodness is *Jiva*. This is called the limiting or differentiating view [for it sets up a boundary, so to speak, between Iswara and *Jiva* according to an *Avacheda Vadi*.]

Non-duality is the business of the *Vedanta*; in other words, the supreme and individual self are one, this is what the *Vedanta* teaches; hence in whatever manner such knowledge is produced in an enquirer, though that may be true to him, yet the commentator of the *Upadesh Sahesri*, and *Vakyabritti*, has mentioned only the view of the reflected shadow (*Avasvad*), so that the principal theme, is the *Atma*. According to his standpoint, *Maya* and the reflected shadow (of Intelligence) in *Maya*, and the abiding intelligence of *Maya* is Iswara, with the attributes of omnipotency, omnisciency and the rest, and that is indicated by the word 'That'; while the reflected shadow (of Intelligence) in the distributive aggregate of Ignorance, and its abiding intelligence is *Jiva* with the attributes, parvipotence, parviscience etc., and indicated by the word 'Thou.'

To regard 'That' and 'Thou' of the phrase "That art Thou," to be identically one is not tenable, hence by abandoning the contradictory element of their signification constituted by the reflected shadow of intelligence with *Maya*, and the creation of omnipotence omniscience etc., by *Maya*, and the relation of that non-conflicting portion, intelligence, is indicated by the word 'That' (according to the canons of Rhetoric of abandoning a part). In the same way, if the reflected shadow along with the particle of Ignorance and the Ignorance created parvipotence and parviscience are abandoned, the remaining non-conflicting intelligence is indicated by 'Thou.' Therefore the words 'That and Thou' hold the relation of Indication and Indicated with respect to the non-conflicting term Intelligence, common to both; and this oneness of the Intelligence is indicated by the phrase 'That art Thou,' which is to be known.

Similarly in the transcendental phrase "My Self *(Atma)* is *Brahma*" the indication of Self (*Atma*) is *Jiva*; and that of *Brahma* is Iswara; of *Brahma* not a predicate only is Iswara, but is the Indicator.—This has already been mentioned in the fourth Chapter.

Similar to the first [That art Thou], the indication indicated by both the words Self, and *Brahma* is not visible, and to establish that visibility, the term Self has been used. *Ayam*, is called the visible *Atma* (self) of all, same with *Brahma*; this is its signification.*

"I am *Brahma*." Here 'I' signifies *Jiva*, and *Brahma* signifies Iswara. The Intelligence of both Iswara and *Jiva* is indicated by the phrase "I am *Brahma*."

"*Prajnanam ananda Brahma*." Self, non-different from *Brahma* is blissfulness. Here *Prajnana* [from '*Pra*' exceeding and '*jnana*' knowledge = exceeding knowledge] means *Jiva*, and *Brahma*, Iswara. But as in the prior instances, the Indication of the Indicator *Brahma* does not possess bliss, but is blissfulness itself; to indicate it, the term (*ananda*) bliss has been made use of, and the phrase means "*Brahma* non-different from Self is blissfulness." That is the expressed signification.

As in the construing of a transcendental phrase, the indication of abandoning a part of the signification is applied, so in other phrases the words truth, knowledge, and bliss are, by the same indication, used to point out the Pure *Brahma*, and not by the force (inherent in words). Because the Pure *Brahma* is not the predicate of any term. This is a natural conclusion, consequently it is the subject of all words. 'Pure' is termed an indicator, truth subservient to *Maya*, and truth independent of Intelligence, the two combined, are the expressed signification of the word 'truth'; but its indication is, truth independent of intelligence;—knowledge formed by the function of

---

* Here self and *Brahma* are characterised by the conflicting characteristics of visibility and invisibility, therefore by the canons of abandoning the indication of a part, if the visibility and invisibility be abandoned, there remains only intelligence (common), which is the indication of "my self is *Brahma*." In other words to put it algebraically we have the equation Intelligence + visibility = Intelligence + Invisibility. Now visibility and its reverse are created by ignorance, therefore we do away with them, and we have Intelligence = Intelligence. The equality being that of identity.

intellect, and self-manifested knowledge, both combined, express the signification of knowledge; but the self-manifested part is what is indicated by it. The modification of the mental function moulded into the shape of material well being, and procuring happiness by its good quality, and felicity in the form of tasting the supreme love, both of them, are the expressed signification of the term 'bliss,' but after abandoning the functional part, 'to determine the natural part, is its Indication. In this manner, the Indication of 'pure' in connection with all terms has been explained in the *Shariraka Sutras.*

An epitome of the above Indications is thus being versified :—

> "A village in the Ganges" is an illustration of Indicative Indication.
>
> In the "Red is running" know the signs of Inclusive Indication.
>
> "That is this" is an Indication of abandoning a part;
> Another name for which is *Jahati-Ajahati.*
>
> To abandon a part of the indication in "That art Thou" Constitutes the Indication called *Juhati-Ajahati.*
>
> *Brahma* is not the predicate of any term, says the *Veda.* *
>
> In this way, know the rules of Indication in all terms.
>
> Truth subservient to, or abiding in *Maya*, and Truth abiding in *Brahma*,
>
> The two, constitute the predicate of Truth, so says the sage.
>
> Of them [abandon the first] *the second* is the Indicated Indication.
>
> The literal signification of knowledge is that formed,

---

* It is the same with *Jahati-Ajahati lakshana*, which means that it is a combination of these two varieties *Jahat* and *Ajahat* or *Jahatswartha* and *Ajahatswartha* or *Ajahat lakshana.*

By the function of Intellect and Intelligence.

But destroy the function of Intellect and Intelligence is the Indication.

Bliss literally signifies felicity, personal and material;

Abandoning the last, blissfulness of Self is what is Indicated.

For removing contradiction implied by the literal signification of the transcendental phrase, it is necessary to construe it, by the Indicative Indication. But then, it is said, the admission of that Indication in one term is enough and there is no occasion of introducing it in both terms of the phrase, for freeing it from incongruity.

Why ?

Says the learned, to introduce Indication in one term, Is enough to dispel contradiction; to admit in two is futile.

Those who understand best, regard the admission of Indication in construing the signification of a transcendental phrase is enough to remove all inconsistencies which are implied by its literal signification, hence it is futile to construe both the terms in that way. Why ? Because, if omniscience and parviscience cannot be established to be identical or equal, yet with the subject of pure Indication of one term, can be established that identity. For instance, " a Sudra person is a Brahman." Here is an antagonism, in regarding a person endowed with the attribute of a Sudra, to be equal to, or identical with one, who has the attributes of a Brahman ; but in reference to another, who has them not, is not a Sudra, but belongs to the Brahman caste; there is no such antagonism in calling him a Brahman without his being endowed with the attributes of a Sudra, but possessing the distinguishing marks of Brahman in his person. In the same way, intelligence distinguished with parviscience is opposed to intelligence endowed with omnipotence, but if out of the literal significations of the terms *Jiva* and Iswara, the part represented by intelligence be alone taken as what is indicated, then to regard it in both Iswara and *Jiva* as identical or equal, implies no contradiction [That is to say, intelligence *plus* parviscience is not equal to Intelligence *plus* omniscience, but by deleting the attributes of parviscience and omuiscience created by ignorance, hence unreal, we have Intelligence = Intelligence]. Thus there is no reason for admitting Indication in both the terms.

But it is cleared in the following verse :—

> When there is Indication in one term admitted.
> Let this be asked of him, who so does admit. Of two terms in which is it admitted ?
> If in the first, or second it be said ; say unto him,
> What antagonism is created in words, is a mark of stupidity.
> In all the three phrases* the subject of the first word is *Jiva*.
> In " That art Thou" the subject of first term indicates Iswara.
> How can indication not be applied to both its terms ?
> So asks one who is marked with indication of good [or who is well acquainted with Indication.]

When a person is inclined to admit the canons of Indication in one term of a phrase, he is to be asked of the two, which is an Indicator ; if he says the Indication is to be applied to the first term of all transcendental phrases, and not to the second, and that in other expressions, an Indication resides in the second term and not in the first: to him, pupil, you are to reply, that the attribution of Indication in the first term is a sign of stupidity or ignorance. If Indication be applied in construing a sentence to either the first or second term, that will introduce a reciprocal contradiction in its signification ; for in the three sentences, " I am *Brahma*" etc. The subject of *Jiva* is the first term, while in "That art Thou" the Indication of the first term is Iswara. Now if Indication in the first term of all three phrases be admitted, that will signify intelligence endowed with the attributes of omniscience, omnipotence, and the rest, unrelated to the world, [independent of birth and death] to be the (Iswara) Lord ; and " That art Thou" would express intelligence distinguished with parviscience etc., and wordly, to be the *Jiva* ; for in all the three instances, intelligence of the predicate of the first word "*Jiva*" is Indicated, and the literal signification

---

* The three phrases referred to are "My self is *Brahma*," "I am *Brahma*," and " The blissfulness of self is *Brahma*."

of the second term, Iswara, is to be accepted, but in "That art Thou" the literal signification of the first word 'That' is Iswara, whose intelligence is the indicated signification, while the literal signification of 'Thou,' *Jiva*, is to be accepted. In this manner, to put the Indication in the first term of the sentence will create a discord in the meaning of "That art Thou." Similarly in the construction of the other three phrases, to put up in the second will amount to this,—that the literal signification of the first word *jiva*, is to be accepted, and intelligence (part) of the next word is to be the Indicated Indication, so that intelligence will be distinguished with the properties, parviscience and the rest: such then will be the signification of the three sentences.

Moreover in "That art Thou" the accepting of the literal signification of the first word 'That'—Iswara—and the Intelligence part of the second 'Thou'—*Jiva*—as what is indicated, will mark that intelligence with the attributes of omniscience etc. From such a construction of "That art Thou," there will be created a mutual antagonism; hence to say that the first or the second word is the Indicator, is clearly absurd. To avoid it, a proposer, who has all the signs of goodness in him says, both words are Indicators.

Then again, if any one were to assert, there is no rule for placing Indication either in the first or second term of a sentence; but that word whose subject is Iswara, in all the (three) sentences, is the Indicator; and the rule is whether that term be the first or the second word of a sentence, there will be no contradiction introduced in the meaning. This is cleared in the following manner:—

> To say the word Iswara, is the Indicator in the signification of all sentences.
>
> Will render the utterance of the *Sruti* on what is to be known as the purport of human life, futile.

If that word whose literal signification or subject is Iswara, be regarded as the Indicator or what is Indicated, then a *Jiva* will be rendered perfectly helpless, he will remain ignorant of the utterances of the *Sruti*, and cease from wishing to be released; parviscience, dependence, subject to birth and death, and the other ills of wordly existence will be attributed to the individual and his end and aim in life will be rendered futile. That is to say, in admitting Indication in the word, whose literal signification is *Iswara*, "That art Thou" would fail to impart the perception of non-duality, which they are intended to produce in the mind of an enquirer. For the indication of ' That' the secondless, unassociated intelligence in *Maya* devoid of its impurities, agent or instrument, dependent on Ignorance, parviscient, finite, shall be subject to virtue and vice, birth and death, and coming and going (transmigration), and to an endless series of other worthless things. If that were the meaning of the transcendental phrase, an enquirer must necessarily be obliged to fix in his intellect, a conscious perception of such signification, so that, with his intellect fixed in that manner, after death, he is re-born and continues to exist and die in the manner aforesaid, to the end of time; and the 'emancipation,' which the *Vedas*, instruct their pupils to acquire by means of knowledge, shall be rendered futile. Hence to hold, indication lies in the term whose subject is *Iswara*, and not in that other term, whose literal signification is *Jiva* is untenable. And those who say that in all transcendental phrases, in the signification of *Jiva* is indication applicable, and not in *Iswara*, and such a consideration does not render emancipation futile; for, in admitting Indication in the subject of the term *Jiva*, the meaning of ' That art Thou' will amount to this:—The indication 'Thou' shall refer to his (part of) intelligence which is omnipotent, omniscient, distinct, unborn, and eternal, and identically the same with *Iswara*. Thus then, in this view of attributing Indication to the subject of the word *Jiva*, an enquirer will have the facility of acquiring the condition of *Iswara*, by fixing in his intellect, the signification of ' That art Thou' in the manner just mentioned, and with this view, they have made it a rule to apply that indication to *Jiva*.

    But it is an error, so to believe, as will appear from the sequel.

        How can the Indication of 'Thou,' witness, be called identical with *Iswara*,

        The prince and best of *Sanyasis* Jati, says in that, there is indication of both terms.

    It is impossible to hold the indication of the word ' Thou'—

witness—identically one with *Iswara*. Consequently the prince and best of *Sanyasis* (ascetics) Jati Swami, says, there is indication in it, of both terms. That is to say:—If indication be only regarded in the literal signification of the word 'Thou'—*Jiva*—and not in 'That' —*Iswara*—by any person; he is to be asked if the indication of 'Thou' refers to the pervading intelligence or to the witnessing intelligence associated with *Jiva*, and situated along with him in the same region. It is impossible to hold the first view, for, when the literal signification can interpret a word, the Indication of abandoning a part is also applicable, but that literal signification cannot have any reference to the all-pervading intelligence; it indicates only the associated intelligence, or witnessing intelligence of the *Jiva* formed by its associate, situated in the same region with him, hence it has reference only to the witnessing and not the pervading intelligence; and as such, the witness cannot be the internal controller of all hearts, nor can it pervade throughout this vast material expanse, so as to be identically equal to *Iswara*. Moreover, witness is always visible, then to regard him equally invisible with *Iswara's* Intelligence is also impossible. Further, to speak of one who is bereft of *Maya*, as one possessed of it, is also as unreasonable as to speak of a person who has not a stick to be one with a stick, or of a child without the rites of consecration as one consecrated. Thus then by regarding a non-difference of the witnessing Intelligence with *Iswara*, an improbable interpretation of " That art Thou" will follow.

But there is no defect in holding Indication in both the terms 'That' and 'Thou.' Because by abandoning the conflicting portion, the non-conflicting portion, Intelligence without any attributes, common to both the terms, indicated by their indication, will establish their identical equality. Though there is difference in the properties of Intelligence caused by its associate and not in the Intelligence itself; by abandoning the associates, it is possible for the Indication of both the terms to establish the oneness of Intelligence, just as in regard to the jar-ether, it cannot be regarded to be identical with the ether pervading a temple, when the first is abandoned; but if both the connections of a jar and temple are abandoned, they are perceived to be identically equal.

'That,' 'Thou;' 'Thou,' 'That,' is the rule in all* sentences
What is invisible, destroys the condition of Finite.

In all sentences by recognizing the rule of connection as 'That,' 'Thou;' 'Thou,' 'That;'† the mistaken conceptions of visibility and finity, in their signification are removed. If it be said, let the word 'That' indicate the signification of 'Thou,' so that the identity of their signification may be established, but the indication of 'Thou' is the witnessing intelligence, eternal and visible, consequently the distinguishing trait of invisibility is destroyed from such a consideration, and if it be said, let the word 'Thou' refer the signification of 'That' and create an identity with it, but the word 'That' means the pervading intelligence consequently it removes the finity of 'Thou.' Similarly in the instances " I am *Brahma*," " Intelligence is *Brahma*," "Self is *Brohma*" injury will be done to the condition of finite, and in the expressions " *Brahma* am I," " *Brahma* is intelligence," " *Brahma* is Self" the invisibility will be destroyed.

> That oneness of *Jiva* and *Brahma* expounded in the *Sruti* and *Smriti*
> Pupil know it to be caused by abandoning the Indication of a part

Pupil it is for you to know what the *Vedas* and *Smriti* expound about non-duality, have the Indication of abandoning a part.

---

* All sentences signify such as have been referred *viz.*, I am *Brahma* &c.

† And it must not be said, let the word 'That' or 'Thou' abandon the incongruous portion of its meaning of invisibility and visibility respectively and retaining the other portion *viz.*, that of intelligence, indicate the meaning of the word 'Thou' or 'That' respectively; then there will be no need of explaining it in another way as *'Bhagtiag Laskhna'* or the indicating of a " portion ;" for, it is impossible for one word to indicate a portion of its own meaning and that of another word; and, further, there is no expectation of the perception of the meaning of either word again by means of indication, when its meaning has been already perceived by the use of a separate word.

Thus, a pupil receiving instruction (on non-duality by the literal signification, and Indications of 'That art Thou') from his spiritual preceptor.

Is cured of all his defects and impurities; as iron is freed from rust by being hammered on an anvil.

The false preceptor Surbani made this instruction in his work.

Listening and practising which, destroys darkness (ignorance); of that the present is a vernacular rendering.

To the Deva Agradha in his dream, imparted a Guru this instruction.

Destroy the source of all miseries, abandon the attraction of the false wood (of a world).

"Attractions" are being explained in another way.

Says Agradha :—

Bhagaban ! this work that you have taught
Have been understood with its meaning.
Yet the world with its miseries I perceive.
Say the remedy that will destroy.

Replies the Guru, after hearing the word of the pupil :—

Listen to what destroys this wood ;
There is not another remedy like it.
It alone is the cause of the world's destruction.
By ascertaining the signification of 'That art Thou,'
He comes to know, I call myself Agradha ; that is false
On second thoughts, and reflecting again,
He removes self from the connection of his name (body etc.)
Then he discovers Self to be free from faults ;
The work of the Guru of the woods, destroys them all.
Becomes full of bliss, by sacrificing miseries of the wood.
And what he is* actually that attains.

---

* Non-distinct from *Brahma*; that is the actual or normal condition of all beings ; ignorance prevents its conscious perception ; with the advent of knowledge when it is thoroughly realized, the barrier for emancipation is removed and the individual is delivered in life. For him actions have no effect whatever to cause an objective re-birth again after death.

As the miseries of the world were created to Agradha in
    dream,
So are the world's miseries created in Self by ignorance.
And as an unreal (because dream created) Guru destroyed
    the miseries of the false world by a word,
So do you, by having recourse to the false Guru, the *Veda*
    seek the destruction of this false world.
Knowing the indication of the phrases,
An enquirer of knowledge became firm.
Denuded of the envelopment of Ignorance art 'Thou'
[Preceptor] kind and merciful to the poor.

Thus ends the discourse of the Guru on the attribution of falsity to the utterances of the *Vedas*.

SECTION VII.

Victory be to Ram.

The eldest, second and youngest, all three
Hearing such instruction from the preceptor; [of them]
The eldest said, *Brahma* is Self, I know,
And have no trace of doubt left about that.

The preceptor imparted his course of instruction equally to all three, yet it failed to produce a direct effect in the two others. Tatwadrishti, the eldest profited by it, and his perception of non-duality was a tangible realization.

Who wanders, as in the wind does a dried fig leaf,
By the consummation of fructescent works (*Prarabdha*)
Is he compelled to see actions again.
Like a performance of magic show
Sees gardens and orchards,
Towns and cities, and again left alone; sometimes he
Has the good things of the world to enjoy, dress, bed and food,
At others, in the solitary cavern of a rock, he
Puts himself up to spend the night with stone.
With salutations is he received and worshipped.
There he sees men, hundreds of thousand; thousands calling him
Deprived of both abodes,—this and the next.
Say some, he is emancipated.
That he may be adored,
Is a result of his accumulated good works.
Who sees him with defects,
Commits a sin, and suffers accordingly.
Such a one, practises, accustomed works from force of habit,
Never attributes them to the body, nor mistakes it, for Self.
He has nothing proper for him to do; in him the difference of duality has ceased.

He knows from the proofs of the Vedas "I am *Brahma*" without a second.

In the practice of the Wise, some finds rules [but he is without them].

Avoids he, the source of all miseries and with love, centres himself in meditation.

What practice has been left in him, to beg for his daily bread and drink,

Does not make him forget the bliss of meditation or cast a slur on the 'three sheaths.'

That is why, the wise use their endeavours repeatedly for meditation.

Who wanders away from it, becomes a demon in hell.

What Gourpad Muni has described about meditation,

The wise abandons* distraction and takes the essence of all.

Without the eight parts, there is no meditation—source of all bliss.

Now listen to the component eight, which support it [They are].—

'Forbearance'† five, 'Canons' five,‡ and 'postures'§ several;

'Regulating¶ the vital airs' is of several sorts, and think of 'restraining the senses.'

---

* *Vikshepa* is projection or evolution; it is nothing else than misapprehension and is thus defined in the Vedanta Sara. "This is identical with powers of creating. It is always present with envelopement [or *Avarana*], as ignorance regarding a rope creates a snake on it, so that ignorance which creates the illusion or mistaken impression of ether and the other elements on the enshrouded *Atma* is called *Vikshepa*.—Dhole's *Vedanta Sara*, pp. 18-19. But it means distraction here.

† '*Yama.*' ‡ *Niyama.* § *Asana.*

¶ *Pranayam* and *Prutyahar.*

'*Forbearance*' includes harmlessness, speaking the truth, not to be addicted to thieving, control over the passions and not to accept any gifts. The canons to be observed are cleanliness, contentment, restraining the mind, repeating mentally the *mantras* given by a Guru; and venerating Brahma.

'Fixed* attention' is the sixth, and contemplation† and conscious meditation‡ [are two more].

These are the eight means of unconscious meditation.

Hearing the propriety of meditation, Tatwadrishti laughs.

Replies he not, but appears as one demented or possessed by the devil.

Like a person possessed by an evil spirit talking incoherently, Tatwadrishti on hearing of 'Samadhi' that it was something proper to be done, began to laugh. Now the meaning of the above piece of poetical effusion is this—A person possessed of knowledge, has no rule to make a practical use of his body; for in practice he is without ignorance, and the difference created by its products, that is to say, anger, spite and desire he has none; he has simply the defects of fructescent works—works that have commenced to bear fruits, they are instrumental to his practice; and as they vary according to the diversity of persons, hence the man of knowledge has no need to observe any rules in his person for fructescent works. This is what the *Sidhanti* says.

There are others who say, there is no rule why a wise person should undertake actions or be engaged in usual works; on the other hand, there are rules for cessation or destroying them. If there be any inclination, it is confined to begging for daily wants and the narrowest strip, just enough to cover the unexposed portion of the body. There is no other inclination left in him; for, prior to the arising of knowledge while simply in his noviciate, enquiring for truth, he

---

* "*Dharana*" is to concentrate the heart on the Real *Brahma* without a Second.

† '*Dhyana*' is the uninterrupted current of the mental function towards the Real *Brahma* without a Second.

‡ Conscious meditation or *Savikalpa Samadhi* is to realize the *Brahma* without a second by concentrating the mind which has assumed the shape of the Impartite and by indivisibly resting its function there, with the distinction of knower and knowledge; that is to say, with the retention of individual consciousness (as to worsipper and the object worshipped).— Duole's *Vedanta Sara*, pp. 47-49.

had been indifferent to the acquisition of material well-being; for, the enjoyment they bring forth is impermanent: since knowledge, that is, subsequent to its growth, his indifference has traced other defects, it has found out that the attribution of happiness to wealth and property, to family and wife, relations and connections is merely a false perception in the intellect—a perception, that is visibly false. There is no true perception in a substance, nor is there any passion present when regarded as faulty, and desire follows that passion, but for a man of knowledge, passion is impossible; and the usual nourishment needed for the maintenance of the body comes to him, as a result of fructescent works—works done in a prior existence that have begun to bear fruit—hence there is no necessity for either passion, or its excited product, a desire, in him,

Works (actions) are of three varieties. *Sanchit* or 'accummulated'; *Prarabdha* or 'fructescent,' and *Agami** or future. In the bodies of the elementals or elementary spirits, past actions are not productive of fruits, but are simply accumulated. Future acts are called *Agami*. In elements, the source of the present body in past works is called fructescent. Of these the 'accumulated' are destroyed by knowledge, and as a wise man never errs in considering Self to be an agent (or doer of works), therefore future works do not apply to him; and as the fructescent works have produced his present body, they produce in him, an inclination to beg for his daily food to make the body last. Fructescent works are only consumed by enjoying their fruits, they are never destroyed by knowledge; but elsewhere it is mentioned that like the accumulated and future works, the fructescent also disappear for him; hence it is quite possible that the wise should still retain an inclination for eating, etc. In other words, what is meant by it, from the standpoint of the wise, Self is quite unrelated with works or their fruits; and as all works have been interdicted, the fructescent are also included in that interdiction: and the fructescent actions done prior to the production of

---

* *Kriyamana* or 'current' is the third variety of works mentioned in the Systems. Our author makes *agami* the second, whereas fructescent is the second. Hence I have put the second in its proper place and made *agami* the third.

knowledge, bring forth no fruits for him to enjoy in the present body. With this object, the fructescent have not been interdicted,* because the author of the *Sutras* says, the accumulated are destroyed by knowledge in the wise, 'future' are quite unrelated; and 'fructescent' are exhausted by enjoying their fruits; hence by the force of the fructescent works, the wise maintain their bodies, and no more. But when works are said to be various, one of them can produce a succession of bodies; hence if the first produced *Karmaic* body of a person can acquire knowledge [of *Brahma* and a person's identity with It], yet he must inherit a fresh body after death, because the works that have already begun to produce fruit can only be exhausted by consummation. Thus then, one act leads to a succession of future re-births; and though knowledge may arise in the first body of the series, yet for reaping the fruits of works, even subsequent to that knowledge, the individual has to live again in another body; and there can be no exception in favor of one who is a theosophist; he must have a subjective future existence too. Moreover, if it be said, the fructescent works must continue to produce the usual number of bodies as their results in the theosophist also; but, as the fructescent are exhausted by enjoyment, therefore, the wise succeed in emancipating themselves from future re-births. But that assertion is clearly contra-indicated. Because, the *Vedas* proclaim: the *Prana* (vital air) of a wise does not go to any other abode in the twenty-one† regions, but is blended into, or merges in

---

* The *Vedanta* doctrine regarding works is this :—True knowledge of *Brahma* and non-duality or identity of a person with it, destroys the accumulated and cancels the results of current works ; the fruits of fructescent must be consumed during the present life, then emancipation follows at death. These last cannot be destroyed by the knowledge of *Brahma* ; but according to the Yoga, the meditation which is styled in that system (*Asamprajnata*) meditation without an object, can destroy them, and so it is considered by Yogins to be superior to knowledge.

† Bhur, Bhavar, Swar, Mahar, Janas, Tapas, and Satya the seven upper, and Atala, Vitala, Sutala, Rusatala, Talatala, Mahatala and Patala are the seven lower regions. What the other seven are, we find no mention in the *Vedanta Sara*.

the internal organ of the body, where it dwelleth with the organs of sense and action. As without the exit of the *Prana*, there can be no succeeding re-birth, consequently after the exhaustion of the fructescent works, the adepts have no more bodies to inherit; and where an action pre-determines a succession of several bodies, knowledge arises in a subsequent body and not in a prior life; because the fructescent works, inasmuch as they are the source of successive lives, are an obstacle to the growth of knowledge. As to one bent after the acquisition of wealth, want of faith in the *Vedic* utterances serves as an obstacle to knowledge by undoing his notions of duality—of difference between him and *Brahma*—so are fructescent works distinctly preventive of knowledge; and as such, they are removed by the 'means' of knowledge, 'hearing' and the rest; so that, the practice of these means in the first life produces knowledge in the next objective life. As in Bamdeva, the practice of 'hearing' in a prior life, and the exhaustion of fructescent works in one body, produced no knowledge, but with the fall of that body, and after the inheritance of another body, after death, the 'hearing' and the other means of knowledge practised in that prior life, gave him knowledge while *in utero*, consequently after knowledge has arisen, there can be no relation with another body, and the endeavours and exertions of the present life are attributable to fructescent works and these serve to maintain the body. Excess of exertion, from passion and desire, there is no occasion for, hence he—the wise—is without all inclinations. In this way, his principal aim is to cause a cessation of all endeavours and works, and this forms the practical part of his existence.

But it may be said in this connection, that as the mind is ever active and cannot rest without a site, but must have something wherein to fix itself, therefore, for procuring a site for the mind, the wise must have a certain inclination or endeavour; but such an assertion is easily removed. A man without meditation may have his activity of mind, but the wise gains victory over it, by resting on meditation, hence he has no inclination left in him. And that meditation can only be done by the eight means mentioned below:—

(1) Forbearance, (2) Canons, (3) Posture, (4) Regulation of the

Vital airs, (5) Restraint of the organs of sense, (6) Fixed attention, (7) Contemplation and (8) Conscious meditation.

(1). Forbearance consists in harmlessness or sparing life, truthfulness, not stealing, chastity and non-acceptance of gifts.

(2). The Canons to be observed are cleanliness, contentment, restraining the mind, endurance of hardships, inaudible repetition of words, and concentration of thought on *Iswara*, The *Jnana Samadhi* describes ten acts of forbearance and two minor religious observances or canons, according to the method of the *Puranas*. But the followers of the *Vedanta* divide each of them into five.

(3). Posture is said to be infinite in variety of which the following are mentioned in works on Yoga.*

(a). Swastica.
(b). Gomukha.
(c). Bira.
(d). Kurma.
(e). Padma.
(f). Kukuta.
(g). Utan.
(h). Kurmaka.
(i). Dhanush.
(j). Matsya.
(k). Pshavamtan.
(l). Mayura.
(m). Sav.
(n). Singha.
(o). Vadra.
(p). Sidha etc.

The signs of these postures have been fully described in *Yoga Philosophy*, but for fear of unnecessarily extending the work, and as they are not requisite in any exposition of the Vedanta, I have purposely refrained from describing their indications; [suffice it to say], that the principal of them are Singha, Vadra, Padma, and Sidhi—and of these four, the last mentioned is Sidhi. It is superior to all the rest.

It is practised by putting the sole of the left foot firmly in the central *ruphi* of the perinaeum, and pressing the pubic region with the sole of the right foot fixing the sight in the interspace between the two eye-brows. 'Sidhasana' is to keep the body fixed in an unrestrained position like a post. There are others, who assert, that

---

* The ascetic posture admits of 84 varieties each more uncomfortable than the last, but in which the Yogin must by degree become quite easy.

Yoga Philosophy, edited by Takaram Tatia, p. xii.

the sole of the left foot is not to be applied to the central *raphi* of the perinaeum in the interspace of the anus and genitals, but it should be put above the penis and the right sole over that. But this 'Sidhasana' like that first mentioned, is the principal posture; because many of the postures cause a removal of disease, while there are others which serve as a means to help the regulation of breath and meditation; but Sidhasana is superior to all the rest, inasmuch as it is present during meditation. It is likewise termed 'Bajrâsana,' 'Muktâsana' and 'Guptâsana.'

(4). Regulation of breath is to be practised subsequent to achieving an ascendency over posture. It is of several varieties; a short description is requisite to enable its comprehension. It consists of three separate parts, viz., *Puraka*, *Rechaka*, and *Kumbhaka*.

    (*a*). *Puraka* is inspiration. It is done by breathing through the left nostril [and stopping the right by the tip of the thumb] by the vessel known as *Ida*.

    (*b*). *Rechaka* is expiring through the right nostril [gently and stopping the left by the index finger, or it and the middle].

    (*c*). Holding the breath in the vessel called *Sushmuna* is *Kumbhaka*.

To inspire, expire, and hold the breath in this manner, is called the 'Regulating of the vital airs.' There are two varieties of it. *Agarva* and *Sagarva*.

    (*a*). 'Regulating the vital airs' without promising 'Om' is called *Agarbha Pranayam*, the unjoined, and

    (*b*). 'Regulating the vital airs' with the pronounciation of 'Om' is called *Sagarbha* or the joint method.

(5). Restraining the organs of sense consists in drawing them away from their several objects.

(6). 'Fixed attention' is the fixing of the internal organ upon the secondless *Brahma* without an impediment.

(7). 'Contemplation' is the unceasing current of the internal organ on the secondless Reality *Brahma*, with an impediment [*i. e.*, at intervals in times of worship etc.]

(8). 'Meditation' is the pursuit of that one object, *Brahma*, after the mind has assumed that modification in which ideas inconsistent with It are excluded, but ideas consistent with the secondless Reality are continued.

'Meditation' is of two kinds :—

    (1). 'Conscious' *i. e.*, with recognition of subject and object, (*Savikalpa*) and

    (2). 'Unconscious' without recognition of subject and object (*Nirvikalpa*).

(1). Conscious meditation is that in which there are present knowledge, knower, and object to be known ; with these three, to rest the mental function on the secondless *Brahma* is called meditation with recognition of subject and object.

Now this conscious meditation is of two kinds.

    (*a*). '*Shabdanuvidha*' or with words.

    (*b*). '*Shabdan-nuvidha*' or without words,

(*a*). When there is a conscious perception of "I am *Brahma*," along with the meditation with recognition of subject and object— the conscious variety—It is called *Shabdanuvidha* [this word is derived from '*Shabda*,' a word and '*anuvidha*' perceived, therefore it means perception from words.

(*b*). When there is no perception of the words "I am *Brahma*" in that conscious meditation, it is called *Shabdan-nubidha* or without words.

(2.) Unconscious meditation is the resting of the mental function after it has assumed the shape of the Impartite *Brahma*, without consciousness of knowledge, knower and object, *i. e.*, without recognition of subject and object.

This then is the difference between conscious and unconscious meditation. The first is a means to that end, the second is the result [of the first].

Though there is a perception of duality in the conscious variety of meditation, inasmuch as there is distinct recognition of subject and object, yet the duality only helps to know the *Brahma* ; in the same way, as in an earthen object, there is a perception of earth, though there be an appearance of an earthen jar etc. ; so too, is there the perception of the secondless Reality *Brahma* alone, even though there be an appearance of duality.

Like the conscious variety, there is also an appearance of duality in the unconscious meditation too, constituted by the distinctions of knowledge, knower and object to be known, but just as in a saline solution, the salt assumes the shape of water, and is no longer perceptible as salt, and nothing appears but the water* [so, by the disappearance of the modification of the internal organ after it has assumed the shape of the Impartite, nothing appears but *Brahma*].

In this manner, the difference between the two kinds of meditation is established; that is to say, in the meditation with recognition of subject and object, there is a perception of duality with that of *Brahma*, and in the meditation without recognition of subject and object, there is no conscious perception of the three integral constituents, knower, knowledge and object to be known; likewise with the state of profound slumber and this second variety of meditation, there is this difference, that in the former, there is an absence of the modification of the mental function in the shape of *Brahma*, while in the latter, there is that modification present, though there is no perception of it. Thus then, there is an entire absence of the internal organ with its function in profound slumber, while in the unconscious meditation there is only a want of the perception, though the internal organ and its function are modified into the shape of the *Brahma*; now this modification proceeds from the practice of the conscious variety of meditation; hence that is reckoned as one of the eight means, whose result is this meditation without recognition of subject and object.

Unconscious meditation is of two kinds :—

(1) Non-dual mental perception.
(2) Non-dual form of resting in *Brahma*.

(1) When the non-dual modification of the internal organ after it has assumed the shape of the *Brahma* arises with the unknown function, it is called a form of non-dual mental perception of unconscious meditation. Here much practice in needed, so that the functional modification of *Brahma* also ceases; and

---

* *Vide Chhandogya Upanishad* v. 13.

(2) When the function has been completely done away with, it constitutes the non-dual condition of unconscious meditation. Then, just as water sprinkled on red hot iron is absorbed into the body of the metal, so by much persevering and firm practice of the non-dual perceptional form of the unconscious meditation, the function merges into the extremely manifested *Brahma*; and this resting on the non-dual *Brahma* form of unconscious meditation, is the chief result of which the first, or perceptional is a means only.

Between that non-dual resting and profound slumber, the difference consists in the merging of the mental function in Ignorance in the latter, and the merging of the same function into the extremely tangible *Brahma* in the former; the felicity of the latter is enveloped in Ignorance, while the blissfulness of *Brahma* perceived in the former, is entirely devoid of covering.

Unconscious meditation is apt to meet with four obstacles which are to be avoided, and they are:—

1. Mental inactivity (*Laya*),
2. Mental distraction (*Vikshepa*),
3. Passion and desires (*Kashaya*); and
4. The tasting of enjoyment (*Rasaswad*).

(1) Mental inactivity is the absence or want of function, either from drowsiness or sleep.* It produces a condition similar to that of profound slumber, and there is no consciousness of the blissfulness of *Brahma*, so that when from drowsiness or sleep the function merges into its proximate cause—the internal organ—the Yogi should be careful, he should restrain that sleep, and stir up the function.† In this way, to stir up the mental function by stopping sleep and inactivity, and to awaken its continued current is by Gourpad‡ Acharya called "addressing the Intelligence."

---

* The *Vedanta Sara* defines it to be drowsiness of the mental perception after it has failed in its endeavour to rest on the Impartite Reality, *Brahma* without a second.—DHOLE'S *Vedanta Sara*, p. 50.

† When the mind succumbs to inactivity it should be stirred up. (*Sruti*.)

‡ He was the Supreme Guru or Guru of Guru of the venerable Sankar Acharya.

(2). Mental distraction is thus defined :—When a sparrow pursued by the fear of a hawk, or cat, restlessly enters a house to find an asylum, there is for the time being, no defect or fault attached to the house ; but finding no rest therein, issues out again and is either overtaken with fear or death ; in the same manner, knowing the substances which are not self, to be productive of grief, the direction of the mental function internally for the perception of felicity of *Brahma*, and as the subject of that function, intelligence, is very subtle, therefore without resting the function for a certain time, in that intelligence, the perception of felicity in the form of intelligence cannot immediately be had or attained ; consequently the function is directed away or excluded from it. Thus then, the exclusion of the mental function is called direction. [In short it is the resting of the mind on something else than *Brahma*.]

Now, without a resting of that function, there can be no perception of true felicity, hence, even when the function is directed internally, but has not been modified into the shape of *Brahma*, till then, a Yogin excludes the function from all the external objects, lest the mind be distracted and rests it firmly there. The struggle for keeping off 'distraction' is by Gourpad Acharya called (*Sama*) passivity, which is an antagonist of mental distraction.

(3). Passions and desires are lust, affection etc.

They are of two kinds :—

(*a*). External, and
(*b*). Internal,

(*a*). The 'external' is the present affection for a wife, son, wealth, etc.

(*b*). The 'internal' is a prospective or future speculation in which the mind dwells in the object of its desire and builds its hopes accordingly.

None of the two can cause impediment to a Yogi already engaged in meditation. Because the mind has five conditions of being as follows :—

(*a*). (*Kshepa*) Unsteadiness.
(*b*). (*Mudhata*) Silliness.

(c). (*Vikshepa*) Distraction.
(d). (*Ekagrata*) Undisturbed attention or earnestness, and
(e). (*Nirodha*) Impediment.

(a). 'Unsteadiness' is that state of modification of desire when there is an ardent wish for attaining abodes, bodies, *Shastras* or learning etc., in short, for every thing else, except self. It is a product of the active quality.

(b). 'Silliness' is the modification of laziness, etc., produced by the quality of darkness.

(c). 'Distraction' is the rare turning away of the mind inclined to, or engaged in contemplation, by the stimulus of an external object.

(d). 'Undisturbed attention' is that modification of the internal organ when the past and present assume an identical equality of shape. Patanjali has described its indication in his *Yoga Sutra*. Its purport is this 'During the time of meditation' there is undisturbed attention of the internal organ in a Yogi, it is therefore not an absence of function; but then all the modifications of the mental function, during such meditation, assume the shape of the *Brahma*, consequently the past and present are all moulded in that way, making *Brahma* their subject, and the identical equality of shape refers to this modification after the shape of *Brahma* only.

(e). 'Impediment' is an increase of undisturbed attention.

These are the five mental conditions. They are likewise termed '*Kshipta*,' '*Mudha*,' '*Vikshipita*,' '*Ekagra*,' and '*Nirodha*,' consecutively. The first two of them cannot affect the internal organ during meditation; distraction does so, and the two last continue also. So says *Yoga* Philosophy.

When the mind is unfixed or rendered unsteady, it cannot qualify itself for *Yoga*; hence it cannot be asserted that passions are a source of obstacle to meditation. For, when the external and internal desires, etc., continue in an unsteady condition of the mind, it cannot at all qualify itself for *Yoga*; because the experience of desire, envy, spite and the rest, acquired in prior lives, leaves their subtle conception in the distracted mind, (hence envy and desire are not included in passions, they are not so called, their conceptions are called passions) so that so long as the mind lasts, that conception cannot be removed, consequently in the time of meditation also, it continues to remain in the internal organ, without affecting it; but on the other hand, the conceptions derived from passions, envy, lust, desire and the rest are quite opposed to meditation, and those which are underived are not inimical to it.

'Derived' signifies produced from, and 'underived,' unproduced. The conceptions produced from passions, envy, etc., to a person engaged in meditation are all directed to material objects and must be buried or overpowered there and then.

Between 'distraction' and 'passion' there is this difference. Function moulded into the shape of external objects is called distraction; and when from a Yogi's endeavour, the function is directed inwards, but from the derivative conception of passions—desire and the rest, the internally directed function is obstructed or impeded, and makes out *Brahma* its subject, it is called passion (*Kashaya*). Now this is destroyed by attacking the usual defects present in all external or material objects; and a Yogi endeavours to remove passion by looking all objects (which are not self) in their true light of impermanency and a productive source of misery; and he succeeds in curbing all desires by them.

(4). 'Tasting of enjoyment.' A Yogi has experience or perception of the blissfulness of *Brahma*, as also that of destruction of the miseries of 'distraction'; sometimes from the destruction of misery, happiness follows, as for instance in the case of person carrying a load, when his burden is removed, he experiences ease and happiness; and for that happiness, there is no other cause except the easing of his load, which therefore is called a source of pain; so that when he is so eased, he expresses himself, "I feel happy," hence cessation of pain is a source of happiness. Similarly the miseries caused by distraction, when removed during meditation, in the person of a Yogi, he experiences happiness and this is called 'Tasting of enjoyment.' If he were to separate his intellect from the experience of felicity for causing a destruction of pain, then, as during meditation, there is an absence of the mental function (for it has assumed the modification of unassociated *Brahma*) he should not experience that blissfulness; hence the tasting of enjoyment caused by a removal of pain and experience of felicity, is an obstacle to meditation.

Without the possession of a desired object, to cause a procurement of happiness, by the destruction of that which is inimical to it is illustrated as follows:—

Gems are found in earth, and if a gem were guarded by a powerfully venomed snake, then prior to its acquisition, the destruction of the snake which stood in the way of its acquisition, is sure to procure pleasure; and if the intellect or perception of happiness derived from a destruction of the snake be satiated, then there will be no attempt to acquire the gem; hence the supreme happiness, which the possession of the gem would have brought forth, will be wanting; so the non-dual *Brahma* is a gem, and the mistaken attribution of self to the physical body and other substances, foreign to him, is the snake of distraction; and the tasting of enjoyment is the experience of felicity, by causing the destruction of the snake of distraction: and as such experience stands an obstacle to the aquirement of the supreme felicity to be experienced in the acquisition of the non-dual *Brahma*, it is called an impediment or obstacle. Or ' tasting of enjoyment may mean—

Unconscious meditation follows the conscious; now there is recognition of knowledge, knower, and object in the conscious; consequently its felicity is associated with the three integral constituents of the conscious Ego, for which it is called associated; but in unconscious meditation they are absent, hence its felicity is unassociated; thus then, in the beginning of unconscious meditation, it is not probable to abandon the perception of associated happiness attendant on conscious meditation, but to follow it, so that the experience of felicity proceeding from a removal of mental distraction or the experience of the felicity of conscious meditation is called (*Rasasuwad*) ' Tasting of enjoyment.' Now both of these varieties cause an impediment to the experience of supreme felicity of unconscious meditation, for which they are regarded as obstacles and as such, they are to be abandoned.

Unconscious meditation is liable to be affected by four similar obstacles, at its commencement, which should all be surmounted, ore the supreme felicity of *Brahma* is to be experienced ; * and he who does experience it is called the "liberated in life." These are the reasons, why the mind of a wise is never wanting a site, and on rising from his meditation, by the strength of fructescent works, he remembers the supreme felicity he was enjoying then. Hence even then, his mind is never unoccupied, and what inclination there remains in him for eating etc., is simply a product of actions which already have commenced to bear fruit; and that inclination is to him, a matter of pain, as it interferes with the experience of felicity in meditation, to which it is inimical ; and one to whom even an inclination of eating, is a matter of pain, can have no more inclination for any thing else ; hence many preceptors have maintained this doctrine in their writings. Moreover, the felicity of the 'liberated in life' can never be produced by a desire of external objects, but rather by their destruction or removal, hence a wise person, desirous of tasting the pleasurable feelings of the 'liberated in life' has also no inclination for external objects; but in the case of a wise person, their cessation holds good for him ; because, either in a tendency or predilection for its removal and destruction, the commandments of the *Vedas* are to be observed, but they do not apply to him ; hence he has his rules of practice regulated by fructescent works (that is to say, the actions he has been destined to, can be

---

* When the mind comes to centre all its thoughts on the Impartite (Universal) Consciousness, after having surmounted the four obstacles (cited before), like the unflickering light of a lamp, by devout and profound meditation it is called the *Nirvikalpa Samadhi* ; on this subject the evidence of the *Sruti* is "When the mind succumbs to inactivity, it is to be stirred up ; when it is distracted, it should be quieted ; when inflamed with passions and desires, it should be prevented from acting under their influence, by knowledge ; when it comes to centre its thoughts on the Impartite Reality *Brahma*—it should not be moved any more ; then it should abstain from enjoying the pleasurable feelings which follow the conscious meditation and dissociate its attachment from all other things by discrimination" [literally the abnegation of Self and engrossment in the Absolute]. And again "To be in a conditional identity with the unflickering light of a lamp."

continued without at all interfering with his knowledge of Self or emancipation) and he is unrestrained and free, and his works are a product of the fructescent. *

Such a wise person, who has only an inclination to maintain his body by begging alms from the force of fructescent works, that begging of food is their result; and in whom, fructescent works are a source of many enjoyments, then he must have the requisite inclination for them also. Moreover if it be said that in a person where the fructescent produce only an inclination to beg his food, there only can knowledge arise ; and who has been accustomed to

---

* There are two opposite doctrines in regard to this matter, one maintains a liberty of action, while the other puts a restriction to that liberty. —The first is distinguished by the name of *Yateshtacharana*. Sureswar the reputed disciple of *Sankar* disapproves it. It is likewise the doctrine of *Panchedasi and Vedantasara*. There it is mentioned " If with sun a knowledge of the Real *Brahma* without a second, the individual follows the bent of his inclinations and acts as he choses, then where is the difference between him and a dog in regard to eating impure food. Such an individual is not one 'liberated in life,' he may be styled a knower of Self." The other doctrine holds an absence of such inclination as above mentioned and his actions are governed by fructescent works.

The Revd. K. M. Bannerji in his *Dialogues* on Hindu Philosophy p. 381 says "*Vedantic* authors have boldly asserted that they are subject to no law, no rule and there is no such thing as virtue or vice, injunction or prohibition," and this is said because of the *dictum* that the knower of *Brahma* may act as he likes. It is needless to add, when a person has acquired the supreme knowledge, there is no more inclination left in him for action ; only the usual acts of nature, hunger and thirst are followed in practice as a part of acquired habit, but they cannot subject him to re-birth inasmuch as the material for that, Ignorance or Matter, is destroyed in knowledge.

In the *Brihadaranyaka Upanishad* (4. 3. 22) is mentioned in reference to knowledge. Here a thief is no more so, a Chandala ceases to be a Chandal the Paullkasa and the sacred mendicant are no more so. They are neither followed by good nor bad works. For the Wise has at last parted beyond all sorrows of his heart."

practise many works, from the same source, can have possibly no knowledge, so that beyond begging—begging alms to procure a daily meal—any other practice is hurtful to knowledge, is quite untenable; for we find Yagnyavalka, Janak and others deservedly called wise; yet the first had the practice [habit] of collecting wealth by gaining victory over his rivals in debate in the ordinary manner, and the second had been in the habit of governing his kingdom. This has been said of them. Likewise in *Vashista* is contained an account of several theosophists who had been accustomed to practise a variety of actions; hence it follows, that in their case, there is no rule one way or the other, either for practice or its discontinuance.

Though Yagnyavalka subsequent to his triumph over rivals assembled in a body for carrying on the controversy about *Brahma Vidya*, turned into an ascetic, thus virtually relinquishing all practices and causing their destruction, and has assigned several faults to inclination and endeavour, yet it cannot be said of him, that prior to his turning into an ascetic he had no knowledge in him; but on the other hand, he had knowledge from the beginning. The fact is, prior to his asceticism he had not acquired the felicity experienced by the liberated in life, so that for its acquisition, he abandoned all his accumulated wealth. * It may be said of him, that his fructescent works were a source of unusually longer period of enjoyment for him in the first period and of lesser enjoyments in the subsequent period of his sojourn in life, so that his longer enjoyment was not attributable to any faults; and its subsequent cessation was brought about, when he found that happiness to be defective. And in the case of Janak, his life-sovereignty was a

---

* He divided it equally amongst his two wives Kartyani and Maitreyi, the former of whom enquired of him where was he going ? The reply was to enjoy happiness, he wanted to be an ascetic. Then she said that wealth is perfectly useless for such a purpose, and she will have it not, but with kindness impart me the necessary knowledge that will procure me the ineffable happiness. So he began to give her the course of instruction which is embodied in the *Brihadaranyaka Upanishad*.

result of fructescent works too, and here also there is a want of abandoning all, but to attribute defects to enjoyments is not appropriate.

In the case of Bamdeva and others, the same fructescent works were a cause of enjoyment for a shorter period, and for this attribution of defects to all enjoyments, it is said, they had no desire for them. In *Vasishta* is mentioned, the instance of Shikuradhaja who had, after the acquisition of knowledge, an intense desire for more extensive enjoyments. Thus then, we find very contradictory doctrines being maintained by several authorities as to the nature of practice which the wise should continue to have. But in all these different considerations, knowledge is regarded in the same light equally, and the successful products which it produces are also said to be equal; and likewise there is a difference of results in practice according to a difference of fructescent works. That is to say, the less he practises, the more happiness a person liberated in life experiences, and a greater amount of practice only reduces that happiness. But it may create misapprehension; some may be inclined to believe, if a liberated person were to engage himself in practising actions, such as he has been accustomed to, by abandoning happiness, his emancipation after the separation of his body will likewise be abandoned, and there will only be an [intense] desire for acquiring the blissful abode of *Vishnu—Vaikuntha.* But so it never happens. Because the abandonment of happiness by a liberated in life, an inclination for work in a wise, are all due to fructescent works of which they are mere results, and the abandonment of emancipation after the separation of the body or desire to inherit some of the blissful abodes in heaven, can never be produced from them, or independently; inasmuch as the vital airs of the wise do not go out; consequently without that he cannot be subjected to a future existence; neither is it possible that there should be abandonment of emancipation, for knowledge destroys ignorance, and subsequent to the exhaustion of fructescent works in that present life, there is no material out of which the future body is to be created; for the source of the physical, and subtle body, is Ignorance (matter) which has already been destroyed by knowledge.

Emancipation after separation of the body is nothing else but a merging into Intelligence (the Absolute *Brahma*, the collective aggregate of *Brahmaic* Intelligence) and that is sure to follow; and if there be any remaining of the primordial Ignorance [undifferentiated cosmic matter], or if the already destroyed Ignorance were to revive, then only, such emancipation is not to take place. But as that primordial Ignorance is inimical to knowledge, it cannot last after knowledge has already been acquired,* hence it does not remain, nor can the destroyed ignorance be revivified: since that destruction had been caused by mature consideration, weighing of proofs, and analysis based on the arguments used in the sacred writings, hence there is no want of emancipation after separation of the body, nor is he liable to abandon his desire of release and beget a desire for inheriting the blissful abode of heaven and the rest; for his desire proceeds as a result of fructescent works, and the requisite materials necessary for his continuance of life are only created by these works and nothing additional. And as no enjoyment can follow without a prior desire for it, hence his desire is not a result of fructescent actions nor can they entail upon him a subjective or objective existence in any of the twenty-one places of abode; [this has already been explained in a previous portion of the present section] hence the wise never abandons a desire of emancipation after the separation of his body, nor does he beget a desire to go into another abode.

The 'liberated in life,' by his present body which is inimical to the enjoyment of felicity, can have a desire for a larger share of enjoyment, in the same way, as there is present an inclination for begging alms for providing food; so that it is quite possible for king Janak to have such a desire in him. When we say so, we mean that an external inclination of the wise is not inimical to cause his liberation in life, but his separate felicity is so. Because Self is eternal

---

* According to Sankhyakara, Undifferentiated cosmic matter is incapable of producing anything, hence its continuance cannot produce a new body, so long as it is not acted upon by 'Purusha' (Force) so as to disturb its equipoise by inducing change.

and free, and bondage is attributed to him from want of knowledge; but with the advent of knowledge, the mistake that he is subject to re-birth is removed by the destruction of ignorance, and that illusion is never reproduced;—and such a destruction of the illusion of bondage constitutes what is called a person liberated in life. From the presence or absence of inclination, he can never mistake Self to be a subject of re-birth, consequently an external inclination cannot affect his liberation in life, nor can it procure that distinct felicity, [which is the blissfulness of *Brahma*]. Earnestness, or sustained and undisturbed attention,—a modification of the mind—produces happiness, but it never arises from external inclination. In this way, according to a difference in fructescent works, there is difference in the practice, amongst the wise. And when they are a source of excessive inclination or endeavour, the fructescent are called bad, because excess of inclination is inimical to undisturbed attention. Then again, without that 'undisturbed attention,' there can be no perception of unassociated felicity (this has already been mentioned when speaking of *Samadhi*). Moreover, what has been said about the perception of falsity in material objects, so that the wise can have no desire for them, hence inclination is also wanting in him, is untenable; for we find, that even with the knowledge that his body is impermanent and unreal, still is he seen to beg for his daily bread, and to support that body accordingly, from a force of fructescent works. In the same way, when a wise person has an excess of fructescent actions for a large share of enjoyment, he has an excess of inclination too; like the inclination for seeing a magic performance, though every one knows it to be false, it is quite possible to have inclination, though he knows all material objects to be false.

But if it be asserted that when a person has found a substance to be defective and faulty, he has no inclination for it, and to say that as a wise person regards all material objects in the light of unreality, hence he has no desire for them; consequently inclination too, must be equally wanting is untenable. Because as such a person having ascertained the consequence of unwholesome food, yet from the force of fructescent works, he has inclination for it, and commits an indiscretion, so in the case of the wise, notwithstanding his knowledge as to the falsity and defective nature of material objects, he has yet an inclination left in him, from the force of the same fructescent works. Vidyarana Swami* has in his treatise ['Triptivipa'] fully expounded the tenet as to the want of a fixed rule for the wise to follow in practice, in this manner; consequently as Tatwadrishti was devoid of it, he was surprised to hear that it was fit that he should practise meditation, and—that made him laugh.

> Wanders Tatwadrishti the good and wise, for a certain time,
> To exhaust his fructescent works; then merges he into [the Absolute].

Subsequent to the exhaustion of fructescent works, by enjoying their results in the present life, the vital airs of the wise do not go out elsewhere; hence, it is said in the verse, that *Tatwadrishti's* breath merged [and not escaped]. Then again, the wise has no need of waiting for a particular time to part with his body; it may happen either when the Sun is in the North or South of the equator; everywhere emancipation is sure to come on. In the same way, his nativity or a foreign country, Benares, or a dirty town, can affect him not: when and where he parts with his body, then and there, he is emancipated. Nor is there any necessity for maintaining a particular posture, he may either be seated on the earth, or on the cremating ground, or he may maintain the position of *Sidhasana*,—all are equally indifferent, so far as his interests are concerned: he may die with all his attention engrossed in the thought of *Brahma* or he may give loud vent to expressions of pain caused by disease, in the full agony of death. All these can affect his emancipation in no manner. When and wherever, he may die, that emancipation proceeds as a matter of course, and has no dependence on the accidents of time and locality, posture and thought etc.,—because his emancipation dates from the period of his rising of knowledge, and the destruction of Ignorance.

---

* The Author of the *Panchadashi* of which *Triptidvipa* is one of the fifteen treatises.

And as the wise waits not for an auspicious moment, or place, or posture to part with his body, so he waits not for them for the purpose of hearing the precepts of the *Vedas*, or the instruction of his spiritual preceptor. But they are necessary for one engaged in devotional exercise. Though Vishnwa and others have been reckoned amongst the wise, and they did not part with their breath till the sun's path was in the north of the equator, yet they were qualified persons, so that a man engaged in devotion is required to wait for an auspicious moment for parting with his breath. Vashishta was also a qualified person and that is why both of them were subjected to several re-births consecutively. Because, the fructescent works of qualified individuals are exhausted during the period of time covered by a *Kalpa* ;* and without a termination of that *Kalpa* his emancipation [*Bideha mukti*] after death never proceeds, but he is successively to inherit a successive series of bodies during all that period ; yet even then, he never regards his Self to be subject either to birth or death, hence he can be called one 'delivered in life.' And the practices of such a qualified person are kept up only to afford instruction to others, but in regard to the practice of other wise persons, this rule does not prevail, hence in reference to the dissolution of body, the usual rules as to time and place etc., do not apply to Tatwadrishti.

> The second pupil Adrishta on the auspicious banks of the sacred Ganges.
> A region too holy,—did he, contemplate on *Brahma*.
> He parted with his body after the manner of the Sacred Writings said before,
> Merged into *Brahma* and found much to animate.

As for the wise, time and place are not needed, so on the contrary, a worshipper waits for a good place and auspicious moment when the sun shall be in the north of the equator to part with his

---

* *Kalpa* is a period of 43,2000,000 years equal to one day of *Brahmā*,—one of the third, or *Trimurti* the creator of the universe, which is called *Brahma's* egg or *Brahmānda*.

body. If he dies in the east of the place, where he used to contemplate, he is sure to remember the object of contemplation, and thus enjoy the fruit of his devotion. And like the recollection of the object of his devotion, when that is *Brahma*, he attains to that *Brahma*, in the way already described, when explaining *Deva marga*,* and it is necessary there should be a remembrance of that road. It constitutes a part of devotional exercise.

For the production of knowledge by means of 'hearing,' there is no need of choosing time, place, posture; but for a person given to contemplation, a good spot, constant practice, and maintaining of the *Sidhasana* are required; hence Adrishta fixed himself on the banks of the Ganges, and parted he with his body, according to the rules laid down in the *Shastras*, for the purpose.

> Tarkadrishti, the third pupil, receiving the verbal instructions of the Guru,
> On the eighteen *Prasthana*, bathed well in them;
> Avoided the words opposed to them, and came to
> Know, Knowledge is the source of emancipation. Parted he with ignorance.

The third pupil, Tarkadrishti, hearing the instruction from his preceptor wanted to confirm it, by ascertaining the drift of other sacred writings, and to do away with the contradiction which apparently they contained, so he studies them and finds 'emancipation' to be the chief necessity laid down everywhere. *That* emancipation can only be had through knowledge which is a means to it. Now this knowledge must be of the non-dual kind. Duality is not knowledge. All the *Shastras* either directly, or indirectly, produce a knowledge of *Brahma*. In Sanscrit, there are eighteen *Prasthans* (*Shastras*). Some treat of actions, others treat of the means which procure the supreme blissfuness of *Brahma*. Some expound the worship of other Devas besides *Brahma*; then again the *Nyaya* produces knowledge, but that knowledge is of the form of duality, which it holds to

---

† Theosophists call it Devachana; in Sanscrit works, it is called Devayana. *Vide* Section V.

be true. Thus then, all the Sacred Scriptures do not expound the view of non-duality. But their authors had been omniscient and kind; the original *Sutras* have been drawn up according to the *Vedas*, but their commentaries have been the source of error, inasmuch as these explanatory notes have widely diverged from the original *Sutras* of their several authors; it was never intended that the *Sutras* would have a meaning quite opposed to what the *Vedas* say. On the contrary, all the Sacred Writings have been drawn up according to the Vedic doctrine. For his good sense, Tarkadrishti ascertained it.

The eighteen Prasthans for knowledge are :—the Four Vedas, Four Upavedas, Six Vedangas, Puranas, Nyaya, Mimansa, etc., Dharma Shastra. These are the eighteen different works on Sanscrit, and as each has a separate subject to treat, from a different standpoint called 'Prasthana' [meaning parting from one place], so we have eighteen different doctrines.

The four *Vedas* are the Rhig, Yayura, Sam and Atharva. In some places, they treat of *Brahma* as what is to be known; in every object there is *Brahma*. In others, they deal on contemplation, and what is to be contemplated; and elsewhere they treat of actions or works. Now where the Vedas expound 'works' the chief necessity is said to be knowledge, for works purify the internal organ and pave the way to it; there is no mention about inclination, and it was never intended there should be any; on the other hand, for restraining a natural inclination for forbidden works, there is much stress, so that when the Vedas say about works which cause the destruction of another (*Abhichara*) the purport is to destroy an inclination for them. If there be an inclination for destroying an enemy from malice or spite, it is not done in the ordinary manner by beheading or burning him, hence in the *Abhichara*, the sacrificial offerings for the purpose are laid down. The means or works for destroying an enemy are termed *Abhichara*, as the 'Swain Yagna' or sacrifice. In the exposition of the 'Swain' sacrifice, the utterance of the Vedas, do not signify that a person having a spite against his enemy, should have inclination for causing his removal, and undertake its performance; what it means is, that a person actuated with such a desire of destroying his enemy should undertake no other works besides it: thus then the Vedic texts on the 'Swain Yajna' have only that one signification to make a man desist from causing an injury to his enemy, by removing his spite, and not stimulate his inclination in the opposite way. For, inclination is produced from spite, and the text does not intend that spite to go elsewhere, and destroy an enemy. In this way, the end of *Vedic* texts is to cause a destruction of inclination; moreover in reference to works, it is intended, they should be undertaken to purify the internal organ, and thus pave the way to knowledge. Similarly there are four additional (*Upa*) *Vedas Ayur, Dhanur, Gandhurba,* and *Atharva*. The authors of the *Ayur* are Brahmá, Prajapati, Asvinikoomar, Dhanantari, etc. It comprises the several works on the science of medicine *viz.,* Charak, Bavat etc., as well as the *Kam Shastra* of Vatsayan. We say, the Kam is included in the 'Ayur Veda' because we find the several experiments of Dumb-founding etc., which it treats of, are also spoken of in the medical works by Charak etc. But the purport of 'Ayur Veda' is to produce an indifference to worldly enjoyments. Because, it seeks the cessation of disease, and as it arises again after being removed once, men will regard the usual remedies as worthless, and that is the purpose of the 'Ayur Veda.' Then again, medicines and gifts are a means of purifying the mind, which again is a source of knowledge.

The same may be said of the 'Dhunur Veda' of Viswamitra. He divides all armour and arms into four classes—

(1). (*Mukta*) Released.

(2). (*Amukta*) Unreleased.

(3). (*Mukta-mukta*) Both.

(4). (*Jantra mukta*)Released by machinery.

(1). 'Mukta' comprises those arms which are thrust by the hand, as wheel etc., [it is called 'released' because an arm of this class must go out of the hand, before it can strike an enemy etc.]

(2). 'Amukta' includes a sword, and other weapons which strike by being retained in the hand.

(3). 'Mukta-mukta.' A javelin and spear, come under this class, they may be used by thrusting or casting, so that they may either be held in the hand or thrown away.

(4). 'Jantra Mukta.' A ball etc., projected from a cannon or other fire-arms are included in this class.

Of them, the arms included in the first class are called missile weapons, (*Astra*); those of the second denomination are termed (*Shastra*) or cutting weapons. All these have their respective deities in Brahmâ, Vishnu, Pashupati, Agni, Varun etc., who are likewise called Mantras. The son of a Kshetrya is qualified for them, and a Brahman and another person may be called qualified, if they would follow the usual method of instruction.

But there are four sorts of qualified persons.

(1). Infantry, or a soldier of the line.
(2). Charioteer, or soldier fighting from a chariot.
(3). Cavalry, those who fight on horseback, and
(4). Elephant ridden soldiers.

In battle there are oaths and benedictions which soldiers express (vehemently). The First of the four portions of the 'Dhanur Veda' treats on this subject, and the signs of a professor; that is to say, the method of instruction which a professor has to impart is fully treated in the Second Division. The Third, treats on the practical and successful use of arms, by the professor in association with his pupils, and how the Devas and Mantras are propitiated; and the Fourth treats on the use of the successful Mantras. Now all these are indicated in the 'Dhanur Veda.' Viswamitra first had them from Brahmâ, Prajapati, and the other Devas and he is therefore a discoverer, and not their real author. It expounds the duty of a Kshetrya—to guard and protect his subjects from robbers, and other villainous outlaws. Here even, the chief purport of the 'Dhanur Veda,' is to purify the mind, and render it fit for knowledge.

Bharat first brought 'Gandhurba Veda' to light. The description on the use of tune, pause etc., with musical accompaniments in dancing and singing which it contains, has its chief purport in producing an undisturbed or earnest attention, whereby to procure knowledge for being emancipated.

The 'Artha Veda' has also a similar signification. It is divided into several classes; and treats of a variety of subjects as, horse, arts of manufacturing industry, and cooking, and all other means of acquiring wealth; but the acquisition of wealth has much to depend on the good fortune or luck of an individual. He may be well versed in everything, and yet very poor, hence the 'Artha Veda' seeks to produce an indifference to all worldly acquisition.

The six limbs of the four 'Vedas' (Vedangas) have likewise a similar signification. They are

(1). *Siksha.*
(2). *Kalpa.*
(3). *Vyakaran* (Grammar).
(4). *Nirukta.*
(5). *Jyotisha* (Astronomy).
(6). *Pingol.*

As they are helpful to the *Veda,* they are called its members (*Vedanga*). Panini is the author of 'Siksha.' It teaches the proper use of alphabets in *Vedic* words, their signification, derivation, and application. It likewise helps to understand the several Commentaries of the *Vedas* which are called so many branch works.

From the '*Kalpa Sutras*,' the 'works' expounded in *Vedas* are known and understood. A Brahman who undertakes to make another person perform the rite of 'sacrifice' and similar other works is called Rutvak. And the *Kalpa Sutras* indicate the various actions which are fit to be performed. Its authors are Katyana, Asvalaya, and other sages. As *Kalpa* is helpful to *Veda* it is called one of its members; for similar reasons (Vyakaran), Grammar is also a member. Its author is Panini; from his Grammar, we are enabled to understand the proper signification of words used in the *Vedas,* and thus come to a right interpretation of the *Vedic* utterances. Panini's Grammar received commentaries and annotations from the pen of Patanjali. [But all other grammars are not similar to Panini's in interpreting *Vedic* words] and as they contain a proper construction of words in general, they are helpful to the understanding of the *Puranas* etc., of which they can be called auxiliaries. Thus then, for a successful and right interpretation of the *Vedic* words, Panini's Grammar is absolutely requisite, hence it is included in the *Vedanga*. His work is divided into eight chapters.

The sage Yaska is the author of Nirukta. It has thirteen chapters. It explains the mantras and remarkable sentences of the *Vedas* and thus helps to their knowledge; for this reason, it is properly regarded as one of its members. It includes the five sections of the other work, of the same author, which has for its subject the determination and interpretations of names. Likewise the Dictionary of Amar Singh (Amar-kosh) is included in it.

Pingal is the author of eight chapters of his work on Prosody. It helps to a knowledge of the *Gaitri* and other *Vedic* metres (*chhanda*). Hence Pingal's *Sutras* are a part of the *Vedas*.

Astronomy is likewise a part of *Vedas*. Its authors are Aditya, Garga, and others; for, in the commencement of a ritualistic work, the proper time of performance must be ascertained and as astronomy alone can give that true knowledge of time, it is included in the *Vedanga*.

Now these Six *Vedangas* have the same purport as the *Vedas*. That is to say, they are guided by the same incentive 'necessity'; though it may be said, that all of them do not help the interpretation of the *Vedas*, yet the fact is, in spite of a difference in their subject-matter, they establish the *Vedic* doctrine in the way of discourse [in a fragmentary way] and not directly.

There are eighteen *Puranas*; all written by Vyas viz.:—

1	Brahma	7.	Markandya	13.	Skanda
2.	Padma	8.	Agneya	14.	Vaman
3.	Vaisnava	9.	Bhavishya	15.	Koormya
4.	Saiva	10.	Brahmavaivarta	16.	Matsya
5.	Bhagvat	11.	Linga	17.	Garura
6.	Naradiya	12.	Baraha	18.	Brahmanda

Besides them, there are several additional *Puranas* known by the name of Upapuran as *Kalipuran* etc. Some call the additional

Puranas 'Eighteen' but that is not the rule. For they are many in number. There are two Bhagvats, of which one is Vaishnav Bhagvat, and the other Bhagvati Bhagvat. Both have an equal number of verses *viz.*, eighteen thousand, and twelve sections (*skandha*). But one of them is a *Puran* and the other *Upapurana*. Both of them are written by Vyas, hence confirmatory of one another. As Vyas is the author of the *Puranas*, the *Upapuranas* have been written by other Vyases. Some of them are the productions of the all-knowing Parasar Muni and others; hence they also are proofs. With the *Puranas* they signify the same meaning as the *Upanishads* as will be shown in the sequel.

Gautama is the author of the *Nyaya Sutras*. It has five chapters, and deals with arguments based on analogy and reason. Arguments sharpen the intellect; their 'consideration' is easily accomplished; hence *Nyaya Sutras* by the arguments used in them, produce the capacity of consideration and lead to knowledge [of the conclusions] of the *Vedas*.

Kanad is the author of the *Vaisheshika Sutras*. They are divided into ten chapters, and are subordinate to the *Nyaya* Philosophy.

Mimansa is of two different sorts. One is 'Dharma Mimansa' and the other 'Brahma Mimansa.' The former is also called 'Purva Mimansa,' and the latter 'Utara Mimansa.' It has twelve chapters and Jaimini is their author. Practice of works is the subject which he expounds in them. Hence an inclination for lawful actions is the result produced by 'Dharma Mimansa.' Actions purify the internal organ, and lead to knowledge, which in its turn produces a desire of release. Hence emancipation is the result of 'Dharma Mimansa.' Then again, there is a difference in the signification of its several chapters, and as the subject is very difficult, I have abstained from introducing it here.

Jaimini is the author of the treatise *Sankarshan Kanda*. It deals on devotional exercise and worship, and is subordinate to the 'Dharma Mimansa.'

'Brahma Mimansa' contains four sections, its authorship belongs to Vyas; each section is divided into four parts. The subject of the first section is the exposition of *Brahma* according to the *Upanishads* and nothing else; but as men may misunderstand the meaning inculcated to imply contradictions, it is removed in the second section. The third treats exclusively on the means of knowledge and worship, which have been fully weighed with arguments for and against. The fourth treats on the effects of knowledge and worship. It is called the 'Shariraka Shastra,' and is superior to all sacred writings. For a person desirous of release, it is the excellent. It has been annotated and commented upon by several authors, but Sankara's edition is the best of them all, and one that an emancipated person should think as fit to be heard; there, knowledge has been plainly established as the means for emancipation.

The *Smriti* has been written after the standard of the Vedas by various omniscient sages [of whom the following are worthy of mention] Menu, Yagnyavalka, Vishnu, Yam, Angira, Vashista, Daksha, Samant, Sham, Tàtap, Parasur, Gautam, Sankhya, Hârit, Apastav, Shukra, Brihspati, Vyas, Katyana, Devala, Narad etc. The *Smriti* is likewise called the 'Dharma Shastra.'

It contains an account of the division of caste and society, and the several stations occupied by individuals, whose bodily, oral and mental Dharma forms its subject. It produces knowledge by purifying the internal organ, thus leading to emancipation which is the purport or necessity of *Smriti*.

Vyasa is the author of *Mahabharat*, and Valmika wrote the *Ramayana*. These two works are also included in the 'Dharma Shastras.' Then again, the *Mantra Shastra* which contains the sacred texts for the worship of the Devas is also included in the Dharma Shastras. Now worship is necessary for clearing the mind of all blemishes and faults. Similarly Sankhya, Yoga, Vaisnav-Tantra, and Siva-Tantra etc., are also included in the Dharma Shastras, inasmuch as they ascertain the *Manas Dharma*.

Kapila is the author of the 'Sankhya philosophy' it is divided into six sections of which the first treats on the subject, and the second gives an account of Mahatatwa, Egoism etc., which are products of Prakriti, or matter, likewise called Pradhana. The third treats of indifference [to worldly enjoyments], the fourth gives an account of persons indifferent to worldly enjoyments, the fifth weighs the arguments against the author, and sets them at nought, [in short, he refutes them in his usual clear style based on reason and analogy.] The sixth is an epitome or brief summary of the five preceding sections and what they mean. Discrimination of Matter and Spirit (force) is the purport of Sankhya, and their knowledge is called unassociated [in short, same as that of *Brahma*, of the *Vedanta*]. And that knowledge, as it helps to clear by Indication the signification of the Vedic word 'Thou,' is a source of emancipation.*

Patanjali is the author of *Yoga Philosophy*, it is divided into four parts. Now Patanjali is regarded as the last of the Avatars (incarnation of the Deity); [the history of his birth is given in the following words]. A Rishi (Saint) was engaged in his devotional exercise and repeating the Sandhya, when Patanjali issuing out of his finger fell into the earth, for which he is called by that name. He is also the author of a work on medicine and the Commentator of Panini's [Science of] Grammar. He has removed faulty pronounciation of words which before his time was very prevalent. In the same manner, he has removed by his authorship of the Yoga Sutras, the mental defect caused by distraction of the mind,—the first part of his 'Yoga' has for its subject 'meditation' by withholding the function of the mind, or resting it there, and its means and the ways of practice. It likewise treats on 'indifference.' The second part speaks about the eight means of meditation to be undertaken by a person whose mind is distracted *viz.* :—'forbearance,' 'cannons to be observed,' 'posture,' 'regulation of breath,' 'non-acceptance of gift,' 'restraint of the senses' and 'contemplation.' The emblishments of Yoga are described in the third part; the fourth has for its subject 'emancipation'—a result of Yoga. Thus then the Yoga Shastra is a means of acquiring knowledge by concentrating attention; and therefore a source of emancipation. Moreover the refutations on

---

* Wilson in his Dictionary gives quite a different account, "Having fallen from heaven, it is said in the shape of a small snake into the hands of the saint Panini as he was performing this act of reverence." *Vide* Wilson's Dictionary page 515 third edition.

the Sankhya Yoga, mentioned in the *Shariraka Sutras*, bear exclusive reference to the exposition of the commentaries, where they set up doctrines antagonistic to the *Upanishads*, and have no concern with the Sutras themselves. We have similar commentaries, refuting the doctrines of the Nyayikas and Vaishesikas. Narad is the author of the Tantra known by the name of 'Panchrâtra', or 'Five Nights.' There, he speaks of resting the internal organ on Vasudeva, which also leads to emancipation by procuring knowledge. All works which set up Vishnu worship are included in the Panchrâtra, which again forms a part of the Dharma Shastra.

In the same way, worship of Siva (Pashupati) is set forth in the Tantra which goes by his name, after its author Pashupati. It likewise produces an unswerving fixedness of the mind, and leads to knowledge, which in its turn, produces the fruit—emancipation. All works dealing on the worship of Siva are included in this Tantra.

Similarly those works which deal on the worship of Ganesh, Sun etc., produce a fixed condition of the mind, requisite for the acquirement of knowledge; and knowledge results in emancipation. All of them form a portion of the 'Dharma Shastra' in which they are included.

In regard to the works which expound the worship of Devi, there are two sects called respectively the Southern and Northern sects. The latter are said to be the followers of the left road (*Bam marga*) and the religious books which contain their especial doctrines are all opposed to the teachings of the Dharma Shastra, for which they form no part of it. On the other hand, the religious works of the Southern Sect are all included in it, and they are called the followers of the right road. Thus then, the books of the northerners are unconfirmatory. Though the *Bam Tantra* owes its authorship to Siva, yet as it is opposed to all the Shastras and Vedas, it is therefore no proof [confirmatory of them]. As the atheistical writings of Buddha—incarnation of Vishnu—go the opposite way and are no proofs [of the Dharma Shastra or Vedas] so is Siva's *Bam Tantra* extremely opposed to them; for there, drinking of spirits is maintained along with other dirty substances which are called good, only to deceive men. For instance, wine is called a place of pilgrimage, meat is termed 'pure' and the drinking cup is designated 'lotus;' onions and garlic are known by the [euphonious] names of Vyas and Sookhdev respectively. A wine merchant is "initiated," a prostitute, an attending maid; and a female of the leather-carrying and Chandal caste is respectively called by the names of Prayag, Sair, and Benares, Savi, and when they are seated in a Bacchanalian circle, they are then called Brahman, and the most shameless prostitute receives the appellation of Yogini, while the worthless whore-monger is a Yogi. Many of the interdicted actions form a daily part of practice, and in time of worship the woman of many crimes is called superior Sakti (goddess of force Durga). A low caste *Paria* (Chandal) woman, of the worst character, in her menses, is worshipped as a Devi, and the remnant of her cup of spirits is quaffed with eagerness. If perchance, the drinking be carried into excess, so that there be vomiting, it is not allowed to touch the ground, but held in a platter, and is next eaten by the officiating priest or preceptor in company with the others, with great care; and the ejecta is called Vairavi. The tongue is applied to the female organ while recanting the *mantras* [for that especial] worship.

The five elements of that worship are:—

1. Spirits.
2. Meat.
3. Fish
4. *Mundra* (a form of intertwining the fingers in religious worship).
5. *Mantra.*

These are the five substances which constitute the 'M' (*makar*) form of worship,* for the desire of release. They designate the first two 'M's' by the application of words little known. All their practices commencing with them (spirit and meat) are subversive of good, present and future. But for the allurements of present

---

* Every one of the five words begins in the Sanscrit and vernacular with the letter 'M' hence it is called *Makar pancha* or the five 'M's.'

enjoyment (many Yogis belonging to the sect of those who have their ears drilled) Avadhout Gossains, Sanyasis, Brahmans and others follow the left road; and as they know that worship has been reviled in the Vedas, they keep it a secret. Suffice it to say, even when a Melacha (unclean) hears the mode of their worship with its usual practices, it makes his hairs stand. So very hateful it is, that everywhere, when a person is found to partake of unclean food, he is reckoned as a follower of the left road, and as it is unfit to be written I have refrained from making a particular mention of their rests and practices. The *Bam Tantra* is always worthy of abandoning, so is atheism to be avoided.

Atheists are divided into six sects or classes—

(1). Madhyamika
(2). Yogachar.
(3). Sontrantika.
(4). Vaibhasika.
(5). Charvaka.
(6). Digambar.

They do not regard the Veda as authority, and admit not its proofs, but have each their especial doctrines. A Madhyamik is an asserter of 'Nothing' or non-being' [as the primary substance from which has been produced the phenomenal world]. According to the doctrine of a Yogachari, all substances are non-different from knowledge (*Vijnana*) which is considered to be the primary element (*Tatwa*), and that knowledge is transient in duration.

According to the doctrine of a Sontrantika, knowledge can only be in connection with a substance that has shape, in short all external objects; so that cognition follows from inference derived by knowledge. Hence the phenomenal world is a subject of inferential and not visible proof, neither is it fixed, but on the other hand transient.

A Vaibhasika says though it is transient, yet an external object is a subject of visible proof. This is their difference. These four doctrines are known by the name of *Sugut*.

A Charvak says external objects are not transient, but they have each a different spirit (*Atma*) in them.

A Digambar says the physical body is not his Self, but he is something distinct from it; and so long as the body is subject to change, Self is likewise modified by that change. In this manner, we find each of them has a different doctrine. Now this difference is noticeable in several other points also, and as they are all opposed to the teachings of the *Vedas*, they are called atheists or believers of 'nothing.' It is quite unnecessary to enter into a refutation of their arguments and doctrines. And though the followers of the 'left road' and atheists have their works written in Sanscrit, yet they are dis-reputable; consequently the 'eighteen Prasthans' are the only ones which follow the *Vedas*.

All works on literature are included in the *Kam Shastra*. Poetry is subordinate either to 'Kam or Dharma Shastra' hence the eighteen Prasthanas for acquiring knowledge or learning are only so many means for the acquisition of *Brahma jnana* whereby to be emancipated; that some of them directly, and others indirectly by their interdependence upon one another, produce knowledge, Tarkadrishti came full well to know. Except the 'Uttarmimansa' all other *Shastras* can be profitably used by a seeker of truth. Notwithstanding this assertion of the Commentator of the 'Shariraka Sutras,' all of them cannot be equally regarded as means suitable for emancipation, and Tarkadrishti with a view of making himself acquainted with their essence,

Repairs to a man celebrated for his learning;
Acquaints him with his personal views and ascertains all.

For fixing his intellect and making it steady and firm he rested it on the signification of what instructions he had heard from the mouth of his preceptor, and ascertains the drift of all the *Shastras*. Uncertain whether they bore the same meaning which he knew, or something different, and actuated with a doubt on this point Tarkadrishti 'the qualified' repairs to another learned person to remove his doubts and know the real truth about them.

Hearing what Tarkadrishti had to say, the learned

Replies:—What you have spoken to me, know them to be true.

They will remove your doubts, and make *Brahma* visibly precepted.

As the world is in a state of non-being, so are bondage and emancipation.

The remnant of fructescent works produce [in Tarkadrishti] inclination

And continue the relationship of a father and mother for the time being.

The ordinary practices of the wise resemble those of the ignorant, simply for the fructescent works; hence it is quite possible for an inclination to exist; but in some of the *Shastras* an opposite doctrine is inculcated, and it is said, the wise has no inclination. Now that does not mean the internal organ of a wise person never undergoes any modification by desire. Because the internal organ is the seat of desire and the rest, which are its attributes; and though it is said to be derived from the good quality of the elements ether and the rest, yet there is an admixture of the two other qualities, active and dark, hence it is not a product of the purely good quality; for if it were so, unsteadiness would not form one of its characteristic trait; moreover anger, passion, lust etc.,—a productive result of the active quality, as also dullness, stupidity etc.,—products of darkness, will be absent. Thus then, the internal organ is not a product of the purely good quality, but there is an admixture of the active and dark with an abundance of 'goodness' in its cause elements, and for this presence of all the three qualities (force or *gunas*) but notably the 'active,' a person cannot be entirely devoid of desire so long as the organ whose property it is, continues to exist; consequently it cannot be said that a wise person has no desire: but what is meant by such an expression 'of absence of desire' is, that an ignorant and wise person are equally actuated with desire, but the former attributes desire to Self whose property or attribute he considers it to be, while the latter never knows it in that way, when any desire possesses him. He regards passions, determination, doubt, faith, fear and desire etc., as modifications of the internal organ, and its attributes consequently.

Thus then, as desires proceed in the manner above indicated, and have no concern with Self, and perceived so by the wise, it is said that he is not without desire. In the same way, whatever actions he practises either by the mind, or word are not known to proceed from Self, but from their respective sources. He knows Self to be unassociated, hence though an agent, yet he is not a doer or actor. To this end, the *Sruti* testimony is "Subsequent to the arising of knowledge, good and bad actions can produce neither virtue nor vice to the present body [of a theosophist]. The strength of fructescent works can possibly bring forth an inclination for, and practice of all sorts of actions, even in the wise, as happens to an ordinary ignorant person. A King by the name of Suva-Santati was abandoned by his three sons, of whom mention has been made up to the present moment; the father shall occupy us now.

<blockquote>
Seeing his sons depart, the father felt pain in his heart,
For he had no sharp Indifference to enjoyment, in him.
</blockquote>

As the Rajah felt pain at the departure of his sons from a want of active indifference, he is said to be badly indifferent. There can be no pleasure felt in such a state of mind from enjoyment of material happiness, and as he had ere long expressed a desire to abandon family, home and sovereignty, but his sons went away, he could not make up his mind to go, leaving an empty throne behind, that also produced pain; if his indifference to worldly enjoyment were intense, he would not have desisted from going, no matter whether his sovereignty had a master or not, but his 'indifference' was of an ordinary nature and he could not go. Moreover as an inclination for gratification of pleasure was also wanting, that was another cause of his distress.

The effects of an indifferent disregard for worldly gratification are now being declared in connection with the object of worship.

That father Suvasantati was very fortunate.
From the first, his regard for enjoyment was indifferent.
Questions arise in his mind,
Concerning Him, who is contemplated by Devas.
Sends he for the learned to know,
Seated, in an ascetic posture, and asks:
Who that Deva is, that neither sleeps nor wakes?
That seeks to procure the good of his creatures?
For whom there should be reverence in heart.
Hearing such questions,
From the sovereign, Lord of Earth,
One of them, very clever, replies:—
Listen to me, King, I speak unto you of Devas
Siva and Brahmâ. Who continue to serve
Him, with the emblem of conch and wheel—a benefactor
And the lotus and rod,—rendering assistance to others:
[The form of] Vishnu—always kind.
He always looks upon his worshippers with mercy.
Sakti, Ganes, Siva, Sun all obey his commands,
Bharat, Padma-Puran and Tapui unanimously proclaims him.
From Vishnu are derived all, therefore
His feet are sought by them.
Incarnated he, in various forms,
To assist the other Devas.
Thus then you must worship him,
There is not another like him.
A Vaisnava calls Siva, good
Yet him, he worships not.
For his form is unpropitious like a corpse;
Him I contemplate not, then,
Because he is equally unauspicious.
He keeps a Dumroo, an elephant's hide, and a begging bowl
In his hands. His son Ganes is no better;
At once both a man and animal in form.
The Goddess,—running with hairs floating, to hurt,
Attended by her maids, equally horrible to look at

Is unclean, impure and unholy, with exquisite
Cunning; of that she has a mine in her.
In acts she is never independent; her I wish not to have.
Who wants to worship such a goddess is welcome to do it.
The Sun wanders all day and night along,
Waits he not for a moment in one place;
Who worships him, runs ever and anon, to and fro,
Like him, whom he worships.
But he who serves Hari (Vishnu)
Abandons all others, and worships him alone,
In the prescribed order, as laid down
By Narad in his *Pancha Ratra.*

If the four other forms of worship, excluding that of Vishnu are interdicted, then virtually that interdiction applies to *Smarta Upasana.* Because 'Smarta Upasana' consists in worshipping all the five with an equal eye, and not to attach any superiority to one of them. Consequently if the worship of Ganes, Sun, Siva and Devi were disallowed, it will amount to a virtual interdiction of Vishnu worship, for they are all equal—and interdiction of five must include the fifth *viz.,* Vishnu.

When the saint hears about the worship of Siva,
In anger turns away, and exclaims:
The Rajah has not attended to one word of mine,
For which there are proofs, ten millions.
Call that another, an equal of Siva,
Who gives away whatever is asked of him.
He gave away all his power [glory] to Hari,
Turned into a beggar, covering his body with ashes.
A bowl and skin are his companions hence.
Thinks he equal all the good and bad,
Take my advice, so long as you are a king,
Practice indifference, for no happiness is equal to it.

To attribute dis-reputability to the skin and bowl of Siva is improper, and is refuted easily. He is remarkable for his utter disregard of the good; happiness and pain, good and bad, are alike to him, and he discriminates them not. Hence his bowl and skin are only emblems of that supreme indifference.

> To do charity freely,
> To die in Benares,
> Emancipate men and women,
> From the pain of uterine existence;
> Like a Siva, when he accepts
> The offerings of good things from men and women, all.
> I have this secondless advice to give.
> Leave off worshipping Linga, that *Brahma* may enter,
> There is no high or low [in his sight]
> For emancipation, is alike in all.
> There is not another king
> More charitable than he,
> To his followers, and those that are not,
> He showers his favors equally.
> Of Vishnu, I have heard,
> Nature is the source of difference,
> Good and bad, devout and undevout.
> All are from nature. This is the universal rule.
> By serving Hari, Har is worshipped,
> Worship Ramchunder or Rameswar;
> Vyas in the *Skandha Purana* says,
> Hari to be worshipper and Har worshipped.
> In the *Bharat* and *Padmapuran*,
> What is said [by the worshipper of Vishnu]
> About Hari's being the Supreme deity and chief
> Its purport is not correctly understood

Vaisnavas [Vishnuvites] say:—According to the authority of the *Mahabharat*, Vishnu is worshipped by all Gods. But this assertion is untenable, for if a proper construction be put on the meaning of the texts of the *Mahabharat*, it will appear that Siva is the Lord (Iswara), according to the version of Apya Dichhit, [a very learned Pandit].

Now this is established from the following anecdote contained in Bharât. When Asvathama used his Narayana and Agnaya Astra (weapons of war belonging to Narayan and Agni) he found none of the Pandavas were killed, though they caused heavy destruction elsewhere in the enemy's line. He was very much disappointed and sorely annoyed. He left the field, rebuking his professor and the *Vedas* for the inutility of his weapons, of which so much had been made by them, and went to the wood. There he found Vyasa, who reprimanded him for his indiscriminate abuse, and pointed out that Arjuna and Krishna—Nara and Narayana—were unhurt, simply because, they had spent long years in worshipping Siva ; he was entirely bound in their love, and ever present in front of their war-chariot. Consequently whatever missiles of destruction are used against them, Mahadeva destroys them. Thus then, according to this version, Krishna's powers have all been derived from the kindness of Mahadeva, whom he propitiated with his worship. Here the superiority of Mahadeva is established clearly, and for this reason the author of *Krishna Charita* expounds the superiority of Siva over all the other Devas, inasmuch as he maintains the worship of Vishnu, who is asserted to be a follower of Mahadeva in the above anecdote.

And for his devotion to Siva, Vishnu was transformed into an object of worship himself, Siva is therefore the Supreme object of worship. This is the way in which Apya Dichhit expounds the superiority of Mahadeva.

> Siva is demonstrated by all the *Shastras*, wherein it is said,
> Vishnu is the Chief of his followers.
> He alone is called the great (Maha),
> And everywhere that surname is added to his name.

While other Devas are known by their individual names, the terms 'great' is ever and everywhere used as his surname. Hence he is called Mahadeva (or great god) Maheswar and Mahes.

> Those distinct from Siva (emancipation)
> Can bring forth no good,

> He alone is goodness,
> And if a man utters his name,
> When immersed in water,
> Wakes he up sure and certain.

Siva is said to be the source of goodness. He is a benefactor showering his beneficience on all his creatures, so that, the other gods (*Devas*) who are distinct from him must have necessarily a distinction in the quality; hence they are not good, therefore attend on them not, but worship Siva only.

> When sight of poison terrified all,
> He quaffed it and brought their fears to end.
> That son of his, called Ganes,
> Destroys obstacles there and then.
> In an action, the quality of its cause is present.
> Them Siva destroys; the obstruction,—root and all.
> The pangs of birth and death are the obstacles
> Which contemplation of Siva destroys.
> He alone is fit to be worshipped always;
> With offering and discrimination, do you meditate,
> After the manner of *Pashupati Tantra*,
>
> Worship him, by contemplation.
> What Narada in his *Panch Ratra* says, is untrue.
> Adopt this pure method and follow it.
> Who serves Siva, in this manner,
> Obtains he his end,— what he wants.

The doctrine of Narad inculcated in the *Panch Ratra* has been refuted by the Commentator. In the same way, Ramanuja, and others have in their commentaries of *Kalpa Taru* and *Parmad* done away with the worship of Vishnu.

> Ganesh the son of Siva attached
> The properties of cause to its effect;
> Hearing it, his servant,
> Was so enraged as to shake the throne of the other saints

When to the king he said, both of you are false.
Hear my word that is true.
They say, Ganes is the son of Siva,
That makes him a dependent of his father.

Hear what I have to say, a story
Written by Bhagavan Vyas:—
Hari, Har, and the other Devas,
All went to destroy Tripur.
They made no worship of Ganes; and
Suffered defeat at his hands;
Disappointed, then offer him worship,
For the destruction of Tripur.
Got strength for it, from him, whom they worshipped;
He alone is fit for worship, and not a second.
As Ram, Dasarath's son removes
Obstacles, so does the son of Siva.

Vyas wrote Ganes-Purana
And did all to worship him, with
Hari, Har, Sun and Shakti.
By producing *Toondi*
He who contemplates him for a moment
Has his obstacles destroyed by Ganes.
Who watches by day and night,
And with love continually worships him,
Has no more obstacles to fear,
All are destroyed by Ganes.

Hearing the source of Ganes is Shakti
Thus says a worshipper of Bhagavati:—
Hear my word of truth. Oh king!
All that is said of the three, is untrue
Without 'Shakti' all Devas are
As a body without breath,
Sakti is the Strength
Without that, how is work to follow?

> Who worships her holds much strength,
> Becomes qualified in all worships.
> Of Hari, Har, Sun and Ganes she is the first;
> You find her everywhere in various ways.
> What people call Shakti
> Is no other than Bhagavati.

Bhagavati has two forms, the ordinary and particular. The strength of producing action which resides in all substances is her ordinary form, and the particular form is that with eight-hands. The first is unlimited and infinite. A thing that has a small amount of force is called strong, or very powerful. In Vishnu, Siva etc., there is large proportion of force, hence they are called powerful and mighty. That is to say, for a large share of the ordinary force of Bhagavati in them, they are powerful, and if force were to be absent, then as a body without breath or vitality is reduced to a perfectly helpless condition, so will the Devas be without the particle of force from Bhagavati. Hence for a larger share of that force, the Devas are justly celebrated for their powers; but virtually those powers are due to Shakti and not to the Devas. Vishnu, Siva and the other Devas have performed worship of the ordinary form of Bhagavati; hence they have a large amount of force. This is meant by the worshippers of Bhagavati in the aforesaid work (Bhagavat). As the formless form of Bhagavati's force is infinitely divided so is her particular form infinite too, of whom Kali is principal; and of her other forms, Maheswari, Vaishnavi, Souri, Ganesi are important. Vishnu worshipped Bhagavati in one form for which she has been called Vaishnavi. Similarly her other names had been derived.

Vishnu and Siva are the chief of her worshippers, inasmuch as the supreme object of worship is the acquisition of the form of the object worshipped, and both Vishnu and Siva had succeeded by worship to have that form. The two and half lines of the last verse bear this meaning.

> Of the hundred thousands and ten millions.
> Written by worthy men in the *Tantra*.

Kali is superior to Maheshwari and others.
Hari, Har, and Brahma, all worship her,
Each derives his own part through her mercy.
When the worshipper got his form,

From the object of his worship;
There came the worship of Siva, from that time,
In the form of a female, as also that of Vishnu
Casting aside their male forms.

In the act of churning nectar
Hari assumed the form of Mohini
Siva had in half his body
The form of the Devi.

When nectar was procured by churning, dispute arose amongst Siva and the Asuras, which Vishnu could not settle. With an earnest head and settled mind made he the worship of Bhagavati to help him in his difficulty, when Vishnu was transformed into her image, and from the magic influence of that form, the Asuras came to his help. Similarly, Siva in his meditation, contemplated Bhagavati, when one half of his body assumed her shape. As if from distraction, there was an absence of meditation, hence his whole body was not so transformed.

Thus then, we find all the Devas are worshippers of Bhagavati, and that worship is to be done in two ways, called respectively the Southern and Northern *Amnayat*.

The former is first spoken of and the latter next, in the following verse:—

When Hari and Har are worshippers of Bhagavati
Whom to worship then?

By Mahamaya's worship
A person obtains immediate success,

There is not in the world, another worship like her's;
For both enjoyment and emancipation, result at once.

Enjoyment in the present life, after that,
There is no more return to the world.

Siva, sings of it in his *Tantra*
Devotion to Bhagavati produces extreme happiness.
All the principal (old) writers speak of the five 'M' worship
And follow this golden method

The Devas Krishna and Baladeva are Wise.
Who drink from the first,

And have no faith in the principal *Purans*,
They only follow the method of the five 'M.'
The rules of their worship,
Siva, himself says are good.

Who keeps faith in his words,
  Obtains enjoyment and release in one birth.
Bhagavat was written by Vyas.
Upapuran Kali and other works;

Speak they all of devotion to Bhagavati,
And lay down rules of that worship.
All contemplate Bhagavati
From Hari, Har, Sun to all the rest,

They first drink and then worship
Bhagavati with mind deeply intent.
She only is the mother of Universe,
Whose worshipper acquires supreme bliss.

Sun is her devotee. When this was said,
A sage inflamed with anger replied

King! listen to one word of mine,
All these statements are untrue.

Their words are sinful and low
And their hearing does no good.
A man of merit if he says so,
Loses his merit at once and for ever.

The dirty wine, they call to be a pilgrim's resort;
And meat is called by the name of pure,
And what contrary things they speak of,
All the *Tantras* have similar rules.

The Southern sect is another,
Though that is better.
Yet without the Sun, all other worships are half done,
And whom these doctrines do bind,

Are illumined by the sun, who lights everywhere.
Without him, it is all darkness
And those other discoverers, besides him,
Are all parts of him everywhere;

Who, save him, is more beneficient?
Wanders he for doing good to others.

Actions all are dependent on time;
That time is of three kinds, so says the professor:—
In the present, future and the past,
The sun works all through.

Thus then, all are derived from the Sun,
And reduced to ashes, when he is enraged

Recognize in that his two aspects:—
Formless and with Form.

Formless yet manifested;
With nature and form he is all-pervading.

He abides alone in everything.
The world is only a modification to one without discrimination;
When the function arises " I am the Sun,"
Then is destroyed all darkness in that discovery.

The sun has two aspects; one formless, and the other with form; and manifestibility is common to both conditions. In both of them, manifestibility without form pervades everywhere in all things, that have name and form; this is expressed by the Vedantic term 'knowledge,' but this is his ordinary form, and abides everywhere, which ignorance modifies or transforms into the universe; and that formless manifestibility with its reflection or reflected shadow in the function of the internal organ is called 'knowledge.' When the mental function is so modified by this reflected shadow as to perceive "I am the Sun," then by the destruction of ignorance, the world is reduced to a condition of non-existence.

> Now listen to that other aspect of the Sun with form,
> Whose portions are in the moon and stars,
> And in other various bodies,
> And gives them light to illuminate.
> This creates two varieties in the Sun,
> What is to be known, and contemplated; their difference to know,
> All the Vedas speak. Of them
> Form, manifestibility and truth are his.

The sun is differently regarded, and that difference is created by form and formlessness. Of these two, the formless is what is to be known, and that with form is an object of contemplation. In the Vedanta this has been spoken of as 'with attributes' 'and without attributes' or Personal and Impersonal *Brahma*.

> He who has no trace of ignorance in him,
> Regards the world and its contents are unreal.
> He never sleeps over it, who has awakened that perception.
> But contemplates, and his luck is good.
> And others there are, who though awake,
> Regard the world real. They are themselves false (ignorant).
> Thus did the followers of the five worships, speak
> On the merit of their own and demerit of other worships.
> The Pandits and others who came,
> Spoke of their own doctrines good.

As each of the five Pandits tried to establish the superiority of his individual worship by attributing demerits to his rivals, and contending against them, so there are others equally learned who hold views opposed to the *Vedas*. Now as the aforesaid five Pandits maintained doctrines opposed to each other, but a 'Smartha Pandit' maintains the doctrine of equality of worship of the five **Devas**, Vishnu, Siva, Ganes, Surya, Shakti, he does not make any difference;

consequently his doctrine is opposed to all five of them. Because a Vaisnav holds there is not another Deva equal to Vishnu; and all are his followers. That his several designations Ram, Krishna, Narayan etc., if considered equal to the names of other Devas, a man, who regards that equality commits a guilt, and never derives any true benefit, which the pronounciation of Ram, and Krishna alone brings forth.

Similarly a Sivite regards his own deity to be superior to all others and there is not another equal to him, and the pronunciation of Siva's name produces results, which the name of Vishnu pronounced in the same way, can never bring forth. Thus then, from the standpoint of each sect, his own deity is secondless; consequently his doctrine is opposed to the four others. Similarly, the respective doctrines of the six *Shastras* inculcated by Kapila in his *Sankhya*, and Patanjali in his *Yoga*, and by the Vaishesikas, Purva Mimansakas and Uttar Mimansaka, are all opposed to one another, inasmuch as in the *Sankhya* there is no admission of Iswara; Yoga is not required for emancipation which is a product of knowledge produced by or derived from a discrimination of Matter and Spirit (Prakriti and Purush). In the *Patanjal Shastras* there is an admission of Iswara, but non-admission of meditation (*Samadhi*); this is their difference. Between *Nyaya* and the doctrine of the Vaishesika there is a difference in the number of proofs (*Praman*). The first hold them to be four, and the last two in number. Besides it, there are seven other points of difference, but they are not requisite to an enquirer of knowledge, hence it is unnecessary for me to mention them. In the Purva Mimansa, Iswara is denied, and emancipation in the shape of eternal bliss is also admitted, but material well-being as a product of action, is regarded as the principal end of existence. In the Uttar Mimansa both the existence of Iswara and emancipation are admitted; there is likewise no consideration about material prosperity being the highest end of human life. Thus then, the views inculcated in the works of the Uttar Mimansa are consistent with and included in the present treatise and all other *Shastras* opposed to it. In other works, difference of views has been established, but in the present all those differences have been refuted;

thus then, we find the conclusions of all *Shastras* are directly opposed to one another.

> When the Raja heard of opposing views,
> Doubts arose in his mind.
> Who of these (men) speaks the truth ?
> Their arguments and reasons are equally good.
>
> In mind, was he pained with doubts:
> Who is the proper Deva fit for worship ?
> When myself am puzzled with doubts
> Whom then to speak about them,
>
> The learned in the Shastras, of the world,
> All talk against each other.
> Thinking in this manner, had he spent long
> When Tarkadrishti came to see him.
>
> Saw they [father and son] both each other.
> The son paid his respects,
> To the father in the usual manner
> Who blessed him as he gave a seat with love.
>
> Seeing the father immersed in thought,
> Listen to my word said the son ;
> Why do you look so thoughtful and unhappy ?
> Subhasautati heard his son and
>
> Began to open his thoughts ;
> Explained the reason why he was thoughtful
> He had not found out whom to worship.
> Tarkadrishti heard what the father had to say,
>
> Replied to make him happy, and explained
> The Cause of All, is to be worshipped.
> Actions—regard them as worthless, and avoid.
> Put faith upon this conclusion of the *Vedas*
>
> He is alone to be worshipped ; about
> Him there are no doctrines several,
> You understand not what the Pandits say,
> And how they refute each other's doctrine.

Nilkant Pandit, the wisest of them
Wrote his commentaries on *Bharat,*
Wherein is mentioned the discussion;
That the conclusion of the 'Sruti' is unassailable.

Though Vyas wrote all the 'Purans,' and in the 'Skanda Puran' is mentioned Siva is truth and blissfulness, in short he has the attributes of Iswara, and from his mercy and favour Vishnu and the other Devas got their extraordinary powers and glory, so that they are no better than Jiva, with his attributes; yet in the 'Vishnu' and 'Padma Puran,' the superiority of Vishnu over the other Devas has been clearly indicated and he has been pointed out as the Iswara; in the same way, other Devas have been respectively pointed out in the Purans. For instance, Ganes has been elsewhere declared as the only Iswara to be served. Thus then, an antagonism is set up amongst worshippers as to their objects of worship. But that is cleared in the following manner. Everywhere there is Iswara, and all these Devas are Iswara. It is not intended by the author, when he was discussing about the superiority of one especial Deva, that the other Devas are to be thrown away; but the declamations about Siva and others in the 'Vishnu Puran' are only for the purpose of producing an inclination in the worship of Siva. If the author's intention were to cause the abandonment of other worships, while discussing about the superiority of an especial Deva, in one part of the work, then there would be an abandonment of all worships, because all of them had been declaimed in turn. Hence such declamations are not made for the purpose of abandoning the worship of the Deva, who had been spoken of disparagingly.

Here is an example to the point. The Vedas fix two periods of time for the Agnihotri (giver of sacrificial offerings to fire), either before sun-rise, or subsequent to it. While discussing the merit of that offering in a subsequent period, they repudiate it entirely; but the declamation is not for abandonment of the second form of offering; in the same way when pointing out the advisability and superiority of making the *Homa** after sun-rise, it seeks to disparage

---

* Offering of clarified butter to fire for propitiating the gods.

the practice of making such an offering before the sun has risen. Thus then, if the Shastras meant to discard, that will virtually apply to both the periods, and there will be a perfect discontinuance of offerings of clarified butter to fire. But there is no possibility of a discontinuance of the 'daily rites;' hence for worshipping before sun-rise, the other has been spoken of disparagingly and *vice versa*. Similarly the disparaging statements about the worship of other Devas, while discussing the superiority of a particular one, are not for causing an abandonment of other worships, or for actually pointing out their demerits. As a difference in the sects makes them give their offerings to fire either before sun-rise or subsequent to it, but the results attained are equally identical, so the five worships performed from a difference in the desire of the worshipper produce the identical result, an abode in Brahmaloka; where after enjoying all enjoyments, emancipation follows with the parting of the body.

Though it is said, the worship of Vishnu, Siva and the rest produce an abode in Vaikuntha, and not that of Brahmaloka, yet a good worshipper is qualified to emancipation after the separation of the body; and by the Devajan road, there is a progressive progression ultimately leading to the Brahmaloka which a Vishnuvite knows by the name of Vaikuntha, and other people, as the abode of the four-armed (Chaturvuja), where the worshipper assumes the form of Vishnu (the four-armed). Similarly Brahmaloka is known to a Sivite as Sivaloka, where all the inhabitants have three eyes, and he himself is to get there. Thus then, each sect identifies Brahmaloka as the abode of his own deity; for it is the rule, when a person is taken by another road than that of Devajan, he is subjected to re-birth; Devajan alone leads to the Brahmaloka, hence those worshippers who are fit to be emancipated go there.

Now the story of Brahmaloka is unrivalled, and wonderful to relate; immediately with a desire, all the objects of such desire are created, for him to enjoy; thus he knows, and with such knowledge he conforms himself. In this manner, all the worshippers of the five deities desire equal results from their individual worship without any difference whatever. But it may be asserted, since the five

Devas have each a distinct name and form and they are so many, while Iswara is one, how can one Iswara possibly have so many forms ? The reply is :—In point of truth, and as a matter of fact, the supreme Self has neither name nor form ; to attribute name and form for setting up a particular worship, owing to the dull intellect of the worshipper is a creation of Maya (Illusion), hence that illusion sets him up in a variety of forms with a variety of names; thus then, there is actually no antagonism implied in the *Purans* when it disclaims one worship in favour of another, and disclaiming that again in turn, and so on with the five methods of worship. Then again, the seeming contradiction can be all removed in quite another way and which may be looked upon as the principal. Vishnu, Siva, Ganes and the rest are all indications of *Brahma*. For as a cause endowed with *Maya* is called *Brahma*, so *Brahma* is the cause of Siva. Vishnu and the rest is indicated by the products Sun, Ganes, Bhagavati and Siva. Therefore the five terms indicate *Brahma*, as *Brahma* is their indicator and their respective significations of Narayan, Nilkanta, Bighnes, Shakti and Bhanu and an endless variety of names are all conceivable into 'Karan Brahma' and 'Karya Brahma' both of which are indicated by them, as these two indicate them. In some places, 'Karya Brahma' indicate 'Karan Brahma'; in the same way, as the signification of the terms 'Sandhub' and 'Aswa' signify salt in connection with eating, and when used in connection with progression, 'Sandhav' signifies a horse which is the indication of 'Aswa' ; so the several terms 'Vishnu' 'Narayan' etc., made use of, in the Vishnu Upasana are indications of *Brahma* as the cause, (Karan Brahma) ; and the words Siva, Ganes, Sakti and Surya, indicate 'Karya Brahma' : consequently Vyas never meant to deny the worship of Siva etc., and maintain that of Vishnu in his 'Vishnu Puran' ; he intended to show that 'Karan Brahma' and not 'Karya Brahma' is what is to be worshipped. Similarly in the 'Skandha Puran' and elsewhere, the terms Siva, Mahes etc., are indicative significations of 'Karan Brahma,' Vishnu, and Ganes respectively imply 'Karya Brahma,' so that, here even, the same doctrine of worshipping 'Karan Brahma' and not 'Karya Brahma' is maintained by praising the first and decrying the last.

The same holds true in respect to the indication of the word Ganesa in Ganes Puran to 'Karana Brahma' while the term Siva and the rest are predicate of 'Karya Brahma,' so that there is inculcated the praise of the 'Karana Brahma' and disapprobation of 'Karya Brahma.' Similarly Kali and Devi, terms used in 'Kali Puran' signify 'Karana Brahma', while the predicate of the words Siva and the rest is 'Karya Brahma', consequently there is praise of the first and disapprobation of the last mentioned *Brahma*. Thus then, there is a difference implied in all the *Purans*, between cause and its product, but in reference to the identity of their meanings, there is hardly any ground of its non-admission. In all *Purans*, the worship of 'Karan Brahma' is admitted to be excellent, while that of 'Karya Brahma' is worthless, therefore they all inculcate the worship of that one *Brahma* who is the cause, and there is no antagonism in their several parts.

Though the respective forms of Vishnu with four hands, Siva with three eyes, and the elephant trunk of Ganes are all created by *Maya* (illusion) whose modifications they are, and as they are transformed products of intelligence, therefore they are all productive results of that Intelligence, and their worship has been spoken of, yet the cause of all these forms endowed with *Maya*, is virtually non-different from them, hence by excluding the several forms to worship the cause, is the object which the author of the *Purans* has in view; because form is a product hence worthless; and cause is truth; and where the dull intellect of a person rests in form, he should continue that worship after the method of the *Shastras*, so that subsequently his intellect may be enlarged, ultimately to rest on the formless cause *Brahma*.

The worship of 'Karan Brahma' is spoken of in this way :—

Brahma is the cause of the universe; It is true desire, true determination, all-knowing and distinct, the internal controller of all, and kind; where the 'Shastras' insist upon Iswara's worship they simply mean to think upon these attributes and not on any particular form; and the mention of several forms in an endless variety is not for the purpose that men should be engaged in their worship but infer the worship of their cause, the One *Brahma*.

Now inference is thus explained :—When a thing resides in the same region with another, and that even seldom, and what is encompassed or surrounded (included) by it is called inferred. For example, in the sentence, "That one with the crow is Devadatta's house," the inference of Devadatta's house is crow; for the crow is situated in the same region with the house, and that even seldom and not always; and in another's house, Devadatta's is enclosed. Similarly in the creative source of the universe, *Brahma* [or more properly 'Karan Brahma' or Iswara] there is present form "in one region, and that even seldom, and the forms of four hands (Chaturbhuja), three eyes and the rest are subjects of 'Karan Brahma', and not of an another's and thus being included in it, that *Brahma* is inferred in the personal worship of Vishnu, Siva etc. That is to say, in the designation of the several objects of worship, one *Brahma* is alone specified. This is called *Upalakshna*. Its purport is to specify or make known the nature of a particular object. As Devadatta's house is known from the crow, and there is no other purport in it, so from the form of Chaturbhuja and others, proceed knowledge of the Impersonal and formless *Brahma* ; and for the sake of worship, there is a necessity for explaining forms, and nothing else ; but dull persons without understanding the drift of the *Shastras*, betake to the worship of forms (idolatry) and always quarrel amongst themselves, like a brother-in-law and dog, as in the instance given below.

A person had a brother-in-law by the name of Utphal, who had an enemy that bore the name of Dhabak. His house-dog was also called Dhabak, and a neighbour's dog answered to the name of Utphal; when that person's wife first came to live at her father-in-law's house, she found both the dogs fighting, her husband and father-in-law scolding Utphal, abusing him, and calling their own dog Dhabak by several fond names and caressing him too. She mistook the abuse to the dog for her brothers, for they bore the same name, and the praise bestowed on Dhabak bore reference to his enemy. This grieved her much, and made her speak to the husband, when the usual explanations cleared her mistake, caused by an identity of name. Similarly in all works supporting the worship of Vishnu, the worship of other Devas, Siva and the rest, have been interdicted, but that interdiction applies to the 'Karya Brahma'; and the different sects not understanding this meaning, have been grieved to find their favorite worships spoken of with slight and contumely: and the Vaishnav feels aggrieved, because he is unaware that 'Karya Brahma' is meant by Vishnu. Moreover all the *Purans* intended to establish the worship of 'Karan Brahma' and the abandonment of 'Karya Brahma.'

Intelligence associated with *Maya* is called *Karana*, while intelligence endowed in bodies produced from *Maya* is called 'Karya Brahma.' This has been set-forth in the commencement of notes on *Bharat*, which is identical with the *Vedanta* doctrine.

> Subhasantati having heard his son's words
> Found some consolation in his mind.
> Again he asks of the son,
> To speak about the contradiction of the Shastras.

When the antagonism of the *Purans* has been cleared away in the above manner, the Raja found a great load eased from his mind, and felt happy; but his doubts about the six Shastras have not been cleared, hence he had only a perception of happiness partly, and not in its entirety.

> Which of the Shastras are true speak unto me,
> So that I may hold the meaning in my intellect.
> Tarkadrishti hearing his father's words,
> Said with proofs positive from text,
> The instruction of the Uttarmimansa.
> It is not at all opposed to the Vedas.
> The other Shastras five, are opposed to them.
> Know them therefore to be incorrect.
> A part only is according to the Veda,
> I find in various works; that disqualifies them.

Since the authors of the several Shastras are said to be all-knowing, the author of *Sankhya*, Kapila; of *Patanjal*, Patanjali—the last of the incarnated;—of *Nyaya*, Goutama; of the *Vaishesika Shastra* Kanad; *Purvamimansa*, Jaimini; *Uttarmimansa*, Vyas; all of whom are justly celebrated, consequently their words which form the text of the Shastra ought to be identical everywhere in being the proof. But then, the authority of the Vedas stands in the highest pedestal of proofs strong, inasmuch as their author Iswara is all-knowing and infallible, and is not liable to the usual defects which attend the composition of a Brahman, who as the reputed author of each of these Shastras, is a *Jiva*; and what is said of the omniscience of the several authors is due to their greatness, or the high dignity of their *Atma*; so that they have been wise from Yoga or 'Jnanayogi,' while Iswara's omniscience is natural. He is 'Yukta' Yogi.

Now 'Jnanayogi' means by thinking of whom knowledge of substances is derived; and one who is recognized to be invisibly present in all substances, with whom he is intimately combined, is called 'Yukta Yogi.' And Iswara is that 'Yukta Yogi,' for which, the utterance of the Veda is infalliable; while the Shastras are weak, because they are the productions of 'Janana Yogi.' Hence those Shastras which follow the Vedas are called proofs, and which set up a contrary doctrine are no proofs; as, the five Shastras opposed to the Vedas as evidenced by the 'Shariraka Sutras' and the rest; and the 'Uttarmimansa' which is now here opposed to them. Moreover some portions of other 'Shastras' also support the Vedas and dull persons seeing that, put their faith in them; but a greater portion of them are opposed to the Vedas, hence they are to be abandoned. If those portions which tally with the Vedas are to be regarded as instructive, then the 'Jain Shastra' which insists upon the non-destruction of animal life, thus resembling the Vedas in that one point, may also be taken as a model for instruction; but actually it is worthy of being discarded, hence not instructive.

If Sugat be an incarnation of Iswara—what is called Boodha—his words must also require proofs similar to the Vedas; but the incarnation of Boodha has only been for talking much, hence his utterances are always wanting in proof. Now much talking with a desire to cheat or misleading is called 'Bipralipsa.' Thus then, the 'Uttarmimansa,' for its complete identity with the Vedas is always excellent for a person desirous of release ; though it is written by Vyas in the form of Sutras, and several authors have added commentaries and explained the text in various ways, yet the version of that most worshipful fect, Sankar's, follows the Vedas thoroughly, and is the only one of its kind, as I have had occasion to speak of in the fifth section ; hence the other five 'Shastras' are not proofs ; and if any one were to say all the 'Shastras' which I have been speaking of, in the present Section, tend to emancipation, that can only apply to them in the manner in which Tarkadrishti has set forth. As a person, being wounded by a sword cut from his enemy, is bled profusely and accidently relieved of a (chronic) disease, then a person who draws the essence of a thing may consider the sword cut to be beneficial to that person. Similarly, by means of the other 'Shastras,' the internal organ is purified in some way or other, or it is rendered firm, so that a person by ascertaining the doctrine set forth in the Vedas finally obtains release ; and if he continues to devote his attention to those 'Shastras' only he is sure to ruin himself like a blind boy sticking to a bullock's tail as in the following example. Hence by abandoning 'Shastras' and following the instruction of the 'Uttarmimansa,' as it is helpful to the knowledge of non-duality, emancipation can be obtained.

Now for the illustration. A rich person's son was kidnapped with all the ornaments on his person ; the son was despoiled of his ornaments, and left starving in a wood with his eyes struck out ; the poor boy was crying with pain, when a heartless ruffian made him catch the tail of a mad bullock, and asked him not to let it go, telling, it will reach you to the village. The poor boy, believing his word, did as he was advised and died after suffering much pain. Similarly material prosperity is the thief that destroys discrimination which resembles the eyes, and leaves a person in the wood of this world, there he is met by a deceiver,—a dualist—who induces in him a desire to follow the doctrine of the other 'Shastras,' and speaks to him in the following manner, " My instructions will procure you supreme bliss, so do not part with them ;" and, thus believing his word, is ultimately deprived of emancipation, and subjected to experience the pain of re-birth and death. Therefore the other *Shastras* are to be avoided.

> Hearing the words of Tarkadrishti,
> Subhasantati his father,
> Had all his doubts removed,
> And obtained tranquillity of mind.
> To the worship of the Impersonal *Brahma** he lends his heart,
> Lo! Tarkadrishti raised to the post of a preceptor in the Raja's circle.

Though Tarkadrishti was the king's son, yet for the invaluable instruction that he offered to his father, he was raised to the post of a Guru; such is the superior dignity of *Brahma* knowledge, and the father gave him all he had.

> Some time elapsed when the Raja departed this life,
> And went to the abode of *Brahma*, where goes the sage in contemplation.

The time and place of the Raja's death are not mentioned, because for a worshipper of Impersonal *Brahma*, neither auspicious time nor place are required. No matter whether he dies in daylight or in night time, whether during the sun's transit in the north or south of the Equator, whether in a holy or impure place, by the strength of his devotional exercises he attains progressively through Devjan to the Bramaloka, and what has been mentioned in a prior portion of the present work, while discussing this subject with Adrishta about their requisition, has been done according to the commentator of the *Sutras*.—

> Then he succeeded to the throne,
> And took up the work,
> Tarkadrishti the able.
> Resumed he work, like an ordinary king.
> But, with full knowledge of *Brahma* ascertained,
> Got the fixed abode,
> Self merged into the Supreme Self;
> And the body turned into ashes.

---

* *Karan Brahma* is Impersonal worship or Pantheism, *Karya Brahma* is personal or anthropomorphic.

Here Self refers to the inherent Witnessing Intelligence non-different from the Supreme Self (*Paramatma*). Now though they are non-different always, yet for a difference in their respective associates, there is a distinction between them, so that with a destruction of that associate, the existing difference is also removed, and the purport of what has been implied by that non-distinction between Self and Supreme Self, is the equality with Iswara of a person who is emancipated with separation of life from the present body; and not with the pure Intelligence of *Brahma*. Such is the assertion of the commentator of the *Shariraka Sutras* (Vide Chapt. IV). It is there mentioned, " In emancipation with the cessation of the present life, there is an attainment of truth, determination etc., [in other words Iswara] according to Jaimini; and according to Dellmaka, there is a want of them; and according to the Sidhanta both their presence and want are maintained." Now the purport is, there is a virtual equality and non-difference with Iswara; and the true determination of Iswara are transferred to the emancipated there to be used; and in the light of true existence that Iswara is said to be pure, and without any attributes,—that is to say, Impersonal,—hence without any true determination. Though in relation to worldly existence, a *Jiva* is virtually without attributes and pure; yet in relation to that existence, from the presence of (*Avidya*) A-knowledge there is perception of an agent and instrument, which perception never accrues to Iswara, either in regard to Self or in regard to another substance—perception of worldly existence—hence he is always unassociated or un-related, without any attributes or properties, and pure—so that the non-distinction of Iswara with *Jiva*, is in regard to the pure (Intelligence). Moreover if this non-distinction with Iswara be not admitted to be identical with non-distinction of that pure Intelligence; and if it be said, Iswara can never aspire to the pure intelligence of *Brahma*, because like the *Jiva*, Iswara never stands in need of instruction, for knowledge to arise, whence emancipation after death is to result; and his ordinary form is not pure; so that he is always something less than a *Jiva* ; consequently, it is fit to believe, Iswara is without the envelopment of ignorance, then he stands in no need of instruction for knowledge to arise; and in the absence of envelopment, he is never subject to illusion; hence he is eternal, omniscient, and always free. Illusion and its product cannot affect Him so, that there may be any misconception as to the nature of Self, or any connection in the form of an agent or instrument; for which, he is un-related or un-associated and pure. In this manner, is shown what is non-distinct from Iswara is non-different from the pure Intelligence of *Brahma.* Now this non-difference can likewise be established from illustration as in the following example; as in the absence of a jar in a temple, the space covered by the jar blends with the space inside a temple, and not with the infinite body of ether occupying all space [for there is the barrier of the temple to exclude] but then, as in the space or ether of the temple, the space occupied by the jar was absorbed, and their non-difference is established, so that, space of the temple is only a form or part of the infinite ether existing everywhere; in the same way, the products of a theosophist's body are destroyed in the (*Brahmanda*) *Brahma's* egg which again is included in Iswara's body, *Maya*: and as a theosophist's *Atma* never goes out during his emancipation with the parting of the body, therefore his Self is non-different from Iswara. But as in the example of the jar-ether, and its non-difference with the temple-ether, which again is only a form of the infinite ether (*Mahakas*) so when there is non-difference with Iswara and a theosophist's *Atma*, and when Iswara is non-different from the pure *Brahma,* consequently a theosophist attains to *Brahma.*

CONCLUSION.

In this manner is written the *Vichar Sagar,*
Which contains many gems.
Conclusions derived from the esoteric signification of *Vedas.*
A man of discrimination receives them with profound [faith]
Spent much labour in *Sankhya* and *Nyaya,*
Read Grammar without end.
Read works on *Adwaita* doctrine,
Have left not one unread.
Difficult are the other obligations,
In which there is a difference in doctrine;

With labor has he dived,
Nischal Das [into] the *Vedas*.
In the vernacular, has he written this work.
In writing it, he felt no shame,
For which, there is this one cause:—
Mercy and Religion are the crown.
Without grammar, cannot be read
Sanscrit works by the dull.
They do read this with ease
And obtain the Supreme bliss.

To the west of Delhi
Eighteen *kos* is the vi'lage.
Where is his residence,
By name called Kehrowli.
The wise in departing this life during emancipation
With what to become one.
The Dadu, original State—[the one existence]
That speaks the *Vedas*;
Name and form are misused
And subservient to that Secondless One
That is the indication of the term 'Dadu.'
Existence is perceived as dear.

This brings to a close and with it, the 7th Section including a description of that form of emancipation, which accrues to one liberated in life, with the separation of his body.

THE END.

www.ingramcontent.com/pod-product-compliance
Lightning Source LLC
Chambersburg PA
CBHW051723300426
44115CB00007B/436